The Jewish Apocalyptic Heritage
in Early Christianity

Compendia Rerum Iudaicarum ad Novum Testamentum

SECTION III

JEWISH TRADITIONS IN EARLY CHRISTIAN LITERATURE

Volume 1
PAUL AND THE JEWISH LAW; HALAKHA IN THE LETTERS
OF THE APOSTLE TO THE GENTILES
Peter J. Tomson

Volume 2
JEWISH HISTORIOGRAPHY AND ICONOGRAPHY
IN EARLY AND MEDIEVAL CHRISTIANITY
Heinz Schreckenberg – Kurt Schubert
Translations from the German: Paul A. Cathey

Volume 3
PHILO IN EARLY CHRISTIAN LITERATURE; A SURVEY
David T. Runia

Volume 4
THE JEWISH APOCALYPTIC HERITAGE IN EARLY CHRISTIANITY
Edited by James C. VanderKam and William Adler

Published under the auspices of the
Foundation Compendia Rerum Iudaicarum ad Novum Testamentum
Amsterdam

The Jewish Apocalyptic Heritage in Early Christianity

Edited by
James C. VanderKam and William Adler

1996
Van Gorcum, Assen
Fortress Press, Minneapolis

CIP-DATA KONINKLIJKE BIBLIOTHEEK, THE HAGUE, THE NETHERLANDS

Jewish

The Jewish apocalyptic heritage in early Christianity / ed. by James C. VanderKam and William Adler. – Assen: Van Gorcum; Minneapolis: Fortress Press. – (Compendia rerum judaicarum ad Novum Testamentum. Section 3, Jewish traditions in early Christian literature; vol 4)
Publ. under auspices of the Foundation Compendia Rerum Iudaicarum ad Novum Testamentum.
NUGI 611
Subject headings: early Christianity / Jewish apocalyptic heritage.

ISBN 90-232-2913-4 bound

Library of Congress Cataloging-in-Publication Data

VanderKam, James, C.

The Jewish apocalyptic heritage in early Christianity / edited by James C. VanderKam and William Adler.
        (Compendia Rerum Iudaicarum ad Novum Testamentum. Section 3. Jewish' Traditions in Early Christian Literature; v. 4) Includes bibliographical references and index.
ISBN 0-8006-2972-8 (alk. paper)
1. Apocalyptic literature. 2. Apocryphal books (Old Testament). 3. Ethiopic book of Enoch. 4. Bible. O.T. Apocrypha. Esdras, 2nd-Relation to the New Testament. 5. Bible. O.T. Daniel IX, 24-27--Criticism, interpretation, etc.--History--Early church, ca. 30-600. 6. Christian literature, Early. 7. Christianity and other religions--Judaism. 8. Judaism--Relations--Christianity. 9 . Church history--Primitive and early church, ca. 30-600. I. VanderKam, James C. II. Adler, William, 1951- III. Series.
BS1705.J48 1995   95-43608
220'.046--dc20   CIP

Printed in The Netherlands by Van Gorcum, Assen

Contents

Preface

Early Christians found themselves in a paradoxical relationship with Jews and Judaism. On the one hand, they saw the Jewish people, especially the religious leaders, as their staunchest opponents. Though they embraced the Torah and the Prophets, which the Christians believed spoke eloquently of Jesus the Messiah, they had rejected him and now opposed his followers. On the other hand, most of the very first Christians were themselves Jewish and almost all members of the church recognized in Judaism their deepest spiritual roots. As time passed, the percentage of Jewish Christians became negligible, but even when the Church had become almost entirely non-Jewish in membership the Jewish contribution to the new faith could hardly be denied.

One major component of that rich Jewish heritage was the broad, diverse apocalyptic tradition. There can be no doubt that many early Christian writers found Jewish apocalyptic texts, modes of thought, characters, and themes to be particularly valuable as they elaborated their theologies, cosmologies, and philosophies of history. The New Testament itself gives eloquent witness to the heavy influence from Jewish apocalypticism. Several passages in it qualify as apocalypses (e.g., the Synoptic apocalypses), and apocalypse as the name of a literary genre comes from the Greek title of the Revelation of John. But the legacy of the Jewish apocalypses by no means ended with the New Testament period; it continued in varied ways for centuries and has left a permanent imprint on Christian theology.

The Jewish and, to a lesser extent, the early Christian apocalypses have become the object of innumerable studies in recent decades. Scholarship in these areas has been reinvigorated in part by discovery of the Dead Sea Scrolls, among which significant portions of key apocalyptic books such as 1 Enoch were found, and by the Nag Hammadi codices in which several apocalypses appear. The apocalypses have been studied from diverse angles and with different scholarly methods. Thus textual, exegetical, and recensional issues have been addressed; and definitions of key terms, isolation of characteristic ways of thinking, and identification of possible social settings have all occupied much time and space in contemporary scholarship. It is fair to say, however, that amid this flurry of activity the Christian appropriation of Jewish apocalypticism has not received as much attention as it deserves or requires. The present book is offered as a contribution toward filling that need. The five essays in it have been designed, not to offer comprehensive coverage of this massive topic, but more as a series of probes into important aspects of the early Christian employment, adaptation, and preservation of Jewish apocalyptic traditions. It seemed wise to select a limited number of significant topics and to pursue them – especially through major examples – in order to gain a greater understanding of the subject. In general, the essays cover the first three or four centuries of the Common Era, although in some cases it was necessary to move beyond these limits.

The introduction surveys ancient perceptions of the apocalypses as well as their function, authority, and survival in the early Church. The second chapter focuses on a specific tradition by exploring the status of the Enoch literature, use of the fallen angel motif, and identification of Enoch as an eschatological witness. A chapter is also devoted to Christian transmission of Jewish texts – a topic whose significance is more and more being recognized. 4-6 Ezra serve as examples of what could and did happen to such works as they were copied and edited. The use and influence of Jewish apocalyptic texts and themes among sectarian Christian groups in Asia Minor and especially Egypt form the subjects of the fourth chapter, while the fifth analyzes early Christian appropriation and reinterpretation of Jewish apocalyptic chronologies.

A word of thanks is due to the Board of Editors for their initiative to include this volume in Section III of the Compendia series, and to Professor Peter J. Tomson for his gentle guidance, prompting, and encouragement as the volume gradually took shape. Words of gratitude to the contributors are also in order. Each one of them has taken time from busy schedules to produce major new studies in areas in which they specialize. Thanks are also extended to the Rev. Les Walck for his important assistance at an early point in the research which lies behind chap. 2.

It is hoped that this volume will enhance the appreciation of the debt the Christian Church owes to its mother religion, and that it will stimulate added reflection on the complex cultural relationships in the early history of both religions.

James C. VanderKam
William Adler

Chapter One

Introduction

William Adler

Jewish Apocalypses in Christian Settings

Recent work on the Jewish apocalypses has devoted considerable energy to the kinds of Judaism that gave birth to this literature, and its social setting and function. Virtually every Jewish party or sect has at one time or another been identified as possibly responsible for its composition. One reason for the lack of success in locating the apocalypses has to do with the conditions under which these works survive. Because most of the Jewish apocalypses received a generally unfavorable reception in post-70 Judaism, there does not exist a developed tradition of Jewish interpretation to contextualize these documents or provide a framework for their analysis.[1]

Like much Jewish literature of the second temple period, the apocalypses owe their survival almost entirely to early Christianity. In most cases, the extant Christianized form of a Jewish apocalypse is the product of a long prior history of transmission, the particulars of which can be quite murky. Since the Christian groups who copied and transmitted the Jewish apocalypses are either unknown or removed from the conventional avenues of research pursued by the student of early Judaism, the function of these documents for the religious communities that preserved them is often a matter of speculation. It is true that the discovery of fragments of Jewish apocalypses at Qumran has partially filled the vacuum. But these fragments are minuscule in comparison with the vast number of apocalyptic texts preserved by the early Church. And the relationship of these compositions to the sectarian writings of Qumran is still unclear.[2] Theorizing about the social setting and function of the Jewish apocalypses must at some point acknowledge the fact that the context in which these apocalypses survive is a Christian one.

---

[1] On rabbinic views toward apocalyptic literature, see Saldarini, 'Apocalypses and "Apocalyptic"'; id, 'Apocalyptic and Rabbinic Literature'; Ginzberg, 'Some Observations'.
[2] See Martinez, *Qumran and Apocalyptic*; Collins, 'Was the Dead Sea Sect an Apocalyptic Movement?'; id, *Apocalyptic Imagination*, 115-141; Stegemann, 'Die Bedeutung der Qumranfunde'; Stone, 'Apocalyptic Literature', 423-27.

The Christian Use of the Jewish Apocalyptic Tradition

APPROACHES TO THE QUESTION

Although formally recognized, the Christian environment in which the Jewish apocalypses were preserved is often treated as a regrettable accident of history standing in the way of the recovery of the original text in its earliest setting. The numerous demonstrably Christian apocalypses that appeared after the first century have also suffered relative neglect.[3] The late date and derivative character of many of the Christian sources partially explain this disinterest. But it also has to do with a widespread preconception that 'real' apocalypses originated in a discrete and identifiable movement in early Judaism and Christianity, a defining characteristic of which was a 'radical eschatologization of the understanding of one's history'.[4]

Because there is broad consensus that primitive Christianity took root on the same soil that produced the Jewish apocalyptic literature, specimens like the 'synoptic apocalypse' and the Book of Revelation are generally understood as products of the same movement. But despite their generic affinities with their Jewish counterparts, the Christian apocalypses that appeared after the first century tend to be treated as step-children, heirs to the form but not the 'thought-world' of their Jewish prototypes. Typically, they are dismissed as a kind of literary epiphenomenon, not reflective of genuine apocalyptic thinking, but rather a product of other religious impulses in late Antiquity. It is surely significant in this regard that the Book of Revelation, the one Christian apocalypse to receive more than its fair share of attention, is almost invariably compared with Jewish, not Christian, works of the same literary genre.[5]

This supposition of a coherent ideology and movement defined by its radically dualist eschatology has decisively shaped the study of the apocalyptic literature, both Jewish and Christian. Until recently, the Jewish apocalypses have functioned mainly as an aid for better understanding the eschatological proclamations of Jesus and the early Church. Insofar as the use of the Jewish apocalypses as 'background literature' refracts the investigation of them through the lens of material in the New Testament, it can sometimes lead to overarching and misleading assertions about the 'basic character of Jewish apocalyptic'.

---

[3] For a survey of the contents of the later Christian apocalypses one still finds Weinel, 'Die spätere christliche Apokalyptik', now 70 years old, cited as the standard work on the subject. For pre-fourth century apocalypses, see A.Y. Collins, 'The Early Christian Apocalypses'. Schüssler Fiorenza, 'The Phenomenon of Early Christian Apocalyptic' is more concerned with methodological issues than specific texts.

[4] See K. Müller, 'Die Ansätze der Apokalyptik', 32. This position was defended recently by U. Müller, 'Apocalyptic Currents', 284.

[5] As Klaus Koch notes (*Rediscovery of Apocalyptic*, 19f) Jewish apocalypses are considered by many scholars to be 'much richer in content and show a greater depth of thought'.

P. VIELHAUER AND EARLY CHRISTIAN 'APOCALYPTIC'

An example of this latter approach is P. Vielhauer's programmatic survey of the origins and development of 'apocalyptic' in early Christianity.[6] Since in his view Christianity 'took over the genre of the Apocalypse from Palestinian Judaism', Vielhauer set out to compare Christian apocalyptic material with its Jewish antecedents, in order to ascertain 'affinities and differences'.[7] While acknowledging that the Jewish apocalypses were not designated by any common title, Vielhauer believed that it was nonetheless possible to identify enough fixed characteristics of this literature to justify the nomenclature of a literary genre. These features included pseudonymity, accounts of a vision or audition, historical surveys in the form of *vaticinium ex eventu*, and more formal literary features such as wisdom sayings, prayers and parenesis. From a list of themes compiled from diverse sources, Vielhauer distilled what he considered to be the apocalyptic 'world of ideas' that gave birth to this literature: pessimism; doctrine of the two ages; universalism; determinism; and imminent expectation of the end of the world. Like many other students of this literature, Vielhauer ascribed the social and religious origins of this literature to crisis and persecution. As products of 'eschatologically-stimulated circles' in post-exilic Judaism whose opposition to the developing 'non-eschatological theocracy' forced them into a sectarian existence, the apocalypses functioned primarily to strengthen these religious communities, especially in times of oppression.[8]

Although Vielhauer conceded that Jesus' preaching about the imminent coming of the kingdom of God may have retained some faint vestiges of Jewish apocalypticism, the content and authority of his message were 'too high to be rendered in categories suitable to eschatological expectation'.[9] In place of the apocalyptic notions of eschatological salvation and the clear temporal distinction of the two ages, Jesus proclaimed a divine sovereignty that shattered the traditional two-age scheme of the Jewish apocalyptist. The same concept rendered superfluous the kind of end-time speculation familiar from many of the apocalypses. Nor did Jesus' teaching seek enhanced status through the typical revelatory vehicles of the apocalyptic genre, namely a pseudonymous figure of the past or an *angelus interpres*. The authority that flowed from the message itself was self-authenticating.[10]

---

[6] Vielhauer's two essays on this subject, entitled 'Apocalyptic' and 'Apocalyptic in Early Christianity', are included in Hennecke-Schneemelcher, *NTA* 2. In the 1990-92 English edition of this work the two essays have been revised and updated by G. Strecker. Unless otherwise indicated, references to Vielhauer's essays are based on the 1976 English version (vol 2, 581-600; 608-642). All other references to *NTA* are based on the most recent edition. See also n20.

[7] Vielhauer, 'Apocalyptic', 581.

[8] Vielhauer, 'Apocalyptic', 595-98, following the suggestion of Plöger, *Theokratie und Eschatologie*, 36-68.

[9] Vielhauer, 'Apocalyptic in Early Christianity,' 609.

[10] ib 608f.

Following this overall perspective, Vielhauer argued that evolving Christian ideas about the parousia determined the form and content of material borrowed from a store of Jewish apocalyptic materials, in the shape either of documents or traditions.[11] As its eschatology began to depart from the fundamentally non-apocalyptic teachings of its founder, the early Church incrementally absorbed apocalyptic material from its Jewish environment. The 'momentous influx' of Jewish apocalyptic ideas commenced with the post-Easter proclamation of Jesus' death and resurrection and his exaltation as an eschatological Savior. Because this idea transformed Jesus' preaching about the kingdom of God into an expectation of Christ's return, the early Church was now able to embrace apocalyptic ideas foreign to Jesus' original teachings, in particular the temporal distinction between this age and the new age and the correlative conception of an eschatological 'son of man'.[12]

The reshaping of the forms of apocalyptic instruction introduced for Vielhauer yet another phase in the transformation of Christian apocalyptic thinking. Since the earliest apostles and missionaries saw themselves only as transmitters of the tradition, not as bearers of new ideas, apocalyptic themes initially found expression through the 'saying of Jesus'. But when in the post-apostolic period the apostles became the vehicles and guarantors of apocalyptic tradition, fictitious letters and apocalypses began to circulate under the name of an apostle, thereby enabling the early Church to absorb from Jewish models another literary element – pseudonymity.[13] The systematization of eschatological expectations also accelerated the adaptation of apocalyptic subject matter from Jewish tradition. These included more elaborate accounts of the parousia and the signs preceding it, and apocalyptic surveys stretching from the present time to the end. The apocalyptic descriptions already in evidence in 1 Thess. 4:16-5:3 and the synoptic apocalypse reveal that quite early the primitive Church lent vividness and color to its thinking about the parousia by assimilating material from Jewish antecedents.

The early Church's self-understanding as an interim eschatological community and the actual persecutions that it experienced further hastened the absorption of Jewish apocalyptic ideas about the eschatological woes preceding the end-times. Motifs from Jewish apocalyptic associated with war and famine, the ruin of families, the increase of tribulation, the Antichrist and the great apostasy thus found ready acceptance within the apocalyptic thinking of early Christianity. When, in Vielhauer's view, the early Church had lost confidence in the imminent end, apocalyptic motifs were even used to dampen eschatological expectation (see, for example, the use of the 'Antichrist' motif in 2 Thessalo-

---

[11] ib 600.

[12] ib 609.

[13] ib 610. It is difficult to see why this feature of the Christian apocalypses requires a Jewish model, especially since pseudonymous documents of all kinds claiming apostolic authorship proliferated in the early Church.

nians 2). As Christian thinking about the end became increasingly estranged from any relationship to 'Christian existence', eschatological doctrines were systematized and repeated artificially as dogma. As a result, what had once been a vital, imminent hope hardened into a 'traditional picture of the future'. In the final stages of this development, interest in the parousia was itself super-seded by fascination with heavenly journeys and the Beyond. From the middle of the second century, the Antichrist and the afterlife, at best subsidiary themes of the parousia expectation in the New Testament, became the dominant elements of Christian apocalyptic thinking.[14]

EARLY CHRISTIANITY AS THE BEARER OF THE JEWISH APOCALYPTIC TRADITION

Fundamental to Vielhauer's program was his reconstruction of a pervasive and fairly static apocalyptic structure behind its diverse literary manifestations. This enabled him to postulate a linear correlation between 'apocalyptic' as a 'literary phenomenon', as the 'realm of ideas from which this literature emanates', and as the social ideology of 'eschatologically-excited communities' supposedly responsible for its composition. As in many older studies of apocalyptic literature, his understanding of the word 'apocalyptic' actually comprehended three distinct, but overlapping, categories: apocalypse as a literary form, apocalyptic eschatology as a theological perspective, and apocalypticism as the ideology of a socio-religious movement.

As has often been pointed out more recently, this all-encompassing use of the word is responsible for much of the current disarray in the research on the literature.[15] Apocalyptic eschatology, a subject neither peculiar to the apoc-alypses nor uniquely defining of the apocalyptic literature, covers a range of positions much wider than Vielhauer's 'basic structure' would tolerate. The doctrine of two ages, for example, which for Vielhauer underpinned the apoc-alyptic world view, may actually represent a later stage in the development of apocalyptic thinking not generalizable to the entire corpus.[16] Because eschatol-ogy defined for him the essential nature of 'apocalyptic', Vielhauer was re-

---

[14] Vielhauer, 'Apocalyptic', 600; id, 'Apocalyptic in Early Christianity', 613. For his treatment of the Antichrist theme in early Christianity and its Jewish antecedents, Vielhauer relied largely on Gunkel, *Schöpfung und Chaos*, and especially Bousset, *Der Antichrist*. For a recent critique of their reconstruction of the Antichrist myth, see Jenks, *Origins*.

[15] For discussion of this matter, see Collins, 'Introduction', 3; id, *Apocalyptic Imagination*, 2.

[16] On the problems of extracting a unified eschatological picture from the literature, see Rowland, *Open Heaven*, 23-29. The example usually given in support of the two-age doctrine is 4 Ezra 7:50. But as Barr notes ('Jewish Apocalyptic', 35) the conditions under which 4 Ezra was written make it difficult to extrapolate this view for the whole of apocalyptic literature. For general discussion of the problems of treating apocalyptic eschatology in terms of the idea of a definite end or two periods, see Collins, 'Apocalyptic Eschatology'.

quired to reduce non-eschatological material in the apocalypses to the status of 'coloring', that is, secondary by-products of the conventicle-like and distressed social conditions under which the apocalypses were produced.[17] But esotericism and speculative wisdom, subjects that figure much more importantly in many of the early apocalypses than is often acknowledged, can hardly be dismissed as literary embellishment. What Jonathan Smith has described as apocalyptic 'scribal knowledge' suggests an international dimension to this literature hardly expected of the oppressed sectarian communities allegedly responsible for its composition.[18] Above all, the sociological description of the apocalypses as sectarian literature created by groups under persecution and crisis needs to be reexamined.[19]

The motive for Vielhauer's relatively fixed picture of 'Jewish apocalyptic' was that it offered a convenient backdrop against which to demonstrate Jesus' transcendence of the apocalyptic environment in which he carried on his ministry. Here the overriding objective of Vielhauer's study was to dissociate, to the extent possible, Jesus' teachings from Jewish eschatological hopes or national aspirations. As Klaus Koch has noted, the influence of Bultmannian theory was so thoroughgoing that it sometimes stood in for historical evidence. Thus, Vielhauer was prepared to dismiss the primitive gospel traditions about the eschatological 'son of man' as not genuine, insofar as they reflected a temporal dualism incompatible with Jesus' message of divine sovereignty.[20] The same dogmatism influenced his selection of 'apocalyptic' material. Unlike his reconstruction of 'Jewish apocalyptic', which drew entirely on the literary apocalypses, the Christian source material serving as a basis of comparison comprised a much more diverse collection of sources: eschatological logia, epistles, and church orders, as well as the later Christian genre apocalypses. As a result, Vielhauer's conclusions about the uniqueness of Jesus' preaching on the basis of formal differences from the Jewish genre apocalypses were potentially misleading. It is certainly true that many of the recurring features of the Jewish apocalypses (historical surveys, divisions of history, speculation about the time of the end and pseudonymity) are lacking in the sayings about the kingdom of God attributed to Jesus in the gospels. But one may well challenge the appropriateness of his drawing weighty theological conclusions about the unique au-

---

[17] Vielhauer, 'Apocalyptic', 598.

[18] J.Z. Smith, 'Wisdom and Apocalyptic'; see also Betz, 'Religio-Historical Understanding', 136; Stone, 'Lists of Revealed Things'; id, *Scriptures, Sects*, 42-47.

[19] On the difficulties of classifying the apocalypses as 'conventicle literature', see Collins, 'The Genre Apocalypse', 546; id, *Apocalyptic Imagination*, 29.

[20] Of Vielhauer's rejection of the authenticity of the son of man sayings, Koch notes: 'Here the dogmatic conceptuality behind the demythologizing movement is acting as sponsor for the historical questions' (*Rediscovery of Apocalyptic*, 68). It will be noted that, in his revision of Vielhauer for the most recent edition of *NTA*, G. Strecker (vol 2 p569f) seems to distance himself from this view, at the same time softening some of Vielhauer's more controversial claims about Jesus' transcendence of his Jewish environment.

thority of Jesus' proclamation of the kingdom of God and the existential demands of his ministry on the basis of uneven comparisons between the fully developed Jewish genre apocalypses and eschatological logia embedded in the gospel tradition.

In line with his overall definition of 'apocalyptic', Vielhauer understood the early Church's use of Jewish apocalyptic sources as almost entirely conditioned by its eschatological hopes. If certain motifs (for example, the apocalyptic historical survey) from Jewish prototypes did not find their way into the Christian apocalypses, it was only because the Church's singleminded focus on the parousia of Christ crowded out themes not directly applicable to this subject. The same criteria predisposed Vielhauer to disqualify *tout court* those Christian apocalypses that did not fit his definition. A genuine apocalypse not only had to embrace certain eschatological doctrines; as 'resistance literature', it also had to be occasioned by a real crisis. Since the later apocalypses failed to satisfy either criteria, they owed their contents (especially their ideas concerning the afterlife) mainly to 'gnostic or pagan' influence.[21] The Shepherd of Hermas was delegitimized for other reasons. Although Hermas held certain features in common with the older apocalypses (for example, parenesis and allegory), these were not 'eschatologically determined' and hence 'stylistic elements' only. Inasmuch as Hermas 'included no disclosures of the eschatological future or the world beyond', the work had to be categorized as a pseudo-Apocalypse.[22]

SCOPE AND METHOD OF THE PRESENT STUDY

In Vielhauer's study, imprecise use of the word 'apocalyptic' as a hybrid set of literary, theological and sociological features created a picture that was at once too diffuse and too narrow. By adducing as examples of Christian 'apocalyptic' texts that were not apocalypses in the formal literary sense, it risked turning the discussion into an amorphous study of Christian eschatology. On the other hand, sources that satisfied the literary desiderata of an apocalypse were invalidated because they did not meet certain preconceived theological ('eschatology') or socio-political ('crisis' or 'persecution') criteria. As a result, the analy-

---

[21] Vielhauer, 'Apocalyptic', 600. See also his *Geschichte der urchristlichen Literatur*, 528 where he argues that because these later apocalypses 'no longer arise from actual occasions' and do not represent 'resistance literature', they are only the 'expectations of more or less speculative groups'. The contention that the tours of heaven and hell in the Christian apocalypses derive from pagan sources has been recently challenged in several studies. See Himmelfarb, *Tours of Hell*; Bauckham, 'Early Jewish Visions of Hell'.

[22] Vielhauer, 'Apocalyptic in Early Christianity', 630, 638. For discussion of the genre of Hermas, see also David Hellholm, *Das Visionsbuch des Hermas*, 96-197.

sis lent itself to circular questions about which apocalypses were genuine and which were not.[23]

To avoid the confusion that would otherwise set in, the current study does not represent itself as an examination of Jewish and Christian 'apocalyptic', but rather of the Jewish apocalypses in their Christian settings. It is curious that the wealth of scholarship on early Christianity as an 'apocalyptic' movement within first-century Judaism has yielded so little research on this question, or in fact on any of the Jewish pseudepigrapha preserved by Christians.[24] It would, of course, be unrealistic to suppose that a single study could do complete justice to a problem as complex and multifaceted as this one. The Christian transmission, use and reworking of any one of the better known Jewish apocalypses would probably deserve an entire volume. In the limited compass of one book, what can at most be accomplished is to examine several representative issues. The following discussion attempts to lay out in broad strokes issues treated in more detail in the remainder of the study. How did Christians perceive and classify this literary legacy? What function and status did these documents have in the Christian communities that preserved them? How were they expanded upon and adapted for Christian use?

Early Christian Perceptions of the Jewish Apocalypses

THE USE OF THE WORD ἀποκάλυψις

Studies of apocalyptic literature commonly designate certain Jewish texts as apocalypses on the basis of some modern conception of the genre. Although useful for purposes of categorization and analysis, these classification schemes are strictly scholarly exercises. None of the various Jewish works now known as apocalypses referred to itself by this or by any other single title. The first work actually to describe itself as an apocalypse was a Christian writing, the Book of Revelation.[25] Moreover, it was not until the end of the second century

---

[23] For a critique of this approach, see also Rowland, *Open Heaven*, 24: 'Not only has the original significance of the word as a particular literary type become less important, but also those apocalypses which do not give evidence of a particular type of piety are excluded from the category of apocalyptic.' For an extreme application of this approach, see Schmithals, *Apocalyptic Movement*. Since for Schmithals the 'apocalyptic thought world' is largely independent of the apocalyptic form (188f), he considers most of the apocalypses, both Jewish and Christian, as incidental to the apocalyptic movement. Of the Christian apocalypses, for example, Schmithals asserts that because many of them have no interest in the end of history, they bear only 'very little connection, or none at all, with actual (*sic*) apocalyptic' (207). Unfortunately, the idea of defining 'apocalyptic' as a theological concept that can somehow be divorced from apocalyptic literature persists in more recent scholarship; see, for example, Sturm, 'Defining the Word "Apocalyptic"', esp p37f.

[24] For general remarks on the importance of this subject, see Stone, *Scriptures, Sects*, 109-111.

[25] Rev 1:1, 'Αποκάλυψις 'Ιησοῦ Χριστοῦ, ἣν ἔδωκεν αὐτῷ ὁ Θεός.

that Christian copyists and commentators, anticipating modern attempts at classification, first bestowed the term 'apocalypse' on a select corpus of Jewish sources. Over time the same title was conferred on other Jewish documents as well.[26]

Before the end of the second century, the disparate Christian citations from the Jewish apocalypses do not recognize anything particularly distinctive about this literature. References to 1 Enoch, for example, the best attested non-canonical Jewish apocalypse, are either unattributed or introduced with the words 'Enoch says'.[27] Formulaic citations of the work with expressions such as λέγει ἡ γραφή or γέγραπται suggest that in select circles the work may have been considered sacred Scripture.[28] Another sign of the high regard for certain apocalypses is the characterization of their authors as 'prophets'. Jude's much-discussed citation from 1 Enoch 1:9 is prefaced with the words 'Enoch ...prophesied (ἐπροφήτευσεν)'. Similarly, Clement's quotation of 4 Ezra 5:35 concludes with the words: Ἐσδρας ὁ προφήτης λέγει.[29] Although equally laudatory descriptions persist after the second century, increasingly neutral or negative characterizations of the Jewish apocalypses reflect heightened awareness of their uncertain status.

While the identity of the groups who first labelled Jewish sources as apocalypses is uncertain, the designation of Jewish texts by this nomenclature occurred at a time when the use of the term to designate a literary genre was becoming increasingly fashionable. Most modern definitions of the term apocalypse would have to be stretched quite far to encompass the various Jewish, Christian, Gnostic, and pagan works of late Antiquity that were known by this title. One may thus reasonably assume that when ancient writers referred to documents as 'apocalypses', they understood something rather different from the modern technical understanding of the word. For that reason, it is all the more important to have a clear understanding of what Christians meant when they first began classifying documents by this title.

In some ways, the use of the Greek term ἀποκάλυψις is unexpected. As Morton Smith has pointed out, before the end of the first century, the term was rarely, if ever, used of written documents.[30] In modern parlance, the word 'apocalypse' usually connotes the idea of a revelation through a vision or audition of a supernatural reality in the sphere of human existence. Classical Greek

---

[26] See Vielhauer, 'Apocalyptic', 582; Smith, 'On the History', 19.

[27] See Barn. 4:3a (ed and tr Prigent-Kraft): ὡς Ἐνὼχ λέγει; Clement, Selections from the Prophets 53.4 (ed Stählin-Früchtel-Treu, vol 3) Ἐνώχ φῆσιν.

[28] Barn. 4:3a; 16:5b. For discussion see below, p.35-39.

[29] Clement, Stromateis 3.16.100.3 (ed Stählin-Früchtel, vol 2); also 5.11.77.2, where Clement cites from the Apocalypse of Zephaniah with the words 'Zephaniah the prophet'. See also Barn. 12:1 (possibly a quotation from 4 Ezra 4:33; 5:5): ἐν ἄλλῳ προφήτῃ.

[30] Smith, 'On the History', 17: 'Down to Domitian's time, or perhaps well thereafter (if we reject the traditional date of the canonical Apocalypse), the preserved Christian uses of ἀποκαλύπτω and ἀποκάλυψις are, with few exceptions, not apocalyptic.'

had many words to express this and related ideas, but ἀποκάλυψις was not among them.³¹ Nor is the term a likely lexical choice to express the visionary experiences commonly associated with apocalyptic revelations. In his study of the word, Oepke took note of this point with some surprise. Observing that an understanding of ἀποκάλυψις and cognate forms as divine revelation was 'fundamentally alien to the Greeks', he offered the unsubstantiated conjecture that later pagan use of ἀποκάλυψις in the 'technical sense' of divine revelation was 'imported from the Orient', possibly either directly or indirectly from the Greek Bible.³² But as Smith has shown, the Old Greek translation does not as a rule use the word to refer to divine revelations or visions, much less revelatory literature.³³ In sum, there is no evidence that the pagan writers who applied the term to religious texts borrowed this linguistic practice from Jewish, Christian, or Oriental sources.

Smith proposes that sometime in the last centuries BCE the earlier meaning of the term ἀποκάλυψις as simply 'uncovering' was extended to include the uncovering of divine secrets. By the third century CE, it is the element of secrecy that is paramount. The word ἀποκάλυψις embraced mysteries and occult lore and books of all kinds, among them cultic ritual, alchemy, astrology, and other esoteric wisdom.³⁴ As a term designating the disclosure of hidden or ineffable wisdom, ἀποκάλυψις appears frequently with other words expressing the same idea: τὰ μυστήρια, τὰ αἰνίγματα, τὰ ἀπόρρητα, τὰ κρυπτά.³⁵

CHRISTIAN IDENTIFICATION OF AN APOCALYPTIC 'GENRE'

There is no reason to suppose that when Christians used the word ἀποκάλυψις to denote a corpus of Jewish literary texts, they used the word in a substantially different way from their pagan counterparts. To the contrary, ἀποκάλυψις often appears in conjunction with the same cluster of words to denote secrecy and ineffability. A relatively early illustration of this understanding of ἀπο-κάλυψις and cognate forms appears in Theodotion's translation of Daniel (2nd

---

³¹ See Kaufmann, 'Apokalyptik', 1143; Oepke, καλύπτω, κτλ', 565-7, 70f. As Oepke notes, the Greek words commonly used to convey the idea of divine revelation are ἐπίδειξις and σημαίνω.
³² Oepke, καλύπτω, 571.
³³ Smith, 'On the History', 10: '...the Septuagint does not use ἀποκάλυψις to refer to what we should call "an apocalypse" nor, in fact to any sort of divine revelation.' For the translation of Ben Sira, this observation does not hold true. In this latter case, the grandson does use the word ἀποκαλύπτω in connection with the revelation of hidden divine mysteries; see, for example, Sir 42:19 (ἀποκαλύπτων ἴχνη ἀποκρύφων).
³⁴ For the texts, see Oepke, καλύπτω, 571. By the late fourth century, Synesius can speak of an abundance (συχνοί) of 'priests and laymen who have fabricated some dreams, which they call "apocalypses"'; see Synesius, Epistles 54.1, in Hercher, Epistolographi Graeci. Smith ib 18 thinks Synesius is referring here to pagan priests.
³⁵ See Oepke, καλύπτω, 570f.

cent. CE). The Old Greek version of Daniel is not consistent in its lexical choices for words to express the revelation of the divine mystery. To render גלה into Greek, it uses forms of ἐκφαίνω (2:19,30,47), δηλόω (2:47), ἀνακαλύπτω (2:22) or δείκνυμι (10:1). At these same verses, however, Theodotion consistently prefers the word ἀποκαλύπτω, producing expressions such as τὸ μυστήριον ἀπεκαλύφθη (2:19) and ἀποκαλύπτει βαθέα καὶ ἀπόκρυφα (2:22) As Smith notes, Theodotion's translation first gave to Daniel the 'linguistic claim to be an apocalypse'.[36]

An especially illustrative example of the use of the word ἀποκάλυψις in connection with the disclosure of divine secrets comes from the Cologne Mani Codex, an account of Mani's early life in the Jewish-Christian Elchasaite sect.[37] As a young man, Mani is said to have received a series of overpowering ἀποκαλύψεις. They are described in much the same way as pagan writers described revelations of hidden higher wisdom: a 'secret mystery (τὸ ἀπόρρητον μυστήριον)', 'exceedingly great secrets (τὰ ἀπόρρητα ταῦτα καὶ μέγιστα)', 'mysteries...which are not permitted for anyone to see or hear', and 'hidden and secret (κρυπτὰς καὶ ἀπορρήτους) things'.[38]

The narration of his visions offers an extremely valuable witness to the role that the Jewish/Christian apocalyptic tradition played in shaping Mani's understanding of his own mission. In the Mani Codex, Baraies the Teacher enumerates a succession of 'saviors, evangelists, and prophets' who had, like Mani, experienced terrifying revelations.[39] The visionaries that are cited – Adam, Seth, Enosh, Enoch, Shem and Paul – had by the third century CE a rich Jewish/Christian apocalyptic tradition associated with their names. What is notable in the description of their revelations is the overriding importance that is attached to the preservation of their heavenly mysteries in a fixed written form. When Baraies refers to the 'apocalypses' of Mani's forerunners, he means in every case a book or some other permanent record of their visions. 'Each one spoke and wrote for a memoir (πρὸς ὑπομνηματισμόν) as well as about his rapture'.[40] Often it is an angel who instructs the seer to commit these mysteries to writing. After receiving his revelation, Adam is instructed to record what he had seen as a permanent legacy, to be preserved in an 'incorruptible' form on papyrus. Seth recorded in his writings the very great mysteries (μέγιστα

---

[36] Smith, 'On the History', 19. See also Bockmuehl, *Revelation and Mystery*, 100-103.

[37] The text of the codex (hereafter abbreviated CMC), edited by Henrichs and Koenen, has appeared in several volumes of the *ZPE*: 19(1975) 1-85; 32(1978) 87-199; 44(1981) 201-318; 48 (1982) 1-59. It is now available in one volume: Koenen-Römer, *Der Kölner Mani-Kodex*. The text and English translation of the portion of the document cited here is by Cameron and Dewey, *The Cologne Mani Codex*. The codex dates from the fourth or fifth century CE.

[38] CMC 11 (7.12), 25 (26.8), 31 (36.1), 35(43.4); 55 (68.4). For discussion of secrecy in the Mani codex, see Stroumsa, 'Esotericism', esp 157-59.

[39] CMC 49 (62.1). On the relationship of the CMC to Jewish/Christian apocalypticism, see Gruenwald, 'Manichaeism and Judaism', 30-35.

[40] CMC 37 (48.1).

μυστήρια) that he had learned.[41] Enosh is told to record 'all these hidden things
(ταῦτα...πάντα τὰ ἀπόκρυφα)' in bronze tablets and store them up in the
desert land'.[42] Whatever Enoch learned from the angels, he would 'inscribe in
his writings'.[43] After Paul himself was snatched up into heaven, he recorded
what he had 'seen and heard in riddles (αἰνιγματωδῶς) for the fellow initiates
of the hidden mysteries (τῶν ἀποκρύφων)'.[44] As part of the same tradition,
Mani also composed in an 'immortal gospel' the vision that he beheld and 'the
most glorious revelation revealed to me (ἐνδοξοτάτης ἀποκαλύψεως τῆς
ἀποκαλυφθείσης μοι)'.[45]

THE JEWISH APOCALYPSES AS 'ESOTERIC BOOK WISDOM'

This fairly fixed description of the archetypal apocalypse suggests that Mani's
conception of the apocalypse as 'esoteric book wisdom' was firmly embedded
in the religious traditions of his community. Indeed, these two features – secret
wisdom and the authority of the written text – typify much of the Jewish
apocalyptic legacy inherited by early Christianity. Although it would be extreme to characterize, *pace* Bornkamm, the disclosure of divine secrets as 'the
true theme of later Jewish apocalyptic', we should not be surprised if the Christian communities who transmitted and enlarged upon this literature identified
the concept of secret wisdom as a defining feature of the Jewish apocalypses.[46]
It is a theme that pervades much of the literature. In Daniel, God is the one who
'reveals mysteries' (2:19) and 'deep and hidden things' (2:22). In 1 Enoch, the
power of God 'exposes every deep thing from generation to generation'; the
divine mysteries are all 'deep and numberless'.[47] As Bornkamm notes, the
interest in encyclopedic learning characteristic of many of the apocalypses
arises from the same self-understanding. 'The disclosure of mysteries,' he
writes, 'involves the revelation of the secret names, measurements, times and
numerical relationships which make up the whole. The "total" character of
mysteries is also plainly expressed in the common phrase "all mysteries".'[48]
    One corollary to this was that these secrets were to be entrusted only to the
wise and those capable of receiving and understanding their meaning. Unlike
the Hebrew prophets, who conveyed the divine message through the spoken
word, apocalyptic seers like Enoch and Ezra were preeminently scribes who

---

[41] CMC 41 (52.1).
[42] CMC 43 (54.1).
[43] CMC 47 (59.8).
[44] CMC 49 (62.4).
[45] CMC 52 (68.1).
[46] On the importance of secrecy in the Jewish apocalypses, see Bornkamm, μυστήριον, 815f;
Rowland, *Open Heaven*, 21f; Volz, *Eschatologie*, 5; Bockmuehl, *Revelation and Mystery*, 24-41.
[47] 1 Enoch 63:3.
[48] Bornkamm, μυστήριον, 815.

received and recorded heavenly secrets for the benefit of future generations.[49] The preservation of the revelation in a book guaranteed its immutability. After reading and recording heavenly tablets, Enoch, the 'scribe of righteousness' and the 'wisest of men', entrusted his book to Methuselah as a legacy to be preserved with the utmost care and delivered to the generations of the world.[50] Because the very words of the revelation are inviolable, the book must be carefully preserved and zealously guarded against sinners who pervert the words of his revelation and 'alter and take away from my words'.[51]

Above all, the written text was the means to assure its secrecy. It is common to find in the apocalypses the view that the recorded revelations of the apocalyptic seer were transmitted through covert channels and available only to a select few. In 4 Ezra, the seer, upon receiving an explanation of the eagle vision, is told that as the one who is 'alone worthy to learn this secret of the Most High,' he should 'write all these things that you have seen in a book, and put it in a hidden place; and you shall teach them to the wise among your people, whose hearts you know are able to comprehend and keep the secret'.[52] The question that now must be asked is: how did this perception of the Jewish apocalypses as written records of hidden higher wisdom affect their standing and use in the Christian communities that used them?

Possible Functions of the Jewish Apocalypses in Early Christianity

ESOTERICISM AS A LITERARY MOTIF

The motive behind the esotericism of the Jewish apocalypses has been variously interpreted. Both Stone and Collins have expressed doubts whether esotericism proves that apocalyptic literature was a product of communities that deliberately chose to sequester themselves from the world. As Collins notes, the 'public hortatory function' of many of the apocalypses does not correspond with the ideology of a religious conventicle.[53] What purpose, then, did these pretensions of secrecy serve? Collins maintains that esotericism is only a by-

---

[49] See 4 Ezra 12:36-38. Russell, *Method and Message*, 118f suggests that this change in emphasis coincides with the codification of the 'law and the prophets' in literary form and a corresponding suspicion of oral revelations.

[50] 1 Enoch 12:4; 15:1; 82:1; 92:1.

[51] 1 Enoch 104:10-11. See Nickelsburg, 'Apocalyptic Message'. See also 2 Enoch 33:11-12, where the scribe enjoins that his words and the writings of his fathers Adam and Seth are to be zealously guarded so that they might survive the flood and remain until the final days. For discussion of the secrecy formula in the apocalypses, see Hutter, 'Halte diese Worte geheim!'

[52] 4 Ezra 12:36-38 (trans. Stone, *Fourth Ezra*); see also 4 Ezra 14:5-6. For discussion, see Stone, 'Apocalyptic Literature', 432; Bornkamm, μυστήριον, 816.

[53] Collins, 'Pseudonymity', 341; Stone, 'Apocalyptic Literature', 431-33.

product of pseudonymity, whereby the author cloaked his writing in secrecy in order to explain how a composition of alleged antiquity managed to elude public notice for a long time.[54] But as a rule secrecy did not function in the Jewish apocalypses in this way. Authors of pseudonymous works in Antiquity who appealed to secrecy to authenticate authorship typically offered elaborate explanations about the circumstances of the work's concealment and its rediscovery after a long period of obscurity. Attempts to establish apostolic authorship through such devices do appear in some of the later Christian apocalypses.[55] But they rarely occur in their earlier Jewish counterparts.

Affectations of secrecy were, of course, hardly unique to the apocalypses. Jewish groups like the Essenes, who deliberately insulated themselves from the outside world, were known to be jealous guardians of secret rites, doctrines and books.[56] Secret books claiming access to a higher wisdom available only through supernatural channels were widespread in the Hellenistic world. The recipients of these well-guarded secrets were thus beneficiaries of the highest wisdom. Under the name of Comarius, supposedly a philosopher, high-priest and teacher of Cleopatra, an alchemical treatise speaks of 'the mystery of the philosophers', which 'our fathers have sworn to us not to reveal and promulgate among the masses (τοῦ μὴ ἀποκαλύψαι αὐτὸ καὶ δημιοσιεῦσαι)'.[57] Frequently, such books heightened their mystique by stressing the difficulties of decipherment and by issuing solemn warnings against translating or disseminating them too widely, especially among the impure or those deemed unworthy to receive them. Because this secret wisdom was profound and even terrifying, unlawful disclosure was sometimes represented as an act of betrayal leading to dire consequences. The fate of the world might even hang in the balance. As long as the ineffable mysteries in Abydus are never revealed (τὰ ἐν Ἀβύδῳ (ἀδύτῳ?) ἀπόρρητα οὐδέποτε ἀποκαλύπτεται), the neo-Platonist Iamblichus writes, all things remain perfect and whole.[58]

---

[54] Collins, 'Pseudonymity', 340f.

[55] For discussion of the use of these techniques to authenticate pseudepigraphic writings, see Speyer, *Die literarische Fälschung*, 67-70.

[56] On the Essene vows of secrecy, see Josephus, J.W. 2.141ff. For discussion of secrecy in Essenism and other early Jewish movements, see M. Smith, *Secret Gospel of Mark*, 197f; Jeremias, *Eucharistic Words*, 74-78; Stroumsa, 'Esotericism', 157-60; Powell, 'Arkandisziplin', 1f. On esotericism in rabbinic literature, see Wewers, *Geheimnis und Geheimhaltung*; Bockmuehl, *Revelation and Mystery*, 42-56.

[57] In Berthelot-Ruelle, *Collection* 3, 296.

[58] See Iamblichus, Mysteries 6.7 (ed des Places); see also 6.5. For discussion of esoteric wisdom as a characteristic of religion in later Antiquity, see Hengel, *Judaism and Hellenism* 1, 210-8. Among the examples that he cites is a Hermetic text communicated by Asclepius to Ammon, in which the god 'forbade any translation of the wisdom communicated to him, so that these mysteries would not reach the Greeks and the arrogant, impotent and elaborate talk of the Greeks would not destroy the honorable, terse and powerful expression of the words' (CH 16.1, ed Nock-Festugière vol 2, 23f). For discussion of revealed books and the prohibitions imposed against their dissemination, see also Festugière, *La Révélation* 1, 309-54; Norden, *Agnostos Theos*, 290-2. On the use of this theme in Egyptian magical texts see, for example, Hopfner, *Offenbarungszauber* vol 2, 1, 49-57 (nos. 35-40).

Jewish and Christian apocalypses invoke the same sanctions. In 1 Enoch's widely retold narrative of the fallen Watchers, the chief transgression of this exalted class of angels consisted of their illicit disclosure of hidden and divine mysteries, an act that results in universal destruction. 'You were (once) in heaven,' Enoch is instructed to tell the Watchers, 'but not all the mysteries (of heaven) are open to you, and you (only) know the rejected mysteries. Those ones you have broadcast to the women in the hardness of your hearts and by those mysteries the women and men multiply evil deeds upon the earth.'[59] Since legitimately received divine revelations were the property of a select few, esotericism functioned in part to heighten the prestige of those in possession of this secret learning.[60] It is telling that, although the apocalypses often demand that the words of the seers be sealed up or hidden away, they could be quite emphatic in specifying the conditions under which the book was to be made public. Sometimes, these conditions were tied to eschatological fulfillment. In Dan 12:4, for example, the seer is commanded to 'shut up the words and seal the book until the end of the time'. The effect of this command is to alert the audience that in hearing these words they were participating in a momentous event of the last days.[61] In this way, esotericism functioned to intensify the impact on those receiving the words of the revelation for the first time.

A particularly difficult text to understand in this regard is 2 Enoch. In chap. 35, Enoch is told that the 'books in your handwriting' are not to become publicly known until the last days.[62] Since the eschatological horizon of 2 Enoch is far off, the message conveyed by this decree is that those who received the revelation were party to a mystery whose full disclosure would not occur until some appointed time in the future.[63] Curiously, however, the text seems to negate its own warning, when the seer later instructs his sons that the books 'which I have given to you, do not hide them. To all who wish, recite them, so that they may know about the extremely marvelous acts of the Lord.'[64] Although the contradiction may be simply a result of the fragmentary and confused state of the text at this point, it highlights a tension between the demands for secrecy and the more public and hortatory use of the apocalypse.

---

[59] 1 Enoch 16:3 (tr E. Isaac in Charlesworth, *OTP* 1, 5-89); see also 65:11: 'And those will have no haven forever, because they have revealed to them the things which are secret.' Clement's summary of the legend grasped this essential point about the illicit disclosure of hidden secrets: 'The angels who had received superior rank, after succumbing to pleasures, revealed forbidden secrets (τὰ ἀπόρρητα) to the women, which had come to their knowledge, while the other angels concealed them or rather protected them up to the arrival of the Lord' (Stromata 5.1.10.1-2).

[60] See, for example, 2 Bar 48:3: 'Only you know the length of the generations, and you do not reveal your secrets to many.'

[61] See also Dan 8:26: 'As for you, seal up the vision, for it refers to many days from now.'

[62] 2 Enoch 35:2.

[63] On the eschatological plan of 2 Enoch, see 33:1-2, where 7000 years are assigned to the 'epoch of the world'.

[64] 2 Enoch 54.

The effect of esotericism would obviously have been blunted if the words of the apocalypse were proclaimed in a large open forum, but neither was it to be sealed up in a religious cloister.

As for the Christian apocalypses, the degree of secrecy is in part determined by their purpose and setting. The composition of the Book of Revelation in the form of a circular letter implies, of course, that it was meant for public consumption. Along with certain other unique features of this work (for example, lack of pseudonymity), this element of the book has been traced to an eschatological perspective fundamentally different from that of its Jewish counterparts.[65] But despite Revelation's intended public dissemination, its fondness for cryptic language and esoteric formulae suggests that the work, for whatever reason, sought deliberately to conceal its meaning from those lacking insight; its secrets are accessible only to those with the wisdom to understand them.[66] Understandably, the later Christian apocalypses that feature visions of the torments of the wicked in hell express greater interest in popular moral edification. In the Apocalypse of Paul, for example, Paul is instructed to make his revelation 'known and reveal it to men'. But upon writing down the apocalypse in a roll, he lacked the time to 'reveal this mystery'. Subsequently, he is commanded to reveal what he had recorded 'so that men may read it and turn to the way of truth that they may not come into these bitter torments'.[67] It is clear that in this case, the motif of secrecy functioned only to explain how Paul's record of his visionary experiences managed to escape public discovery for so long.[68] Yet even in this type of apocalypse, there are warnings against indiscriminate dissemination among the unworthy. In the Questions of Bartholomew (3rd cent. ?), Bartholomew asks Jesus if it is 'lawful for me to reveal to every man these mysteries (χρή <με> ἀποκαλύψαι τὰ μυστήρια ταῦτα)' about the punishments of the damned. Jesus' response is that only the faithful and those 'able to keep them to themselves (φυλάξαι καθ' ἑαυτούς)' may receive these revelations. The reason they are to be kept secret (ἀπόκρυφα) is because of those who are 'unable to contain them'.[69]

---

[65] The explanation often given is that John's certainty that the critical eschatological moment had already arrived with Christ's ministry allowed him to dispense with certain well known literary features of apocalyptic literature, among them esotericism, pseudonymity and *ex eventu* prophecy. For discussion, see Collins, 'Pseudonymity'; Schüssler Fiorenza, 'Phenomenon', 310.

[66] Rev 13:9, 18; 17:9.

[67] Apoc. Paul 51 (*NTA* 2, 743).

[68] Apoc. Paul 1-2 (*NTA* 2, 716-17). The use of secrecy to validate the work's genuineness is further illustrated by the description of the book's discovery. An angel appears in a dream to a man living in Tarsus and compels him to break up the foundations his house. Upon doing so, he discovers a marble box sealed with lead. It is only through the intervention of the Emperor Theodosius that the box containing the original manuscript of Paul's apocalypse is finally opened.

[69] Questions of Bartholomew 4.66-68, ed Bonwetsch, 'Apokryphen Fragen'.

APOCALYPTIC WRITINGS IN SECTARIAN SELF-DEFINITION

It is perhaps predictable that in the sectarian Christian movements of the second and third centuries, the possession of secret apocalyptic writings came to be regarded as a sign of the highest form of election. Mani, a religious reformer with an acute sense both of his own mission and of his participation in an apocalyptic tradition, self-consciously emphasized restricted access to his revelations. In the Cologne Mani Codex, they are characterized as 'secrets hidden and covered from the sects and the heathen (τὰ ἀπόρρητα...ἔκ τε τῶν δογμάτων καὶ τῶν ἐθνῶν)', and 'mysteries hidden to the world (μυστήρια τὰ λεληθότα τὸν κόσμον), which are not permitted for anyone to see or hear'. The reason why Mani hesitated to 'reveal this mystery (τὸ μυστήριον τοῦτο ἀποκαλύψαι)' was that his own community was 'entangled in error'.[70] But just as the apocalyptic seers who preceded him had consigned their revelations to a small inner circle, so did Mani entrust a record of his mysteries to the 'elect that he has chosen'.[71]

Other sectarian communities used the esoteric tradition of the Jewish/Christian apocalypses in much the same way. In order to call attention to the privilege conferred upon those who receive and understand their mysteries, Gnostic texts are fond of deliberately paradoxical statements about their accessibility. Hippolytus describes the Naasene mystery in the following way: 'the great and hidden unknown mystery of the universe...unrevealed and revealed (τὸ μέγα καὶ κρύφιον τῶν ὅλων ἄγνωστον μυστήριον ... κεκαλυμμένον καὶ ἀνακεκαλυμμένον)'.[72] Gnostic apocalypses exhibit the same characteristic. Among the apocalypses from Nag Hammadi, for example, one frequently finds grave prohibitions against public circulation among those not fit to receive them. Thus, the apocalypse entitled Melchizedek imposes a ban against divulging 'these revelations to anyone in the flesh,...unless it is revealed to you to do so'.[73] In the Apocryphon of John, the Savior instructs that the mysteries he reveals are to be written down and given secretly to others in the community; a curse is pronounced on anyone who barters the written document for personal gain.[74] Yet in spite of these prohibitions against public dissemination, it is not unusual to find alongside calls for secrecy additional narrative about the oral communication of the mysteries to other disciples, who in turn proclaim a

---

[70] CMC 27 (31.4). As a result, 'none of them recognized him... or what he had received or what had been revealed to him' (CMC 59 [74.1]).

[71] CMC 53 (67.1).

[72] Hippolytus, Refutatio 5.7.27 (ed Wendland); see also 5.8.7: λαλοῦν μυστήριον ἄρρητον.

[73] Melch. 27, in *NHL* 403.

[74] Ap. John 31 (*NHL* 116). See also the Apoc. Adam 85 (*NHL* 264), where Seth after receiving the 'hidden knowledge' of Adam made it known to his seed. In 1 Apoc. Jas. 36 (*NHL* 247) James is to 'hide these things within you and... keep silence'. He is then to reveal them to Addai, who in the tenth year will write them down.

gospel based upon these secret teachings.[75] Certainly, Gnostic groups did not keep their apocalypses strictly to themselves. Porphyry speaks with some irritation about Christians appearing at the school of Plotinus armed with a host of books and 'apocalypses in the name of Zoroaster, Zostrianus, Nicotheus, Allogenes and Messus'. Fearing that many were being misled by what he regarded as their erroneous teachings, Plotinus had to write a refutation of the Gnostics. Porphyry contributed his part by exposing the Apocalypse of Zoroaster as a fraud.[76]

A good illustration of the role that the esoteric 'book wisdom' of the Jewish/Christian apocalypses played in sectarian self-definition and the promulgation of sectarian ideology is found in the so-called Book of Elchasai, an apocalypse in the possession of the Jewish Christian community to which Mani belonged.[77] A recurring feature of this apocalypse is its secrecy and the status accruing to those who owned and understood it. According to Hippolytus, the site of the revelation was 'Seres', an exotic, even mythical region somewhere in the remote Orient.[78] There, in the third year of Trajan's rule (101), Elchasai received the book from an angel of towering stature.[79] Elchasai is said by Hippolytus to have advised his disciples to guard the 'great and ineffable mysteries (ἀπόρρητα μυστήρια)' of his revelations as if they were 'valuable pearls'. For that reason they were not to be 'transmitted to many', 'because not all men are faithful, nor all women upright'.[80] Although the book was probably composed in Aramaic, the Greek translation still managed to retain some of the mystique of the original language. In it is found a deliberately cryptic Aramaic invocation, and a strict warning against trying to understand or translate it. To decode the invocation, the reader of the Greek version would have had to work outward from the middle and reverse the order of the Aramaic letters.[81]

Given the fascination of late Antiquity with occult wisdom, a warning against making a book public was bound to elevate the cachet of the group in possession of it. Elchasai and his co-religionists must have recognized this, for the book served as a prop for missionaries. After Elchasai received the book, he began to proclaim a 'gospel of forgiveness' for the person who is 'converted

---

[75] See Gospel of Mary 19 (*NHL* 474); 1 Apoc. Jas. 42 (*NHL* 248).

[76] Life of Plotinus 16 (ed Volkmann). On Gnostic self-styled apocalypses, see Pearson, 'Jewish Sources', 445-447.

[77] Christian heresiologists describe the work both as a book and as an apocalypse. On the latter designation, see Epiphanius, Panarion 19.1.7 (ed Holl). Epiphanius states that Elchasai 'smuggles in some fantastic ideas allegedly from an apocalypse (δῆθεν <ἐξ> ἀποκαλύψεως)'. The fragments of the book preserved by Hippolytus and Epiphanius are collected in Irmscher, 'Book of Elchasai'. Greek text and translation of the relevant texts are also found in Luttikhuizen, *Revelation of Elchasai*, 41-53 (Hippolytus), 82-113 (Epiphanius).

[78] See Reinink, 'Das Land "Seiris"'; Luttikhuizen ib 60f.

[79] Hippolytus, Refutatio 9.13.1-3.

[80] Hippolytus, Refutatio 9.17.1.

[81] Epiphanius, Panarion 19.4.3.

and listens to the book and believes in it'.[82] By the third century it was available in a Greek version and was known and disseminated as far west as Rome by Elchasaite missionaries. In a paradoxical way, the secrecy of the Book of Elchasai was an invitation to outsiders to join a priviliged elite.

The Jewish Apocalypses and the Question of their Authority

THE SELF-VALIDATING CLAIMS OF THE JEWISH APOCALYPSES

What survives of the Book of Elchasai is a miscellany of astrological speculation, incantations, prescriptions for community organization, and warnings about future troubles. The rather inconclusive attempts to classify the Elchasaites on the basis of the fragmentary remains of the Book of Elchasai underscore the difficulties of correlating Jewish or Christian apocalypses to a coherent and recognizable religious ideology.[83] This observation is broadly true of most of the apocalypses. The contents of the Gnostic apocalypses are diverse and not necessarily related to Gnostic doctrines. Mani's description of the apocalyptic visions of his predecessors includes very little that is singularly Manichean.[84] And although the earlier Jewish apocalypses are often presented as products of groups with a strongly sectarian identity, they are in fact not especially forthcoming about the kinds of Judaism that produced them. While it is occasionally possible to detect in them traces of religious polemic, there is very little in them that can be described as 'doctrine' in the systematic sense of the word. For that reason, attempts to link the apocalypses to some known Jewish party have been mostly disappointing.[85] If, then, this literature does not reveal any uniform, pervasive, or readily identifiable ideological stance, one may well ask what was it about these documents that engendered general disapproval from developing 'orthodox' Christian circles.

It may be suggested here that the resistance to this literature had less to with objections to its 'heretical' contents than it did with the nature of the apoc-

---

[82] Hippolytus, Refutatio 9.13.3-4.

[83] The contents of the book included ritual immersion for baptism and healing, and the strict observance of most Jewish laws. Irmscher's description, *NTA* 2, 686, of the book typifies the futility of modern attempts to classify the work. Although he describes the basic character of the book as 'Jewish, but ...a syncretistic and not a pure Judaism', he also discerns in the work Christian ideas mixed 'together with a strong tinge of Gnosticism', as well as ideas of pagan origin.

[84] See Pearson, 'Jewish Sources', 451. Of Mani's description of the apocalypses of his predecessors, he writes: 'There is nothing specifically Gnostic about the material quoted; these apocalypses could easily be lost apocryphal works.' See also Henrichs, 'Literary Criticism', 725.

[85] See Koch, *The Rediscovery of Apocalyptic*, 21; Collins, 'Apocalyptic Literature', 356-58. After examining the diverse contents of the apocalyptic literature, Russell, *Method and Message*, 27 concluded that the apocalypses may have come from 'many parties, known and unknown, and among men who owed allegiance to no party at all'.

alyptic claim to authority based on direct divine inspiration. Such claims are implicit in many of the apocalypses. In Revelation, for example, the seer is commanded to 'write in a book what you see' (1:11). Since it is the Spirit that is speaking directly to the churches, the words of the revelation demand immediate assent (2:7). At the close of the work, the binding authority of the apocalypse's words is sealed by the solemn warning, unique in the New Testament, against adding to or subtracting from the seer's words (22:18). This same sense of autonomy underlies the book's allusive use of Scripture. Numerous allusions to and phrases from the Old Testament permeate the work, but like other apocalypses, it does not seek confirmation through direct quotations from the biblical text.[86]

In some cases, as in a much-quoted passage at the close of 4 Ezra, claims to surpassing authority were forthright. As Michael Stone has noted, 4 Ezra contains nothing that would enable an unambiguous identification with some known Jewish group or party.[87] What is striking, however, is the author's bold claim to an authority self-consciously patterned upon the revelation to Moses at Sinai. Following a divine injunction, Ezra takes five men to a field, whereupon Ezra receives wisdom and understanding. For 40 days, the men in his company recorded 94 books 'in characters which they did not know'. Ezra is then commissioned to 'make public the 24 books that you wrote first and let the worthy and the unworthy read them'. But the 70 others that were written last were to be kept secret and revealed only to the wise. 'For in them are the springs of understanding, the fountains of wisdom, and the river of knowledge.'[88]

The message conveyed by this injunction is that possession of these hidden books granted access to a secret store of wisdom that might complete or even surpass more publicly accessible forms of religious knowledge, represented by the 24 books of the traditional canon. Mani's own narration of the paradigmatic experiences of the seers who preceded him aptly illustrates how the self-validating claims of the Jewish/Christian apocalyptic tradition figured in the legitimation of his divine commission. After each of his predecessors was 'snatched up', Mani says, '[all these things which he beheld] and heard he wrote down and set forth, and he himself *became a witness of his own revelation* (αὐτοῦ [τ]ῆς ἀποκαλύψεως μάρτυς ἐγένετο). But his disciples became a seal of his apostleship.'[89] Mani again invokes the same tradition when he writes in a letter to Edessa that, like the seers who preceded him, he 'received it not from me,

---

[86] On this dimension of the Jewish and Christian apocalypses, see Stone, 'Apocalyptic Literature', 428; von Campenhausen, *Formation*, 218. As von Campenhausen points out, only in the Apocalypse of Peter does the principle of not citing biblical texts 'start to become blurred'. In the fourth chapter of the work, there is a citation from Ezek 37:4.

[87] Stone, *Fourth Ezra*, 38f.

[88] 4 Ezra 14:37-47 (tr Stone).

[89] CMC 57 (72.1).

nor from fleshly creatures, not even from my studies in Scriptures'.[90] Here Mani represents himself as part of a long continuum of secret and self-authenticating revelations that superseded all other sources of religious knowledge.

THE UNCERTAIN STATUS OF THE JEWISH APOCALYPSES

The question now arises as to how these perceptions of the Jewish apocalypses figured in internal Christian controversies over canon and authority in the second and third centuries. It is highly probable that the esotericism and autonomy of the apocalyptic text would have found a welcome reception in sectarian Christian communities interested in circumventing the orthodox models of institutional authority developing in the second and third centuries CE. Increasingly acerbic characterizations of them by their opponents show that the apocalyptic claim to higher wisdom based on secret instruction was a source of growing contention.[91] Repeatedly, Christian heresiologists seek to undermine the authority of the apocalypses with derisive exposés of the real circumstances of their composition. A tactic used to blunt the impact of secret revelations was one that Christian writers had tried against other esoteric literature and rites: openly to disclose what these hidden mysteries contained.[92] Thus, Hippolytus, who made it his business to divulge publicly all the confidential teachings of the heretics, exposes the secret instructions and incantations based on Elcha-

---

[90] CMC 51 (64.12).

[91] Some sense of the controversy may be inferred from an exchange between Peter and the arch-heretic Simon Magus recorded in Hom. 17 of the pseudo-Clementine Homilies (ed Rehm-Irmscher). The debate ponders the question: what is the true ἀποκάλυψις? Simon first claims that religious instruction through supernatural experience is more reliable than that acquired through the senses. It is generally assumed that readers would recognize here the claims made by the supporters of Paul in favor of the overriding authority of Paul's apocalyptic visions. Peter's response points to the kinds of arguments that might be posed against those claiming special insights based on apocalyptic visions. He argues that it is the impious, not the righteous, who have visionary experiences and that these visions occur 'as to an enemy'. True revelation comes not 'through riddles, and visions and apparitions', but through the kind of direct encounter with Jesus that Peter himself experienced. This encounter gave Peter knowledge of the true δύναμις ἀποκαλύψεως, namely 'knowledge gained without instruction, and without apparitions and dreams' (17.18.1,2). If then, Simon Magus considered himself a true apostle of Jesus, he would not oppose Peter, 'a firm rock' and 'foundation of the Church'.

[92] For Christian use of this tactic against the Greek mystery cults, see Clement of Alexandria, Protrepticus 2.14.1 (ed Stählin, vol 1): 'I publish without reserve what has been involved in secrecy, not ashamed to tell what you are not ashamed to worship.' On the importance of maintaining silence about the rites of the mystery cults as a motif in Greek religious and philosophical texts, see Casel, De philosophorum Graecorum silentio mystico; Mensching, Das heilige Schweigen, esp 125-33. For the application of this same technique against heretics, see the pseudo-Clementine Homilies (18.12.3), where the arch-heretic Simon Magus angrily accuses Peter of impudence for artlessly revealing (ἐκφαίνων ἀτέχνως) Simon's secret doctrines (τὰ ἀπόρρητα) before the ignorant masses (ὄχλων ἀμαθῶν).

sai's revelations. 'We shall not be silent about these things (ὧν οὐδὲ ταῦτα σιωπήσομεν),' he writes.[93] Epiphanius pursues the same strategy. After noting the Elchasaite prohibition against divulging the meaning of the Aramaic prayer, he freely offers his own rendering of the formula into Greek. As if this were not enough, he then provides for those 'who would like to hear precise translation' a word-for-word rendering, juxtaposing each Aramaic word to a Greek equivalent.[94]

Two examples from Jewish documents will serve to illustrate how a comparable perception of the older Jewish apocalypses influenced their standing and reception in early Christianity. The first is a work known in the early Church as the Assumption or Ascension of Moses. In his Stromata, Clement of Alexandria shows the highest regard for traditions originating in this work. In one instance, he recounts Joshua's vision of Moses' two bodies as a symbol of the ability of only a privileged few to attain true gnosis.[95] Elsewhere, he discusses a tradition about the heavenly name of Moses ('Melchi') after his ascension into heaven. Although the ultimate source of both of these references was presumably a written document, Clement names as his immediate informants a circle of religious savants whom he characterizes only as 'the initiated' (οἱ μύσται).[96] His testimony implies that already by the end of the second century, religious elites within the early Church valued the teachings of the Assumption of Moses as a conduit for hidden higher wisdom.

The context of Clement's discussion makes it clear that the μύσται were the allegorical exegetes of Alexandria, those who 'see through to the thoughts and what is signified by the names' in Scripture.[97] Indeed, Origen, Clement's successor in Alexandria, later derived the same allegorical significance from the story about Moses' two bodies. Joshua's vision of Moses' two bodies, Origen writes, refers allegorically to the material and the spiritual law. But there is a

---

[93] Hippolytus, Refutatio 9.14.2; see also 9.13.6. On Hippolytus' promise to expose all the secrets of the heretics, see Refutatio 1, proem. 2-5. The justification given here for revealing the secret doctrines and rites of the heretics is that, because they keep silent (σιωπᾶν) and hide their ineffable mysteries (τὰ ἄρρητα ... μυστήρια), many believe they are worshiping God. But cf. Hippolytus' own respect for secret traditions in his work On the Antichrist (29). Here he expresses great apprehension about openly disclosing eschatological secrets concerning which earlier prophets had only 'spoken in a concealed way (ἀποκρύφως)' and 'in mysteries (μυστικῶς) through parables and riddles'. The reason for their unwillingness was out of fear that open proclamation of these secrets would disturb people's mental state (12.16-22; ed Bonwetsch-Achelis).

[94] Epiphanius, Panarion 19.4.

[95] Clement, Stromata 6.15.132.2-3.

[96] Clement, Stromata 1.23.153.1; see also 1.23.154.1. For conflicting views on the relationship of this material to the incompletely preserved Assumption (or Testament) of Moses, see Tromp, *Assumption of Moses*, 270-85. Tromp believes that these traditions about the heavenly Moses originated in the lost ending of that work. For an opposing reconstruction, see Bauckham, *Jude*, 235-80. See also Beckwith, *Old Testament Canon*, 398; Denis, *Introduction*, 131; Schürer, *Geschichte* 3, 303.

[97] Clement, Stromata 6.15.132.3. For discussion, see Hanson, *Origen's Doctrine*, 53-72.

crucial difference in Origen's treatment of this legend. In contrast to Clement, who reveals no uncertainty about the legitimacy of the tradition, Origen expresses some misgivings about its authority. The tradition about Moses' two bodies, he writes, comes from a 'certain little book, in which, although it is not contained in the canon, a figure of this mystery is described'.[98] Already one can detect here an escalating tension between the promise of higher wisdom from a book of secret revelation, and the lack of official or formal recognition of it.[99] By the fourth century, the momentum had definitely shifted against the work. When the bishop Evodius refers to the tradition about Moses' two bodies in one of his epistles to Augustine, he is now careful to hedge his quotations with an emphatic disclaimer. This tradition, he writes, comes from 'the hidden and secret books of Moses himself, a writing that is lacking authority (*caret auctoritate*)'.[100]

One reason why the Assumption of Moses provoked so much uncertainty was its apparent independent confirmation from the New Testament epistle of Jude, something that supporters of the book did not fail to mention.[101] A similar argument was mounted on behalf of 1 Enoch, one of the books investigated in this volume. Of all the Jewish apocalypses, 1 Enoch was probably the most scrutinized. In the first and second centuries, it was quoted without apology as a work of prophecy by Jude, Barnabas, and Clement.[102] A marked change in attitude sets in, however, by the early third century. Tertullian can now no longer assume that his readers will embrace the book with the same alacrity that he does. Origen's enthusiasm for the work was also waning. Although his earlier citations from Enoch reveal no ambivalence, his later allusions to the book are increasingly dismissive. By the fourth century, those Christian writers who do cite the book rarely do so without extensive explanation or equivocation.[103]

When Jerome later tried to explain 1 Enoch's loss of credibility, he attributed it to the work's prominence among heretics (especially the Manichees) and a growing incredulity about 1 Enoch's story of the birth of giants from the intercourse of angels and women.[104] Although these factors may have contributed

---

[98] Origen, Homilies on Joshua 2.1 (ed Baehrens): '... in libello quodam, in quo, licet in canone non habeatur, mysterii tamen huius figura describitur....'

[99] For Origen's knowledge of secret Jewish books, see also his Commentary on Matthew, ser. 28 (on Matt 23:37-39).

[100] Evodius, Ep. 158.6, in Goldbacher, *S. Augustini Epistulae* (CSEL 44).

[101] See Clement, Adumbrationes in epistolas canonicas (In epistola Iudae catholica) 2.24-26 (ed Stählin, vol 3); Origen, De principiis 3.2.1 (ed Koetschau, GCS 22).

[102] See above p9.

[103] See below 47-59.

[104] Jerome, Homily on Psalm 132 (ed Morin) 280.137-281.15. Here Jerome denounces as Manichean the idea that spirits descended into bodily form in order to mingle with women. He also questions a 'certain apocryphal book (quendam librum apocryphum)' that the Manichees use to conform their heretical beliefs; see also Augustine, City of God 15.23. On Manichean use of 1 Enoch, especially the Enochic Book of Giants, see most recently Reeves, *Jewish Lore in Manichaean Cosmogony*.

to the erosion of the work's status, they have the ring of justification after the fact. An 'orthodox' interpretation of Genesis 6 did not solidify until the fourth century, and even after that time, there were those who did not find 1 Enoch incompatible with this interpretation.[105] Moreover, the Church became aware of heretical use of the book well after 1 Enoch's legitimacy was already in doubt. Significantly, the earliest opposition to the work seems to have been unrelated to suspicions about the rectitude of the work's doctrines. Even when his assessment of it begins to sour, Origen does not object to the orthodoxy of the book or the groups who used it. The same observation holds true in Carthage. Tertullian's own interest in the work preceded his alliance with the Montanists and was unrelated to Montanist teachings. Moreover, the critics of the book whom Tertullian sets out to refute did not find anything objectionable about the work's contents or the groups that used it; what they questioned was its genuineness. How then can we account for the book's decline?

We should not be misled by the handful of citations from 1 Enoch in the first two centuries CE. While numerous allusions to the story of the fallen angels attest the popularity of this legend in the early Church, explicit citation of the work by only three writers does not invite the conclusion that the work was widely known or read outside of a few select circles. It would, of course, be anachronistic to inquire into an 'official' position on the book in the first and early second century. The writers who quote the book do not raise this issue, and it is unlikely that the matter was much discussed. But when the question of 1 Enoch's status was first broached, the book's limited dissemination proved most disquieting. In Against Celsus, Origen dismissed the work as 'some book or other', which does not 'circulate very much as divine scriptures (οὐ πάνυ φέρεται ὡς θεῖα τὰ ἐπιγεγραμμένα)'.[106] Nor, he says elsewhere, was it found in the Jewish Bible.[107] Of itself, this latter observation could hardly have constituted for Origen a decisive indictment of the work's legitimacy. Elsewhere, he chides Julius Africanus for suggesting that the Bible of the Jews should dictate standards in such matters.[108] But in the case of 1 Enoch, the Jewish rejection of the book could only have heightened suspicions that the document was confined to a comparatively small circle of readers.[109]

In early Judaism and Christianity, Enoch was a popular figure upon whom to foist secret books. The number of works that survive apparently constitute only a fraction of the many books that circulated in his name. Like other apocalyptic seers, the source of his authority derived from his prestige as a scribe who recorded his heavenly revelations with the utmost care. Wide publication and

---

[105] For discussion, see Wickham, 'The Sons of God'.
[106] Origen, Against Celsus 5.54-55 (ed Koetschau, GCS 3).
[107] Origen, Homilies on Numbers 28.2 (ed Baehrens, GCS 30).
[108] See Origen, Letter to Africanus 3-4 (PG 11, 51-55).
[109] On Origen's views on the Enoch literature, see below 54-59; also Ruwet, 'Les "Antilegomena"', 48-50; id, 'Les apocryphes', 155-57.

acceptance of 1 Enoch, inclusion in a canon, or legitimation through some other channel of institutional authority would have been largely irrelevant to those who accepted his books as secret and inspired.[110] Origen's wavering assessment of the book captures the inherent dilemma created by a work whose allure rested on its esotericism. For even when he can no longer recommend the book to his readers, Origen is still willing to praise the many 'secrets and mysteries' contained in Enoch's writings.[111] Tertullian's own uncertain attempts to procure official acceptance for the book are equally instructive. There is no doubt that Tertullian considered 1 Enoch inspired. In answer to those who do not 'receive' the book, he calls its author a prophet, the 'oldest prophet' (*antiquissimum propheten*) in fact, and suggests to sceptics the possibility that Noah restored the book after the flood 'under the inspiration of the spirit'.[112] The rejection of the book by the Jews, he says, counts for little. Jude's citation of the work attests for him the merit of a work that proclaims Christ. But despite his forceful arguments on behalf of the book's legitimacy, Tertullian does not press for the work's inclusion in the Christian Bible. His discussion of the books of the Old Testament reveals no dissent from what he knows to be the 'orthodox' canon, notwithstanding its omission of a work he privately admired. His chief concern is simply that he and others of like mind be allowed to appeal to a work that he considers inspired and edifying.[113]

The relative ease with which the Church in the fourth century officially ceded 1 Enoch to its enemies reflects the consequences of views like Tertullian's. Many books were vigorously contested in the struggle between 'orthodoxy' and 'heresy'. But the very fact that by the fourth century the church surrendered 1 Enoch without much of a struggle implies that there was not a groundswell of popular or official support for the work in the first place.

The Survival and 'Christianization' of Older Jewish Apocalypses

It would be extreme, of course, to conclude from this that the nature of the apocalyptic claim to authority either precluded official acceptance or uniformly

---

[110] On this aspect of the apocalypse, see von Campenhausen, *Formation*, 217f.

[111] Origen, Homilies on Numbers 28.2. This ambivalence seems to describe Origen's overall attitude toward secret Jewish books. In his Commentary on Matthew (ser. 28), for example, Origen refers to traditions 'ex libris secretioribus qui apud Iudaeos feruntur' in order to explain Jesus' polemic against the Jews in Matt 23:37-39 (ed Klostermann vol 11). At the same time, however, he warns against placing too much confidence in these books, because the Jews might have falsified some of them in order to subvert Christian scriptures. Later, he suggests that Paul may have issued his warning against eschatological speculation in 2 Thessalonians 2 as a counterblast against Jews in his day who claimed to have received 'from books knowledge about the time of the end or (other) secrets' (ser. 55, on Matt 24:36). On Origen's attitude toward secret tradition, see Hanson, *Origen's Doctrine*, 73-90.

[112] Tertullian, De idol. 15.6; De cultu fem. 1.3.1.

[113] De cultu fem. 3.1.

condemned them to marginality. Some of the Jewish apocalypses did in fact receive 'canonical' recognition. 4 Ezra (also known as 2 Esdras) is included in most modern editions of the Vulgate. Canon lists of the Ethiopian Orthodox Church include 1 Enoch and 4 Ezra.[114] Among the Christian apocalypses, the Book of Revelation managed to survive doubts about the work's contested authorship, questionable millennialism, and use by Montanists. The Apocalypse of Peter was recognized in the Muratorian canon, and the Shepherd of Hermas seems to have acquired some measure of formal recognition.

Well after the third century, select Jewish apocalypses managed to find their champions. In Egypt, where 1 Enoch seems to have circulated most widely, the work continued to be known and cited by monastics and practitioners of occult or specialized disciplines.[115] In the latter half of the fourth century, Priscillian of Avila mounted a spirited plea on behalf of 1 Enoch and 4 Ezra. Arguing that inspiration by the Spirit was not bounded by the canon, Priscillian defended these books as genuinely prophetic works, whose worth and edification were certified by apostolic tradition.[116] Later commentators sometimes found enough of value in these works to overrule any doubts about their authenticity or orthodoxy. In the seventh century, for example, the Syriac polymath Jacob of Edessa defended 1 Enoch on the grounds that earlier proscriptions against it were only a reflection of the troubles that the Church once faced in combatting heresy. In the time of Athanasius, he writes, the abuse of secret books by heretics required a blanket condemnation of all of them. But now that the crisis was past, the genuine books, notably Enoch, could be rehabilitated for legitimate purposes.[117]

But these are the exceptional cases. Were it not for passing references in canon lists or quotations from early Christian writers, a substantial number of apocalypses of uncertain origin would now be entirely unknown.[118] Many of those that do survive are translations two or even three times removed from the original. The uneven conditions of their preservation have had a profound im-

---

[114] See Cowley, 'Biblical Canon'.

[115] On the use of 1 Enoch by the Egyptian alchemist Zosimus see below 83f. On 1 Enoch's popularity in Egyptian monasticism, see Lawlor, 'The Book of Enoch', 178-183; Nickelsburg, 'Two Enochic Manuscripts'.

[116] Priscillian, Tractatus 3.56-57, 68 (ed Schepps). In defense of 1 Enoch, Priscillian furnishes arguments similar to Tertullian's, namely Jude's reference to it and its value as witness to Christ. On behalf of 4 Ezra, he observes that it reports the rewriting of the Hebrew Bible after it was burned (see 4 Ezra 14), something not mentioned in the canonical books of the Bible. For discussion, see Chadwick, *Priscillian*, 74, 80-83.

[117] Syriac text in Wright, 'Two Epistles of Mar Jacob'. For French translation of the Syriac text, see Nau, 'Traduction'. Jacob's defense of 1 Enoch is found in Ep. 13.2 (114v; Nau ib 206).

[118] See Russell, *Method and Message*, 66-69; James, *Lost Apocrypha*. For more recent discussion, see Beckwith, *The Old Testament Canon*, 398. Useful observations on the hardening of Christian attitudes to the apocalypses and other Jewish pseudepigrapha after the second century may be found most recently in Kraft, 'The Pseudepigrapha in Christianity', 63-66.

pact on the study of the Jewish apocalypses, especially as it involves the recovery of the lost 'original' text behind its preserved Christian form.

Of all of the Jewish literature inherited by early Christianity, apocalypses and related literary genres (oracles and testaments) proved to be especially vulnerable to editorial reworking. The stern injunctions that some of the apocalypses issue about preserving intact the precise words of the revelation suggest that their authors recognized the temptation to tamper with the text.[119] As early as the second century, pagan opponents of Christianity were already able to identify what must have been extensive and fairly egregious Christian additions to the Sibylline Oracles.[120] But while it is generally recognized that the Jewish apocalypses have been subject to varying degrees of Christian reworking, it is not always an easy matter to establish criteria to distinguish a Jewish source from a Christian interpolation or addition. Many apocalypses survive in recensions often varying quite considerably from one another. The channels through which these documents were transmitted and preserved are still imperfectly understood. Although new textual editions have benefited from a much expanded manuscript base, the initial or transitional stages in the translation and transmission of these documents are in most cases still obscure. When the rare occasion does arise to compare a Christian version of an apocalypse with the same document in an earlier Jewish version, the results can be sobering. In the case of 1 Enoch, for example, the discovery of fragments of that work from Qumran required a complete reevaluation of the Christian and Manichean textual transmission of the work.[121]

Typically, the supposition of an underlying Semitic text, the absence of overtly Christian doctrines or allusions, and the presence of material difficult to explain in a Christian context are adduced as proof of a work's non-Christian origin. But the application of these criteria can be extremely imprecise. Since many of the apocalypses were ascribed to worthies of the distant past, Semitisms and content seemingly incompatible with a Christian religious outlook may only be antiquarian touches designed to enhance the work's credibility. Early Judaism and Christianity were far from homogeneous, and the boundaries between the two religions remained fluid and uncertain for a long time. It would be naïve to suppose that distinctions between 'Jewish' and 'Christian' could not, therefore, vary substantially from one region to the next.[122]

One apocalypse especially illustrative of the difficulties of establishing meaningful criteria for authorship and origin is the mysterious work known as 2

---

[119] See, for example, Rev 22:18-19.

[120] See the observations on this matter attributed to Celsus in Origen's Against Celsus 7.53. For a survey of Christian reworking of the apocalypses and other Jewish pseudepigrapha, see Charlesworth, 'Christian and Jewish Self-Definition'.

[121] For discussion, see Stone, 'Apocalyptic Literature', 395-406; VanderKam, 'Some Major Issues'.

[122] On this problems of differentiating Jewish from Christian, see especially Kraft, 'The Multiform Jewish Heritage', 177-88.

(Slavonic) Enoch. Almost nothing certain can be said about its provenance, date, or original language. The manuscript witnesses, none of which pre-date the 14th century, survive in longer and shorter recensions whose textual relationships have yet to be unravelled. Although 2 Enoch, like much Christian literature preserved in Slavonic, was probably translated from a Greek original, numerous Semitisms at least raise the possibility of an earlier Aramaic or Hebrew version. Dated anywhere from the first century BCE to the tenth century CE, it has been attributed to a bewildering variety of Christian and Jewish groups.[123]

Late word usages in the underlying Greek text, possible dependence on and allusions to Christian sources, and references to the Julian calendar have suggested to some the possibility of Christian authorship well after 70 CE.[124] The absence of anything unmistakably Christian in the work has, however, generally tipped the scale in favor of Jewish authorship. But if it can be granted that the work does not reveal any identifiably 'Christian' characteristics, the same might be said of its 'Jewish' content as well. It is Enoch's secret writings, not Moses', that embody divine wisdom. Neither Jewish nor even post-diluvian history of any sort is part of the work's purview. Apart from vigorously championing an ethical monotheism, the apocalypse shows very little interest in or knowledge of specifically 'Jewish' practices and beliefs. On the basis of a reference in the work to the preparation of animal sacrifices (2 Enoch 59:2-3), R. H. Charles concluded that the composition of the work was 'earlier than the destruction of the Temple, A.D. 70'.[125] But the apocalypse's prescriptions for the right methods of sacrifice – binding the four legs of the sacrificial animal together – actually contradict temple sacrificial customs described in the Mishnah.[126] If 2 Enoch does originate in pre-70 Judaism, independent documentation for the kind of Judaism it reflects is very slight.

2 Enoch exemplifies the difficulties that often arise in identifying an apocalypse's Jewish or Christian provenance on the basis of inconclusive internal evidence. How much recognizable difference would one expect to discover between a Jewish and Christian work recounting revelations to an antediluvian hero? Would not a Christian or Jewish writer (pre- or post-70) seek to endow his work with authenticity through deliberately archaizing descriptions of out-

---

[123] Charles-Morfill, *Secrets of Enoch*, xxv-xxvi: 'Egyptian Judaism'; Vaillant, *Secrets d'Hénoch*, x-xi: 'Jewish Christianity' with Hellenistic elements; Milik, *Books of Enoch*, 109: a Christian monk of Byzantium.

[124] See Milik, *Books of Enoch*, 107-116. Milik dates 2 Enoch to the ninth or tenth century CE. F.I. Andersen's introduction to his translation of 2 Enoch (*OTP* 1, 94-97) contains a useful discussion of the problems; see also Collins, 'The Genre Apocalypse', 533.

[125] Charles and Morfill, *Secrets of Enoch*, ad loc.

[126] See Pines, 'Eschatology and the Concept of Time', 75.

moded religious practices?[127] The problems associated with this apocalypse fully justify F. C. Burkitt's observation that 'the whole question of the channels by which rare and curious literature found their way into Slavonic requires fresh and independent investigation'.[128] They also illustrate the need to deepen our knowledge of the types of Christian communities that used the apocalyptic literature and their reasons for perserving it.[129]

Apocalyptic Themes in Non-Apocalyptic Genres

The final subject examined in this volume concerns the use of apocalyptic themes in non-apocalyptic genres, in this case the adaptation of the apocalyptic review of history by Christian apologists and historians.

As has already been noted, the early Church produced on its own a sizable number of apocalypses sharing at least in formal terms similarities with their Jewish counterparts. Conspicuously absent from the Christian apocalypses, however, are certain of the better-known features of their older Jewish counterparts. One of these is the review of history. The highly schematized reviews of history found in some of this literature were not simple exercises in antiquarianism. By contextualizing a contemporary crisis in a larger historical framework, the historical survey helped to demonstrate that the upheaval of the apocalyptist's time, far from being a meaningless or random event, represented the final phase in an irrevocable chain of events. In order to convey the idea of history as predetermined, the surveys of history were typically cast in the form of ex eventu prophecy and periodized into historical or chronological epochs. Because of their popularization by early Christian writers, the 70-year weeks and the four kingdoms of Daniel are probably the better known examples of such schemes. However, related schemes are attested in other Jewish apocalypses, among them 1 Enoch, 4 Ezra and 2 Baruch.[130]

While the diminished role of the outlines of history in Christian and Gnostic apocalypses has been generally explained on theological grounds, the absence

---

[127] As Burkitt, *Jewish and Christian Apocalypses*, 76 writes: '...the whole book is supposed to be written before the Flood, long before the promulgation of the Mosaic Law. Enoch's "sons" are all mankind, and the book actually closes with an account of Methusalem's sacrifice to the Lord on the occasion of his father Enoch's translation... I do not know that a Christian romance of Enoch need differ very much from a Jewish romance of Enoch'.

[128] Burkitt ib.

[129] For discussion of the problem of identifying Jewish materials preserved in a Christian context, see Kraft, 'The Pseudepigrapha in Christianity', 60-63.

[130] See 1 Enoch 83-90 (the 'animal apocalypse'); 91:12-17; 93 (the 'apocalypse of weeks'); 4 Ezra; 2 Baruch 53-74; Apocalypse of Abraham 21-32. For discussion of the historical survey in apocalyptic literature, see Hall, *Revealed Histories*, 61-170.

of the historical survey may not be strictly a result of internal developments.[131]
It should first be noted that the reason why this feature of the apocalypses has
been accorded such significance by modern scholarship has to do with its
prominence in Daniel and the support it gives to an eschatological definition of
the genre. But sweeping surveys of history were not a *sine qua non* of the
Jewish apocalypses. They are at best marginally attested in apocalypses that
feature otherworldly journeys.[132] Although the evolution of the Jewish apocalypses is by no means linear and the factors responsible for shaping this
development are uncertain, the popularity of the heavenly journey in many of
the later Jewish apocalypses corresponds to a marked increase in late Antiquity's appetite for revelatory literature of this kind. The fact that otherworldly
excursions, visions and auditions increasingly dominate the Christian apocalypses may thus have less to do with fundamental changes in theological
perspective than with broader religious trends in the Greco-Roman world.[133] At
any rate, one consequence of this was that the historical survey, which was
never an important element of the apocalyptic heavenly journey, fell into obso-
lescence.

Whatever the reasons for their absence from the Christian apocalypses, surveys of history found ready acceptance in other literary forms, especially the
Christian universal chronicle. From its very inception, the universal chronicle
embraced a theory of history very similar to the Jewish apocalyptist's. After
having been disappointed in their expectations of the imminent arrival of the
kingdom, early Christian writers based their eschatological hopes on the belief
that the world was destined to run its course after six millennia.[134] But whereas
this was initially stated simply as a matter of conviction, the first Christian

---

[131] Vielhauer ('Apocalyptic', *NTA* 2, 600) conjectured that an increasing Christian fascination with
the parousia precluded elements of the Jewish apocalyptic tradition that were not directly relevant
to the signs of the end time. The decline of the historical survey has also been attributed to a
fundamentally altered Christian conception of the meaning of history. The conviction that the
culmination of history had already taken place in the coming of Christ meant that Christian apoc-
alyptists no longer felt the need to relate some current crisis to past history through ex eventu
prophecy. The critical moment was already past; see Schmithals, *Apocalyptic Movement*, 208-9;
Schüssler Fiorenza, 'Phenomenon', 310f; Collins, 'Pseudonymity', 338f, 342 offers the same explanation, but denies that this represents any fundamental change in perspective. The absence of the
historical survey from the Gnostic apocalypses has been traced to Gnostic pessimism and alienation
from the world that necessarily entailed disinterest in historical processes; see, for example,
Schmithals, *Apocalyptic Movement*, 89-110, 208f; but cf Kippenberg, 'Ein Vergleich'.

[132] See Collins, 'The Jewish Apocalypses', 22-25. He notes (23) that the Apocalypse of Abraham
15-32 is the only Jewish apocalypse with an otherworldly journey and a review of history.

[133] For discussion of the otherworldly journey in Greco-Roman literature, see Attridge, 'Greek and
Latin Apocalypses', 159-68.

[134] See Barn. 15:1-5; Irenaeus, Against Heresies 5.28.3; Justin Martyr, Dialogue with Trypho
80.5-81.4; Hippolytus, Commentary on Daniel 4.24; Lactantius, Divine Institutes 7.14. For discussion, see Daniélou, 'La typologie millénariste'. On the Jewish background, see Str-B 4.2, 989-
94.

chroniclers determined to give it an empirical foundation by subsuming all of world history under this 6000-year span. In setting out to encompass the broad sweep of history from its very beginnings, the Christian chroniclers conceived of their task on an order of magnitude unthinkable in Greek historiography. It is not surprising that in their efforts to harness world events to this form of historical determinism, Christian chroniclers seized on some of the better known schemes in the Jewish apocalypses.[135]

The Jewish apocalyptist's interest in the past was not derived strictly from theodicy and eschatology. One aspect of the speculative and encyclopedic dimension of the Jewish apocalypses, perhaps best represented by 1 Enoch, was a fascination with the origins of things. In 1 Enoch, this expressed itself in curiosity about the discovery of the calendar, the measurement of time, and the origins of wisdom, both depraved and legitimate. These traditions were readily received by Christian apologists and chroniclers with interests in the same matters. 1 Enoch's legend about the origins of the reckoning of time and the Watchers' introduction of unlawful wisdom into the world became integral elements of their attempts to piece together a coherent narrative of the origins of civilization, particularly as it involved the measurement of time.[136] At the same time, Christian redactors were not above inserting chronological or historical details designed to make them more agreeable to later sensibilities.[137] Excerpts from 1 Enoch, along with other Jewish pseudepigrapha, in Syriac and Byzantine chronicles, testify to the continuing vitality of some of the Jewish apocalypses long after their official prohibition.[138]

---

[135] For discussion, see most recently Palmer, *The Seventh Century*, xxvi-xxviii; see also below 221-23, 236-38.

[136] This is already evident in Clement's Stromata 5.1.10.1-2, where the origin of the false wisdom of the Greeks is traced to the unlawfully revealed heavenly secrets of the Watchers.

[137] For discussion of chronological insertions into the text of the longer recension of 2 Enoch adapted from the Christian universal chronographers, see Vaillant, *Secrets d'Hénoch*, xxi-xxii, 117 n1.

[138] For discussion see Adler, *Time Immemorial* 80-97, 117-22, 175-231.

Chapter Two

1 Enoch, Enochic Motifs, and Enoch in Early Christian Literature

James C. VanderKam

The Status of Enochic Literature in Early Christianity

INTRODUCTION

From early times there were booklets which circulated under the name of
Enoch. Scholars have long recognized that several of these are pre-Christian in
date, but the recovery of significant parts of this corpus among the Dead Sea
Scrolls has added decisive evidence for the antiquity of most of 1 Enoch. It
appears that the five booklets which constitute this work belong in the following chronological order:

1. The Astronomical Book (1 Enoch 72-82= AB):   3rd century BCE.
2. The Book of the Watchers (1 Enoch 1-36= BW):   3rd century BCE.
3. The Epistle of Enoch (1 Enoch 91-108= EE):   2nd century BCE.
4. The Book of Dreams (1 Enoch 83-90= BD):   2nd century BCE.[1]
5. The Book of Parables (1 Enoch 37-71= BP):   1st century BCE/CE

As is well known, sizable pieces from four of these sections were found among
the fragments of Qumran Cave 4, but not a single scrap of The Book of Parables has been identified. This fact has added fuel to the debate among New
Testament scholars about the relevance of these parables for understanding
Jesus' self-designation 'son of man'. Is the text pre-Christian, or was it written
during or even after New Testament times and hence clearly not a source for
the gospels' 'son of man' usage? In recent times opinions about the date of 1
Enoch 37-71 have ranged from the first century BCE to the first century CE.[2]
Whatever one decides about this issue, it is clear that several Enochic texts
were available for reading by the time of Jesus and the early church. The
Qumran library has divulged that there was an Enochic Book of Giants (BG) as

---

[1] For discussion of the paleographical data and other dating considerations, see Milik, *The Books of
Enoch*, 4-59; and VanderKam, *Enoch and the Growth*, 76-178.

2 For references, see Knibb, 'The Date of the Parables'. Milik, *The Books of Enoch*, 89-98 has
stimulated the most recent discussion with his contention that the Parables were written in the third
century CE.

well.[3] It is noteworthy, too, that some copies of the Enoch material combined several booklets in a single scroll:

4QEn^c:	BW, BG, BD, EE[4]	last third of the first century BCE[5]
4QEn^d:	BW, BD	last third of the first century BCE[6]
4QEn^e:	BW, BG(?), BD	first half of the first century BCE[7]

There are two other books which bear the name Enoch, but both of them belong to later times. 2 (Slavonic) Enoch may have been written in the late first century CE.[8] No MS of it antedates the fourteenth century, however.[9] G. Nickelsburg notes that a date in the first century CE is often suggested but it is uncertain.[10] It was probably written in Greek and comes from Egypt.[11] 3 (Hebrew Apocalypse of) Enoch, which is a work from perhaps the fifth or sixth century CE, falls outside the purview of this study.[12]

The survey that follows will adduce the surviving evidence regarding the assessments given the writings of Enoch by those early Christian authors who mention them.[13] The major concern here will not be to identify the places where an Enochic theme or phrase may lie behind an expression in a text written by a Christian; rather the focus will be on those relatively few passages from which we can glean something about the status Enochic writings had for a particular author. Clearly, only limited conclusions may be drawn from the sparse evidence. It hardly follows from one writer's lofty claims about the value of Enoch's books that all those in his area at that time shared his opinion. Nevertheless, it is undeniable that some early Christian authors accorded high, indeed scriptural standing to the writings of Enoch. The order of the ensuing survey is chronological, and where possible the geographical locations of the authors are specified.

---

[3] It may have been composed in the second century BCE (Milik ib 58).

[4] On inclusion of the BG, see Milik ib 57f.

[5] ib 5.

[6] ib.

[7] ib 5, 227.

[8] This is the date indicated in the title of the translation of it in *OTP* 1, 91. F.I. Andersen, the translator, however, writes (97): 'In every respect 2 Enoch remains an enigma. So long as the date and location remain unknown, no use can be made of it for historical purposes. The present writer is inclined to place the book – or at least its original nucleus – early rather than late; and in a Jewish rather than a Christian community.'

[9] Andersen ib 94.

[10] Nickelsburg, *Jewish Literature*, 188.

[11] ib 185, 188.

[12] For the dates see P.S. Alexander in *OTP* 1, 225-29.

[13] It should be kept in mind that early readers of Enochic literature may have had available only a single part of it, not the full collection that is now designated 1 Enoch.

CHRONOLOGICAL SURVEY

Jude (Palestine?; second half of the first century). The Letter of Jude, which identifies itself as being written by 'a servant of Jesus Christ and brother of James' (v1),[14] is often thought to be among the latest of the New Testament writings;[15] and the early canon lists evidence some uncertainty within different parts of the church regarding its standing. It appears among canonical works in the Muratorian Canon, and both Tertullian and Clement of Alexandria recognize it. Nevertheless, as late as the fourth century, Eusebius placed it among the disputed writings. It seems that Jude's use of traditions from documents not found in the most widely accepted forms of the Old Testament had something to do with its tenuous status.[16] Among these traditions are, of course, words attributed explicitly to Enoch.

Much of the little epistle consists of examples which illustrate divine punishments in the past or evils like those committed by the writer's opponents: 1) those who were saved from Egypt were later destroyed when they failed to believe (v5); 2) the 'angels who did not keep their own postion, but left their proper dwelling, he has kept in eternal chains in deepest darkness for the judgment of the great Day' (v6) – a clear allusion to material in 1 Enoch 6-11;[17] 3) Sodom, Gomorrah and surrounding cities (v7). Here, then, he has aligned references to episodes in Exodus/Numbers, 1 Enoch, and Genesis. Nothing is said about the status of any of these works, nor is it said that one was ranked higher or lower in authority than another. Each is considered an appropriate source of information about the Lord's punishing acts in the past. That is, like Genesis and Exodus/Numbers, 1 Enoch is a source of facts about what God has done.

Jude then proceeds to indict 'certain intruders' (v4) for slander and for pursuing the way of Cain, Balaam, and Korah (vv8-11) – examples from Genesis and Numbers. At an earlier point he had noted about them that they were '...people who long ago were designated for this condemnation as ungodly' (v4),[18] and to

---

[14] All biblical citations are from the NRSV.

[15] Cf Kümmel, *Introduction*, 300-302; but see Bauckham, *Jude, 2 Peter*, 13f, who puts it in the second half of the first century CE and even remarks: 'All the same, once one has cast off the spell of the early catholic and antignostic reading of Jude, the letter does give a general impression of primitiveness. Its character is such that it might very plausibly be dated in the 50's, and nothing requires a later date.' As the destination for the letter, he notes (16) Syria, although it was not accepted there. Asia Minor or Egypt are also possibilities. The author himself, Bauckham thinks, may have been from Palestinian apocalyptic circles. See most recently his 'Jude, Epistle of'.

[16] See Beckwith, *Old Testament Canon*, 400f. He cites Didymus the Blind and Jerome in support of this point. Bauckham, *Jude, 2 Peter*, 17 mentions Origen, Eusebius, Didymus, and Jerome as attesting to doubts about the book because it used apocryphal material.

[17] So Charles, *Book of Enoch*, xcv. Odeberg, 'ENΩX' claims that Jude 4 cites 1 Enoch 48:10. If so, the allusion would be vague (it has to do with denying the Lord and Messiah). The reference is more likely to 1 Enoch 67:10; see Osburn, '1 Enoch 80:2-8', 300-2.

[18] Cf Bauckham, *Jude, 2 Peter*, 97.

this point he returns in his famous citation from 1 Enoch 1:9:[19]

> It was also about these that Enoch, in the seventh generation from Adam, prophesied [ἐπροφήτευσεν], saying, "See, the Lord is coming with ten thousands of his holy ones, to execute judgment on all, and to convict everyone of all the deeds of ungodliness that they have committed in such an ungodly way, and of all the harsh things that ungodly sinners have spoken against him." (vv14-15)

Several items in this passage should be highlighted. First, Enoch is credited with 'prophesying'[20] and the sense of the verb here is that he predicted because, though he was the seventh from Adam, he had already spoken about the ungodly intruders who so severely exercised Jude.[21] Second, in his prediction, Enoch had in view not only Jude's impious foes but also the eschatological judgment. From his vantage point before the flood, Enoch spoke of the final courtroom and the sentence that those who slander the Lord would there receive. Thus, Jude knew several parts of The Book of the Watchers (chaps. 1, 6-11 at least), and believed that in prophetic fashion the ancient patriarch had spoken these words. It is also worth mentioning that in calling Enoch ἕβδομος ἀπὸ 'Αδάμ Jude uses a phrase[22] found in 1 Enoch 60:8 – though it may be a simple inference from Genesis 5.[23]

The Epistle of Barnabas (Alexandria; second half of the first century). The letter, though falsely attributed to Paul's colleague Barnabas,[24] is nevertheless among the earliest surviving specimens of Christian literature. Scholars place its date of composition between ca. 70 and 100 CE. It was written in Greek, perhaps in Alexandria. Its general purpose was to show that the Old Testament scriptures, far from enjoining the practices current among the Jews, actually provided advance testimonies about Christ – if only they were read correctly and not as the Jews understood them.[25] Thus he cites passages which show that

---

[19] This is the only place in which he quotes a source and uses a standard introductory formula; see Bauckham ib 93. On the wording of the citation – an early witness to the text of 1 Enoch 1:9 – see the comparison in Milik, *The Books of Enoch*, 184-6 on 4QEnᶜ 1 i.15-17; Knibb, *The Ethiopic Book of Enoch* 2, 59f; Bauckham, *Jude, 2 Peter*, 93-98 who thinks that 'Jude *knew* the Greek version, but made his own translation from the Aramaic'; and Osburn, 'The Christological Use'.

[20] Bauckham ib 96: 'While this word indicates that Jude regarded the prophecies in *1 Enoch* as inspired by God, it need not imply that he regarded the book as canonical scripture. At Qumran, for example, the Enoch literature and other apocryphal works were evidently valued without being included in the canon of Scripture.' So too Beckwith, *Old Testament Canon*, 403. Their claims about a Qumran canon are highly dubious.

[21] Note the repeated use of ungodliness/ungodly and the same word for these opponents in v4.

[22] 2 Peter, which many think is dependent on Jude, lacks the explicit citation from 1 Enoch but refers to the ancient condemnation of deceptive teachers/prophets (2 Pet 2:3), while 2:4 refers to the Watcher story. Beckwith, *Old Testament Canon*, 401f thinks the absence of a direct reference shows the writer's suspicion about pseudepigrapha.

[23] Charles, *The Book of Enoch*, xcvi; Odeberg, 'ΕΝΩΧ', 559; see Bauckham, *Jude, 2 Peter*, 96; cf 1 Enoch 93:3; Jub. 7:39 but neither one is phrased as here; only 1 Enoch 60:8 is.

[24] By Clement of Alexandria, for example.

[25] See J.B. Lightfoot, *Apostolic Fathers*, 133.

the Lord wanted neither sacrifices (par. 2) nor fasts (par. 3). In the fourth
paragraph he urges the readers to flee from the works of lawlessness and adds:
'The final stumbling-block is at hand of which it was written, as Enoch says,
"For to this end the Lord has cut short the hours and the days, that his beloved
should make haste and come to his inheritance"' (4:3).[26] Elsewhere in Barnabas, when an authority is named, the cited material follows rather than precedes
the reference.[27] Yet, the statement that Barnabas relates to Enoch is the first
part, according to a number of scholars. It reads in this way: τὸ τέλειον σκάνδαλον ἤγγικεν, περὶ οὗ γέγραπται. While Barnabas' reference to a written
work that circulated under the name of Enoch seems clear, the passage to which
he is referring is not. As R. H. Charles wrote about it: 'Not in our Enoch'[28] –
that is, this exact statement does not appear in the extant texts of 1 Enoch.[29]
Milik[30] suggests that it, like the reference to Enoch's writing in Barn. 16:5, is a
summary, 'a recapitulatory note to En. 106:19-107:1, where the word γέγραπται refers to the contents of the heavenly Tablets...' The passage to which he
alludes occurs in Enoch's response to Methuselah regarding the meaning of
Noah's remarkable nature already at the moment of birth. He predicts,

> But after this [i.e. the flood] there will be yet greater iniquity than that which was
> committed in the earth before. For I know the mysteries of the holy ones, for that
> Lord showed (them) to me and made (them) known to me, and I read (them) in the
> tablets of heaven. And I saw written on them that generation upon generation will do
> wrong until a generation of righteousness shall arise, and wrongdoing shall be de-
> stroyed, and sin shall depart from the earth, and everything good shall come upon
> it.[31]

It is true that these verses refer to something written, but no σκάνδαλον, much
less the final one, figures here, nor is there any prediction that one has drawn
near (if Enoch's words are contained in the first part of the passage). It is
possible that Barnabas is not citing but paraphrasing or summarizing, as Milik
proposes; but one must also remember that the text of 1 Enoch has in places
been altered in transmission. Or, possibly Barnabas is not referring to something in 1 Enoch. Of these various possibilities, it seems safest to say, given the
character of the references later in Barnabas, that the writer is referring to
teachings in 1 Enoch – a book dominated by concerns with the growth of evil

---

[26] Translations of Barnabas are from Lake, *Apostolic Fathers*. Lake identifies the Enochic words as
those that follow 'as Enoch says', not those which precede, unlike many commentators. Cf *ANF* 1,
138. Lake notes in the margin that the passages intended are 1 Enoch 89:61-64; 90:17. Both have to
do with the shepherds' excesses and their punishment; neither resembles Barnabas' words literally
or in content.
[27] On this point see Reeves, 'An Enochic Citation'.
[28] Charles, *The Book of Enoch*, lxxxi.
[29] Nor does it figure in any other Enochic text.
[30] Milik, *The Books of Enoch*, 73f.
[31] All English citations from 1 Enoch are from Knibb, *The Ethiopic Book of Enoch*.

until the final judgment. In addition, there are several references in it to the belief that the end is drawing nigh.[32] The material summarized from 1 Enoch would then be the words which come after 'as Enoch says' – thus conforming with the practice in Barnabas.

The context in Barnabas 4 also includes references to Daniel,[33] Exodus,[34] Isaiah,[35] Matthew[36] and allusions to some New Testament epistles. The setting, then, shows that Enoch's words are among those γέγραπται, and they are aligned with references to other books widely recognized as scriptural.

The same author resorts to the writings of Enoch again in chap. 16, where his subject is the temple. He wishes to 'show how the wretched men erred by putting their hope on the building, and not on the God who made them, and is the true house of God'. (16:1) He proceeds to quote from Isa. 40:12; 66:1; and 49:17 in order to demonstrate his point (16:2-3). He alludes to the destruction of the temple at the end of the revolt (70 CE) as more confirmation of Old Testament sentiments about the building that could not contain the Lord. In 16:5-6 he writes:

> Again, it was made manifest that the city and the Temple and the people of Israel were to be delivered up. For the Scripture says [λέγει γὰρ ἡ γραφή], "And it shall come to pass in the last days that the Lord shall deliver the sheep of his pasture, and the sheepfold, and their tower to destruction." And it took place according to what the Lord said. But let us inquire if a temple of God exists. Yes, it exists, where he himself said that he makes and perfects it. For it is written [γέγραπται γάρ], "And it shall come to pass when the week is ended that a temple of God shall be built gloriously in the name of the Lord."

Charles[37] identified these references as drawn from 1 Enoch 89:56 for Barn. 16:5 and 91:13 for 16:6. In 1 Enoch 89:56, part of the second dream vision of Enoch in which Israel is represented as sheep, one reads: 'And I [=Enoch] saw how he left that house of theirs and their tower and gave them all into the hands of the lions, that they might tear them in pieces and devour them, into the hands of all the animals.'[38] 1 Enoch 91:13[39] adds: 'And at its end they will acquire

---

[32] See, for example, 45:6 ('for the sinners my judgment draws near before me'); 47:2; 51:2; 91:6; 93:9 (which places the final apostasy in the seventh week – apparently the author's time, after the destruction of Jerusalem and the temple had occurred at the end of the sixth week); 94:6-7; 95:6; 96:1; 97:10; and 98:15. R. Kraft has emphasized, in an oral discussion of the present chapter, that at least in the manuscript tradition of a work such as the Testaments of the Twelve Patriarchs the names of the person to whom a statement is attributed change from manuscript family to manuscript family.

[33] Dan 7:24 and 7:7f.

[34] Exod 34:28; 32:7.

[35] Isa 5:21; 33:18.

[36] Matt 22:14.

[37] Charles, *The Book of Enoch*, lxxxi; cf 199.

[38] Cf 89:54 in which the house of the Lord of the sheep and the tower are mentioned together with their pastures.

[39] Part of the description of the eighth week in the Apocalypse of Weeks.

houses because of their righteousness, and a house will be built for the great king *in glory* for ever.' M. Black[40] makes the same identification of Barnabas' words in 16:5 and writes: 'In spite of its being introduced as a scriptural quotation, the verse in Barnabas looks more like a free reminiscence of vss. 55, 56 here. It appears to be drawing on a Greek version: νομή = מרעיתא, πύργος = מגדלא(?)'[41] One can make a good case that Barnabas, who seems fairly loose in his citations of passages, has something like this context in 1 Enoch in mind because he mentions each of the items which the images in the second dream vision symbolize.[42]

city   = house/pasture/sheepfold – cf 89:54, 66-67[43]
temple   = tower
people   = sheep

It is transparent from Enoch's dream, however, that the temple is the first temple; the time is therefore not the last days. This is one reason why Milik has demurred regarding the standard theory: '...the Book of Dreams is quoted only once [in early Christian literature], in a recapitulatory manner, by the Epistle of Barnabas 16:5 ...this quotation is generally compared with En 89:56-74. But the precise detail, "at the end of time", which was essential for the author of the Epistle makes me think rather of En 90:26-8:[44] "And I saw at that time a precipice... And these blinded sheep were brought and they were ...cast into this abyss of fire and they burned... And I rose to watch until they folded up that old house (sc. Jerusalem) and all the columns were swept away... and they were cast into a place to the right of the earth."'[45] There is no doubt that Milik is right: Barnabas' introductory words require an eschatological source; but it is awkward for Milik's case that the temple, the point of Barnabas' remark, is not mentioned in 90:26-29, since the house is Jerusalem in this vision, not the temple. It is not impossible that the original mentioned the tower/temple, but the extant texts do not.[46] More acceptable is Milik's remark that 16:5 is '... a conglomerate of expressions scattered all over our Enochic writing'.[47]

As for Barn. 16:6, there is also some uncertainty regarding the passage in-

---

[40] Black, *The Book of Enoch*, 270. Beckwith, *Old Testament Canon*, 396 suggests 1 Enoch 91:5-7, but this is unlikely.

[41] There is no Greek version for this section of 1 Enoch.

[42] Lawlor, 'Early Citations' studies this passage in connection with Testament of Judah 18 where, he believes, 1 Enoch 89:53f is under consideration, and where the Testament introduces the words of Enoch with ἐπ' ἐσχάταις ἡμέραις: 'The conclusion seems irresistible that somewhere in En lxxxix.53-56 the words "in the last days" occurred, though they have disappeared from the text now in our hands' (171).

[43] For sheepfolds in the desert period, see 89:34-35 (לדיריהון in 4QEn^c 4.6,8). Cf Charles, *The Book of Enoch*, 198, comment on 89:50 and T. Levi 10:4; but see Milik, *The Books of Enoch*, 46f, who thinks he misinterpreted it.

[44] ib 73 he writes 90:26-29.

[45] ib 46.

[46] 89:73 does mention the building of the second temple.

[47] Milik, *The Books of Enoch*, 47.

tended, but, as in 16:5, 1 Enoch is the most likely source for the statement if not for the precise formulation: 'And it shall come to pass when the week is ended that a temple shall be built gloriously in the name of the Lord.' These words appear nowhere verbatim in 1 Enoch, but the reference to *a week*, especially the end of one, reminds one of a repeated phenomenon in the Apocalypse of Weeks. Thus Charles[48] finds echoes of 91:13 here: 'And at its end they will acquire houses because of their righteousness, and a house will be built for the great king [God] *in glory* for ever.' The verses in Barnabas and 1 Enoch share the mention of a week, of the 'weekend,' and a temple built gloriously for the Lord. Much of this verse now is available in Aramaic in 4QEn[g] 1 iv 17-18:

17   ועם סופה יקנון נכסין בקשוט

18   ויתבנא היכל [מ]ל[נ]כ[ו]ת רבא ברבות יוה לכול דרי עלמין

[13]And with its end they shall acquire riches in righteousness, and there shall be built the royal Temple of the Great One in His glorious splendour, for all generations forever.[49]

Milik comments that רבא, 'the Great One,' 'by itself is a substitute for the name of God',[50] and that Barnabas refers to the name of God. Therefore, it is surprising to find Milik opting for 1 Enoch 90:29,[51] which shares with Barnabas only the reference to the house. But in 90:29 the house is Jerusalem, not the temple.

There is no doubt that in these two places in chap. 16 the author is alluding to, though not citing from 1 Enoch. For the present purposes the most significant fact about the context is that Barnabas, after several quotations from Isaiah, introduces the Enochic material with, 'For Scripture says'. For this ancient writer, then – perhaps from Alexandria[52] – 1 Enoch constituted scripture and hence its teaching could be used to establish points that he wished to convey to his Christian audience so that they would, in this case, have a proper understanding of the Old Testament temple.

The two works just surveyed exhaust the first-century Christian references to the writings of Enoch. Jude cannot be located with certainty but may come from Syria/Palestine; Barnabas is somewhat more securely situated in Egypt. The writers of both works accord high status to Enoch's words – they are prophecy and scripture. How widespread their views may have been cannot be determined, but at least these two authors greatly valued Enoch's words and expected use of them to be acceptable to their audiences, since neither defends his practice of citing from them.

Athenagoras, Embassy for the Christians (Alexandria; 176-80 CE). The Embassy of the apologist Athenagoras can be dated quite precisely to 176-80 by its

---

[48] Charles, *The Book of Enoch*, lxxxi.
[49] Milik, *The Books of Enoch*, text, 266; translation, 267.
[50] ib 268.
[51] ib 46.
[52] See Lake, *Apostolic Fathers*, 337.

address to the two emperors – Marcus Aurelius and Commodus – who were associated in office for those years.[53] The sources place him in Alexandria.[54] His Embassy defends Christians against the charges of atheism, cannabalism and incest – charges that arose from popular perceptions of Christian rituals and practices.

As he rebuts the charge of atheism, Athenagoras defends Christian monotheism and opposes statues of pagan gods. At par. 23, he turns to a new objection which might be raised against his position: 'Your surpassing wisdoms [the emperors] might ask me: How do some of the idols show activity, if those are not gods to whom we set up statues?'[55] He then adduces Plato's accommodation of his philosophical view regarding the one God with the popular notion of Zeus. In par. 24 he explains the Christian concept of God[56] and refers to angels to whom God entrusted the regulation of the material world. These angels had the ability to choose good or evil: some selected well, others did not.

> ...Some remained at the task for which they were created and to which they were appointed by God (for they had received free will from God), while others acted wantonly towards their own nature and their charge, that is, the ruler of this realm of matter and of the forms that are in it, and others that were in charge of the first firmament. Pray, realize that we tell of nothing without evidence, but expound what the prophets have declared (ἃ τοῖς προφήταις ἐκφώνηται). Well, then, these angels fell a-lusting after maidens and yielded to fleshly desires, and he, the chief of them, became heedless and wicked in the administration of his charge. Thus by those that went after maidens were the so-called giants begotten, and it is no marvel that an account, though incomplete, of the giants was told by the poets. Earthly wisdom differs from that of the prophets as a likely tale does from the truth: the one is earth bound and under the rule of matter, the other is from heaven. (par. 24)

Such spirits, he later[57] explains, draw people toward idols.

In this citation, Athenagoras indicates his familiarity with the myth of the angels who descended and mated with women. The giants who were engendered have souls which 'are those spirits that wander about the world'[58] and produce evil in people. Though the angel story has its exegetical base in Gen 6:1-4, Athenagoras transparently knows a more developed form of it – specifically, the elaborations best known from 1 Enoch. Crehan refers to the account in Jub. 4:22; 5:1-9[59] and does not mention 1 Enoch. In fact, he notes in connection with the first instance of the word *prophet* (above): 'The prophets were held to include Moses as their chief (Deut. 18:15) and hence Gen 6:1-4, which is the source of the myth about the fornicating angels, might be said to come

---

[53] Crehan, *Athenagoras*, 9-11; Barnard, *Athenagoras*, 19-22.
[54] Barnard ib 13-17; Crehan ib 4-7.
[55] Translations of Athenagoras are from Crehan ib.
[56] He mentions Father, Son, and Spirit.
[57] Par. 26.
[58] Par. 25.
[59] Crehan, *Athenagoras*, 154 n208.

from the prophets.'[60] But he misses the point that Moses can hardly be said to be the prophetic source of the angel story which Athenagoras presents. This raises the possibility – a rather likely one – that among the *prophets* to whom he refers is Enoch. Barnard correctly appeals to 1 Enoch 15:3.[61] Others have also concluded that Enoch is meant among the prophets.[62] One cannot be certain about the conclusion, because the watcher myth is more widely attested, though 1 Enoch is the earliest, most developed source for it. Nevertheless, it is probable that Athenagoras, like Jude, classified Enoch as a prophet.[63]

Irenaeus (Gaul; ca. 130 – ca. 200). Irenaeus mentions Enoch in Against Heresies 4.16.2.[64] In chap. 16, he deals with Old Testament laws such as circumcision and sabbath. Both meant more than their literal signification. Moreover, people were not justified by such ordinances, as the examples of Abraham, Lot, and Noah show. The next model for his point is Enoch: 'Enoch, too, pleasing to God, without circumcision, discharged the office of God's legate to the angels although he was a man, and was translated, and is preserved until now as a witness of the just judgment of God, because the angels when they had transgressed fell to the earth for judgment, but the man who pleased [God] was translated for salvation.'[65] Lawlor[66] saw here a reference to 1 Enoch 12, 13, 6ff., and 10; Charles[67] listed 12:4, 6; 13; 14:3-7; and 15; and 16. The source for Irenaeus' allusion is not in doubt, but the context in which he places it is of greater interest. None of his other examples in this section goes beyond the givens of Genesis; only the lines about Enoch do. This suggests that Irenaeus understood Genesis 5:21-24; 6:1-4 in the light of 1 Enoch and placed its account of Enoch on the same plane as the other scriptural references.

The first example mentions Enoch by name but elsewhere Irenaeus shows that he knows the Watcher story, even if he does not attribute it to Enoch. In a remarkable passage, after summarizing the Gnostic systems, the Bishop of Lyon sketches the one Christian faith confessed by believers throughout the world on the basis of what they have received from the apostles and disciples. His résumé follows the triune pattern. Here the section on the Holy Spirit is of special interest:

---

[60] ib 154 n209.

[61] Barnard, *Athenagoras*, 114. He also notes the Jubilees passage.

[62] Lawlor, 'Early Citations', 177; Charles, *The Book of Enoch*, lxxxii-lxxxiii. He adds 1 Enoch 6:7; 13:5; 14:5; 15:8-10.

[63] It is clear, however, that his reference to angelic control over the lower realm is not from 1 Enoch.

[64] See *ANF* 1,312; the work was written during the bishopric of Eleutherus, who held the office in Rome during these years.

[65] *ANF* 1, 481; The full text is available only in Latin, but parts of it are extant in Greek, and some also in Syriac and Armenian (see the article 'Irenaeus', in Cross-Livingstone, *Oxford Dictionary*, 713f.

[66] Lawlor, 'Early Citations', 195f.

[67] Charles, *The Book of Enoch*, lxxxiii.

...And in the Holy Spirit, who proclaimed through the prophets the dispensations of God, and the advents, and the birth from a virgin, and the passion, and the resurrection from the dead, and the ascension into heaven in the flesh of the beloved Christ Jesus, our Lord, and His [future] manifestation from heaven in the glory of the Father "to gather all things in one," [Eph 1:10] and to raise up anew all flesh of the whole human race, in order that to Christ Jesus, our Lord, and God, and Saviour, and King, according to the will of the invisible Father, "every knee shall bow, of things in heaven, and things in earth, and things under the earth, and that every tongue should confess" [Phil 2:10-11] to Him, and that He should execute just judgment towards all; that he may send "spiritual wickednesses", [τὰ μὲν πνευματικὰ τῆς πονή-ριας]^{68} [=Eph 6:12] and the angels who transgressed and became apostates [καὶ ἀγγέλους [τοὺς] παραβεβηκότας, καὶ ἐν ἀποστασίᾳ γεγονότας], together with the ungodly, and unrighteous, and wicked, and profane among men, into everlasting fire...[69]

It is not impossible that Irenaeus, in the wording of his lines about the angels, is thinking of 2 Pet 2:4 and Jude 6, but the language he uses does not reproduce their vocabulary very closely. There is, however, some verbal similarity with 1 Enoch. For example, at 1 Enoch 106:14, in reference to the angels, Enoch says to Methuselah: καὶ ἰδοὺ ἁμαρτάνουσιν καὶ παραβαίνουσιν^{70} τὸ ἔθος – the very verb used by Irenaeus. 1 Enoch 106:13 does the same.[71] If Irenaeus is here reflecting the Watcher story, he is attributing it to the Holy Spirit's inspiration of the prophets and including it within a brief statement of the Christian faith shared throughout the scattered churches.

Irenaeus makes clear in several other passages that he knows this story and accepts it in his system. In Against Heresies 1.15.6 he notes the words of a certain 'divine elder and preacher of the truth' who says of the gnostic Marcus that he is involved in the 'black arts of magic' and signs and wonders

Which Satan, thy true father, enables thee still to accomplish
By means of Azazel, that fallen and yet mighty angel.[72]

Or, in 4.36.4 he writes: 'And in the days of Noah He justly brought on the deluge for the purpose of extinguishing that most famous race of men then existant, who would not bring forth fruit to God, since the angels that sinned had commingled with them, and [acted as He did] in order that he might put a check upon the sins of these men, ...'[73]

---

[68] The Greek is cited from Black, *Apocalypsis Henochi*, 11.

[69] *ANF* 1, 330f.

[70] 4QEn^c 5 ii.17 has ועבןריך (Milik, *The Books of Enoch*, 209).

[71] There the Greek has παρέβησαν = עברו in 4QEn^c 5 ii.18 (Milik ib).

[72] *ANF* 1, 340.

[73] *ANF* 1, 516. The Latin has 'commiati fuissent' = 1 Enoch 7:1. So Lawlor, 'Early Citations', 196. Cf 4.37.1, where angels are rational beings with moral choice, like humans; or 5.29.2: the beast with the number 666 in the Apocalypse has their number, '...since he sums up in his own person all the commixture of wickedness which took place previous to the deluge, due to the apostasy of the angels.' *ANF* 1, 558.

Clement of Alexandria (Egypt; ca. 150 – ca. 215). Clement begins his Selections from the Prophets (ἐϰ τῶν προφητιϰῶν ἐϰλογαί)[74] by citing several summonses to praise found in the Danielic hymn of the three young men,[75] referring to it as part of αἱ γραφαί (1.1). In par. 2.1 he quotes Dan 3:54 (= θ'):

> εὐλογημένος εἶ ὁ βλέπων ἀβύσσους, ϰαθήμενος ἐπὶ χερουβίμ.
> Blessed are you who look into the depths from your throne on the cherubim.

To the quotation he adds the words:

> ὁ Δανιὴλ λέγει, ὁμοδοξῶν τῷ Ἐνὼχ τῷ εἰρηϰότι· »ϰαὶ εἶδον τάς ὕλας πα-
> σας«[76]
> Daniel says, agreeing with Enoch who had said: "I saw all the matter."

The short extract is attributed specifically to Enoch, but its location has caused some debate. A. Dillmann believed that Clement was quoting from 1 Enoch 19:3: 'And I, Enoch, alone saw the sight, the ends of everything; and no man has seen what I have seen.' The Greek has: ϰἀγὼ Ἐνὼχ ἴδον τὰ θεωρήματα μόνος, τὰ πέρατα πάντων, ϰαὶ οὐ μὴ ἴδῃ οὐδὲ εἷς ἀνθρώπων ὡς ἐγὼ ἴδον.[77] His suggestion has often been repeated, despite the clear fact that the two do not match all that closely.[78] Lawlor,[79] however, had already observed that Clement '...assigns to Enoch a saying which is nowhere found in our Book...' He concluded as he frequently did: 'The passage therefore must be added to the list of extracts from the Book of Enoch not found in our present text.'[80]

The citation should, nevertheless, be read in context. As Lawlor said,[81] Clement pairs the citations from Daniel and Enoch – two prophets – in order to show that the terms ἀβύσσους in the former and ὕλας in the latter are synonymous. The sequel further explicates the two words:

> ἄβυσσος γὰρ τὸ ἀπεράτωτον ϰατὰ τὴν ἰδίαν ὑπόστασιν, περαιούμενον δὲ τῇ
> δυνάμει τοῦ θεοῦ. αἱ τοίνυν οὐσίαι ὑλιϰαί, ἀφ' ὧν τὰ ἐπὶ μέρους γένη ϰαὶ τὰ
> τούτων εἴδη γίνεται, ἄβυσσοι εἴρηνται· ἐπεὶ μόνον τὸ ὕδωρ οὐϰ ἂν εἶπεν
> ἄβυσσον. ϰαίτοι ϰαὶ ὕδωρ ἄβυσσος ἢ ὕλη ἀλληγορεῖται. (2.2-3)
> For "abyss" is the unlimited according to its own essence, but bounded by the power
> of God. Hence the material properties from which the individual types and their
> forms come are called "abysses", since he would not have called the water alone
> "abyss". Yet water is allegorized as "abyss" or "matter".

---

[74] For the Greek text, see Stählin-Früchtel-Treu, *Clemens Alexandrinus*, vol. 3.

[75] Dan 3:59, 58, 60, 61-63, 90; so Stählin ib 137.

[76] See below for Origen's use of the same passage.

[77] G² = εἶδον. Black, *Apocalypsis Henochi*, 32. The passage is not preserved in Aramaic. Milik, *The Books of Enoch*, 145 notes the use of קצות for extremities = all, entirety, as in קצות ארעא.

[78] Charles, *The Book of Enoch*, 43; Black, *Apocalypsis Henochi*, 11; see also his *The Book of Enoch*, 161; Beckwith, *Old Testament Canon*, 397.

[79] 'Early Citations', 182.

[80] ib.

[81] ib.

Here one is reminded of words from 1 Enoch 19:3: τὰ πέρατα πάντων. That is, Clement draws a distinction between the singular ἄβυσσος = τὸ ἀπερ-άτωτον and plural ἄβυσσοι (in the Enochic quotation) = αἱ οὐσίαι ὑλικαί. Consequently, when Enoch is cited as saying that he saw τὰς ὕλας πάντας, whereas the passage in 1 Enoch says τὰ πέρατα πάντων, the two are the same. Clement has drawn information from this passage in 1 Enoch without citing it verbatim. If this explanation is correct, it also renders superfluous the additional claim that 2 Enoch 40:1,12 may be behind Clement's attribution.[82] Those verses are farther removed from Clement's text. In 40:1, Enoch claims: 'I know everything; for either from the lips of the Lord or else my eyes have seen from the beginning even to the end, and from the end to their recom-mencement.'[83] This appears to be an explication of words such as those in 1 Enoch 19:3. 2 Enoch 40:12 simply notes that Enoch saw where hell was. The explanation given above also entails that Milik's thesis is unnecessary in this case. Here again he infers from the difference in wording between what Clem-ent writes and what is found in extant texts of 1 Enoch 19:3 that the Christian author was not citing a text of Enoch: 'At the very most one might envisage it as an explanatory gloss of the Enochic passage [the position defended above] indicated; note in particular the philosophical meaning of ὕλη, a term which one just would not expect in a literal translation of a work of Enoch. Such an explanatory phrase – in which an attempt is made to elucidate the rather unclear expression, τὰ πέρατα πάντων, which is moreover, a mistranslation[84] – would have its appropriate place in a collection of Old Testament quotations, enriched with glosses, exegetical notes, summaries, etc.'[85] It seems simpler to say that Clement was referring to 1 Enoch 19:3 and explaining the word ἄβυσσοι from the terms used in that verse, i.e., he provided the explanatory gloss.

A larger inference may be drawn from Clement's use of 1 Enoch here: he refers to it in clarification of a term in Daniel and locates it in a work entitled 'Selections from the Prophets'. Thus Clement joins the early Christian witness-es (Jude, apparently Athenagoras and Irenaeus) to the belief that Enoch was among the prophets.

In Selections from the Prophets 53.4 one encounters another early Christian reference to the angel myth, and again it is attributed to Enoch. The passage is set in a context in which Ps 19:2 is under discussion. The verse reads:

> Day to day pours forth speech
> and night to night declares knowledge.

In explanation, Clement notes that the demons have special knowledge:

---

[82] So Stählin, *Clemens Alexandrinus*, 137; Black, *Apocalypsis Henochi*, 11.
[83] So recension J; A is almost identical (translation of F.I. Andersen in *OTP* 1, 164f).
[84] See Milik, *The Books of Enoch*, 35.
[85] ib 73.

"νὺξ νυκτί·" πάντες οἱ δαίμονες ἔγνωσαν ὅτι κύριος ἦν ὁ ἀναστὰς μετὰ τὸ
πάθος. ἤδη δὲ καὶ Ἐνώχ φησιν τοὺς παραβάντας ἀγγέλους διδάξαι τοὺς
ἀνθώπους ἀστρονομίαν καὶ μαντικὴν καὶ τὰς ἄλλας τέχνας. "Night to night":
All the demons knew that it was the Lord who arose after the passion, for Enoch
already said that the angels who transgressed taught humanity astronomy, divination,
and the other arts.

It is undoubted that Clement has in mind the various arts, enumerated in 1
Enoch 7:1-8:3,[86] which the fallen angels taught to humans. The three categories
that he mentions – astronomy, manticism, and the other arts – are not named in
those very words and in that precise order in 1 Enoch 7:1-8:3, but all appear to
be there. The first category is largely undefined, but ἀστρονομία = ἀστρολο-
γίας (=8:3); cf also τὰ σημειωτικά, ἀστεροσκοπία, σεληναγωγία. The form
ἀστρολογίαν actually occurs in Syncellus' version of 8:3. The Aramaic fragments have preserved this verse partially,[87] and in them some terms explicating
Clement's μαντική appear:

4QEnª 1 iv.2-4	כ]שפו וחרטמו[	'magic, sorcery'[88]
	נ]חשי כוכבין[	'signs of the stars'[89]
	נחשי שמ]ש	'the signs of the sun'[90]

cf 4QEnᵇ 1 iii.2-4.[91]

So, in this instance, too, an early Christian writer alludes to rather than quotes 1
Enoch, but he gives sufficient information so that the object of the allusion can
be identified. The Book of Enoch could, therefore, be used to explain a phrase
in a psalm. Also, Clement's use of ἤδη indicates that he regarded the book, not
as a recent forgery, but as an ancient work. This ancient work was, on this
point, a reliable source of information.

Stromata 5.1.10,1-2 differs from the preceding instances in that Clement does
not name Enoch here, but he once more alludes to the angel story in a way that
expresses his confidence in it. Indeed he mentions it in a context in which
Moses and the prophets appear. The general subject is Greek theft from the Old
Testament:

And we showed in the first Miscellany[92] that the philosophers of the Greeks are
called thieves, inasmuch as they have taken without acknowledgement their principal
dogmas from Moses and the prophets (παρὰ Μωυσέως καὶ τῶν προφητῶν τὰ
κυριώτατα τῶν δογμάτων οὐκ εὐχαρίστως εἰληφότας). To which also we shall
add that the angels who had obtained the superior rank, having sunk into pleasures,
told to the women the secrets which had come to their knowledge; while the rest of

---

[86] So Lawlor, 'Early Citations', 182; Beckwith, *Old Testament Canon*, 397; Charles, *The Book of Enoch*, lxxxv, 19 – he mentions only 8:2,3; Black, *Apocalypsis Henochi*, 11 notes 8:1-3.

[87] Enª and Enᵇ.

[88] Milik, *The Books of Enoch*, 157f.

[89] ib.

[90] ib; see his general comment on p160.

[91] ib 170.

[92] = Stromata 1.17.87,2.

the angels concealed them, or rather, kept them against the coming of the Lord. Thence emanated the doctrine of providence, and the revelation of high things; and prophecy having already been imparted to the philosophers of the Greeks, the treatment of dogma arose among the philosophers, sometimes true when they hit the mark, and sometimes erroneous, when they comphrehended not the secret of the prophetic allegory.[93]

Lawlor finds here a reference to 1 Enoch 16:3, where Enoch is ordered to say to the angels:[94]

You were in heaven, but (its) secrets had not yet been revealed to you and a worthless mystery you knew [μυστήριον ⸢τὸ ἐκ τοῦ θεοῦ γεγενημένον⸣ ἔγνωτε·][95]. This you made known to the women in the hardness of your hearts, and through this mystery the women and the men cause evil to increase on the earth.[96]

It is likely that Clement had this verse (and the general story in 1 Enoch 6-16) in mind when he penned these lines. It is not obvious, however, that he meant to include the Enochic material within the literary categories 'Moses and the prophets'. In fact one might more convincingly argue that he considered the contents of the book a truthful supplement to Moses and the prophets in that he writes, directly after noting the Greek theft from them: οἷς δὴ κἀκεῖνα προσθήσομεν. Then follows the Enochic material. What is happening here is that Clement is surveying the various means by which the Greeks stole the truth from the Old Testament authorities and other sources: the demonic angels, about whom one learns the truth in 1 Enoch, were another such source. As a result, here, unlike in the Ekloge, Clement may not be including Enoch among the prophets.

Tertullian (North Africa; ca. 160 – ca. 220). Tertullian converted to Christianity in 195 or 196 CE and went back to his native Carthage. He became a Montanist in ca. 207. He is of special interest as a fervent defender of Christianity for whom the authenticity of the Book of Enoch was worth supporting and from which he cites as from a great authority. There is substantial disagreement about the dates for Tertullian's various writings (within very limited chronological confines), but all of the texts in which he uses 1 Enoch antedate his Montanist phase, with the possible exception of On Idolatry.

Barnes dates the Apology to 'autumn 197 or later'.[97] As he deals with 'the existence of certain spiritual essences,'[98] Tertullian cites the support of Socrates

---

[93] *ANF* 2, 446.
[94] 'Early Citations', 182; so, too, Charles, *The Book of Enoch*, 37; Stählin, *Clemens Alexandrinus*, 332, n. to lines 16-20 = *Stromata Bücher I-IV* (GCS 52/2); Black, *Apocalypsis Henochi*, 11, 30; id, *The Book of Enoch*, 155; Martin, *Le livre d'Hénoch*, cxxv.
[95] Charles, *The Ethiopic Version*, 47 noted that E read ἐξουθενημένον. Black, *The Book of Enoch*, 155 accepts this explanation.
[96] Cf 9:6-8
[97] Barnes, *Tertullian*, 55.
[98] *ANF* 3, 36.

and Plato and then adds (22): 'We are instructed, moreover, by our sacred books how from certain angels who fell of their own free-will, there sprang a more wicked demon-brood, condemned of God along with the authors of their race, and that chief we have referred to.'[99] As the detail regarding the angels exceeds that of Genesis and reflects clearly what is found in 1 Enoch 6-15, and especially 15:8-9, it is likely that Tertullian is including 1 Enoch among 'our sacred books'.[100]

Scholars have formulated arguments for dating this treatise in 196-197[101] or 198-208,[102] although it has at times been assigned to his Montanist phase. Waszink and van Winden write: '*De idololatria* is a treatise on the practice of Christian life in relation to the (often hidden) religious elements in the heathen world.'[103] In this work, in chaps. 3-23, Tertullian deals with the sundry ramifications of idolatry, and in 3-11 specifically with the sort of idolatry that arises through the arts and professions. Within these general confines, he makes his initial foray into 1 Enoch.

In 4.1 Tertullian cites the decalogue's command against making idols. He then (4.2-3) turns to 1 Enoch.

> 2. Already earlier Enoch had prophesied (*praedicens*) that the demons and spirits, that is the apostate angels, would employ all elements, everything belonging to the world, everything that the heaven, the sea, and the earth contain, for idolatrous purposes, so that they were hallowed, instead of God, against God. Everything, therefore, is worshipped by human error except the Creator of everything Himself. The images of these things are idols, the consecration of the images is idolatry. Every offence committed by idolatry must of necessity be imputed to every maker of every idol.
>
> After all, the same Enoch threatened and forejudges at the same time both the worshippers and the makers of an idol: 3. "And again I swear to you sinners, that unrighteousness has been prepared for the day of the destruction of blood. You, who serve stones and who make images of gold and silver and wood and stone and clay, and serve ghosts and demons and spirits in sanctuaries and all errors, not according to knowledge, you will not find any help for them."[104]

In this case, Tertullian just alludes to Enoch's prophecy that the apostate angels would employ all elements for idolatrous purposes. It has long been suggested that the Latin father here intends 1 Enoch 19:1: 'And Uriel said to me: "The spirits of the angels who were promiscuous with the women will stand here; and they, assuming many forms, made men unclean and will lead men astray so that they sacrifice to demons as gods – (that is,) *until the great judgement day*

---

[99] He has mentioned Satan just before this.
[100] See Charles, *The Book of Enoch*, lxxxiv, 36.
[101] Barnes, *Tertullian*, 55.
[102] Waszink – van Winden, *Tertullianus*, 10-13 say it is probably to be dated between 203 and 206.
[103] ib 9; cf Barnes, *Tertullian*, 96f.
[104] Waszink – van Winden, *Tertullianus*, 27, 29.

on which they will be judged so that an end will be made of them.'" Charles[105]
pointed to this passage and to 99:7[106] (the only two verses in which the word
demons appears in the Greek texts) as the source of Tertullian's remarks. Lawlor had earlier done the same,[107] though he admitted the source was 'not quite
clear'. Typically, however, he seizes upon the differences in wording between
the Ethiopic of 1 Enoch 19:1 and Tertullian's text to conclude that '[e]ither
Tertullian's text of xix.1 was very unlike ours, or he was quoting a passage not
in our Book of Enoch at all.'[108] But Tertullian is clear enough that he is alluding
to, not quoting from, the Book of Enoch in these comments. Waszink and van
Winden, after noting that Charles and Black point to 1 Enoch 19:1, object that
though this is the only passage which exhibits similarity with what Tertullian
says, there are additional items mentioned by Tertullian but not found in 1
Enoch 19:1. They propose that the elements named by Tertullian are from a
passage such as 1 Enoch 80:2-8.

> ...We do best to assume that Tertullian is here expressing in his own words a combi-
> nation of ideas which he had found in the book of Enoch. That the formulation is
> entirely his own is also evident from the structure of the sentence, which bears the
> stamp of Tertullian's style, especially the climax built up by successive parts of the
> sentence.[109]

Thus, it seems likely that Tertullian is more broadly alluding to the contents of
various parts of 1 Enoch. Milik, who agrees that he is referring to 19:1, also
believes that Tertullian's *omnia elementa*, etc. reflects the world as pictured in
the report of Enoch's travels in 1 Enoch 17-36; while his phrase 'quae in caelo
sunt' echoes, not 80:7, but chaps. 33-36.[110] However, the material in 99:6-7 is
similar to Tertullian's reference in 4.2.

The situation is much different for the words in 4.3 because here Tertullian is
clearly quoting. All commentators recognize that he is reproducing a form of 1
Enoch 99:6-7, although it is not identical to the readings in the surviving manu-
scripts of the book.[111] The wording employed by Tertullian is noteworthy.
There is no doubt that he connects the statements with the antediluvian sage.[112]
These he considers prophetic --apparently in the sense of prediction. Moreover,

---

[105] Charles, *The Book of Enoch*, 42f; see, too, Martin, *Le livre d'Hénoch*, cxxvi; Black, *The Book of Enoch*, 161; Beckwith, *Old Testament Canon*, 397 (who suggests either 19:1 or 65:6-8, but the latter is unlikely to be the source).

[106] Tertullian quotes this passage in the next paragraph.

[107] Lawlor, 'Early Citations', 181.

[108] ib.

[109] Waszink – van Winden, *Tertullianus*, 116.

[110] Milik, *The Books of Enoch*, 79.

[111] For comparisons, see especially Milik ib and Waszink – van Winden, *Tertullianus*, 117-9. Milik ib 80 concludes from Tertullian's uses of 1 Enoch that he had a manuscript which contained both the Book of the Watchers and the Epistle of Enoch.

[112] 'Antecesserat Enoch praedicens' (Waszink – van Winden, *Tertullianus*, 26); cf 'praedamnat' in 4.3 (ib 28).

Enoch is referred to and cited as an authority. The material from 1 Enoch is sandwiched between a citation from the pentateuch[113] and quotations from Isaiah 44:8-9 and Ps 115:8; 135:18,[114] with no indication in the text that Tertullian puts them on different levels. If this were not clear enough, the rhetorical flourish with which he ends the section clinches the case:

> And why should I, a man of limited memory, suggest anything more, why remind you of anything more from Scripture (*de scripturis*)? As if the voice of the Holy Spirit were not sufficient, or as if it deserved any further consideration whether the Lord has not rather cursed and damned the makers themselves of those things, whose worshippers He curses and damns.[115]

In the same work Tertullian again resorts to 1 Enoch but does so in an unexpected manner. Chap. 15 appears within the more general context of his discussions of the kinds of idolatry which come about through participation in social life;[116] 14.6-15.11 deals with the celebrations in which Christians participate. In the paragraph in question the issue is the decoration of doors with lamps and laurel wreaths – a practice (found also among Christians) which Tertullian took to be idolatrous. Enoch is then adduced as an authority on the superstitions which involved the gods of doors, which apparently attract demons.

> Moreover, demons have no name individually but they find a name where they also find a pledge. The Greeks, too, as we read, have in Apollo Thyraeus and the Antelian demons protectors of entrances. Therefore the Holy Spirit, foreseeing this from the beginning, predicted through the intermediary of the oldest prophet, Enoch, that even entrances were to become objects of superstition. For we see that other entrances, too, are worshipped, viz., in the baths. (15.6)[117]

Waszink/van Winden[118] maintain that Tertullian here is recalling his earlier listing (in 4.2) of what the demons would lead people to worship: 'In this conversation Tertullian wants to say: "Enoch also predicts the adoration of doors": hence *etiam ostia*.' Lawlor[119] believed Tertullian had in mind 1 Enoch 19:1 or whatever passage he was referring to in 4.2.[120] Milik[121] demurs, seeing here allusions to 1 Enoch 9:2 and 9:10 '...where the complaints of men, which rise as far as the "doorways of heaven," are mentioned'. But this seems highly implausible, since different doorways are involved.

  If it is acceptable to conclude that Tertullian is referring to the same pas-

---

[113] It is from the decalogue (4.1).
[114] Waszink – van Winden, *Tertullianus*, 119: 4.4.
[115] ib 29.
[116] ib 15f.
[117] ib 53.
[118] ib 244.
[119] Lawlor, 'Early Citations', 181.
[120] Similarly Beckwith, *Old Testament Canon*, 397.
[121] Milik, *The Books of Enoch*, 79.

sage(s) as he was using before, then we find here another strong statement about his view of the Enoch whose words appear in 1 Enoch: he was the most ancient prophet, and the Holy Spirit predicted through him that this kind of idolatry would occur.

There is some disagreement about the unity of the work that goes under the name *De cultu feminarum*. Barnes holds that the second book was written in 196 or 197. Later, before becoming a Montanist, Tertullian 'reworked' this document, the results of which are now presented as the first book, though its original title may have been *De habitu muliebri*.[122] He dates the latter, in which the reference to Enoch occurs, to perhaps 205-206.[123] Turcan, however, considers the whole work a unity and places it in 202.[124] As he opens Book 1, Tertullian reminds women that each of them is an Eve, due to whose transgression the Son of God had to die (1.1). He goes on to explain in the second chapter that the ornaments and finery worn by women are really to be traced back to the angels who '...conferred properly and as it were peculiarly upon women that instrumental means of womanly ostentation, the radiances of jewels wherewith necklaces are variegated, and the circlets of gold wherewith the arms are compressed, and the medicaments of orchil with which wools are coloured, and that black powder itself wherewith the eyelids and eyelashes are made prominent' (1.3).[125] These angels the Christians are some day to judge, according to the Pauline promise (1 Cor 6:3). Reference to the angel story[126] raises in Tertullian's mind the status of the Book of Enoch from which the account comes. To it he then devotes chap. 3 – '...n'étant qu'une parenthèse destinée à prouver l'authenticité du livre d'Énoch, qui affirme cette origine satanique...'[127]

> [1.] I am aware that the Scripture of Enoch [*scripturam Enoch*], which has assigned this order (of action) to angels, is not received by some, because it is not admitted in the Jewish canon [*armarium Iudaicum*] either. I suppose they did not think that, having been published before the deluge, it could have safely survived that worldwide calamity, the abolisher of all things. If that is the reason (for rejecting it), let them recall to their memory that Noah, the survivor of the deluge, was the great-grandson of Enoch himself; and he, of course, had heard and remembered, from domestic renown and hereditary tradition, concerning his own great-grandfather's 'grace in the sight of God,' and concerning all his preachings; since Enoch had given no other charge to Methuselah than that he should hand on the knowledge of them to his posterity. Noah therefore, no doubt, might have succeeded in the trusteeship of (his) preaching; or, had the case been otherwise, he would not have been silent alike concerning the disposition (of things) made by God, his Preserver, and concerning the particular glory of his own house.

---

[122] Barnes, *Tertullian*, 137, cf M. Turcan, *Tertullien*, 20.

[123] Barnes, *Tertullian*, 55.

[124] Turcan, *Tertullien*, 30.

[125] *ANF* 4, 15.

[126] Tertullian turns to it a number of times: De idol. 9; De or. 22; De cult. fem. 1.2 ch. 10; De virg. Vel. 7.

[127] Turcan, *Tertullien*, 21.

[2.] If (Noah) had not had this (conservative power) by so short a route, there would (still) be this (consideration) to warrant our assertion of (the genuineness of) this Scripture [*scripturae*]: he could equally have *renewed* it, under the Spirit's inspiration, after it *had* been destroyed by the violence of the deluge, as, after the destruction of Jerusalem by the Babylonian storming of it, every document of the Jewish literature is generally agreed to have been restored through Ezra.

[3.] But since Enoch in the same Scripture [*scriptura*] has preached likewise concerning the Lord, nothing at all must be rejected *by* us which pertains *to* us; and we read that 'every Scripture [*scripturam*] suitable for edification is divinely inspired'. By the *Jews* it may now seem to have been rejected for that (very) reason, just like all the other (portions) nearly which tell of Christ. Nor, of course, is this fact wonderful, that they did not receive some Scriptures which spake of Him whom even in person, speaking in their presence, they were not to receive. To these considerations is added the fact that Enoch possesses a testimony in the Apostle Jude.[128]

Tertullian's primary concern here is to support the genuineness of the Enochic scripture, which provides him with the basis for his argument about the origin of women's finery. In building his case he formulates four arguments:

a) The flood need not have destroyed the writing because Noah could have preserved his prophetic deposit.[129]

b) If that did not happen, the Spirit could have renewed it through inspiration, just as happened much later with Ezra.[130]

c) Enoch preached or prophesied about the Lord in this book, and Christians must not reject such inspired words, though the Jews, to no one's surprise, do not accept them.

d) Enoch has the support of Jude.

Here, then, for the first time in extant Christian literature one finds arguments for the genuineness or scriptural status of 1 Enoch, which speaks not only about the evil origins of feminine ornamentation but about Christ himself. This latter claim may, as Turcan observes, point to the Similitudes of Enoch[131] in which a judicial Son of Man figures. However, it is also possible that passages such as the theophany in 1:3-9 are meant. It is beyond doubt that Tertullian knows the story in 1 Enoch 6-11, while the allusion to the transmission of Enoch's words through his son Methuselah arises from 1 Enoch 82.

Tertullian opens the second chapter of *De cultu feminarum* with some sarcastic remarks (such as God's forgetting to create purple and scarlet sheep) to show that the deity was not the author of womanly ostentation. Within the paragraph he alludes at some length to 1 Enoch:

So true is it that it is not intrinsic worth, but rarity, which constitutes the goodness (of these things): the excessive labour, moreover, of working them with arts introduced

---

[128] *ANF* 4, 15-16.

[129] Apparently this would have happened through Noah's memory, not by his having the book on the ark; cf also 1 Enoch 68:1.

[130] This entails that Tertullian also found 4 Ezra authoritative or at least accurate on this matter.

[131] Turcan, *Tertullien*, 60.

by the means of the sinful angels, who were the revealers withal of the material substances themselves, joined with their rarity, excited their costliness, and hence a lust on the part of women to possess (that) costliness. But if the self-same angels who disclosed both the material substances of this kind and their charms – of gold, I mean, and lustrous stones – and taught men how to work them, and by and by instructed them, among their other (instructions), in (the virtues of) eyelid-powder and the dyeings of fleeces, have been condemned by God, as Enoch tells us, how shall we please God while we joy in the *things* of those (angels) who, on these accounts, have provoked the *anger* and the *vengeance* of God? (2.10)[132]

The passage to which he refers is 1 Enoch 8:1, the text which he used in 1.2.[133] Though Tertullian draws a number of terms and ideas from this passage in 1 Enoch, he uses the phrase 'ut Enoch refert'[134] specifically in connection with the words 'damnati a Deo sunt'. Here he probably intends 1 Enoch 10.[135] Thus it is the Book of Enoch which contains within it the account of what God did with regard to the sinful angels.

Barnes[136] dates the treatise On the Resurrection of the Flesh to 206-207, still before Tertullian became a Montanist. Ernest Evans[137] outlines the first parts of On the Resurrection of the Flesh in this way: 'The first (paras. 1-4), which almost serves the usual purpose of an exordium, relates the heretical half-beliefs with which Tertullian is in conflict, to the opinions of philosophers and to the prejudices of the general non-Christian public. In part two (paras. 5-17) are set out the general principles which are to govern the interpretation of the relevant passages of Scripture: namely, the dignity of the flesh, the power of God, and the necessary requirements of the divine judgement. Parts three (18-39) and four (40-56) take up the testimony of the Scriptures, first expounding their positive teaching, and then rescuing from perverse misunderstanding or misinterpretation a number of apostolic texts of which the adversaries have claimed the support.'[138] It is within this third part that Tertullian may again resort to the Book of Enoch.

32. But lest it should seem that the only resurrection preached is of those bodies which are consigned to sepulchres, you have it written [*habes scriptum*], "And I will command the fishes of the sea and they shall spew up the bones that are consumed and I will bring joint to joint and bone to bone."[139]

Tertullian then goes on to defend this thesis in the remainder of the paragraph, later saying:

---

[132] *ANF* 4, 23.

[133] See Charles, *The Book of Enoch*, lxxxiv, 19.

[134] Turcan, *Tertullien*, 148.

[135] See especially 10:8; cf also 13:1-2; 14:4-5; chap. 16.

[136] Barnes, *Tertullian*, 38, 55.

[137] Ernest Evans, *Tertullian's Treatise*, xvi-xvii.

[138] ib.

[139] ib 87.

Will any one then, ...who is rather in awe of the divine wisdom than rashly confident of his own, when he hears that God has appointed a certain destiny for flesh and skin and sinews and bones, invent some other meaning for these, as though that which is preached respecting these substances were not the destiny of man?[140]

Once he has argued his point, he begins 33 with: 'That is enough concerning the prophetic document'.[141] Evans notes regarding the way in which Tertullian opens his quotations ('et mandabo', etc.) that this seems as if it should derive from Rev 20:13, but that the line actually comes from 1 Enoch.[142]

Now Tertullian does not here claim to be citing from Enoch, but some scholars identify the source of his words as 1 Enoch 61:5.[143] If it is a paraphrase of this passage, it is not a very tight one:[144] 'And these measurements will reveal all the secrets of the depths of the earth, and those who were destroyed by the desert, and those who were devoured by the fish of the sea and by animals, that they may return and rely on the Chosen One: for no one will be destroyed before the Lord of Spirits, and no one can be destroyed.' The two passages share only a reference to 'fishes of the sea' (in somewhat different settings); and perhaps Tertullian's 'and they shall spew up' is not entirely unlike 'that they may return'. The thought of the two passages is similar but the wording is not. If one is generous and grants that Tertullian is echoing, however loosely, the thrust of 1 Enoch 61:5, then he is once again recognizing its scriptural status, since he attributes the teaching to God and refers to it as *scriptum* and *praedicari*.

Tertullian, then, echoes the high esteem in which earlier writers held 1 Enoch but he, for the first time, as far as one knows today, overtly defends the genuineness of the book. While his arguments articulate only his views, they also reflect the fact that use of the book in the sorts of contexts in which he employed it required defending. Not all may have shared his enthusiasm for it.

Origen (Egypt and Palestine; ca. 185 – ca. 254). In Origen's writings one finds evolving attitudes about the Book of Enoch, and these follow chronological lines. He alludes to the book in four of his writings, all of which can be dated fairly accurately to specific stages in his career.

On First Principles appears to have been completed in about 225 CE,[145] that is, when Origen was still associated with the catechetical school in Alexandria. Though much of this work is extant only in Rufinus' Latin translation, there is

---

[140] ib 89.
[141] ib, though this may refer to Ezekiel, since he has been discussing Ezekiel 37 since par. 29 (see p266).
[142] ib 266; 87 n5.
[143] ib; see also Beckwith, *Old Testament Canon*, 397: '...what appears to be a paraphrase of 1 En. 61:5'.
[144] An angel is answering Enoch's question about the cords which other angels carried.
[145] Butterworth, *Origen*, xxix-xxx.

no reason for doubting that the references to Enoch stood in the original Greek text.

Chap. 3 of Book 1 is devoted to the Holy Spirit; in it Origen adduces various passages from Scripture which attest to the existence of the Holy Spirit. In the third paragraph he handles the question whether there is any substance not created by God and thus coeternal with God. To refute this notion, he first cites the Shepherd of Hermas (Mandate 1) which asserts that God did create everything.

> Similar statements are also made in the book of Enoch [*Sed et in Enoch libro his similia describuntur*]. But up to the present we have been able to find no passage in the Holy scriptures which would warrant us in saying that the Holy Spirit was a being made or created, not even in that manner in which we have shown above that Solomon speaks of wisdom, nor in the manner in which the expressions we have dealt with, such as life, or word, or other titles of the Son of God, are to be understood. (1.3.3)[146]

The passage to which Origen makes reference may be 1 Enoch 2-5,[147] in which one reads: 'And understand in respect of everything and perceive how He who lives for ever made all these things for you...' (5:1) This seems, nevertheless, a rather unlikely source for Origen's plural *similia*. In fact there are not many statements in 1 Enoch about the subject. Milik, however, while conceding the point, adds that the Enochic booklets '...do speak..., in great detail, in the Book of the Watchers and in the Astronomical Book, of terrestrial and celestial worlds, that is of the results of creation, and it is these descriptions which Origen has in mind'.[148] However that may be, it does appear possible that Origen is including Enoch among the sacred books here, as suggested by his subsequent comment about not finding indications in *scripturis sanctis* that the Spirit was made or created.

In the fourth chapter of the fourth book of On First Principles, Origen begins by summarizing sundry trinitarian points that he had earlier clarified.[149] This topic raised the issue of substance, matter and qualities (beginning with par. 5). For him there is no unbegotten or uncreated matter (par. 6); further, he believes '...that a substance never exists without quality, and that it is by the intellect alone that this substance which underlies bodies and is capable of receiving quality is discerned to be matter'.[150] In par. 8 he seeks scriptural warrant for this assertion. One instance he finds in Ps 139:16 (LXX 138:16) which he read in the form, 'Mine eyes have seen thine incompleteness.'[151] He takes God's in-

---

[146] This is Butterworth's rendering of the Latin, ib 31; for the Latin text, see in Görgemanns-Karpp, *Origenes*, 162.

[147] So Görgemanns-Karpp ib 163 n6a. Butterworth, *Origen*, 31 n3 must mean the same section but he writes II.5 – there is no 2:5 in 1 Enoch.

[148] Milik, *The Books of Enoch*, 109.

[149] Or, according to the Greek text, points that he had previously omitted.

[150] Butterworth, *Origen*, 4.4.7.

[151] I.e. he read: τὸ ἀκατέργαστον σου εἴδοσαν οἱ ὀφθαλμοί μου.

completeness to refer to that entity to which qualities are added in order to bring it to completeness.

> Moreover Enoch speaks thus in his book: "I walked until I came to what is incomplete," which I think may also be understood in a similar way, namely, that the prophet's mind, in the course of its investigation and study of every visible thing, came right to the very beginning, where it beheld matter in an incomplete state without qualities. For it is written in the same book, Enoch himself being the speaker: "I perceived every kind of matter." Now this certainly means: "I beheld all the divisions of matter, which from one original have been broken off into all the various species, of men, animals, sky, sun and everything else in the world."[152]

The first citation in the passage is from 1 Enoch 21:1 where the text reads: 'And I went round to a place where there was nothing made'.[153] Görgemanns and Karpp[154] make this identification and note that the Greek term ἀκατασκευάστου appears in LXX Gen 1:2;[155] hence it would have been an especially suggestive term for Origen.[156] Origen took it to mean matter without any qualities. The second quotation from Enoch's book has been noted before: Clement of Alexandria cited it in his Selections from the Prophets 2.1.[157]

The context in which Origen uses these verses from the Book of the Watchers and the way in which he refers to Enoch document the fact that he considered the book inspired and authoritative. It will be recalled that he introduces them in a paragraph in which he is adducing scriptural support for his philosophical point.[158] In addition, he calls Enoch himself a prophet.[159] Origen's attitude toward 1 Enoch will change with time.

In two of his numerous expositions of biblical books Origen also exploits the contents of 1 Enoch. He wrote extensively on the Gospel of John during his Alexandrian phase.[160] In book 6, chap. 25 he draws upon the Book of Enoch. In the context he is highlighting the importance of paying attention to names in

---

[152] Butterworth, *Origen*, 323; the text reads: 'Sed in libro suo Enoch ita ait: "Ambulavi usque ad inperfectum," quod et ipsum puto posse similiter intellegi, quod scilicet "ambulaverit" mens prophetae perscutans et disserens singula quaeque rerum visibilium, usquequo ad principium perveniret illud, in quo "inperfectam" materiam absque qualitatibus pervideret; scriptam namque est in eodem libello, dicente ipso Enoch: "Universas materias perspexi"' (Görgemanns-Karpp, *Origenes*, 806).
[153] Knibb, *The Ethiopic Book of Enoch* 2: wa-'adku 'eska makān xaba 'albotu za-yetgabbar; Greek: καὶ ἐφώδευσα ἕως [Gr²: μέχρι] τῆς ἀκατασκευάστου = Black, *Apocalypsis*, 32.
[154] Görgemanns-Karpp, *Origenes*, 807 n51.
[155] It translates Hebrew בֹהוּ.
[156] For the identification of 21:1 as the verse Origen uses, see also Charles, *The Book of Enoch*, 44n; Butterworth, *Origen*, 323 n2; Beckwith, *Old Testament Canon*, 398; Milik, *The Books of Enoch*, 73.
[157] See above for a discussion; there it was identified as coming from 1 Enoch 19:3, not from 2 Enoch.
[158] 'Sed fortasse requirat aliquis, si possumus etiam *de scripturis* occasionem aliquam intelligentiae huius accipere' (Görgemanns-Karpp, *Origenes*, 806).
[159] 'Mens prophetae perscutans', Görgemanns-Karpp ib.
[160] Butterworth, *Origen*, xxv.

Scripture: 'Names are not to be neglected, since indications may be gathered from them which help in the interpretation of the passages where they occur'.[161] Chap. 25 then opens with an etymology of the name 'Jordan':[162]

> Let us look at the words of the Gospel now before us. "Jordan" means "their going down". "Jared" is etymologically akin to it, if I may say so; it also yields the meaning "going down"; for Jared was born to Maleleel, as it is written in the Book of Enoch – if any one cares[163] to accept that book as sacred – in the days when the sons of God came down to the daughters of men.

He follows with an allegorical interpretation of both the descent and the waters of the Jordan. The explanation of Jared's name occurs at 1 Enoch 6:6; cf 106:13,[164] and the genealogical descent from Maleleel is found in 1 Enoch 37:1; see also 83:3-9. But here already one detects a hesitation in Origen vis-à-vis 1 Enoch: some apparently do not accept it as sacred. Origen, while he is still willing to use it, nevertheless reveals an awareness that not all may be ready to classify it among the sacred works – a hesitation he did not show in On First Principles.[165] In the same commentary (2.25) Origen makes a similar remark about a work called The Prayer of Joseph.[166]

The Homilies on Numbers must come from much later in Origen's life, since he did not allow his homilies to be transcribed and circulated until he was 60 years of age. Most of the more than 200 extant ones survive only in Rufinus' Latin translations.[167] In the twenty-eighth homily on Numbers Origen deals with the fact that the various places in Judea and other neighboring areas have their own particular names. The apostle Paul said that the earthly was a shadow and example of the heavenly realm; thus, there may also be various areas in heaven: the regions and the stars have their own names and signs:

> "Qui enim fecit multitudinem stellarum, ut ait Propheta,[168] omnibus eis nomina vo-cat." De quibus quidem nominibus plurima in libellis qui appellantur Enoch, secreta continentur et arcana; sed quia libelli ipsi non videntur apud Hebraeos in auctoritate haberi, interim nunc ea quae ibi nominantur, ad exemplum vocare differamus.[169]
> For "he makes the multitudes of the stars", as the prophet says, "he gives names to all of them." Regarding these names many secret and hidden matters are also contained in the booklets called "Enoch". But since those booklets do not appear to be regarded as authoritative among the Jews, for the moment we should postpone appealing to those matters that are there mentioned as an example.

---

[161] 6.24; *ANF* 9, 371
[162] He is commenting on John 1:28.
[163] This translation seems a bit strong: ὡς ἐν τῷ Ἐνὼχ γέγραπται, εἴ τῳ φίλον παραδέχεσθαι ὡς ἅγιον τὸ βιβλίον. For the text, see Preuschen, *Origenes*.
[164] See Milik, *The Books of Enoch*, 152; Black, *The Book of Enoch*, 117.
[165] Cf Lawlor, 'Early Citations', 203; Charles, *The Book of Enoch*, lxxxv.
[166] See Beckwith, *Old Testament Canon*, 398.
[167] Butterworth, *Origen*, xxv.
[168] He is quoting Ps 147:4.
[169] PG 12, 802

Lawlor understands this as a reference to 1 Enoch 82:9ff (assuming that the antecedent of 'quibus ... nominibus' is the names of the stars); if the antecedent is the heavenly regions, he thinks it refers to 2 Enoch 21:6; 22:1 (A). But he concludes that Origen is probably referring to both.[170] Milik thinks the passages intended are 1 Enoch 75:3; 82:10 (for the names of the stars); and 77:13 (for the names of the quarters of heaven).[171] While Origen does mention a problem with the status of the books (pl.) of Enoch, that difficulty seems to be only that they are not considered authoritative by the Jews.[172]

Origen's apologetic work was written, according to Eusebius (Hist. eccl. 6.36.2), during the reign of Philip the Arabian (244-49), when Origen was more than sixty years of age. The data suggest that it was composed in ca. 248,[173] that is, later in his career when he was in Caesarea. In this composition Origen mentions the Book of Enoch several times and shows the degree to which his opinion of the book had shifted in a negative direction.[174]

The context in which he comments on 1 Enoch is in Against Celsus 5.52-55. In 5.52 Origen quotes Celsus as saying:[175]

> We leave on one side the many arguments which refute what they say about their teacher: and let us assume that he really was some angel, Was he the first and only one to have come? Or were there also others before him? If they were to say that he is the only one, they would be convicted of telling lies and contradicting themselves. For they say that others also have often come, and, in fact, sixty or seventy at once, who became evil and were punished by being cast under the earth in chains. And they say that their tears are the cause of hot springs.

Commentators have observed that Celsus here mirrors 1 Enoch 6-10 and 67-69;[176] the latter passage (esp. 67:11) is possibly the source for the theory about angels' tears and hot springs, though 1 Enoch does not mention the connection. 1 Enoch 6:6, 8 specify two hundred as the number of angels who descended; Celsus' comment about sixty or seventy may derive from 1 Enoch 89:59-90:25 which chronicles the misdeeds of the seventy shepherds who shared the same judgmental fate as the stars (which represent the angels who descended [90:24-25; cf also 10:12]).

Origen wrote the following sections in reply to this and related claims. In 5.53 he counters that '...no real Christian says that Christ is the only one who has visited mankind...' Later he admits that the Marcionite heretic Apelles did believe Jesus was the only supernatural being who had come to visit human-

---

[170] Lawlor, 'Early Citations', 203.
[171] Milik, *The Books of Enoch*, 20.
[172] See Beckwith, *Old Testament Canon*, 398.
[173] Chadwick, *Origen*, xiv-xv.
[174] See Lawlor, 'Early Citations', 204.
[175] Translation of Chadwick, *Origen*, 305.
[176] Koetschau, *Origenes Werke* 1, 56; Martin, *Le livre d'Hénoch*, cxxvii; Charles, *The Book of Enoch*, lxxxv; Chadwick, *Origen*, 305 n1.

kind, so that Celsus' argument that there were others would be valid against him.

> For Apelles ...does not believe the books of the Jews which relate miracles. He will much less admit what Celsus seems to have affirmed because he misunderstood what is written in the book of Enoch.[177] Nobody, then, convicts us of telling lies and of contradicting ourselves as if we said both that only our Saviour has come and that none the less many others have often come. However, because he was hopelessly muddled in his discussion about the angels who have come to men, he uses the instances, which he failed to understand, that were suggested to him by what is written in the book of Enoch. He seems neither to have read them nor to have been aware that the books entitled Enoch are not generally held to be divine by the churches,[178] although perhaps he took from this source his statement that sixty or seventy angels came down at once and became evil. (54)

Origen goes on to isolate the basis for the words of Enoch in Genesis 6 and cites Philo's allegorical interpretation of the passage.[179] But, after some additional comments, he returns to Celsus' statement about the angels.

> Then he muddles and confuses what he has somehow heard, and what is written in some book or other,[180] whether believed by Christians to be divine or not, saying *that sixty or seventy angels came down at once, and were punished by being cast under the earth in chains.* And he quoted as from Enoch, though he does not name it, *their tears are the cause of hot springs*, a notion neither mentioned nor heard of in the churches of God. For no one has been so stupid as to imagine that the tears of the angels that came down from heaven were physical tears like those of men. If we may be frivolous about objections which Celsus seriously brings against us, we would remark that nobody would say that warm springs, most of which are fresh water, are angels' tears since tears are naturally salt – unless perhaps Celsus' angels weep tears of fresh water!

From these remarks it is unmistakable that, in Origen's opinion, the books (again plural) of Enoch are not generally considered divine in the churches. Moreover, he seems to be almost derogatory toward Enoch's compositions when he calls his writings 'some book or other' (55). He considers it inane to believe angels' tears have anything to do with hot springs, but this need not be a criticism of 1 Enoch since the book does not say they do.

SUMMARY

In the first part of this chapter the writings of seven authors from the first three centuries of Christian history have been studied. All of them show familiarity

---

[177] Koetschau ib: ἀπὸ τῶν ἐν τῷ Ἐνὼχ γεγραμμένων.

[178] *ANF* 4, 507: 'do not at all circulate...' Koetschau, ib: ἀπὸ τῶν ἐν τῷ Ἐνὼχ γεγραμμένων· ἅτινα οὐδ' αὐτὰ φαίνεται ἀναγνοὺς οὐδὲ γνωρίσας ὅτι ἐν ταῖς ἐκκλησίαις οὐ πάνυ φέρεται ὡς θεῖα τὰ ἐπιγεγραμμένα τοῦ Ἐνὼχ βιβλία.

[179] As he does in his Commentary on John; see above on this work, and Chadwick, *Origen*, 307 n1.

[180] καὶ τὰ ὅπου ποτ' οὖν γεγραμμένα, clearly referring to 1 Enoch again.

with Enochic books and accord them authoritative standing (all use words such as *scripture* or *prophet/ prophesy* in connection with them) although in his later works Origen was plainly moving away from this conviction. Jude and the Epistle of Barnabas adduced Enoch's words in connection with the final judgment; later writers (Athenagoras, Irenaeus, Clement, Tertullian, and Origen) found the story of the fallen angels more helpful and applied it to various ends (see the second part of this chapter). Clement and Origen used words from 1 Enoch to clarify philosophical points. Some of the witnesses cannot be located with precision, but four of the seven authors were associated with Alexandria (Barnabas, Athenagoras, Clement, and Origen), and one with Carthage (Tertullian). That is, five of the seven were from two north African cities. Only Jude and Irenaeus fall outside these geographical settings, the former perhaps in Syria/Palestine and the latter in Gaul (though he had come from the East and had studied with Polycarp in Smyrna).[181] It is also noteworthy that Origen seems to have changed his mind about 1 Enoch upon moving from Alexandria to Palestine.[182]

Early Christian Uses of the Enochic Angel Story

INTRODUCTION

Another way in which to gauge the influence of the Enoch traditions on early Christian writers is to select a prominent theme in 1 Enoch and to trace where and how it was employed by the authors whose works have survived. The obvious choice for such a theme is the central Enochic myth of the angels who descended from heaven to earth and married the daughters of men. This familiar exegetical expansion of Gen 6:1-4[183] is elaborated most extensively in the

---

[181] At the end of this section, it should be added that the Book of Giants, which is now known from Qumran, is an Enochic work whose unusual fate betrays the esteem in which it was held: Mani himself, the founder of the highly syncretistic Manichean religion in the mid-third century CE, seems to have revised the Book of Giants (which he may have read during his association with the Elchasaites) and made it one of the authoritative works for his followers. For the evidence, see Henning, 'The Book of Giants'; Milik, *The Books of Enoch*, 57f, 298-339; and Reeves, *Jewish Lore*.

[182] Although little could be derived from it about the authority which early Christians accorded parts of 1 Enoch, it is worthwhile to mention that Eusebius (Hist. eccl. 7.32.19) quotes from the Canons on the Pascha of Anatolius, Bishop of Laodicea (in Syria) who found in the Book of Enoch that for the Hebrews the first month occurs around the time of the equinox. I thank W. Adler and J. Treat for the reference.

[183] Many of the Greek copies of Genesis that might have been available to early Christian writers read ἄγγελοι for Hebrew בני in Gen 6:2 (in the phrase 'the sons of God'); fewer copies attest this reading in v4. For the evidence, see Wevers, *Genesis*. It should also be noted that not all agree that 1 Enoch 6-16 is an expansion of Gen 6:1-4; Milik, *The Books of Enoch*, 30-33 considers 1 Enoch 6-16 to be the older document.

corpus of books that circulated under Enoch's name, though it is, of course, attested elsewhere.[184] The fact that the myth is articulated in other works entails that one should not assume all early Christian allusions to it arose from the authors' knowledge of 1 Enoch. Nevertheless, it is a fact that 1 Enoch is the earliest attested and most extensive presentation of the myth--one that was probably the source for the others; and at times Christian authors identify it as the book from which they drew.

The myth is first set forth in 1 Enoch 6-16 – a work which dates from the third century BCE. According to these chapters, the heavenly angels lusted after the daughters of men, swore an oath to carry out their plan, and descended in the days of Jared on Mt. Hermon – more than 200 of them in all under Shemi-hazah's leadership. Once married, they taught their wives divinatory techniques and engendered from them giants, who in turn devoured people's crops and eventually the people themselves. Azazel, one of the angelic leaders, taught humans the making of armaments, ornaments and cosmetics. All of the evil that resulted from the angelic invasion provoked a human cry to heaven. Four good angels brought the humans' complaint before God himself. God determined to send a flood to punish the giants (after they had slaughtered many of their own number), while the angels (who were immortal) were to be bound under the hills until the final judgment, when their eternal punishment will begin. Enoch himself, who had been hidden before all this, was delegated by the doomed angels to plead their case before God, but that plea was rejected. Later one learns that the death of the giants was not the end of the evil associated with the angelic descent:

> And now the giants who were born from body and flesh will be called evil spirits upon the earth, and on the earth will be their dwelling. And evil spirits came out from their flesh because from above they were created; from the holy Watchers was their origin and first foundation. Evil spirits they will be on the earth, and spirits of the evil ones will they be called... And the spirits of the giants ...which do wrong and are corrupt, and attack and fight and break the earth, and cause sorrow; and they eat no food and do not thirst [unlike the voracious giants], and are not observed. And these spirits *will rise* against the sons of men and against women because they came out from them. (15:8-9, 11-12)

The story of the angels, which even in 1 Enoch 6-16 may be an amalgam of more than one tradition, explains the phenomenal increase of evil on the earth before the flood (the angels and giants caused it) but it also accounts for baleful changes which originated then but continue now and will remain until the final judgment: the angels instructed humanity in divination, warfare, and cosmetics, all of which have evil consequences; and the evil spirits or demons[185] who

---

[184] Examples are Jubilees, the Genesis Apocryphon, and the Testaments of the Twelve Patriarchs. The motif of a positive reason for sending the angels to the earth does not come from 1 Enoch, but it is attested initially in Jub. 5:6.

[185] For use of the word 'demon' for the spirits that issue from the giants' bodies, see 1 Enoch 19:3; 99:7; and Jub. 10:1, 2.

emerge from the corpses of the giants exercise an ongoing and malicious influence on humanity. These themes came to play prominent and diversified roles in ancient Christian literature until the beginning of the fourth century and became much more widespread than the relatively infrequent explicit mentions of the Book of Enoch would lead one to believe. Here, as in the first part of our chapter, the survey will proceed chronologically and if possible, geographical distribution will be noted. Since some of the passages are the same as those cited and analyzed in the first part, they can be handled more briefly in this section.

CHRONOLOGICAL SURVEY

Three New Testament writings make explicit use of the angel story: 1 Peter, 2 Peter, and Jude.

1 Pet 3:19-20. The date of the letter is disputed – a dispute which focuses around whether Peter himself wrote (or was ultimately responsible for) the work, or whether it is a pseudepigraphon. Whatever decision one reaches on the issue, the book is almost certainly a product of the period 60-100 CE. It is quite possible that it was written in Rome – the Babylon of 5:13.[186] In the third chapter, after exhortations to wives[187] and husbands (vv1-7), the writer urges unity for his readers and calls upon them to be ready to suffer, if need be, just as Christ suffered for sins.

> He was put to death in the flesh, but made alive in the spirit, in which also[188] he went and made a proclamation to the spirits in prison, who in former times did not obey, when God waited patiently in the days of Noah, during the building of the ark, in which a few, that is, eight persons, were saved through water. (3:18b-20)

Commentators have pointed out that the spirits to whom Christ preached could hardly be those of individuals who had died. As the reference to the time of the flood shows, they are the imprisoned spirits who, according to 1 Enoch, sinned at the time of Noah. The writer puts the theme to creative use by casting the spirits as the audience for Christ's post-passion proclamation. If this is what the author has in mind, then he is calling the angelic Watchers of 1 Enoch – the ones who were imprisoned in the earth – 'spirits in prison'. The Watchers are indeed said to be spiritual in 1 Enoch 15:4, 6, 7 – at least they were before lust overcame them. It is quite likely, however, that 1 Peter reflects a passage such

---

[186] Cf Kümmel, *Introduction*, 292-99; Donfried, 'Peter', 262f.

[187] Note the reference to adornment, etc in vv3-4.

[188] Some commentators have proposed that in the original form of the Greek text Enoch's name was mentioned here: ἐν ᾧ καὶ ᾿Ενώχ became the present ἐν ᾧ καὶ through homoioarchton. For an analysis and refutation of the suggestion, see Selwyn, *The First Epistle of St. Peter*, 197f.

as 1 Enoch 19:1,[189] where the angel Uriel paints for Enoch a scene of judgment:

> The spirits of the angels who were promiscuous with the women will stand here; and they, assuming many forms, made men unclean and will lead men astray so that they sacrifice to demons as gods – (that is,) *until the great judgement day* on which they will be judged so that an end will be made of them.

Jude 6. The author cites the story of the angels – particularly the judgment which they experienced – as an example of how the Lord, in the past, had destroyed those who had begun in his favor.

> And the angels who did not keep their own position, but left their proper dwelling, he has kept in eternal chains in deepest darkness for the judgment of the great Day. (v6)

The themes articulated in this verse echo the contents of 1 Enoch 12:4; 14:5; 15:2-10 (leaving their proper dwelling) and 10:4-6, 12-14.[190]

2 Pet 2:4. This short epistle has proven notoriously difficult to date and locate. It is reasonable, however, to assign it to the end of the first century (the opponents do not appear to be gnostic and thus it need not have been written in the second century) and to place it in Asia Minor in a locale where the author could be familiar with Jewish and Greek traditions.[191] After warning about false teachers who will arise as deceptive prophets did in the past and declaring that their punishment has been determined long ago (2:1-3), the writer documents his case by citing ancient instances of God's definitive judgments:

> For if God did not spare the angels when they sinned, but cast them into hell [=ταρταρώσας][192] and committed them to chains of deepest darkness to be kept until the judgment; ...then the Lord knows how to rescue the godly from trial, and to keep the unrighteous under punishment until the day of judgment... (vv4, 9)

There can be no doubt that the same Enochic sections which underlie Jude 6 also inspired this passage,[193] although, unlike Jude (one of his sources), the writer never names Enoch as the authority on which his words rest.

Justin Martyr (Syria-Palestine; died ca. 167). Justin Martyr appears to be the first writer outside the New Testament to employ the angel story, but he presses

---

[189] See Charles, *The Book of Enoch*, xcvi. Nickelsburg, 'Two Enochic Manuscripts', 252-54 draws attention to a number of points of contact between Enochic and Petrine traditions as he highlights the fact that Codex Panopolitanus contains extracts from the Gospel of Peter, the Apocalypse of Peter, and large portions of the Book of Watchers in Greek.

[190] Charles, *The Book of Enoch*, xcvi.

[191] See the introductory sections in Neyrey, *2 Peter, Jude* for a discussion of these matters.

[192] Cf 1 Enoch 20:2. Naturally, this term would have special meaning for a reader familiar with Greek myths.

[193] Charles, *The Book of Enoch*, xcvi.

it into service in his own way. There are two principal passages in which the
story surfaces, both of which make the same point.

In his first apology (ca.155) Justin defends the Christians against, among
other slanders, the charge of atheism. He accuses their detractors of not examining what they say and responding with passion under the guidance of evil
demons.

> For the truth shall be spoken; since of old these evil demons, effecting apparitions of
> themselves, both defiled women and corrupted boys, and showed such fearful sights
> to men, that those who did not use their reason in judging of the actions that were
> done, were struck with terror; and being carried away by fear, and not knowing that
> these were demons, they called them gods, and gave to each the name which each of
> the demons chose for himself... For not only among the Greeks did reason (Logos)
> prevail to condemn these things through Socrates [the demons brought about his
> death], but also among the Barbarians were they condemned by Reason (or the
> Word, the Logos) Himself, who took shape, and became man, and was called Jesus
> Christ; and in obedience to Him, we not only deny that they who did such things as
> these are gods, but assert that they are wicked and impious demons, whose actions
> will not bear comparison with those even of men desirous of virtue.[194]

Here Justin argues emphatically that Greek religion is demon-based – a theme
which will emerge among other apologists for the faith.[195] But who are these
demons who through terror induced humans to call them gods? Justin answers
this query in his second apology (ca.161). In it he explains that God entrusted
the care of humanity and all things under heaven to angels:

> But the angels transgressed this appointment, and were captivated by love of women,
> and begat children who are those that are called demons; and besides, they after-
> wards subdued the human race to themselves, partly by magical writings, and partly
> by fears and the punishments they occasioned, and partly by teaching them to offer
> sacrifices, and incense, and libations, of which things they stood in need after they
> were enslaved by lustful passions; among men they sowed murders, wars, adulteries,
> intemperate deeds, and all wickedness. Whence also the poets and the mythologists,
> not knowing that it was the angels and those demons who had been begotten by them
> that did these things to men and women, and cities, and nations, which they related,
> ascribed them to god himself, and to those who were accounted to be his very
> offspring, and to the offspring of those who were called his brothers, Neptune and
> Pluto, and to the children again of these their offspring. For whatever name each of
> the angels had given to himself and his children, by that name they called them.[196]

Justin reproduces several aspects of the angel story – their lust, fatherhood, and
teachings – but also their role in religion. However, in his version the demons
are the offspring of the angels, not apparently the emanations from the giants'
dead bodies. Here, as in 1 Pet 3:19-20, the basis for Justin's claims is 1 Enoch

---

[194] *ANF* 1, 164 = Apology 1.5.
[195] See Athenagoras and Tertullian below; cf Droge, *Homer or Moses?* 54-57.
[196] *ANF* 1, 190

19:1.[197] Justin's point is that the gods of Greek mythology, who committed a host of immoral deeds, were actually the evil demons depicted in the Enochic angel tale.[198]

Tatian (Rome and Antioch; ca. 110-72). Justin's student Tatian also used the Watcher story in his Address to the Greeks, though he does so in less clear form than his mentor. His allusion comes in a section of the Address that is dominated by his views about the demons (from chap. 8 on). Christians have repudiated the demons and follow the one God who created all things (chap. 19). Even if drugs effect cures, one must give the proper thanks to God.

> For the world still draws us down, and through weakness I incline towards matter. For the wings of the soul were the perfect spirit, but having cast this off through sin, it flutters like a nestling and falls to the ground. Having left the heavenly companionship, it hankers after communion with inferior things. The demons were driven forth to another abode; the first created human beings were expelled from their place; the one, indeed, were cast down from heaven; but the other were driven from earth, yet not out of this earth, but from a more excellent order of things than exists here now.[199]

While not all is pellucid in this statement, the parallelism – the demons driven to another abode which is then equated with being cast from heaven – shows that the beings whom Tatian called demons are the angels of 1 Enoch 6-16.[200]

Athenagoras. Much of the segment in question, from the Embassy 24-25, was quoted above in the first part of this chapter. The apologist uses the Watcher story much as Justin did: the angels who sinned with women became the fathers of giants; the souls of these giants are the demons who mislead people and, along with the angels, give rise to false religion. Note the sequel (25-26):

> These angels, then, that fell from heaven, dwell about our earth and sky and can no longer stretch upwards into the regions that are above the heavens. The souls of the giants are those spirits [δαίμονες] that wander about the world, and both classes are productive of motions, the spirits producing motions akin to the natures they have received, and the angels of such desires as those to which they fell victims, while the ruler of this material world guides and directs it in a manner oppposed to the goodness of God, as is evident from what happens...
>
> Now these spirits [δαίμονες] are they that drag men towards idols..., while the gods that catch the popular fancy and give their names to the idols were originally men –

---

[197] 'The spirits of the angels who were promiscuous with women... made men unclean and will lead them astray so that they sacrifice to demons as gods...'

[198] See Droge, *Homer or Moses?* 54-57; and Bauckham, 'The Fall of the Angels', 319. In his Dialogue with Trypho 79.1, Justin quotes Trypho as accusing him of saying that the angels committed evil and apostatized from God (I thank J. Treat for the reference).

[199] *ANF* 2, 74.

[200] Martin, *Le livre d'Hénoch*, cxxiv; Charles, *The Book of Enoch*, lxxxii. Cf also Address to the Greeks 8.

as one can ascertain from their history. That it is the evil spirits who usurp these names one can prove from the cult-operations in each case.[201]

Irenaeus. Irenaeus exhibits his familiarity with the angel story in several passages of his *Against Heresies.* The following were cited above in the first part of the chapter: 1.10.1;[202] 1.15.6;[203] 4.16.2;[204] and 4.36.4.[205] He also mentions it in *In Demonstration of the Apostolic Preaching* 18:

> ...The angels brought as presents to their wives teachings of wickedness, in that they brought them the virtues of roots and herbs, dyeing in colours and cosmetics, the discovery of precious substances, love-potions, amours, concupiscence, constraints of love, spells of bewitchment, and all sorcery and idolatry hateful to God.[206]

Clement of Alexandria. The great Alexandrian scholar not only displays his awareness of the angel myth but also adapts it in his system to a unique purpose. His allusions in *Selections from the Prophets* 53.4 have been cited above.[207] Also, note has been taken of *Stromata* 5.1.10,1-2 where Clement, in innovative fashion, maintains that Greek philosophy arose from the angels who had sinned – one of several opinions he expressed on the issue.[208] This figures in a context where Clement is discussing faith which, he affirms, must not stand alone and passive but needs to be accompanied by investigation.

Clement alludes to the angel myth in a few other contexts. In *The Instructor* 3.2 he lashes out against ornamentation of the body, especially the painstaking hours devoted by women to beautifying themselves. He cites various poets who ridicule such practices[209] and these he reinforces with scriptural references.

---

[201] Crehan, *Athenagoras*, 63-65; placing the good angels higher and the evil ones over the lower parts of the universe may originate in Platonic sources. See Barnard, *Athenagoras*, 111-114 for an explanation of Athenagoras' angelology – entirely set within the overall providence of God. Cf also Martin, *Le livre d'Hénoch*, cxxiv; and Charles, *The Book of Enoch*, lxxxvii-lxxxviii.

[202] '...That he may send ...the angels who transgressed [καὶ ἀγγέλους (τοὺς) παραβεβηκότας] and became apostate, ...into everlasting fire...'

[203] There he mentions magic, signs, and wonders '... which Satan, thy true father, enables thee to accomplish/By means of Azazel, that fallen and yet mighty angel.' Azazel is, of course, one of the two chiefs of the angels in 1 Enoch 6:7; 8:1; 10:4,8; 13:1; there he is charged with teaching various subjects (making weapons, ornaments, make-up [8:1]) and with being responsible for all sin (10:8; 13:2).

[204] Here Enoch is '...God's legate to the angels, ...because the angels when they had transgressed fell to the earth for judgment...'

[205] 'And in the days of Noah He justly brought on the deluge for the purpose of extinguishing that most famous race of men then existant, who would not bring forth fruit to God, since the angels that sinned had commingled with them...' See also 5.29.2 which mentions the prediluvian apostasy of the angels. Cf Martin, *Le livre d'Hénoch*, cxxiv; Charles, *The Book of Enoch*, lxxxiii-lxxxiv.

[206] The translation is from Bauckham, 'The Fall of the Angels', 320.

[207] 'Enoch says that the angels who transgressed taught mankind astronomy, divination, and the other arts' (my translation).

[208] Bauckham, 'The Fall of the Angels', 313-30; Droge, *Homer or Moses?* 138-41; See also *Stromata* 1.81.4-5.

[209] Menander, Antiphanes, and Alexis.

After a series of criticisms on the subject, he rounds it off with the words:

> Heaven delights in two charioteers,[210] by whom alone the chariot of fire is guided. For the mind is carried away by pleasure; and the unsullied principle of reason, when not instructed by the Word, slides down into licentiousness, and gets a fall as the due reward of its transgression. An example of this are the angels, who renounced the beauty of God for a beauty which fades, and so fell from heaven to earth.[211]

At about the same time Tertullian was applying the story to the same end. Elsewhere, in Stromata 3.7. 59, in a section on continence, Clement refers to the angels who lacked this virtue, were overcome by desire, and descended from heaven.[212]

Bardaisan (Syria; 154 222). Bardaisan (Bardesanes) was from Edessa and converted to Christianity in 179. After he was excommunicated from the church, he went to Armenia.[213] In the work The Book of the Laws of Countries (written in Syriac) he (or a disciple) holds that humans have received a freedom which they share with the angels.

> We understand well, that if the angels had not possessed free-will, they would not have had intercourse with the daughters of men, they would not have sinned and would not have fallen from their state.[214]

As Lawlor has observed, the ending of the statement, while it echoes Genesis 6, goes beyond what Genesis says and thus is probably based on the Enochic elaboration of Gen 6:1-4.[215] The story for Bardaisan, then, established a point in his philosophical or theological understanding of the created nature of humans and angels.

Tertullian. Tertullian employs the angel story in several of his compositions, some of which were mentioned above. For instance, in Apology 22 he reports that the sacred books spoke of fallen angels who gave rise to a demon-brood. On Idolatry 4.2-3 charges the apostate angels with using everything in creation for idolatrous purposes (cf. 15.6). Tertullian attributes to the angels who sinned the crime of teaching women about finery, cosmetics, and the like in De cultu feminarum 1.2 (cf. 2.10). To that list a few more should now be added; they are treated here because they appeal to the angel story but do not mention the Book of Enoch explicitly.

---

[210] The image is related to a passage of Homer which he has just quoted.

[211] *ANF* 2, 274 = The Instructor 3.2.14

[212] The editors of the Ante-Nicene Fathers series decided to print the entire book in Latin rather than in English translation, because of its explicit subject matter.

[213] See 'Bardesanes', in Cross-Livingstone, *Oxford Dictionary*, 132; Drijvers, *Bardaisan*, 217f.

[214] Translation of Drijvers, *The Book of the Laws of Countries*, 15. See also Martin, *Le livre d'Hénoch*, cxxv.

[215] Lawlor, 'Early Citations', 194.

The first is the early[216] treatise On Prayer. In chap. 20 Tertullian takes up the issue of women's dress. Naturally, modesty is to be observed, in accord with the teachings of Peter (1 Pet 3:1-6) and Paul (1 Cor 11:1-16). This, however, raises the problem whether Paul's instructions, addressed to *women* (1 Cor 11:5) also apply to virgins (chap. 21). Chap. 22 is Tertullian's answer. He argues that in scriptural usage 'woman' means all of the feminine gender, not just one group of them; hence virgins are included in Paul's teachings on women. Continuing to explicate 1 Cor 11:5 ('but any woman who prays or prophesies with her head unveiled disgraces her head') he writes:

> For indeed it is "on account of the angels" [1 Cor 11:10] that he saith the woman must be veiled, because on account of "the daughters of men" angels revolted from God. Who, then, would contend that *"women" alone* – that is, such as were already wedded and had lost their virginity[217] – were the objects of angelic concupiscence, unless "virgins" are incapable of excelling in beauty and finding lovers? Nay, let us see whether it were not *virgins alone* whom they lusted after; since Scripture saith *"the daughters* of men"; inasmuch as it might have named *"wives* of men", or "females", indifferently. Likewise, in that it saith, "And they took to themselves for wives", it does so on this ground, that, of course, such are "received *for* wives" as are devoid of that title. But it would have expressed itself differently concerning such as were *not* thus devoid. And so (they who are named) are devoid as much of *widow-hood* as of *virginity*. So completely has *Paul* by naming the sex generally, mingled "daughters" and species together in the genus.[218]

Tertullian's insistence that virgins are included in the generic term 'women' leads him to Gen 6:1-4, and nothing he says in this passage (except perhaps 'angelic concupiscence') proves that he knows the greatly enlarged interpretation of these verses in 1 Enoch. However, in a treatise from his Montanist phase – On the Veiling of Virgins (ca. 208/9)[219] – he explores the matter in far greater detail and there leaves no doubt that he reads Genesis through the lens of 1 Enoch – a book whose genuineness he defends, as noted above. 1 Corinthians 11 is again the starting point of the argument.

> If "the woman ought to have power upon the head [= 1 Cor 11:10]", all the more justly ought the *virgin* to whom pertains the essence of the cause (assigned for this assertion). For if (it is) on account of the angels – those, to wit, whom we read of as having fallen down from God and heaven on account of concupiscence after females – who can presume that it was bodies already defiled, and relics of human lust, which such angels yearned after, so as not rather to have been inflamed for *virgins*, whose bloom pleads an excuse for human lust likewise? For thus does Scripture withal suggest: "And it came to pass", it says, "when men had begun to grow more numerous upon the earth, there were withal daughters born them; but the sons of God, having descried the daughters of men, that they were fair, took to themselves

---

[216] Barnes, *Tertullian*, 55 puts it between 198 and 203; see also p117f.
[217] This is a definition of *women* that Tertullian rejects.
[218] *ANF* 3, 688.
[219] So Barnes, *Tertullian*, 47.

wives of all whom they elected'.[220] For here the Greek name of *women* does seem to have the sense "*wives*", inasmuch as mention is made of marriage. When, then, it says "the *daughters* of men", it manifestly purports *virgins*, who would be still reckoned as belonging to their *parents* – for *wedded women* are called their *husbands*' – whereas it *could* have said, "the *wives* of men": in like manner not naming the angels adulterers, but husbands, while they take *unwedded* "daughters of men", who it has above said were "born" thus also signifying their *virginity*: first "born"; but here, wedded to angels. Anything else I know not that they were except "born" and subseqently wedded. So perilous a face, then, ought to be shaded, which has cast stumbling-stones even so far as heaven: that when standing in the presence of God, at whose bar it stands accused of the driving of the angels from the (native) confines, it may blush before the other angels as well; and may repress that former evil liberty of its head – a liberty now to be exhibited not even before human eyes. But even if they were females already contaminated whom those angels had desired, so much the more "on account of the angels" would it have been the duty of virgins to be veiled, as it would have been more possible for virgins to have been the cause of the angels' sinning.[221]

His argument about this practical matter rests upon a combined reading of 1 Corinthians 11 and Genesis 6. But an unusual feature crops up here: the scriptural text from which Tertullian quotes reads 'sons of God,' not 'angels of God'; nevertheless, he understands the phrase as if it did say 'angels of God' and in doing so he moves beyond the literal text. Other elements also show that he does have the more elaborate Enochic version in mind: the angels left heaven because of their lust. Neither of these themes is mentioned in Genesis.

In this context note should also be taken of On Idolatry 9 where he asserts that certain professions are idolatrous. One of these is astrology, and happily an astrologer had recently defended his calling. Against him Tertullian declares:

> 9.1 I only put forward one thing: that it is those angels, apostates from God, lovers of women, who introduced also this inquisitiveness and who are, also for this reason, damned by God. 2. Oh divine sentence which in its working even reaches the earth and to which even those ignorant of it bear testimony: the astrologers are banned just like their angels.[222]

As the editors comment, Tertullian here echoes 1 Enoch 8:3.[223] He expresses a similar thought in Apology 35.12 where he mentions the crafts of astrologers, soothsayers, augurs, and magicians – '...arts which, as made known by the angels who sinned, and forbidden by God, Christians do not even make use of in their own affairs'.[224]

Tertullian, then, more than any other early Christian writer, appeals to the Watcher myth. For him it comes from an authoritative source, proves the de-

---

[220] Gen 6:1-2.
[221] On the Veiling of Virgins 7 = *ANF* 4, 31f.
[222] Waszink – van Winden, *Tertullianus*, 35.
[223] ib 160.
[224] *ANF* 3, 44.

monic origins of pagan religions and some professions, and places appropriate condemnation on the immodest dress and make-up of women.[225]

Gnostic Uses of the Angel Story. A number of texts show that the angel story, first and best known from 1 Enoch, figured prominently in gnostic views about evil and its origins. There is no doubt that this elaboration of Gen 6:1-4 lies behind several key passages, but there is also no denying that the myth was transformed as it was adapted to gnostic forms of thought. Stroumsa writes that the fallen angel theme '...played a major function in the development of Gnostic mythology, and that it is at the very core of the mythological expression of Gnostic consciousness'.[226] In the gnostic system(s), the two biblical stories which could account for the entry of evil into the world – the fall of Adam and Eve in Genesis 3 and the presumed descent of the sons of God in Gen 6:1-4 – were combined to produce new theories about the mixture between the pure and impure worlds from which the current human situation emerged. As Stroumsa puts it: 'The two original myths were integrated into a much broader mythical frame, intended to make manifest the basic pattern of both history and cosmogony: the evil deeds of the lustful demiurge and his associates, the archons. For Gnostic mythology, indeed, evil stemmed from a series of sexual sins. In its new frame the myth focused upon the escape of pure women from the lust of the angels (i.e. the archons). These women, having remained unsoiled, were thus able to transmit the pure seed.'[227] The texts which underlie these comments should now be examined.

A fairly extended borrowing of the angel theme appears in the Apocryphon of John which may date from before ca. 180, since Irenaeus seems to use it or something much like it. The earliest manuscript evidence (ca. 350) contains the Coptic translation of an original (now lost) Greek text.[228] In the Apocryphon the writer devotes some introductory comments to the subjects of God and the structure of the divine world and then turns (in 12.33) to the events of Genesis.

---

[225] Mention should also be made of the references in Five Books in Reply to Marcion, wrongly ascribed to Tertullian, in which the unknown author writes:

Her [the mother, formerly barren] Enoch, signal ornament,
Limb from her body sprung, by counsel strove
To recall peoples gone astray from God
And following misdeed, (while naves on earth)
The horde of robber-renegades, to flee
The giants' sacrilegious cruel race;
Faithful in all himself.
With groaning deep
Did he please God, and by deservèd toil
Translated is reservèd as a pledge,
With honour high. (*ANF* 4, 151).

[226] Stroumsa, *Another Seed*, 32.

[227] ib 33; cf also 171.

[228] B. Layton, *The Gnostic Scriptures*, 23-26. Cf also Wisse, 'The Apocryphon of John', 104; id, 'John, Apocryphon of'; Fallon, 'The Gnostic Apocalypses', 130f.

The framework into which the teachings of the book have been placed is a
dialogue between the resurrected Christ and John the son of Zebedee. The key
passage for the present study is 29.14-30.9. Just before this Christ, in answering
John's question about the origin of the counterfeit spirit, says that the chief
archon, realizing that the perfect race was superior to him, decided to act.

> He made a plan with his authorities, which are his powers, and they committed
> together adultery with Sophia, and bitter fate was begotten through them, which is
> the last of the changeable bonds. And it is of a sort that is interchangeable. And it is
> harder and stronger than she with whom the gods united and the angels and the
> demons and all the generations until this day. For from that fate came forth every sin
> and injustice and blasphemy and the chain of forgetfulness and ignorance and every
> severe command and serious sins and great fears. And thus the whole creation was
> made blind, in order that they may not know God who is above all of them.[229]

Next the chief archon decided to bring a flood, but Noah was supernaturally
warned and told mankind about it. Strangers, however, did not listen to him.
Many from the immovable race did hide with Noah in a luminous cloud amid
the darkness sent by the chief archon.[230] So it was time for the chief archon to
move to his alternative plan:

> And he made a plan with his powers. He sent his angels to the daughters of men, that
> they might take some of them for themselves and raise offspring for their enjoyment.
> And at first they did not succeed. When they had no success, they gathered together
> again and they made a plan together. They created a counterfeit spirit, who resembles
> the Spirit who had descended, so as to pollute the souls through it. And the angels
> changed themselves into their likeness into the likeness of their (the daughters of
> men) mates, filling them with the spirit of darkness, which they had mixed for them,
> and with evil.[231] They brought gold and silver and a gift and copper and iron and
> metal and all kinds of things. And they steered the people who had followed them
> into great troubles, by leading them astray with many deceptions. They (the people)
> became old without having enjoyment. They died, not having found truth and with-
> out knowing the God of truth. And thus the whole creation became enslaved forever,
> from the foundation of the world until now. And they took women and begot chil-
> dren out of the darkness according to the likeness of their spirit. And they closed
> their hearts, and they hardened themselves through the hardness of the counterfeit
> spirit until now.[232]

One can see plainly the major elements of the Watcher myth: angels descend,
couple with daughters of men for the purpose of raising offspring, provide them
with something they did not have before, and terrible evil results. But these
elements are here transformed into a new setting and their contents are some-

---

[229] 28.11-28.29; tr Wisse in *NHL*, 121.

[230] 28.32-29.15.

[231] The reason in Codex III.39.4-5 is 'so that mankind might not think about their immortal Pro-
noia', i.e., their celestial origin.

[232] tr Wisse in *NHL*, 121f = 29.16-30.11. Janssens, 'Le thème de la fornication', 490; and Stroumsa,
Another Seed, 36 have pointed out that all of this occurs after the flood, not before it.

what altered as well. M. Scopello has subjected the passage to a careful, comparative analysis and notes the following: 1) the angels do not fall of their own accord as in 1 Enoch 6; instead they are sent by the chief archon or demiurge; 2) the women are not blamed for enticing the angels as in some forms of the myth.[233] The explanation seems to be that the 'daughters of men' in this text are souls (cf. 29.25-26), and thus the physical theme is irrelevant; 3) the angels' metamorphosis into the image of the women's mates reflects a similar theme found in T. Reub 5:6-7; Philo, Quaestiones in Genesin I.92; Pseudo-Clementine Homily 8.12-13;[234] 4) the angels here do not reveal knowledge and arts to the women; rather, they bring raw materials only. The purpose for this is not noted; only the harmful results are; 5) in 1 Enoch a generation of giants comes from the union of angels and women; in the Apocryphon there is a generation which comes out of darkness – the result, as in 1 Enoch, of the mating of beings with different natures. This sexual sin, like that involved in the fall of the first couple (according to the gnostic story), served to consolidate the rule of fate in the world.[235] One has, then, in this document of Sethian gnosticism, a clear reapplication of the story about the angels who descended.

The angel story figures in several other gnostic texts. The Acts of Thomas was probably written in the first half of the third century, perhaps in Syriac, though Greek and other versions of it have survived.[236] The context for the passage in question is an encounter with a serpent who had killed a young man – the lover of a beautiful maid in whom the serpent is interested. Thomas makes him explain who he is (30-31), and chap. 32 conveys his reply:

> I am a reptile of reptile nature, the baleful son of a baleful father; I am son of him who hurt and smote the four standing brothers; I am son of him who sits upon the throne <and has power over the creation, S> which is under heaven, who takes his own from those who borrow; I am son of him who girds the sphere about; and I am kinsman of him who is outside the ocean, whose tail is set in his own mouth; I am he who entered through the fence into Paradise and said to Eve all the things my father charged me to say to her; I am he who kindled and enflamed Cain to slay his own brother, and because of me thorns and thistles sprang up on the earth; I am he who hurled the angels down from above, and bound them in lusts for women, that earth-born children might come from them and I fulfil my will in them; I am he who hardened Pharaoh's heart...[237]

---

[233] See Pirke R. El. 22; Tg. Ps.-J. Gen 6:2.

[234] Cf Stroumsa, *Another Seed*, 35-38.

[235] Scopello, 'Le mythe de la "chute"', esp 221-8. As Pearson, 'Jewish Sources', 453-5 notes, after tabulating the similarities between the material in the Apocryphon of John and 1 Enoch, the imitation or counterfeit spirit is the 'most substantial deviation from the passage in 1 Enoch 6-8'. In a related essay, Pearson ('Use, Authority', 647-51) characterizes the Apocryphon of John's exegesis of Genesis as similar to the Jewish books of the so-called re-written Bible (eg. 1 Enoch, Jubilees).

[236] Bornkamm, 'The Acts of Thomas', 441; Goodspeed, *A History*, 78, 80; and Attridge, 'Thomas, Acts of', 531. On the theoretical and geographical location of the 'School of St. Thomas', see Layton, *The Gnostic Scriptures*, 359-64.

[237] Translation of Bornkamm ib 460.

The entire pericope demonstrates that the serpent, once he reaches the story of Eve, merely surveys biblical instances of temptation or misleading and attributes them to his influence. The angel section follows the Cain story and precedes that of Pharaoh. But it involves more than Gen 6:1-4 alone provides: angels being hurled from above, lusts for women, and the children of the unions as agents of the serpent. Not all of these come from 1 Enoch either,[238] but in other respects it mirrors the Enochic story.

A Valentinian Exposition is also indebted to the Enochic story.[239] The general setting is a description of Jesus' act of creating: '...He brought [forth] for the All those of the Pleroma and of the syzygy, that [is, the] angels. For simultaneously with the [agreement] of the Pleroma her consort projected the angels, since he abides in the will of the Father' (36.20-28).[240] After additional remarks about putting forth other entities, the text moves to creation of mankind by the demiurge and the role of the devil in the life of the first family:

> [And] Cain [killed] Abel his brother, for [the Demiurge] breathed into [them] his spirit. And there [took place] the struggle with the apostasy of the angels and mankind, those of the right with those of the left, those in heaven with those on earth[,] the spirits of the carnal, and the Devil against God. Therefore the angels lusted after the daughters of men and came down to flesh so that God would cause a flood. And he almost regretted that he had created the world. (38.24-39)

As in the Acts of Thomas 32, the author documents the role of evil and the devil in biblical history. A new note is that the purpose of the angels' descent was to compel God to send a flood. As Stroumsa observes, the passage also connects the myth with the beginnings of humanity.[241]

The text referred to as Untitled Text (On the Origin of the World) may have been written in Alexandria in the early fourth century.[242] 'The cosmogony and anthropogony that follow upon the semi-philosophical beginning are in part oriented to Genesis 1-2, but beyond that to concepts such as those known from Jubilees or the Enoch literature. In general, characteristically Jewish influences dominate, e.g., in the angelology, demonology, and eschatology, as well as in etymologies'.[243] The writer offers an extensive gnostic explanation of the first

---

[238] The hurling theme does not. It is related to the version in the Apocryphon of John (Scopello, 'Le mythe', 226).

[239] Turner, 'Valentinian Exposition', 782 dates the composition between Irenaeus' anti-gnostic writing in ca. 180 and Constantine's edict against heretics in 326 on the ground that it defines its theology over against other Valentinian views, not against that of the Catholic church (a procedure that one would expect after 326).

[240] Translations of this text are from J.D. Turner, 'A Valentinian Exposition' in *NHL*.

[241] Stroumsa, *Another Seed*, 33.

[242] Bethge, 'On the Origin of the World', 170. Perkins, 'World, On the Origin of', 973 writes that the text is '... a rich source for 2nd century cosmological speculation, for gnostic traditions of Genesis exegesis and for other elements of popular mythology'.

[243] Bethge ib 171.

chapters in Genesis. The rulers, who were responsible for much of what Genesis 3 attributes to God, aroused – by their actions and by the curse placed upon
the first couple – the ire of Sophia Zoe who expelled the rulers from their
heavens and threw them into the world to serve as demons upon the earth
(118.17-121.35). There follows a section on the phoenix and then these words:

> Let us return to the aforementioned rulers, so that we may offer some explanation of
> them. Now, when the seven rulers were cast down from their heavens onto the earth,
> they made for themselves angels, numerous, demonic, to serve them. And the latter
> instructed mankind in many kinds of error and magic and potions and worship of
> idols and spilling of blood and altars and temples and sacrifices and libations to all
> the spirits of the earth, having their co-worker fate, who came into existence by the
> concord between the gods of injustice and justice.
> And thus when the world had come into being, it distractedly erred at all times. For
> all men upon earth worshipped the spirits (*daimones*) from the creation to the con-
> summation – both the angels of righteousness and the men of unrighteousness. Thus
> did the world come to exist in distraction, in ignorance, and in a stupor. They all
> erred, until the appearance (*parousia*) of the true man.[244]

The rulers here play the role of the angels in the Enoch story, since they are the
ones who come down from heaven. They in turn made (not engendered) angels
of a demonic character who not only served the unfortunate rulers but also
carried out the teaching function, which in 1 Enoch the angels also perform.
Evil is explained through the misguided pedagogy in which they engaged. It
should be emphasized that in the Untitled Text, as in the writings of Justin and
Clement of Alexandria, the angelic teachings included the elements of false
religion. Moreover, as elsewhere in the gnostic texts, the angel story is brought
into immediate connection with the first couple and their sin.

While there may be several other allusions to the angel story in gnostic works
(Tri. Trac. 135:1-15 [?]; Testim. Truth 41;[245] Gos. Eg. 61.16-22;[246] and Apoc.
Adam 83:14-17[247]), a more important incorporation of elements from the tale
can be found in Pistis Sophia. This work, which probably dates from the late
third or early fourth century,[248] deserves attention because it not only reflects
the angel story but also mentions books written by Enoch himself. The two
passages in which his compositions figure are 2.99 and 3.134. The former

---

[244] Translation of Bethge, Layton, and the Societas Coptica Hierosolymitana, 'On the Origin of the World', in *NHL*, 186f = 123.2-24.

[245] The saw which cut Isaiah into two '...is the word of the Son of Man which separates us from the error of the angels' (tr S. Giversen – B. Pearson, *NHL*, 453 = 41.2-4).

[246] It mentions that Seth saw the 'persecutions of his [the devil's] powers and angels, and their error, that they acted against themselves' (tr A. Böhlig – F. Wisse, *NHL*, 216).

[247] 'Then the peoples will cry out with a great voice saying, "Blessed is the soul of those men [=the chosen] because they have known God with a knowledge of the truth! They shall live forever, because they have not been corrupted by their desires, along with the angels..."' (tr G.W. MacRae, *NHL*, 285 = 83.8-17); cf also 77.18-26. See, too, Paraph. Shem 44.13-17 and Aesclepius 73.5-12.

[248] So Perkins, 'Pistis Sophia', 376.

occurs within a complicated reply by Jesus to Mary Magdalene's question, 'My Lord, how many years of the *world* is a year of the light?'[249] After a detailed explanation, he tells her that '[t]he *mysteries* of these *portions* of the light are exceedingly numerous. You will find them in the two great Books of Jeu.' (2.99) He then continues: '*Now* you have no *need* for the remainder of the inferior *mysteries*, *but* you will find them in the two Books of Jeu which Enoch has written as I spoke with him out of the Tree of Knowledge and out of the Tree of Life in the *paradise* of Adam.'

The second reference is similar. In 3.134 Mary's question concerns how people will know, when they come into contact with erroneous teachings, whether they belong to Jesus. In the course of his reply he says:

> *Now* at this time, for the sake of sinners, I have *troubled* myself. I have come to the *world* that I might save them. Because even for the righteous *themselves* who have never done evil, and have not committed sin at all, it is necessary that they should find the *mysteries* which are in the Books of Jeu, which I caused Enoch to write in *Paradise* when I spoke with him from the Tree of Knowledge and from the Tree of Life. And I caused him to place them in the *rock* of Ararad, and I placed the *archon* Kalapatauroth, which is over Gemmut, upon whose head are the feet of Jeu, and who goes around all the *aeons* and the *Heimarmene*, I placed that *archon* to watch over the Books of Jeu because of the *Flood*, so that none of the *archons* should *envy* them and destroy them ...

Despite the attribution to Enoch, there is no Enochic book whose contents correspond with what is said to be found in these Books of Jeu. In fact, Books of Jeu were discovered in the late nineteenth century and have been published; they have little in common with 1 Enoch.[250]

Though the author's motive for claiming that the Books of Jeu were revealed to Enoch remains unclear, it is evident that he had some acquaintance with the central Enochic myth. The relevant section is in Book 1, chap. 15 – part of the oldest layer of the work.[251] Jesus describes the journey involved in his ascension when he was clothed in a garment of light, the rebellion of the aeons against that light, and their consequent loss of power. The following passage occurs in his account of the rebellion by the tyrants who were in the aeons:

> Now it happened when they *waged war* against the light, they were all exhausted together, and they were cast down into the *aeons*, and they became like the earth-dwellers who are dead and have no breath in them. And I took a third part of all their power so that they should not *work* their wicked *actions*, and in order that when men who are in the *world call upon* them in their *mysteries* – those which the *transgressing angels* brought down, namely their *magic* – that when now they *call upon* them in their wicked *actions*, they are not able to complete them.[252]

---

[249] Quotations from Pistis Sophia are taken from Schmidt (the old text) and MacDermot (a new translation), *Pistis Sophia*.

[250] See Schmidt-MacDermot, *The Books of Jeu*.

[251] Puech, 'The Pistis Sophia', 252 (between 250 and 300).

[252] 'Jeu, the *Overseer* of the Light' is mentioned just a few lines later.

Similar words surface in Book 1, chap. 18 where this magic is related to astrologers, soothsayers, and foretellers. The setting (at the ascension of Jesus) is sharply different, but the contours of the Watcher story are clear: a sinful action leads to the tyrants' (the transgressing angels) being thrown down among humans to whom they teach magic (mysteries) and by whom they are called upon as deities.[253] There is little doubt that the author has inserted the angel myth, not into a creation setting, but into a New Testament scene.

The Pseudo-Clementine Literature. It is convenient to begin a study of third-century sources with two documents which are not categorized as gnostic but have clear gnosticizing tendencies – the Pseudo-Clementine Homilies and Recognitions. The former is a collection of 20 discourses which, according to the pseudepigraphic setting, Clement of Rome sent from the imperial capital to James in Jerusalem. They relate Clement's travels on which he met Peter and witnessed his struggles with Simon Magus. The Recognitions, which are divided into ten books, resemble the Homilies quite strongly. The two texts, which in their present form date from the fourth century, are thought to be revisions of a *Grundschrift* that was composed in the early third century, possibly in Syria.[254] They express a Jewish-Christian viewpoint and at times attack Paul's theology. They are intriguing for the present study because they combine elements of diverse ways in which Gen 6:1- 4 was interpreted in early Christianity. Moreover, in line with their anti-Pauline stance, the Homilies appeal to the angel myth as an explanation for the origin of evil whereas the apostle based his teaching on Genesis 3.[255] The somewhat parallel sections in which the two texts deal with Gen 6:1-4 are Homilies VIII.12-18 and Recognitions I.29 – both of which belong to the presumed *Grundschrift*.[256]

In the pertinent sections of the Homilies, Peter has arrived at Tripolis where, on the second day, he addresses a large crowd about the worship of God, after Simon Magus had earlier corrupted their minds (VIII.8). He draws attention to the eternal law that God had given to the first man and to the abundance enjoyed by humans when they obeyed it. They, however, became ungrateful and were punished. Nothing is said about Adam's sin. Chap. 12 then depicts what happened after ingratitude had set in:

> For of the spirits who inhabit the heaven, the angels who dwell in the lowest region, being grieved at the ingratitude of men to God, asked that they might come into the life of men, that, really becoming men, by more intercourse [*sic*] they might convict those who had acted ungratefully towards Him, and might subject every one to adequate punishment. When, therefore, their petition was granted, they metamor-

---

[253] See Lawlor, 'Early Citations', 182-86.
[254] See Irmscher, 'The Pseudo-Clementines', 533-5; Dexinger, *Sturz der Göttersöhne*, 116-19; and Jones, 'Clementines, Pseudo-', 1061.
[255] Stroumsa, *Another Seed*, 30.
[256] Dexinger, *Sturz der Göttersöhne*, 116f (following G. Strecker).

phosed themselves into every nature; for, being of a more godlike substance, they are able easily to assume any form. So they became precious stones, and goodly pearl, and the most beauteous purple, and choice gold, and all matter that is held in most esteem. And they fell into the hands of some, and into the bosoms of others, and suffered themselves to be stolen by them. They also changed themselves into beasts and reptiles, and fishes and birds, and into whatsoever they pleased. These things also the poets among yourselves, by reason of fearlessness, sing, as they befell, attributing to one the many and diverse doings of all.

13. But when, having assumed these forms, they convicted as covetous those who stole them, and changed themselves into the nature of men, in order that, living holily, and showing the possibility of so living, they might subject the ungrateful to punishment, yet having become in all respects men, they also partook of human lust, and being brought under its subjection, they fell into cohabitation with women; and being involved with them, and sunk in defilement and altogether emptied of their first power, were unable to turn back to the first purity of their proper nature, their members turned away from their fiery substance: for the fire itself, being extinguished by the weight of lust, *and changed* into flesh, they trode the impious path downward. For they themselves, being fettered with the bonds of flesh, were constrained and strongly bound; wherefore they have no more been able to ascend into the heavens.

14. For after the intercourse, being asked to show what they were before, and being no longer able to do so, on account of their being unable to do aught else after their defilement, yet wishing to please their mistresses, instead of themselves, they showed the bowels [literally = the marrow] of the earth; I mean, the choice metals, gold, brass, silver, iron, and the like, with all the most precious stones. And along with these charmed stones, they delivered the arts of the things pertaining to each, and imparted the discovery of magic, and taught astronomy, and the powers of roots, and whatever was impossible to be found out by the human mind; also the melting of gold and silver, and the like, and the various dyeing of garments. And all things, in short, which are for the adornment and delight of women, are the discoveries of these demons bound in flesh.

15. But from their unhallowed intercourse spurious men sprang, much greater in stature than *ordinary* men, whom they afterwards called giants; not those dragon-footed giants who waged war against God, as those blasphemous myths of the Greeks do sing, but wild in manners, and greater than men in size, inasmuch as they were sprung of angels; yet less than angels, as they were born of women. Therefore God, knowing that they were barbarized to brutality, and that the world was not sufficient to satisfy them (for it was created according to the proportion of men and human use), that they might not through want of food turn, contrary to their nature, to the eating of animals, and yet seem to be blameless, as having ventured upon this through necessity, the Almighty God rained manna upon them, suited to their various tastes; and they enjoyed all that they would. But they, on account of their bastard nature, not being pleased with purity of food, longed only after the taste of blood. Wherefore they first tasted flesh.

16. And the men who were with them there for the first time were eager to do the like. Thus, although we are born neither good nor bad, we become *one or the other*; and having formed habits, we are with difficulty drawn from them. But when irrational animals fell short, these bastard men tasted also human flesh. For it was not a long step to the consumption of flesh like their own, having first tasted it in other forms.

17. But by the shedding of much blood, the pure air being defiled with impure vapour, and sickening those who breathed it, rendered them liable to diseases, so that thenceforth men died prematurely. But the earth being by these means greatly defiled, these first teemed with poison-darting and deadly creatures. All things, therefore, going from bad to worse, on account of these brutal demons, God wished to cast them away like an evil leaven, lest each generation from a wicked seed, being like to that before it, and equally impious, should empty the world to come of saved men. And for this purpose, having warned a certain righteous man, with his three sons, together with their wives and their children, to save themselves in an ark, He sent a deluge of water, that all being destroyed, the purified world might be handed over to him who was saved in the ark, in order to [*sic*] a second beginning of life. And thus it came to pass.

18. Since, therefore, the souls of the deceased giants were greater than human souls, inasmuch as they also excelled their bodies, they, as being a new race, were called also by a new name. And to those who survived in the world a law was prescribed of God through an angel, how they should live. For being bastards in race, of the fire of angels and the blood of women, and therefore liable to desire a certain race of their own, they were anticipated by a certain righteous law. For a certain angel was sent to them by God, declaring to them His will, and saying:... [chap. 19 contains that revelation][257]

In this version, the angels who live in the lower celestial regions most nearly in contact with the earth (a theme met before) descend to participate even more closely in human life and to effect punishment for the ingratitude of people. That is, their motive is positive, and to it God gives his imprimatur. The angels metamorphose rather than retaining their angelic nature. The list of entities into which they transformed themselves is highly unusual, but the different kinds of animals into which they are shaped reminds one of 1 Enoch 7:5 where the giants begin '... to sin against birds, and against animals, and against reptiles and against fish...' The 'precious stones, and goodly pearl, and the most beauteous purple, and choice gold, and all matter that is held in most esteem' (chap. 12) overlap with the items in 1 Enoch 8:1: '... bracelets, and ornaments, and the art of making up the eyes and of beautifying the eyelids, and the most precious and choice stones, and all (kinds of) coloured dyes'. The Greek text prefaces 'metals' to the list, and in fact the same word may underlie the Ethiopic for 'after these' in 8:1.[258] Also, Syncellus' version of the passage mentions '... the metals of the earth and gold, how they work (them) and make them into ornaments for women, and silver'.[259] The Homily notes that people stole the precious stones and metals into which the angels were transmogrified. In response, they changed themselves into humans – again for a positive reason: to live virtuous lives, thereby proving that it could be done and punishing the wicked. Alas, by becoming human they also acquired lust. The consequence is the familiar tale of sex and defilement. In their depraved and impure condition,

---

[257] *ANF* 8, 272f.
[258] See Knibb, *The Ethiopic Book of Enoch* 2, 80.
[259] tr Knibb ib. 4QEn[b] 1 ii 27 has כספא.

they were unable to return to their fiery natures and original home. The motif of teaching, too, is somewhat altered: the subjects on which the erstwhile angels instructed women were substitutes for what the latter really wanted – for the angels to show them their original nature. When they proved incapable of doing that, they disclosed to them the insides of the earth, i.e., metals and precious stones. Entailed in these were the arts that accompanied each. In this manner they transmitted the techniques of magic, astronomy, roots (see 1 Enoch 7:1; 8:3), melting gold and silver, dyeing garments (thus including feminine adornment), etc. The author designates the transformed angels 'demons bound in flesh'.

As in 1 Enoch, the children issuing from the unnatural unions were gigantic men. Strangely, God provides for their immense appetites and attempts to prevent their consuming meat (illegal before the flood) by raining manna on them. But the bastards preferred blood and eventually turned to cannibalism (1 Enoch 7:3-4; 9:9). The impure air produced by bloodshed was the cause for diseases and poisonous creatures. God decided to intervene with a flood to rid the earth of the demons. Their large souls, however, survived the deluge that claimed their bodies. To these surviving souls God gave a righteous law communicated through an angel. That law (in chap. 19), which begins in a way reminiscent of the apostolic decree in Acts 15, provides that demons may dominate and receive worship only from those who willingly accept these conditions. The others they were not allowed to touch. In chap. 20 Peter underscores the point that demon worship involves being subject to them. Consequently, the Homily explains the nature of pagan religion as the second-century apologists had.

In the Recognitions, as Peter presents an orderly exposition of the faith for Clement, he begins with a summary of the biblical creation stories (chaps. 27-28). Directly afterwards, without mentioning the events of Genesis 3, he rehearses the story of Gen 6:1-4.

> 29. All things therefore being completed which are in heaven, and in earth, and in the waters, and the human race also having multiplied, in the eighth generation, righteous men, who had lived the life of angels, being allured by the beauty of women, fell into promiscuous and illicit connections with these; and thenceforth acting in all things without discretion, and disorderly, they changed the state of human affairs and the divinely prescribed order of life, so that either by persuasion or force they compelled all men to sin against God their Creator. In the ninth generation are born the giants, so called from of old, not dragon-footed, as the fables of the Greeks relate, but men of immense bodies, whose bones, of enormous size, are still shown in some places for confirmation. But against these the righteous providence of God brought a flood upon the world, that the earth might be purified from their pollution, and every place might be turned into a sea by the destruction of the wicked. Yet there was then found one righteous man, by name Noah, who, being delivered in an ark with his three sons and their wives, became the colonizer of the world after the subsiding of the waters, with those animals and seeds which he had shut up with him.[260]

---

[260] *ANF* 8, 85.

It is surprising that of the parallel versions in Homily VIII.12-18 and Recognitions I.29 the former articulates the angelic interpretation of Gen 6:1-4 while the latter opts for a non-supernatural reading. The writer of the Recognitions must have had the word 'angels' in his biblical text but he reinterpreted it: the righteous *lived the life of angels* until the eighth generation. The nature of their life accounts for Genesis' use of *angels* for them. In the eighth generation, however, the beauty of women seduced men who had followed this manner of life. They not only sinned through the illicit relations but also transformed their conduct in a radical way and induced others to sin. Their children were called giants; God imposed the flood to punish them. As the last pages of the present survey will show, the sort of interpretation found in the Recognitions will come to dominate Christian exegesis of Gen 6:1-4.[261] The first extant evidence for it appears only in the third century; by the fourth century it will, for all practical purposes, have forced the angelic reading from the field.

Julius Africanus (various places; ca. 160-ca. 240). Africanus, who came from Palestine, laid the foundations for Christian world chronologies in his Chronicle which traced events from creation to about 220 CE. The book itself is lost, but extracts from it survive in the writings of Eusebius and the Byzantine chronographer George Syncellus. In one of the passages cited by the latter, Africanus wrote about Gen 6:1-4. In his exposition he shows his awareness of a problem that was more and more to exercise Christian exegetes:

> When mankind became numerous upon the earth, angels of heaven had intercourse with the daughters of men. In some copies, I found: 'the sons of God'. In my opinion, it is recounted that the sons of God are called sons of Seth by the Spirit, since the genealogies of the righteous and the patriarchs up until the Savior are traced from him. But the descendants of Cain it designates as human seeds, as having nothing divine because of the wickedness of their race and the dissimilarity of their nature, so that when they were mingled together, they caused God vexation. But if we take this to mean 'angels,' we would conclude that it refers to those who transmitted knowledge about magic and sorcery, as well as motion of the numbers [and] astronomical phenomena (?), to their wives, from whom they produced the giants; and because of them, depravity came into being, and God resolved to destroy the whole faithless race of living things in a flood.[262]

The great scholar was clearly familiar with the angelic understanding of Gen 6:1-4, but he rejects it, it seems, in favor of the theory that the 'sons of God' are the Sethites and the 'daughters of men' are from the Cainite branch of humanity (a distinction not found in the Pseudo-Clementine Recognitions). His analysis of the passage was informed by manuscript study. He was aware that the copies

---

[261] Dexinger, *Sturz der Göttersöhne*, 119 finds the Pseudo-Clementines to be a 'Kampffeld zwischen der alten Engeldeutung und der neuen Sethitendeutung'.

[262] I thank W. Adler for allowing me to use his forthcoming translation of Syncellus' work. The reference in Syncellus is 19.24-20.4 (ed Mosshammer).

did not agree regarding the proper reading ('sons of God' or 'angels of God/ heaven'). Although he apparently finds the Sethite reading more compelling, he does enumerate some details of the Enochic understanding of the passage.[263]

Origen. The explicit references which Origen made to the Book of Enoch were treated in the first part of the chapter. Among the passages cited there, the only ones in which he displays his knowledge of the angel story as presented in 1 Enoch are his Commentary on John 6.25 and Against Celsus 5.52-55. In the former, his etymological explanation of 'Jordan' (derived from ירד, just as Enoch's father Jared's name was) calls forth a reference to the Book of Enoch:

> ...For Jared was born to Maleleel, as it is written in the *Book of Enoch* – if anyone cares to accept that book as sacred – in the days when the sons of God came down to the daughters of men. Under this descent some have supposed that there is an enigmatical reference to the descent of souls into bodies. Taking the phrase "daughters of men" as a tropical expression for this earthly tabernacle.[264]

Origen, who by this time plainly had reservations about the value of 1 Enoch, here offers a figurative interpretation of the passage. Wickham maintains that the wording of Origen's statement implies that he did not accept the allegorical reading to which he refers (note: '... some have supposed').[265]

In Against Celsus 5.52 he quotes his opponent's allusion to many angels who came to humankind other than Christ – a claim which, according to Celsus, some Christians denied:

> If they were to say that he is the only one, they would be convicted of telling lies and contradicting themselves. For they say that others also have often come, and, in fact, sixty or seventy at once, who became evil and were punished by being cast under the earth in chains. And they say that their tears are the cause of hot springs.

Celsus, then, had heard that some Christians accepted the story about a large group of angels who visited the earth, became corrupt, and were punished. Origen, of course, scoffed at his charge:

> However, because he was hopelessly muddled in his discussion about the angels..., he uses the instances, which he failed to understand, that were suggested to him by what is written in the book of Enoch. He seems neither to have read them nor to have been aware that the books entitled Enoch are not generally held to be divine by the churches, although perhaps he took from this source his statement that sixty or seventy angels came down at once and became evil. (5.54)

After his rebuttal, Origen turns to the interpretation of Gen 6:2, 'which he [Celsus] did not notice'. For the report about the marriages between the sons of

---

[263] Cf Lawlor, 'Early Citations', 212f; Wickham, 'The Sons of God', 144f; and Klijn, *Seth*, 61f. As Dexinger, *Sturz der Göttersöhne*, 106 reports, Africanus had contact with the royal house of Edessa (during the reign of Abgar IX), just as Bardaisan did.
[264] *ANF* 9, 371.
[265] Wickham, 'The Sons of God', 142f.

God and daughters of men he offers a different reading but one supported by precedent:

> ..Nevertheless even here we shall convince those who are able to understand the meaning of the prophet that one of our predecessors referred these words to the doctrine about souls who were afflicted with a desire for life in a human body, which, he said, is figuratively called "daughters of men". Yet whatever the truth may be concerning the sons of God who desired daughters of men, the idea does not help him at all towards showing that Jesus, if an angel, is not the only one who has visited men. Indeed, he has manifestly become Saviour and benefactor of all who change their lives from the flood of iniquity.[266]

The predecessor mentioned here is Philo.[267] In this passage, Origen does not explicitly embrace Philo's exegesis, but for him the more important point is that as always Celsus' argument fails. He simply was ignorant of the Christian texts and how to read them.

Commodian (mid-third century). Commodian was a Latin Christian poet who, though he became a bishop in North Africa, may have had some connection with Palestine.[268] In his Instructiones adversus Gentium Deos pro Christiana Disciplina 3 Commodian, like the earlier apologists, deals with demons in connection with the angel story.

> When Almighty God, to beautify the nature of the world, willed that earth should be visited by angels, when they were sent down they despised his laws. Such was the beauty of women, that it turned them aside; so that, being contaminated, they could not return to heaven. Rebels from God, they uttered words against Him. Then the Highest uttered His judgment against them; and from their seed giants are said to have been born. By them arts were made known in the earth, and they taught the dyeing of wool, and everything which is done; and to them, when they died, men erected images. But the Almighty, because they were of an evil seed, did not approve that, when dead, they should be brought back from death. Whence wandering they now subvert many bodies, and it is such as these especially that ye this day worship and pray to as gods.[269]

It is noteworthy that Commodian sets forth a rather full form of the Watcher myth, but his initial words reveal that he knew a version in which the descent was God's will, not the result of angelic lust from heaven.

Cyprian (Carthage; died 258). The bishop of Carthage, who may have been converted to Christianity as late as 246, was an admirer of Tertullian and

---

[266] tr Chadwick, *Origen*, 307.

[267] ib 307 n1; Wickham, 'The Sons of God', 141f. See Philo, On the Giants 2; cf Questions and Answers on Genesis 1.92.

[268] See 'Commodian', in Cross-Livingstone, *Oxford Dictionary*, 319-20.

[269] *ANF* 4, 203 (the Latin original is in poetry). Commodian's comments about the angels follow a preface and an opening paragraph in which he deals with the prohibition of idol worship in the decalogue.

adopted a number of his teachings. He, too, was concerned about the garb of virgins and devoted a treatise to the subject; and he, like Tertullian, found the Enochic reading of Gen 6:1-4 to suit his needs admirably in this area. In *On the Dress of Virgins*, he rails against the wealthy women who were zealous for all sorts of ostentatious finery (chaps. 7-13). Against them he cites Isa 3:16-24 and charges: 'Having put on silk and purple, they cannot put on Christ; adorned with gold and pearls and necklaces, they have lost the adornments of the heart and soul'.[270]

> For God has not made sheep scarlet or purple, nor has He taught how to tint and color with the juices of herbs and with shell fish, nor has He made necklaces of precious stones set in gold, or of pearls arranged in chains with numerous joinings, wherewith to hide the neck which He has made so that what God has created in man may be covered, and what the devil has invented may be exposed to view. Has God wished that wounds be inflicted on the ears, by which childhood still innocent and without knowledge of the evil of the world may be tortured, so that later from the incisions and holes in the ears precious stones may hang--heavy, although not by their own weight but by their high prices? All these things the sinful and apostate angels brought into being by their own arts, when, haven [sic] fallen into earthly contagion, they lost their heavenly power. They also taught how to paint the eyes by spreading a black substance around them, and to tinge the cheeks with a counterfeit blush, and to change their hair by false colors, and to drive out all truth from the countenance and head by the assault of their corruption. (14)

Cyprian's comments, which betray an attentive eye, attribute numerous corrupt sorts of bejewelment and cosmetics to the teachings of the sinful angels who had fallen from their heavenly home. 1 Enoch 8:1, the passage which underlies his charge, left the way open for the prudish expositor to expand the angelic curriculum. It lists among Azazel's teachings: '... bracelets, and ornaments, and the art of making up the eyes and of beautifying the eyelids, and the most precious and choice stones, and all (kinds of) coloured dyes'.[271]

Zosimus of Panopolis (late third-early fourth century). Zosimus's own writings have perished, but Syncellus has preserved from him a citation that deals with the angelic teachings in an interesting context.

> Thus, for the benefit of those who want them, I have cited these passages from the divine scriptures. But it is also fitting to cite a passage regarding them from Zosimus, the philosopher of Panopolis, from his writings to Theosebeia in the 9th book of *Imouth*, reading as follows: "The holy Scriptures, that is the Bible, say, O woman, that there is a race of demons who avail themselves of women. And Hermes mentioned this in his *Physica*, and nearly every treatise, both public and esoteric, made mention of this. Thus, the ancient and divine scriptures said this, that certain angels lusted after women, and having descended taught them all the works of nature.

---

[270] tr Deferrari, *St. Cyprian*. This passage is on p42, the following one on p43f.
[271] For the textual problems in the verse and the somewhat fuller Greek versions, see Knibb, *The Ethiopic Book of Enoch* 2, 80f.

Having stumbled because of these women, he says, they remained outside of heaven, because they taught mankind everything wicked and nothing benefitting the soul. The same scriptures say that from them the giants were born. So the first tradition of Chemeu concerning these arts is theirs. He called this the book of Chemes, whence also the art is called Alchemy, ... and so forth."[272]

It appears that 'the ancient and divine scriptures' to which Zosimus refers were books such as the writings of Enoch because his comments go well beyond what Genesis says about the angels.[273]

Gen 6:1-4 in the Fourth Century. As seen above, already in the third century some Christian writers (the Pseudo-Clementine Recognitions and Julius Africanus) favored a non-angelic interpretation of Gen 6:1-4. It is abundantly clear that in the fourth century the so-called Sethite interpretation commended itself more and more to expositors. The result was that soon it completely drove the older angelic understanding from the field.

Perhaps the last major writer to embrace the Enoch-inspired exegesis of the passage was Lactantius (ca. 240 – ca. 320) in his Divine Institutes (written from 304-11). He begins his work by affirming divine providence and the unity of God but soon turns to pagan accounts of origins and the evil effects produced by the Greek and Roman cults. The second book of the Divine Institutes focuses on worship of humans and celestial phenomena. As Lactantius tries to explain how such religions began, he bases himself heavily on the Watcher myth, though he fails to name the source from which he drew it. The relevant sections are book 2, chaps. 14-17. It may seem that he places the angel narrative after the flood. He treats that event in chap. 13 and proceeds beyond it to trace ignorance of the deity to the descendants of the accursed Canaan and to charge the Egyptians with being especially inclined to worship the stars and to indulge in other forms of idolatry. However, he closes the thirteenth chapter by saying: 'Now let us return to the beginning of the world'.[274] The opening words of chap. 14 leave no doubt that Gen 6:1 underlies the report: 'When, therefore, the number of men had begun to increase...' Lactantius indicates that God sent the angels to foil the devil, the ruler of the earth. They were to prevent him from corrupting humanity as he had at the first. In spite of God's warnings to the angels 'not to lose the dignity of their celestial substance through contagion with the stain of the earth,' the plan went awry:

> So, while they were dwelling with men, that most astute master of the earth coaxed them little by little according to the same custom to vices, and he stained them by contacts with women. Then, not being received into heaven because of the sins in which they had immersed themselves, they fell to the earth. Thus, the devil made them from angels of God into his satellites and ministers. Those who were sprung

---

[272] tr Adler (forthcoming). The reference in Syncellus is 14.1-14 (ed Mosshammer).

[273] On Zosimus, see Dexinger, *Sturz der Göttersöhne*, 103.

[274] tr McDonald, *Lactantius*.

from these, because they were neither angels nor men, but having a certain middle nature, were not received into the lower world as their parents were not received into heaven. Thus, there were made two classes of spirits, one heavenly, the other earthly. The latter are the unclean spirits, the authors of the evils which are done, and of these the same devil is chief. From this Trismegisthes calls him the *daemoniarch*.

The grammarians say that these were called spirits, like indwelling powers (*daemones*), that is, skilled and knowing things; for they think that these are gods. (14)

Lactantius asserts that the poets and philosophers also deal with demons; from them the magi, too, receive their powers.

These spirits, contaminated and lost, as I say, wander over all the earth, and they work toward a solace of their own perdition by destroying men.

Thus, they fill all things with trickeries, frauds, deceits, and errors. They cling to individual men and they seize all homes, indeed, every last doorway. They take to themselves the name of *genii*, for thus they translate the word *daemonas* into Latin. Men honor them in their inner chambers, and daily for them do they pour out wines. Knowing these demons, they venerate them as though they were terrestrial gods and dispellers of the evils which they themselves make and bring upon them. (14)

He charges that they produce poor health and disturb people's thoughts so that they run for help to them. In chap. 15 he explains the harm that demons can do to those who fear them and conversely the terror that they feel in the presence of the righteous. Hermes and Aesclepius understood all this: 'Each of them in truth affirms that demons are enemies and annoyers of men. Trismegistus calls them "harming angels". Therefore, he was not unaware that from celestial beings they had begun to be depraved earthly ones.' (15) After such sentiments, the reader is not surprised to learn in chap. 16 that divinatory and magical arts are likewise the gift of the demons. Indeed, the magi even summon the demons by name (16; cf. 17) and mislead people by mixing truth with error. They ensnare people in false religions in various ways, including the prodigies which they perform. God merely permits this sham and will inflict appropriate punishment in due time.

Subsequent to the time of Lactantius, a series of writers refer to the Genesis passage but consistently opt for the Sethite interpretation. The attraction of this reading became so strong that the older angelic exegesis could be eventually be called *stupid*[275] or *heresy*.[276] Little is known about what may have motivated the change in reading the biblical text. One possibility is that the Enochic understanding fell prey to Christological arguments according to which Old Testament references to 'sons of God' proved that Christ was the divine Son before the incarnation since others are called sons of God only in a derivative way through their relationship with Christ.[277] But there is reason for thinking that more was being rejected than the older view.

---

[275] It was so characterized by Theodoret in his Questions on Genesis 6.48 (in ca. 466).

[276] So Philaster (d. ca. 397) in On Heresy 108. Chrysostom, Athanasius, and Cyril of Alexandria also wrote against the angelic interpretation. On Theodoret, Philaster and the others, see Dexinger, *Sturz der Göttersöhne*, 106f.

[277] This point is made by Wickham, 'The Sons of God', 145f.

Augustine of Hippo (354-430) discusses the problem, and his analysis is a good point at which to end this survey. He takes up the topic in the fifteenth book of The City of God in which he treats early biblical history in connection with the theme of the two cities. For him the two categories of beings in Gen 6:2 – the sons of God and the daughters of men – belonged to the two cities of his theory, and the mixing of these two produced the evil which Scripture records.

> And by these two names (sons of God and daughters of men) the two cities are sufficiently distinguished. For though the former were by nature children of men, they had come into possession of another name by grace. For in the same Scripture in which the sons of God are said to have loved the daughters of men, thay are also called angels of God; whence many [!] suppose that they were not men but angels. (15.22)[278]

He then turns to this last issue: do angels have bodies such that they could have intercourse with women? He notes that there are scriptural references to tactile angelic bodies and hence he would not rule out the possibility:

> ...But certainly I could by no means believe that God's holy angels could at that time have so fallen, nor can I think that it is of them the Apostle Peter said, "For if God spared not the angels that sinned, but cast them down to hell, and delivered them into chains of darkness, to be reserved unto judgment" [1 Pet 2:4]. I think he rather speaks of those who first apostatized from God, along with their chief the devil, who enviously deceived the first man under the form of a serpent. But the same holy Scripture affords the most ample testimony that even godly men have been called angels; for of John it is written: "Behold, I send my messenger (angel) before Thy face, who shall prepare Thy way." And the prophet Malachi, by a peculiar grace specially communicated to him, was called an angel. (15.23)

He also counters the argument that the gigantic size of the children born from these marriages suggests a supernatural element in their conception. He mentions other very tall individuals whose parents were not of exceptional height. Augustine also makes an exegetical point: Gen 6:4, as he read it ('There were giants in the earth in those days; and also after that, when the sons of God came in unto the daughters of men, and they bare children to them, the same became giants, men of renown'), demonstrates that giants existed before the unions in question. Moreover, in the same pericope, the Scriptures call the same individuals both 'angels of God' (v2) and 'men' (v3: 'My Spirit shall not always strive with these men, for that they also are flesh'). 'For by the Spirit of God they have been made angels of God, and sons of God; but declining towards lower things, they are called men, a name of nature, not of grace; and they are called flesh, as deserters of the Spirit, and by their desertion deserted [by Him]' (15.23).[279] He concludes his study of the issue with a general statement about apocryphal books:

---

[278] tr Dods, The City of God.
[279] Augustine in the sequel discusses the readings of the LXX and Aquila ('sons of gods'). He also cites Ps 82:6, in which he thought the ones called 'gods' are humans.

Let us omit, then, the fables of those scriptures which are called apocryphal, because their obscure origin was unknown to the fathers from whom the authority of the true Scriptures has been transmitted to us by a most certain and well- ascertained succession. For though there is some truth in these apocryphal writings, yet they contain so many false statements, that they have no canonical authority. We cannot deny that Enoch, the seventh from Adam, left some divine writings, for that is asserted by the Apostle Jude in his canonical epistle. But it is not without reason that these writings have no place in that canon of Scripture which was preserved in the temple of the Hebrew people by the diligence of successive priests; for their antiquity brought them under suspicion, and it was impossible to ascertain whether these were his genuine writings, and they were not brought forward as genuine by the persons who were found to have carefully preserved the canonical books by a successive transmission. So that the writings which are produced under his name, and which contain these fables about the giants, saying that their fathers were not men, are properly judged by prudent men to be not genuine; just as many writings are produced by heretics under the names both of other prophets, and, more recently, under the names of the apostles, all of which, after careful examination, have been set apart from canonical authority under the title of Apocrypha. There is therefore no doubt that, according to the Hebrew and Christian canonical Scriptures, there were many giants before the deluge, and that these were citizens of the earthly society of men, and that the sons of God, who were according to the flesh the sons of Seth, sunk into this community when they forsook righteousness. (15.23)

For Augustine, then, Enoch's book was not canonical; hence, it could not dictate the exegesis of sacred Scripture which contained within itself the means for properly interpreting the words of Gen 6:1-4.

SUMMARY

Early Christian appeal to the angel story – whether based on 1 Enoch directly or indirectly – occurs over a wider horizon than explicit appeals to the book itself (see the first part of the chapter). In this case there is stronger evidence from the Syro-Palestinian area (Jude, Justin, Tatian, Bardaisan, Acts of Thomas [?], the Clementine literature, Africanus for a time), while Egypt (Athenagoras, Clement, Origen, the gnostic texts [they were at least found in Egypt, though some may have been composed elsewhere], and Africanus) and North Africa (Tertullian, Commodian, and Cyprian) continue to be well represented. The tradition was present in Rome at an early time (1 Peter; Africanus was also there for some years), and Irenaeus knew it in Gaul. Moreover, 2 Peter may come from Asia Minor, and much later Lactantius wrote about the angel story while he was in Nicomedia in Bithynia; it was in Asia Minor, too, that Irenaeus had received his instruction. Consequently, one may say that Christian employment of the Watcher myth is attested throughout the Roman world, in all the leading centers of the church. The story, in various forms, was used in different ways but a prominent purpose was to account for the angels or demons (Justin, Tatian, Athenagoras, Clement, Tertullian, gnostic texts, the Pseudo-Clementines, and

Lactantius) who gave rise to false teachings, including idolatry (Justin, Athenagoras, Irenaeus, Tertullian, gnostic works, the Pseudo-Clementines, Commodian, and Lactantius).

The Person of Enoch in Early Christian Literature

INTRODUCTION

Enoch himself, one of the more enigmatic characters in the Hebrew Scriptures, also became a productive subject for deployment in various contexts within the early church period. The most intriguing fact about him was, of course, the report of Gen 5:24: 'Enoch walked with God; then he was no more, because God took him'. Whereas all others in the priestly list of long-lived antediluvian patriarchs have their deaths recorded, Enoch alone does not and thus was paired with Elijah as the only Old Testament characters who bypassed death and continued to exist without interruption. Early writers also noted that in Gen 5:24 it was said for a second time that 'Enoch walked with God' and that in this instance, unlike in v22, that sojourn was dated to the end of his 365 years. In both cases of Enoch's walk, he is said to go about with הָאֱלֹהִים, but the one who took or removed him was designated אֱלֹהִים (without the definite article). The definite form was understood to refer to the angels, while the anarthrous term was interpreted as the deity himself. Hence, both during his 365 years (Gen 5:22) and after (5:24), when God took him, Enoch spent time with the angels. According to Jub. 4:23-25 his task after removal had eschatological implications:

> 4:23 He was taken from human society, and we [the angels] led him into the Garden of Eden for (his) greatness and honor. Now he is there writing down the judgment and condemnation of the world and all the wickedness of mankind. 4:24 Because of him the flood water did not come on any of the land of Eden because he was placed there as a sign and to testify against all people in order to tell all the deeds of history until the day of judgment. 4:25 He burned the evening incense of the sanctuary which is acceptable before the Lord on the mountain *of incense*.[280]

1 Enoch, most of which was written before Jubilees, focuses more on Enoch's contacts with the angels during his 365 years, but it, too, knows of his post-removal experience of angelic company (e.g., the entire scene in the Animal Apocalypse after 87:2-4) and his presence at the final judgment (1 Enoch 90:31). With the existence of such traditions about Enoch, it is understandable that early Christian authors incorporated him into their eschatological tableaux.

Enoch is mentioned fairly often in texts from the first three centuries. At

---

[280] tr VanderKam, *Book of Jubilees* 2. For the interpretation of Gen 5:21-24 implied in this passage, see id, *Enoch and the Growth*, 31f, 184-88.

times the authors simply reproduce the genealogy of Genesis 5 or allude to some other feature of the biblical notice about him. The most famous borrowing that New Testament writers made from traditions about the person Enoch was, however, the phrase 'son of man' used of the superhuman eschatological judge in 1 Enoch 37-71 (the Similitudes or Parables of Enoch). It is true that not all contemporary scholars would agree with this statement, since the date of the Similitudes, in which the phrase is employed 16 times (using three expressions), is disputed. It is quite possible, however, that it was written in pre-Christian times and that it was therefore a potential source for the usage of this remarkable self-designation attributed to Jesus in the gospels.[281] But since that set of issues has been canvassed many times and with great thoroughness, and since use of 'son of man' for Jesus is rare outside the canonical gospels (it does figure in some gnostic texts),[282] it seems more profitable simply to mention it here and to turn to another context in which early Christian writers found a role for Enoch as they portrayed the great events that would bring this world to an end. That context is the interpretation of the two witnesses in Revelation 11. In the first three centuries there is a consistent though not very widely attested tradition that those two witnesses were Elijah and Enoch. Later, the more obvious inference that Moses, not Enoch, was Elijah's partner came to dominate exegesis of the passage. In the next paragraphs Revelation 11 will be studied, the texts in which Enoch is one of the witnesses will be adduced, and finally the source(s) for the identification will be sought.

REVELATION 11[283]

The chapter opens at the temple of God. John the seer is told to measure it, the altar, and the worshipers but not the outer court to which the nations could come. The language of measuring the sanctuary and its appurtenances reminds one of Ezekiel 40:3-42:20; but the writer also predicts that the nations '...will trample over the holy city for forty-two months' – a clear citation of Daniel's frequent appeal to days and months totalling three and one-half years (e.g., 7:25; 8:13-14 [where the trampling theme also figures; cf. Luke 21:24]; 9:26-27 [where destruction of temple and city appears]; 12:7, 11, 12). That is, the seer is addressed in words that recall two eschatological works of the Hebrew Bible in

---

[281] For recent discussions of the problems involved and solutions suggested, see Hindley, 'Towards a Date'; Greenfield-Stone, 'The Enochic Pentateuch'; Knibb, 'The Date of the Parables'; Mearns, 'Dating the Similitudes'; and VanderKam, 'Some Major Issues', 89-94.

[282] The literature on this subject is, of course, immense. Much material can be found in Borsch, *The Son of Man*. Later analyses include Donahue, 'Recent Studies'; A.Y. Collins, 'Origin of the Designation'.

[283] For a thorough study of the passage in question, see Haugg, *Die Zwei Zeugen*, 3-34, 84-85 (where the biblical and extra- biblical background for the various elements in the pericope are adduced and discussed).

which temple and city play a role. Within this setting he introduces the two witnesses.

The general context for Rev 11:3-13 is the period between trumpets six and seven (one-six are treated in 8:1-9:21). Rev 10:5-7 had announced that the divine mystery conveyed through the prophets would be fulfilled when the seventh angel, without delay, blew his trumpet; the seventh one is then sounded in 11:15 (just after the two-witnesses section), and it ushers in '...the kingdom of our Lord and of his Messiah'. The two-witnesses pericope is also set within the second of the three woes. Rev 7:13-8:12 presents the first, and 11:14 notes that the second woe has passed with the episode of the witnesses and that the third will come soon. In other words, the two witnesses are located very near to the end of the world.

The passage names several actions that the witnesses perform and attributes a number of qualities to them. First, they receive '...authority to prophesy for one thousand two hundred sixty days, wearing sackcloth' (v3). The danielic number of days (though Daniel never uses this precise figure) reprises the forty-two months of gentile trampling in v2. The backdrop for the prophetic ministry of the two witnesses is, then, the unpromising period when the nations smash Jerusalem and the court of the gentiles. Perhaps their clothing (sackcloth) is conditioned by these circumstances.

Who are the individuals characterized as 'my two witnesses'? The sequel provides a string of clues strongly implying that they are Elijah and Moses. The initial identifying comment seems, at first blush, to be unhelpful: 'These are the two olive trees and the two lampstands that stand before the Lord of the earth'. (v4) The allusion should be to Zechariah 4 (rebuilding the temple is part of the vision) in which the prophet sees *one* lampstand. On it are seven lamps and next to it are two olive trees (Zech 4:2-3). The interpreting angel explains to Zechariah that the seven lamps are '... the eyes of the Lord, which range through the whole earth' (v10), while the two olive trees are '... the two anointed ones who stand by the Lord of the whole earth'. (v14) These last words are repeated in Rev 11:4. However, the single lampstand of Zechariah has become two, and the lampstands and olive trees symbolize the two witnesses.

The light imagery already recalls traditions about Elijah who had, of course, seen his sacrifice devoured by a heavenly bolt (1 Kings 18:38) and had been separated from Elisha by 'a chariot of fire and horses of fire' (2 Kings 2:11). Moreover, the Lord's messenger who like Moses had experienced a flame on Sinai (1 Kings 19:12) was remembered by Ben Sira as '... a prophet like fire, and his word burned like a torch. He brought a famine upon them, and by his zeal made them few in number. By the word of the Lord he shut up the heavens, and also three times brought down fire' (Sir 48:1-3; cf. v9 where the whirlwind which took him up is also said to have been fiery). The lampstand alone, however, probably would not have convinced an ancient reader that one witness was Elijah. But in Rev 11:5-6a the author drops enough hints to remove any doubt that he was the Tishbite. 'And if anyone wants to harm them, fire pours from their mouth and consumes their foes; anyone who wants to harm them must be killed in this manner. They have authority to shut the sky, so that no rain may fall during the days of their prophesying...' Rev 11:5 harks back to 2 Kings 1:10, 12 where Elijah summons celestial fire to consume two military units (cf. v14; Sir 48:3). It should be added, nevertheless, that Jeremiah, too, was associated with similar imagery: '...I am now making my words in your mouth a fire, and this people wood, and the fire shall devour them'. (Jer 5:14) He also was to become a candidate for one of the witnessing positions. Authority to shut the sky so that no rain could fall would remind any reader of Elijah's efforts in 1 Kings 17-18. It is of some interest that the drought in his time lasted into the third year according to 1 Kings 18:1 but that Luke 4:25 and James 5:17 extend it to three and one-half – the same amount of time that the witnesses would prophesy.[284] Rev 11:6b provides the documentation that Moses would be the second witness: '...and they have authority over the waters to turn them into blood, and to strike the earth with every kind of plague, as often as they desire'. The plagues leave no doubt who is meant, and turning water to blood evokes the first of the ten inflicted by Moses on Egypt (see especially Exod 7:17, 19).

These indications have led expositors to identify the two witnesss of Rev 11:3-13 as Elijah and Moses. Their names are also consistent with the fact that they are said to prophesy (11:3, 6); in addition, they were a natural pair as both had fiery experiences at Sinai (note the reference to 40 days and nights in 1 Kings 18:8). Malachi's prophecy associated the two as well. After mentioning the coming day (it will burn the evildoers [Mal 4:1 (Heb. 3:19)]), he urges his readers: 'Remember the teaching of my servant Moses, the statutes and ordinances that I commanded him at Horeb for all Israel. Lo, I will send you the prophet Elijah before the great and terrible day of the Lord comes'. (4:4-5 [Heb. 3:22-23]). These were the two who visited Jesus on the mount of transfiguration (Mt 17:1-9; Mark 9:2-10; Luke 9:28-36; 2 Pet 1:17-18). Elijah's irregular removal from the earth is familiar from 2 Kings 2:11; and Moses' death as told in Deut 34:5-6 has a mysterious quality about it in that it was the Lord who buried him. It gave rise to speculation such as that found in T. Moses 11:4-8 where Moses' tomb is '... from the rising to the setting of the sun, and from the South to the limits of the North, the whole world is your sepulcher' (v8).[285]

Revelation 11, after describing the two witnesses, proceeds to relate their experiences. Once they have finished their testimony (two witnesses were required to convict in some cases: Num 35:30; Deut 17:6; 19:15; 31:19, 21, 26), the beast from the abyss,[286] who is to figure prominently in chaps. 13 and 17, will conquer and kill them, leaving their corpses exposed in Jerusalem for three

---

[284] Charles, *Revelation of St. John* 1, 279f. For the Elijah allusions see, too, Haugg, *Die Zwei Zeugen*, 89-93 (he also adduces the other NT and the rabbinic references to Elijah's return).

[285] tr Priest, 'Testament of Moses', 933.

[286] See Haugg, *Die Zwei Zeugen*, 21f for connections between this creature and the fourth beast of Daniel 7.

and one-half days. The nations gloat over their demise 'because these two prophets had been a torment to the inhabitants of the earth' (v10). After three and one-half days (thus longer than their Lord lay in the tomb), a divine breath revives them, and their resuscitation produces fear in all who see them. A loud voice summons them from heaven (v12): '"Come up here!"' John the seer, who was also a witness, had been called in the same way (1:2; 4:1). They ascend in a cloud as Jesus had after he had commissioned witnesses (Acts 1:8-9). An earthquake, the fall of a tenth of the city, the deaths of 7000, and general terror accompany the event (v13).

CHRONOLOGICAL SURVEY

Early Christian exegetes agreed that Elijah was one of the witnesses, but the other one was identified by some as Enoch, not Moses, despite the clear hints in the text.

The Apocalypse of Peter (second century). There is debate about the date of the Apocalypse, which may be a unified composition though it is attested in different sources (Greek and Ethiopic). It was known by the time of Clement of Alexandria and may have been written in Egypt before 150.[287] Use of the text appears to have been widespread; in fact it is attested in all the major centers of Christianity and copies of it continued to be made for centuries.[288] A substantial amount of space in the document is devoted to Jesus' parable of the fig tree and his explanation of it. As he details the signs of his coming for Peter and his other followers, Jesus mentions the parable: 'But you learn from the fig tree its parable: as soon as its shoot has gone out and its branches have sprouted, then will be the end of the world' (2:1). Peter then requests and receives clarification (2:2-13) within which the two witnesses surface. Apparently a false messiah is to arise (2:8, 10); when some reject him he will lead many to die as martyrs.

> So then the branches of the fig tree will sprout. This is the house of Israel only. There will be martyrs by his hand. Many will die and become martyrs. For Enoch and Elijah will be sent that they might teach them that this (is) the Deceiver who must come into the world and do signs and wonders to deceive. And on account of this those who die by his hands will be martyrs and will be reckoned with the good and righteous martyrs who have pleased God in their life. (2:11-13)

---

[287] Buchholz, *Your Eyes Will Be Opened*, 17. He collects (20-79) the direct and indirect allusions to it and argues (398-412) for a date during the Bar Kochba revolt of 132-35. He also defends the value of the Ethiopic text, about which Bauckham, 'The Martyrdom of Enoch', 454-56 voices some scepticism. The translation used here is that of Buchholz.
[288] Buchholz ib 20-81.

The identification of the two witnesses, listed in chronological order, is assumed, not demonstrated.

Tertullian. Tertullian, whose witness to the text of 1 Enoch and to the Watcher story was noted in the first two parts of this chapter, also employed the exegetical tradition which identified one of the two eschatological prophets in Revelation 11 as Enoch. The manner in which he refers to it suggests that he was not innovating. He was merely reproducing an accepted view. The relevant passage occurs in A Treatise on the Soul, chap. 50, in which he is refuting the opinions of Epicurus, who claimed that humanity owed the deity no natural debt, that is, to die, and of Menander, who maintained that upon baptism his followers became immortal without delay. Tertullian disputes their views but feels the need to deal with some exceptions to the one-hundred percent mortality rate among humans (he mentions Christ and Medea). 'Enoch no doubt was translated, and so was Elijah; nor did they experience death: it was postponed (and only postponed,) most certainly: they are reserved for the suffering of death, that by their blood they may extinguish Antichrist'.[289] So, while the fates mentioned for Enoch and Elijah in the Old Testament make them appear to be exceptions to the requirement that all die, Revelation 11 discloses that their deaths will come at the end when they oppose Antichrist. His short statement betrays a reason for identifying the two witnesses as Enoch and Elijah: they did not die at the expected time. Hence they lived on and were the best candidates to be the witnesses who would still be alive when the Antichrist became manifest. It seems likely that for him Elijah was an obvious choice and Enoch, the only biblical parallel to Elijah, was the logical selection for the other position.

Hippolytus (Rome; ca. 170-236). Hippolytus evoked the theme of the two witnesses in his treatise on Christ and the Antichrist and in his commentary on Daniel. The latter contains his more significant and developed statements about the matter. His exegetical comments demonstrate that he understood Revelation 11 in the light of the teaching in Daniel 9 about the 70 weeks. As noted above, Rev 11:2-3 draws the reader's attention to Daniel by its allusions to 42 months and 1260 days; these numbers are not, however, found in Daniel 9. But Rev 11:9, which mentions the three and one-half days during which the two witnesses' bodies lie unburied in Jerusalem, and 11:11, which tells of their resuscitation after that span of time, would remind one of the detailed account in Dan 9:24-27. Hippolytus, of course, believed that Daniel's 70-week prophecy foretold the coming of Jesus. On his reading, the 62 weeks of Dan 9:25 covered the 434 years that, according to his chronology, transpired between the return from Babylonian exile and the birth of Christ. Since this period is preceded by the first seven weeks, the total of 69 weeks of years left just one remaining (see

---

[289] *ANF* 3, 227f.

13-16). Hippolytus notes that in Dan 9:27 the final week is divided into two parts. The version of this verse that he interpreted read: 'After threescore and two weeks the times will be fulfilled, and one week will make a covenant with many; and in the midst (half) of the week sacrifice and oblation will be removed and in the temple will be the abomination of desolation (21).'[290] At this point he adduces the scene of Revelation 11.

> For when the threescore and two weeks are fulfilled, and Christ is come, and the Gospel is preached in every place, the time being then accomplished, there will remain only one week, the last, in which Elias will appear, and Enoch, and in the midst of it the abomination of desolation will be manifested, viz., Antichrist, announcing desolation to the world. And when he comes the sacrifice and oblation will be removed, which now are offered to God in every place by the nations. (22)

Revelation 11, then, provides additional detail about Daniel's seventieth and last week. The first part of it is the occasion for the appearance of the two witnesses Elijah and Enoch; but afterwards Antichrist (= the abomination of desolation) will arise – the beast from the abyss in Revelation 11. It is noteworthy that at this juncture Hippolytus gives no exegetical warrant for identifying the witnesses as Elijah and Enoch; he simply names them as if the point were self-evident.

He returns to the two when interpreting Daniel 11. He offers identifications for the sundry kings and events in that chapter (see 29-37) and brings the story down to Maccabean times. As he sees it, Daniel turns his attention to the last days in 11:36. Hippolytus thought the verse referred to a new king, not to Alexander Balas who had been under discussion in the previous section (see section 38 where he cites and summarizes Dan 11:36-43). The shameful and blasphemous monarch here described is Antichrist, and with him he associates the witnesses of Revelation 11, though he does not name them in this context (39).

Given the close connection between Antichrist and the two martyrs, it is not surprising that Hippolytus returns to the theme in his treatise on Christ and the Antichrist. There he surveys many biblical passages, especially ones from Isaiah, Daniel, and Revelation. In the sections immediately preceding his first reference to the witnesses, he quotes Revelation 17-18 at considerable length (37-42). In the sequel he delves into the torments of the last times and the period when they will take place. Daniel becomes important for these subjects:

> But it becomes us further diligently to examine and set forth the period at which these things shall come to pass, and how the little horn [Dan 7:8, 11, 20-21, 24-26] shall spring up in their midst. For when the legs of iron have issued in the feet and toes, according to the similitude of the image and that of the terrible beast [Daniel 2 and 7]..., (then shall be the time) when the iron and the clay shall be mingled together. Now Daniel will set forth this subject for us. For he says, "And one week will make a covenant with many, and it shall be that in the midst (half) of the week

---

[290] tr of Hippolytus: *ANF* 5.

my sacrifice and oblation shall cease" [Dan 9:27]. By one week, therefore, he meant
the last week which is to be at the end of the whole world; of which week the two
prophets Enoch and Elias will take up the half. For they will preach 1,260 days
clothed in sackcloth, proclaiming repentance to the people and to all the nations.
(43)[291]

Shortly after this explanation Hippolytus returns to the topic as he discusses the
two advents of the Lord, both of which have a precursor: John the Baptist for
the first, and Elijah the Tishbite for the second (see Mal 3:23-24 [English
4:5-6]). He introduces Elijah in section 46 and, quoting Malachi, he begins
speaking in the plural of ones who will proclaim Christ's manifestation and do
miracles in order to shame people to repentance. This leads to a quotation from
Rev 11:3 (where the two witnesses prophesy for 1260 days in sackcloth) and
the comment: 'That is the half of the week whereof Daniel spake.' (47) He also
cites Rev 11:4-6, which concludes with the death of the two witnesses. For him
the little horn of Daniel 7 was the Antichrist.

The Apocalypse of Elijah (Egypt; third-fourth centuries). Scholars have assigned the Apocalypse of Elijah and the Jewish traditions which may lie behind
it to a variety of dates. The earliest manuscript evidence for it consists of Coptic
and Greek witnesses of the fourth century.[292] It is possible that material in it
served as the source for some very early Christian references to an Elijah
document,[293] but the Christian version of the work probably dates from no
earlier than the third and perhaps from the fourth century.[294]

The Apocalypse of Elijah places the episode of the two witnesses within a
larger eschatological context. It relates that the lawless one, who claims to be
Christ, will arise and be opposed by a series of righteous individuals in Jerusalem. Tabitha comes to Jerusalem to rebuke him and is killed for her efforts (she
later arises and rebukes him again). Elijah and Enoch oppose him but he fights
them for seven days, kills them, and leaves them lying dead for three and one-
half days. On the fourth, however, they once again turn against him; this time
he is not able to overcome them. Some 60 righteous individuals also enter the
lists against the lawless one. The treatment of Elijah and Enoch differs here
from that in other texts through the more extensive speeches that it credits to
them.

---

[291] For Enoch and repentance, see Sir 44:16 (LXX): '...an example of repentance to all generations'.

[292] Pietersma *et al*, *The Apocalypse of Elijah*, 6.

[293] For a survey of these see Schürer, *History* 3, 799-803. He considers it possible that the citation
in 1 Cor 2:9, which according to Origen came from a book of the prophet Elijah, actually does so.
Cf also, Wintermute, 'Apocalypse of Elijah', 728.

[294] Wintermute ib 729f places it between 150 and 275; Jenks, *Origins*, 33f puts it in the second half
of the third century; and Bauckham, 'The Martyrdom of Enoch', 450f prefers a time no earlier than
the fourth century, since its version of the Enoch-Elijah story has the nearest affinities with fourth-
century and later traditions. Cf Haugg, *Die Zwei Zeugen*, 94f. For the most recent treatment of the
texts and date for the book see Frankfurter, *Elijah*, 17-30.

Then when Elijah and Enoch[295] hear that the shameless one has appeared in the holy places, they will come down and wage war against him saying, 'Are you not ashamed seeing that you are estranged constantly? You became an enemy of heavenly beings, now you have acted against those on earth as well. You became an enemy of angels and powers. You are the enemy for all time. You fell from heaven like the morning stars. You have changed. Your substance (?) has been darkened. Are you not ashamed, you who hurl yourself against God? You are the devil.' The shameless one will hear, become angry and wage war against them in the market place of the great city. He will spend seven days fighting with them and kill them. For three and a half days they will lie dead in the market place in full view of all the people. But on the fourth day they will arise again and rebuke him, saying to him, 'O you shameless one, are you not ashamed, you who deceive God's people, for whom you have not suffered? Do you not know that we live in the Lord, in order that we may rebuke you whenever you say, "I have overpowered them?" We will lay aside the flesh of this body and kill you without you being able to utter a sound at that time, because we live in the Lord always, whereas you are a perpetual enemy.' The shameless one will listen in anger and wage war against them. The whole city will surround them. At that time they will raise cries of joy towards heaven, shining forth as the whole world watches them. The lawless one will not prevail against them. (15:8-17:4)[296]

Much later, after the lawless one has suffered various setbacks, Elijah and Enoch annihilate him and his followers.

After that Elijah and Enoch descend. They lay aside the flesh of the world and put on the flesh of the spirit. They pursue the lawless one and kill him without his being able to utter a sound. At that time he will melt before them like ice which melts through fire. (Ach 5:32-33)

Finally, Christ descends and spends a millennium in Jerusalem and creates a new heaven and earth.

The Apocalypse of John (third-fifth centuries). This work, the Greek manuscript of which entitles it Apocalypse of Saint John the Theologian,[297] is of uncertain date. As Jenks notes, it has been located at various times from the third to the fifth centuries.[298] It may, then, come from the end of the period covered by this chapter or from a somewhat later time. At the beginning of the text, John, who is sitting on Mt. Tabor after the ascension, asks the Lord to teach him about his coming, when it will occur, and what will happen then (1). After seven days of prayer, a cloud takes the apostle, sets him before heaven, and tells him to look into it. A voice gives him commands, and, as in the biblical Revelation, a book

---

[295] This reverse order of the names is shared with few texts which reproduce the story. According to Bauckham's chart ('The Martyrdom of Enoch', 449), only Hippolytus in his Christ and the Antichrist, Ephraem 'Graecus', Sermo in adventum Domini, and the Latin Tiburtine Sibyl do likewise among the 24 texts that he lists.

[296] Translations of the document are from Pietersma *et al*, *The Apocalypse of Elijah*, 49, 51, 53. For parallel translations of the Sahidic and Achmimic witnesses see Frankfurter, *Elijah*, 317-19.

[297] The text is in Tischendorf, *Apocalypses Apocryphae*, 70-94.

[298] *Antichrist Myth*, 35 (where there is additional bibliography).

with seven seals is involved. John is given various pieces of information, such
as an account of the Antichrist including a description of his physiognomy (7).
In section 8 John asks how many years Antichrist will operate on the earth, and
the voice answers:

> Those times will be three years, and I will make the three years like three months,
> and the three months like three weeks, and the three weeks like three days, and the
> three days like three hours, and the three hours like three moments – as the prophet
> David said: You have broken down his throne to the earth; you have shortened the
> days of his time; you have poured out shame for him. And then I will send Enoch
> and Elijah for reproving him. They will show that he is a liar and deceiver. He will
> kill them on the altar, as the prophet said: Then they will offer on your altar young
> bulls. (my translation)

In the sequel all human nature dies. The unusual feature here is that the altar is
specified as the place of execution. This may be an inference from Rev 11:1-2
which places the scene at the temple in Jerusalem.

POSSIBLE SOURCES FOR THE IDENTIFICATION OF ENOCH
AS ONE OF THE WITNESSES

There would be no difficulty in extending the survey because the identification
of the two witnesses as Enoch and Elijah continued for some time in Christian
literature. W. Bousset collected references to it and considered it to be a '...fast
einstimmige[] Überlieferung' that they were Enoch and Elijah.[299] Bauckham
has supplemented his list so that it has grown to 24 texts which evidence the
tradition.[300] Most of these, however, are later in date than the period which is
considered in the present survey; hence they need not be included. It should
be stated, though, that this tradition does not seem to have suffered the same
fate as 1 Enoch itself and the Watcher myth in the fourth century and later.
Rather, it continues to be attested for centuries thereafter.[301] What might be the
source(s) of this tradition?

The most obvious answer is, of course, that Enoch and Elijah were presented
in the Old Testament as the only two individuals who bypassed death and
would therefore continue to be alive at the end.[302] Also, Malachi prophesied that
Elijah would be part of the final scenario. In extra-biblical texts the same was
the case for Enoch. Rev 11:2 adds that they are witnesses and that they prophesy. These two characteristics may assist in tracking down items in the traditions
about Enoch that could have inclined early Christian authors to name him as
one of the heroes of the chapter.

First, Jubilees places heavy stress on Enoch's role as witness in the short

---

[299] Bousset, *Antichrist*, 134-39; quotation p134.
[300] Bauckham, 'The Martyrdom of Enoch'.
[301] See also Haugg, *Die Zwei Zeugen*, 96f, 100-102.
[302] ib 98.

pericope which it devotes to him. Jub. 4:18 reports that he '... was the first to write a testimony. He testified to mankind in the generations of the earth'. Moreover, he '... wrote a testimony for himself and placed it upon the earth against all mankind and for their history'. (v19) As in 1 Enoch 12-16, Jubilees makes Enoch testify against the Watchers (v22). When he was translated from earth after his 365 years, the angels escorted him to the Garden of Eden where he writes the '... judgment and condemnation of the world and all the wickedness of mankind' (v23) and his labors serve '... to testify against all people in order to tell all the deeds of history until the day of judgment'. (v24)[303] In other words, for the author, Enoch carried out the role of a witness both during and after his time on earth. His testifying role continues until the final judgment.[304] The motif is reinforced by 4Q227 (copied in the early Herodian period)[305], on which one reads about Enoch:

ויעד על כולם
[וגם על העירים

And he testified against them all
] and also against the Watchers.

There is, then, documentation in pre-Christian times for the theme of Enoch as witness.

One of the early Christian texts cited above – the Apocalypse of Elijah – offers a broader clue regarding a source for identifying one of the witnesses in Revelation 11 as Enoch. The second passage quoted from it (Ach 5:32-33) is immediately preceded by words which betray a dependence on the Animal Apocalypse of 1 Enoch (chaps. 85-90).

> On that day, the Lord will judge the heaven and the earth.
> He will judge those who transgressed in heaven,
> and those who did so on earth.
> He will judge the shepherds of his people.
> He will ask about the flock of sheep,
> and they will be given to him,
> without any deadly guile existing in them. (5:30-31)[306]

The setting at the final assize and the allusions to shepherds who are to be judged and the flock which is to receive divine attention all recall 1 Enoch 89:59-90:36. There in Enoch's dream vision, the oppressors of God's people are shepherds and his people are his sheep. Once the appointed time has arrived, the shepherds who had exceeded their orders in punishing the flock are judged and destroyed, while the sheep – who had become pure – are brought

---

[303] tr VanderKam, *The Book of Jubilees* 2.
[304] Some of these themes are, of course, drawn from 1 Enoch. For a comparison, see VanderKam, 'Enoch Traditions', 231-36. Note in particular 1 Enoch 80-82 and 91-93.
[305] A transcription appears in Milik, *The Books of Enoch*, 12.
[306] tr Wintermute, 'Apocalypse of Elijah', 752.

into their Lord's new house. Enoch himself plays a part in this symbolic drama. The vision, which surveys biblical history, describes Enoch's removal as being brought to a tower from which he is able to view what is to transpire (87:3-4). Once history runs its course and several events of the judgment occur, Enoch returns to the earth. 'And after this those three [angels] who were dressed in white and had taken hold of me by my hand, the ones who had brought me up at first – they, with the hand of that ram also holding me, took me up and put me down in the middle of those sheep before the judgement was held'. (90:31) That is, though the temporal sequence is difficult to follow, Enoch is present on earth while these final events take place.

In this context, an exegetical problem is of special interest: who is the ram who, with the angels, holds Enoch as he is placed amid the sheep? Charles[307] identified him as Elijah who, according to 1 Enoch 89:52, was removed from the earth: 'But one of them [Elijah] was saved and was not killed, and it sprang away and cried out against the sheep, and they wished to kill it; but the Lord of the sheep saved it from the hands of the sheep, and brought it up to me [Enoch], and made it remain *there*.' It would be only natural, one would think, that the two, who are paired in 89:52, would be returned to the earth together as well. One problem is that in 89:52 Elijah is classified as one of the *sheep*, not as a *ram*.[308] Rams are also under consideration in 90:10-11, while in 90:13-16 there appears a special ram who is usually thought to represent Judas Maccabeus.[309] Milik infers from these data that the ram of 90:31 is also Judas.[310] This is not a very likely conclusion though, since, as Black notes, elsewhere in the Animal Apocalypse other leaders are also termed sheep.[311]

As a result, one may conclude that the passage certainly does place Enoch on the scene 'before the judgement was held' (90:31) and the context uses language that is resumed in the Apocalypse of Elijah. It may also bring Elijah into the same situation, though that is uncertain. The Apocalypse of Elijah, as 1 Enoch does certainly for Enoch and possibly for Elijah, also speaks of their returning from above (4:7; 5:32).[312] While there are these connections between

---

[307] Charles, *The Book of Enoch*, 215n.
[308] Martin, *Le livre d'Hénoch*, 233.
[309] See for example Charles, *The Book of Enoch*, 211.
[310] Milik, *The Books of Enoch*, 45.
[311] Black, *The Book of Enoch*, 279; see too his 'The "Two Witnesses"', 227f.
[312] On the subject of the Apocalypse of Elijah and 1 Enoch 90:31, see also Haugg, *Die Zwei Zeugen*, 15, 99f; and Bauckham, 'The Martyrdom of Enoch', 450-52. Bauckham is critical of Rosenstiehl, *L'Apocalypse d'Elie* who argued that the Apocalypse of Elijah was a first-century BCE Essene work, although chap. 2 has expansions from a third-century CE Jewish author.

the two texts, 1 Enoch does not assign any function to Enoch (or Elijah?) at the judgment.[313]

There is, as a consequence, documentary evidence for a pre-Christian Jewish expectation that both Enoch and Elijah, the two men who had escaped death, would return at the time of the final judgment. The author of Revelation has built upon such sources but has added a number of features to them to fashion his own understanding of the eschatological drama.

Conclusion

The foregoing three-part study of Enochic writings, Enochic themes, and Enoch himself in early Christian literature has shown that the writings that circulated under the patriarch's name had a noticeable but limited role to play in the first several centuries of the Common Era. The booklets that comprise 1 Enoch, especially the Book of Watchers, were apparently more popular among Christian readers than among their Jewish contemporaries, or at least the surviving literature suggests as much. In Jewish literature Enoch and themes associated with him nearly disappeared, although they are a major part of the early Jewish apocalyptic heritage.[314] Even among Christians, while Enoch's writings were a legitimate source of authority for some time, by ca. 300 CE they no longer enjoyed the status they once had. Enoch himself is named often in early Christian texts but primarily as the intriguing, enigmatic character found in Gen 5:21-24, not as the more spectacular figure of revelations and the last days as he appears in the Enochic literature. The major exception is the limited but persistent tradition that identifies him as one of the two end-time witnesses in Revelation 11.

The greatest contribution of the Enochic apocalyptic tradition to early Christian thought was its angelic reading of Gen 6:1-4. Its influence can be traced in the various centers of Christianity from New Testament times until the early fourth century. In one form or another it gave Christian writers ammunition for explaining the presence of evil, idolatry, and demons in the world and the certainty with which wickednes would be punished at the judgment. However,

---

[313] Black, 'The "Two witnesses"', 229 conjectures that the curious order of the materials for the judgment scene in 1 Enoch 90 (Enoch [and Elijah] return before the judgment occurred, even though their return is mentioned after it) is purposeful: 'It is possible that the presence of the two Israelite immortals was to be that of witnesses to see that justice was done, on the principle that a valid testimony requires two witnesses (Num. 25:30; Deut. 17:6; Heb. 10:28).' Black ib 230-35 also explores other possible sources for the theme of the eschatological appearance of Enoch and Elijah (2 Esdr 6:25-28 [he gives 8:18ff as the reference]; Bib. Ant. 48:1), but none of these is specific enough to be a plausible source for the picture in the early Christian texts. See also Haugg, *Die Zwei Zeugen*, 14f, 86; Bauckham, 'The Martyrdom of Enoch', 451f.

[314] For brief surveys and further literature see Himmelfarb, 'A Report on Enoch'; VanderKam, *Enoch – A Man for All Generations*, chap. 5.

with the declining popularity of Enochic literature came rising doubt about the angelic reading of Gen 6:1-4. As the Sethite interpretation became more and more dominant, the mythological scenario of the Enochic exegesis lost its appeal and place in the early church. The Enoch literature itself, apart from excerpts here and there, fell out of circulation and would have been lost had it not been for the survival of the Ethiopic translation and the discovery of the Aramaic fragments in Qumran cave 4.

Chapter Three

Christian Influence on the Transmission History of 4, 5, and 6 Ezra

Theodore A. Bergren

4 Ezra (2 Esdras 3-14), a highly sophisticated Jewish apocalypse, was apparently written in Hebrew, in the land of Israel, between 90 and 100 CE.[1] It is pseudonymously ascribed to 'Ezra'. 5 Ezra (2 Esdras 1-2), also an 'Ezra' pseudepigraphon, seems most likely to be a Christian writing of the 2nd or 3rd century; its provenance and original language are uncertain.[2] 6 Ezra (2 Esdras 15-16) is an anonymous work (in its present form) that seems to date from the 3rd century CE; it was probably written in Greek by a Christian living in the eastern Mediterranean region.[3]

Each of these three works has a complex history of transmission. In each case, as is true for most of the 'pseudepigrapha' ascribed to Hebrew biblical figures and for other extra-canonical, 'biblical-type' writings (whether of 'Jewish' or 'Christian' origin), most of the known transmission of the work occurred in a Christian context. Moreover, at many points, 'Christian' interests active in the process of transmission seem to have influenced the disposition and even the contents of the three writings in identifiable ways.

In the Latin tradition, in which alone 5 and 6 Ezra are preserved in their entirety, these three writings came to be associated with one another and, in some cases, even joined into a single literary unit. It is for this reason that this essay treats the three works together. Nevertheless, at least 4 and 6 Ezra possessed literary histories of their own before this connection took place. This

---

[1] Studies of Christian influence on the transmission of the Jewish pseudepigrapha often focus on the Testaments of the Twelve Patriarchs rather than on pseudepigrapha associated with Ezra or other figures. Since, however, the study of the Testaments of the Twelve Patriarchs is mired in considerable controversy at present, it seems preferable to approach the issue from the angle of a different text. Comments on 4 Ezra here and throughout this study depend largely on the recent definitive commentary by Stone, *Fourth Ezra*. I am indebted to Prof. Stone for his helpful comments on an early draft of this paper.

[2] For comments on 5 Ezra see Bergren, *Fifth Ezra*.

essay is largely concerned also with those histories, especially with 'Christian' influences upon them.

Clearly, any intentional modification of a text that occurs within a context of Christian transmission can justifiably be termed, and analyzed as, a 'Christian' modification. It also seems, however, that many such modifications were made for stylistic or narrative reasons that have no demonstrable connection with any specific ideological stance of an editor. Also, for works such as 4 and 6 Ezra that are clearly or possibly of Jewish origin, it is often impossible to determine whether certain modifications to the 'original' text occurred in a 'Jewish' or 'Christian' phase of the transmission process (if it is possible to use such labels). For these reasons, and also for the sake of economy, this essay then will focus on textual modifications that appear to betray *identifiably* 'Christian' biases or interests.

Intentional Christian textual modification of 'pseudepigrapha' or biblical-type writings can be classed under several headings. First, Christians are known to have changed the wording of some texts in a tendentious manner. Second, Christians sometimes made insertions, or interpolations, into texts, in which Christian interests are betrayed. Third, Christians seem at times to have deleted parts of texts that were inconsistent with certain doctrinal points. Fourth, Christians sometimes brought into association texts or textual units that were once separate. Finally, in some cases, Christian editors seem to have rearranged the order of texts, or complexes of texts, for various reasons.[4] It is noteworthy that the transmission histories of 4, 5 and 6 Ezra, as traced below, appear to preserve examples of each of these categories of textual modification.

The Transmission History of 4 Ezra in Hebrew and Greek

Due to the circumstances of its composition and attestation, 4 Ezra presents an unusually useful case for evaluating the extent and character of Christian influence on the transmission of a pseudepigraphic writing. First, as stated above, 4 Ezra is almost certainly, in its original form, a Jewish writing of the last decade of the 1st century CE. Second, it possesses an extraordinarily rich base of textual attestation, being preserved in no fewer than eight tertiary (and several quaternary) language versions; each of these can probably be assumed to have been translated by a Christian and transmitted in a primarily Christian context.[5] Third, a provisional stemma of the versions can be contructed (see below). Thus, although the methodological cautions urged above remain in force, it will be possible, in some cases, to attempt to identify in a reasonable way 'Christian' textual modifications of an originally 'Jewish' writing.

---

[3] For comments on 6 Ezra see Bergren, '6 Ezra'.
[4] Although specifically 'Christian' rationales often cannot be identified for these final two categories of modification, the categories are nevertheless important enough to mention here.

It is almost universally acknowledged that, as noted above, 4 Ezra was composed in Hebrew. However, no traces of a Hebrew text remain. Furthermore, since practically no direct evidence survives of any language version that was translated directly from the Hebrew, the 'original' Hebrew form of 4 Ezra remains, essentially, an unknown factor.

4 Ezra seems to have been translated from Hebrew into Greek at some time before 190 CE, when Clement of Alexandria first quotes the text in Greek. The only direct evidence for a Greek text is three citations that survive in Christian sources.[6] Clement, in Stromateis 3.16.100, 3, apparently written between 190 and 200, quotes 4 Ezra 5:35. (Clement also appears to allude to 4 Ezra 14:18-22 in Stromateis 1.22.149, 3.) The Apostolic Constitutions, the present form of which apparently comes from 4th century Syria, cite 4 Ezra 7:103 (Apost. Constit. 2.14, 9) and 8:23 (Apost. Constit. 8.7, 6).

The form of attribution in Clement's citation is noteworthy: the quote is followed by the phrase 'Ezra the prophet says' (Ἔσδρας ὁ προφήτης λέγει). Although the expression 'Ezra the prophet' is sometimes taken to represent Clement's idea of the title of 4 Ezra, this is uncertain. Clearly, however, Clement views the book and its prophecy as authoritative. Both of the quotations in the Apostolic Constitutions are unattributed.

Although there is no direct evidence for the textual history of the Greek version of 4 Ezra, certain data can be deduced from the eight extant versions that were apparently translated from it (Latin, Syriac, Ethiopic, Georgian, two independent Arabic versions, Armenian and Coptic). Comparison of the translations indicates that the Latin, Syriac and 'Arabic1' versions form one distinct branch of the transmission stemma, while the Georgian, Ethiopic and Coptic constitute a second. (The 'Arabic2' and Armenian versions both seem to represent independent and reworked traditions.) Presumably, the *Vorlage* of each language version was a Greek text. The stemma is usually represented as follows:[7]

---

[5] Stone, *Fourth Ezra*, 207.
[6] For these citations, see Denis, *Introduction*, 194-197; id, *Fragmenta*, 130-132.
[7] See Blake, 'Jerusalem Manuscript', 313; Stone, *Fourth Ezra*, 3.

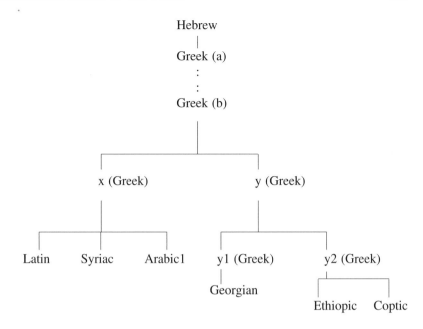

It is clear from this reconstruction that the Greek version of 4 Ezra itself underwent significant processes of redaction. In fact, by comparing the readings of the two main branches of the stemma where they differ, it is often possible to identify or even reconstruct separate Greek readings that lay behind each.[8] Furthermore, M.E. Stone, who has both edited and written a textual commentary on the idiosyncratic Armenian text, has shown that that version, which was translated in the 5th century, was itself based on a Greek text that had already been extensively reworked.[9]

Since knowledge of the Greek text can be gained only by inference from its surviving daughter versions, it is possible to know about the Greek version only beginning at the level of the stemma where we locate 'Greek b', the hyparchetype of those Greek texts that formed the *Vorlagen* for the versions. Presuming that the 'original' Greek translation of 4 Ezra ('Greek a') and 'Greek b' are not identical,[10] that 'original' translation, and any textual modification that occurred between it and 'Greek b', remain, like the hypothetical 'Hebrew original' of 4 Ezra, unknown.

The questions must now be addressed: what was the role of 'Christian'

---

[8] Stone, *Fourth Ezra*, identifies such cases on p106, 118, 125, 163, 176, 179, 190f, 202, 225, 262, 269, 276f, 360 and 381 of his commentary.

[9] See Stone, *The Armenian Version*; id, *A Textual Commentary*; furthermore id, *Fourth Ezra*, 8; id, 'Some Features'.

[10] In theory, of course, they could be identical, or at least very close.

tradition in the transmission of the Greek text; and was there any 'identifiably Christian' textual influence at this level.

It can probably be assumed that the translation of 4 Ezra from Hebrew into Greek was made by a Jew and that the work was disseminated in Greek form in Jewish circles.[11] On the other hand, all surviving citations of or references to the Greek text are in 'Christian' sources, and, as stated above, the translators of all the presently known tertiary versions can probably be assumed to be Christian. Thus, the Greek version presumably circulated in both Jewish and Christian milieus.

There are several ways in which demonstrably Christian influence on a Greek text of 4 Ezra could be shown. One would be to identify a clearly Christian element that was shared by two or more of the tertiary versions (preferably in the same part of the stemma) and that would be unlikely to have arisen independently.

There are at least two readings that could be taken to fulfill this criterion. In 4 Ezra 7:26, where the earliest recoverable text reads 'the city which now is not seen shall appear',[12] the Latin and Syriac versions have 'the bride shall appear, even the city appearing': an original Greek ἡ νῦν μὴ φαινομένη seems to have been misread as ἡ νύμφη φαινομένη.[13] Although, as several critics have pointed-ed out,[14] this corrupted reading might reflect an influence from Rev 21:1-2, 9-10, such influence is not certain.

Second, in 7:28, where the earliest recoverable text seems to read 'my Messiah shall be revealed', the Latin, Syriac and Arabic1 versions have 'my son (or: servant) the Messiah[15] shall be revealed'. Although this reading clearly could be viewed as reflecting Christian interests, the fact that exactly the same words occur in the earliest recoverable text of the next verse shows that it does not necessarily do so.

Another way in which to demonstrate Christian influence in the Greek stage of transmission would be to identify a clearly Christian element in one of the versions that could be argued on internal (e.g. linguistic or paleographic) grounds to have existed in Greek. I know of no such cases in any version aside from the Armenian. Stone, however, has shown that many of the distinctive

---

[11] 4 Ezra was written by a Jew and read originally in a Jewish milieu. If the book were to circulate outside Palestine in a Hellenistic diaspora setting, e.g. Egypt, Asia Minor, or Rome, it would of course have to be translated into Greek. Although it is in theory possible that a translation from Hebrew to Greek was made by a Christian, this sort of translational activity at this period is *a priori* less likely. In fact, to my knowledge there is no direct evidence of any Christian translation of Jewish literature from Hebrew into Greek.

[12] Quotations of 4 Ezra in this study are drawn from Stone, *Fourth Ezra*; Stone's translation is based primarily on the RSV.

[13] See Volkmar, *Das vierte Buch Esrae ad loc*; Violet, *Die Esra-Apokalypse ad loc*; Box, *The Ezra-Apocalypse ad loc*.

[14] For example, Box, *The Apocalypse of Ezra*, 51.

[15] Or, in the Latin version, 'my son Jesus'; see further below.

readings of the Armenian version did exist in the Greek *Vorlage* of that version;[16] on the basis of Stone's arguments, it may be assumed that this applies to some of the distinctively 'Christian' elements of that version as well. In fact, Stone argues that 'the Armenian is generally a faithful translation of a Greek version and most of the reworking to be discerned in it took place in Greek. This reworked Greek version must have existed by the fifth century at the latest and, consequently, we must posit a major reworking of the book before that time. This was the work of a Christian, but there is reason to think that some of the sources available to him may have included ancient, Jewish material.'[17] The 'identifiably Christian' elements in the Armenian version of 4 Ezra are discussed below.

Clearly, it is possible that any or all of the 'Christian' elements discussed below in the tertiary versions (besides the Armenian) existed in the Greek *Vorlage* of that version. However, these elements could equally well have been introduced by the translator from Greek, or at some stage in the transmission of the tertiary version itself.

Christian Influence in the Extant Tertiary Versions of 4 Ezra

THE LATIN VERSION[18]

The Latin version of 4 Ezra, which survives in full in eight independent manuscripts, is often regarded as the most literal and 'accurate' of the extant versions. The earliest indisputable witness to a Latin text is Ambrose (*fl.* 374-97), who quotes 4 Ezra copiously; Tertullian and Cyprian may also allude to the book. The independent manuscripts are: 'S', a two-volume Bible from St. Germain de Prés, France that is dated 821/22 CE; 'A', a 9th century manuscript from Amiens, France that consists of five writings attributed to 'Ezra' (Ezra-Nehemiah; 1 Esdras; 5, 4 and 6 Ezra); 'C', a 9th to 10th century Bible from Alcalà, Spain; 'V', a 12th to 13th century Bible from Avila, Spain; 'L', a 12th century Bible from León, Spain; 'M', an 11th to 12th century Bible from Les Cordeliers, France; 'N', a 12th century Bible from Belgium; and 'E', an 11th century Bible from Echternach, Luxembourg.[19]

4 Ezra is labeled in the latter three manuscripts as '2 Ezra', in C as '3 Ezra', in S, A and V as '4 Ezra', and it is unlabeled in L. In almost every case, it stands in connection with the canonical Ezra-Nehemiah and with 5 and 6 Ezra (further details are given below).

[16] Stone, *Textual Commentary*, x-xiii.
[17] ib ix.
[18] Klijn, *Der lateinische Text*.
[19] There are many other Latin manuscripts of 4 Ezra; all of these, however, can be proved to derive from 'S'. See further below.

To my knowledge, the Latin version has only one textual feature that can clearly be identified as 'Christian'. As stated above, in 7:28, where the earliest recoverable text seems to read 'For my Messiah shall be revealed', the Syriac and Arabic1 texts have 'For my son the Messiah shall be revealed'. All of the Latin manuscripts, however, read 'Revelabitur enim filius meus Iesus' (For my son Jesus shall be revealed).

The Latin transmission history of 4 Ezra, which is extremely complex, is investigated in detail in the final section of this study. For the present, it is worth noting that all of the independent complete Latin texts of 4 Ezra are either in Bibles (mss SCMNEVL) or connected with biblical materials (ms A).

THE SYRIAC VERSION[20]

The Syriac version of 4 Ezra is generally regarded as a reliable witness to the Greek text; Box states that it is 'singularly faithful, though it betrays occasionally a tendency to amplify'.[21] This text survives in a single manuscript, the 6th century Ambrosian Bible codex in Milan. To my knowledge, this is the earliest complete manuscript of 4 Ezra in any language. In this manuscript, 4 Ezra stands between 2 Baruch and the canonical Ezra-Nehemiah (the latter labeled '2 Ezra'). 4 Ezra is entitled at the beginning 'The Book of Ezra the Scribe, who is called Salathiel'; a colophon at the end identifies it as '1 Ezra'.

The Syriac text also has one main feature that seems to be identifiably Christian. In 7:28-29, where the earliest recoverable text reads 'For my Messiah shall be revealed ... and he shall make rejoice those who remain for *four hundred* years, and after these years my son the Messiah shall die...', the Syriac text has '...for *thirty years*...' This reading is most plausibly understood as a reference to Luke 3:23.[22]

THE ETHIOPIC VERSION[23]

4 Ezra survives in Ethiopic in about twenty-five manuscripts. The majority of these are Bibles that postdate the 14th century. According to Box, the Ethiopic version 'is much more paraphrastic than the Syriac, but occasionally attests valuable readings'.[24] The Ethiopic manuscripts label 4 Ezra as '[The book] of the prophet Ezra' or as '1 Ezra'.

---

[20] Bidawid, '4 Esdras'.

[21] Box, *The Apocalypse of Ezra*, x.

[22] It should be noted, however, that such a reference is not absolutely certain: cf Gen 41:46; 2 Sam 5:4; Ezek 1:1; 4 Ezra 3:1, 29; 9:45; 10:45-46.

[23] Dillmann, *Libri Apocryphi*, 154-193.

[24] Box, *The Apocalypse of Ezra*, x.

This version has only one textual feature that is arguably distinctively Christian. In 6:1, where the earliest recoverable text states that 'The beginning [sc. of creation] is through man and the end is through myself [viz. God]', the Ethiopic has 'The beginning (is) through the son of man and after that, (through) I myself'. Since the term used for 'son of man' here is the same as that found in the gospels,[25] and since the stemma suggests that this expression did not stand in the hyparchetypes 'y' or 'Greek b', it is probably a Christian feature.[26]

THE GEORGIAN VERSION[27]

The Georgian version of 4 Ezra survives in incomplete form in two manuscripts, one in a monastery on Mt. Athos and the other in the Greek Patriarchal Library at Jerusalem. The Athos manuscript, written in 978 at the monastery of Oska, contains most of the Old Testament, but has only excerpts from 4 Ezra. The Jerusalem manuscript, which dates to 1050, contains the biblical prophetic books plus 1 Esdras, Nehemiah, and 4 Ezra; of 4 Ezra, only 1:1-9:20 is preserved. The two manuscripts between them have about two-thirds of the text of 4 Ezra. The Georgian translation, which dates from about the 9th century, appears to be fairly literal. 4 Ezra is entitled 'Ezra Sutieli' (the latter word is a variant of 'Salathiel').

There do not seem to be any identifiably Christian features in the Georgian text.

THE ARABIC1 VERSION[28]

The more literal of the two surviving tertiary Arabic versions was edited by H.G.A. Ewald and is often referred to by his name. This version rests on two manuscripts: an original, written in 1354, presently at Oxford; and a copy of it, now in the Vatican. The original contains 4 Ezra (labeled '1 Ezra'), Ezra-Nehemiah (labeled '2 Ezra'), Tobit, and one other non-biblical piece. According to Violet this version is, in comparison with the Latin, Syriac and Ethiopic texts, 'often very free', but not as idiosyncratic as the 'Arabic2' version.[29]

---

[25] Violet, *Die Esra-Apokalypse*, 88 n1.

[26] This is also the view of Stone, *Textual Commentary*, 123. There are several other passages in the Ethiopic version in which potentially Christian features have been identified. In 7:104, for example, where the earliest recoverable text reads 'The day of judgment is *decisive*', the Ethiopic has 'sudden' or 'in an instant'. Violet, *Die Esra-Apokalypse ad loc* points out a similarity to 1 Cor 15:52; however, the influence of this text is not certain. An equally uncertain case of Christian influence lies in 13:52, which states that 'No one of those on earth can *know* (instead of 'see') [God's] son'; to this Violet compares Matt 11:27.

[27] Blake, 'Georgian Version', and 'Georgian Text'.

[28] Ewald, *Das vierte Ezrabuch*.

[29] Violet, *Die Esra-Apokalypse*, xxxvi.

The Arabic1 version contains several potentially Christian elements. In 5:38, where the earliest recoverable text reads 'Who is able to know these things except he whose dwelling is not with men?', Arabic1 has '...except God, who dwelt with men?' Violet interprets this as a reference to the Christian incarnation. In two passages, 7:34 and 7:139, the Arabic1 text inserts, into contexts in which God is described as judge, the phrase '[God,] who takes no account of persons...' (emphasizing God's impartiality). These passages are characterized by Violet as 'Christian additions' made with reference to Rom 2:11; the notion invoked, however, is certainly not exclusively Christian.

In 7:96, the phrase 'and they will see what no eye has seen' is inserted into a description of the joys of the elect. This statement is close to a passage quoted by Paul in 1 Cor 2:9-10 (probably derived from Isa 64:4) and has numerous other parallels in ancient Jewish, Christian and Islamic literature.[30] Although it is not certain that the phrase in Arabic1 derives directly from 1 Corinthians, such an origin is possible.

THE ARABIC2 VERSION[31]

A second Arabic version, edited by J. Gildemeister, is attested in complete form in a 14th century Vatican manuscript and partially in an extract (in Oxford) and a fragment, the latter from a Paris Gospel manuscript dated to 1321. In the Oxford text, 4 Ezra is labeled '1 Ezra'; the other texts lack numeration. According to Violet, this version has a 'less faithful, frequently abridged, often very free, and sometimes intentionally altered text', with several substantial interpolations.[32]

The Arabic2 version again has several potentially Christian textual elements. In 11:42, where the earliest recoverable text refers to 'the meek' and 'the peaceable', Arabic2 has 'the despised' and 'the poor in spirit'; Violet reads the latter as an allusion to Matt 5:3. In 13:35, the earliest recoverable text reads 'But [the Messiah] shall stand on the top of Mount Zion'; the Arabic2 version has 'And a man will arise on Golgotha, which is at Zion'. The latter is most likely a Christian reference (cf Mark 15:22; Matt 27:33; John 19:17).

THE ARMENIAN VERSION[33]

The Armenian version of 4 Ezra is widely recognized as the most idiosyncratic and heavily interpolated of the extant versions. Its textual base consists of

---

[30] See Stone-Strugnell, *The Books of Elijah*, 41-73.
[31] Gildemeister, *Esdrae liber quartus*.
[32] Violet, *Die Esra-Apokalypse*, xxxviii.
[33] Stone, *The Armenian Version*; id, *Textual Commentary*.

twenty-eight manuscripts ranging from the 13th to the 17th centuries; all save one are Bibles. The usual title of 4 Ezra in these manuscripts is '3 Ezra' (1 Esdras is usually designated '1 Ezra'; the canonical Ezra is '2 Ezra'; Nehemiah normally follows the Ezra books). The title 'Salathiel Ezra' is also attested.

As noted above, the Armenian translation was probably made in the 5th century. Stone states that 'the Armenian version is typified by extensive re-working and particularly by some long additions. It seems likely that the re-workings existed for the most part in its Greek *Vorlage* and that the additions, while not preserving parts of 4 Ezra proper, most likely preserve some frag-ments of ancient Ezra literature.'[34] Additional comments by Stone on the back-ground of the Armenian version were given above. In sum, he believes that the Armenian version is 'substantially a faithful rendering of a revision of the book carried out in Greek'.[35]

The Armenian version contains a much larger body of potentially Christian material than any of the other versions, most of it occurring in additions to the text. A long expansion at 5:12 reads in part:

> They shall be seized at the end of time by pains..., for not only did they change the Law, but also the Most High himself, upon the earth [*four corrupt words*]. Because of that, evil will come upon them...

Stone identifies this as a 'Christian addition', presumably taking 'the Most High himself, upon the earth' as a reference to Jesus (cf Armenian 6:1, quoted below).[36]

In 5:40, the expanded Armenian text includes an element similar to that noted above in the Arabic1 version of 7:96:

> ...the good things from him which eye has not seen and ear has not heard and have not occurred to man and man has never considered, which God has prepared for his beloved ones.

The literal approximation of this text to 1 Cor 2:9, which is much closer and more extensive than was the case in Arabic1, makes it almost certain that the Armenian refers to the Pauline passage.

A lengthy expansion in 6:1 provides what seem to be the most explicit Christian references in the Armenian version:

> He [the angel] replied and said to me [Ezra]: "The Most High will come and act and teach, but this people is stiff-necked and uncircumcised in everything and of little faith until the end, for evil will come upon them."
> And I said to him, "How will the Most High come, or when will his coming be?"
> And he said, "First of all, he will come after a little time in the form of a son of man, and he will teach hidden things: and they will dishonor him and they will be rejected

---

[34] Stone, *Fourth Ezra*, 8.
[35] Stone, *Textual Commentary*, xiii.
[36] Stone, *Fourth Ezra*, 106; contrast, however, the statement made by him in *Textual Commentary*, 89.

and they will do themselves evil. And after that, acts of wickedness will increase; the spirit of error will lead them astray..."

This text probably refers to the earthly career of Jesus.

Finally, the Armenian version of 13:32-40 states:

> (32) ...when these signs happen which I told you, the Most High shall appear with great power. He is that man whom you saw, that he ascended from the sea [viz. the messianic figure]. And some of the heathen will destroy the images of their abomination, (33) and when they shall hear about him they shall draw apart so as not to fight with one another. (34) And they will be assembled at one time, an innumerable multitude of all the inhabitants of the earth, to serve the Lord faithfully... (36) For he will come from Zion and will appear to all those who are ready...
> (40C) And I said, "That generation (or: nation) will be more blessed than this people."

The significance of this passage, which is probably a Christian self-reference, can be understood fully only when it is compared to the earliest recoverable text, where the corresponding section describes those whom the Messiah will *destroy*! One may compare with the Armenian the 'majority' text of 4 Ezra 13:34, which states that 'an innumerable multitude shall be gathered together, as you saw, desiring to come and conquer him'. It is also noteworthy that the Armenian version lacks 13:41-50, which in the earliest recoverable text describes the eschatological return of the ten lost tribes of Israel. Presumably, the 'Christian' editor intended the passage quoted above to take the place functionally of that description.

Thus, the identifiably Christian material in the Armenian version appears usually in extensive textual additions or interpolations, but sometimes also in extensive reworking of existing sections of text, often in contexts where the 'earliest recoverable text' invites a Christian interpretation.

In conclusion, the Armenian version itself provides an excellent case study of pervasive Christian influence on a presumably originally Jewish source document.[37]

THE COPTIC VERSION[38]

A Sahidic Coptic version of 4 Ezra survives only in a fragment of a 6th-8th century manuscript now in Berlin. 4 Ezra seems to have been known in Coptic as 'Ezra Southiel'.[39] The extant fragment contains 4 Ezra 13:29-46. The Coptic text of this section, which shows many large gaps and abridgements, contains no distinctively Christian elements.

---

[37] The reader is referred to Stone's *Textual Commentary* for further details.
[38] Leipoldt-Violet, 'Ein säidisches Bruchstück', 138-40.
[39] See Blake, 'Georgian Version', 310f. The second name in the title is a variant of Salathiel.

Several important points emerge from these data. First, virtually every attestation of the text of 4 Ezra in the extant versions is in a Bible or in the context of biblical materials. It could be inferred from this that, at some point in the Greek tradition of 4 Ezra, the book might have existed in association with biblical materials or even have been included in biblical manuscripts. However, no evidence for this possibility survives in Greek biblical manuscripts or canon lists.

Second it is noteworthy that, in the versions, 4 Ezra is sometimes labeled '1 Ezra', being placed before the 'canonical' Ezra-Nehemiah materials (e.g. Syriac, Arabic1), and sometimes '2', '3' or '4 Ezra', being in this case placed after them (e.g. Latin, Armenian). The placement before the canonical Ezra-Nehemiah books presumably derives from the alleged time setting of 4 Ezra (chronologically prior to the events described in Ezra-Nehemiah and 1 Esdras), the placement after them from the fact that 4 Ezra was regarded in some sense as having less authority than the other books.

A third point regards the *types* of 'identifiably Christian' textual modification that are attested in the versions. On the one hand, these modifications tend in most of the versions to involve relatively minor textual alterations, such as the Latin substitution of 'Jesus' for 'Messiah' (7:28), the Syriac substitution of 'thirty' for 'four hundred' (7:28), and the Ethiopic replacement of 'man' with 'son of man' (6:1). On the other hand, the Armenian text presents a dramatic example of large-scale interpolation of clearly Christian materials into textual contexts that either are consistent with the earliest recoverable text of 4 Ezra or are not otherwise identifiably Christian.

Christian Influence in the Latin Transmission History of 4, 5 and 6 Ezra

In the preceding section, some remarks were made about Christian influence on the extant Latin text of 4 Ezra. The transmission history of 4 Ezra in the Latin tradition is, however, an extremely complex one that goes far beyond the scope of the details given above. Moreover, the process of transmission in Latin can be assumed to have taken place entirely within a 'Christian' context. Thus, the Latin transmission history of 4 Ezra furnishes a remarkable model of the different types of influence to which an 'originally Jewish' pseudepigraphon could be subjected in the process of transmission in a 'Christian' context. This section of the study seeks to illuminate this process of transmission.

BACKGROUND

As noted above, the earliest indisputable witness to a Latin text of 4 Ezra is Ambrose; Tertullian and Cyprian may also allude to the book. 4 Ezra was known by several other early Latin Christian authors, including Priscillian (*fl.* ca. 380), Vigilantius (*fl.* ca. 400), Jerome (*fl.* 380- 420), the anonymous author of the Opus imperfectum in Matthaeum (425-475), the anonymous author of the Inventiones Nominum (pre-8th century), and the authors-compilers of the Mozarabic and Roman liturgies (the former specifically in a 10th century manuscript).[40] The 'confession of Ezra' in 8:20-36 was extracted from the text, apparently for liturgical purposes, and appears in numerous Latin liturgical manuscripts, the earliest of which dates from the 8th century.[41]

In addition to the eight complete independent Latin manuscripts described above, which range from the 9th to the 13th centuries, 4 Ezra is also attested in four fragmentary manuscripts that date from the 7th to the 9th centuries.[42]

4 Ezra, in fact, appears in many more Latin manuscripts than the eight complete and four fragmentary ones mentioned above. An account of why only these are used in the textual criticism of it presents a remarkable example of Christian influence on the transmission of the pseudepigrapha.

Every Latin manuscript of 4 Ezra known before 1875 lacked the section now labeled 7:36-106 ('et apparebit ...quoniam rogavit'). In that year, R.L. Bensly made public his discovery of the Amiens manuscript (A), which contains the 'missing fragment'.[43] Moreover, Bensly showed that a page containing precisely this missing section had been physically excised from the St. Germain manuscript. The reason for the excision was apparently dogmatic: the missing section contains a statement denying the efficacy of prayers for the dead (v. 105) – a sentiment that presumably was offensive to some reader. Since every manuscript lacking the 'missing fragment' must have descended, directly or indirectly, from S, none of these manuscripts is of independent value in the textual criticism of 4 Ezra. All eight complete Latin manuscripts listed above contain the missing section (except, of course, S); the four fragmentary ones are early enough to escape suspicion.

The transmission history of 4 Ezra in Latin is closely linked with that of two other works: 6 and 5 Ezra. Each of these books is described briefly in the first part of this essay.

6 Ezra belongs to the genre 'eschatological prophecy': it is similar in style

[40] For the Latin quotations of 4 Ezra, see Violet, *Die Esra-Apokalypse*, 433-8 and Klijn, *Der lateinische Text*, 93-97.
[41] Klijn, *Der lateinische Text*, 15f.
[42] ib 13-17.
[43] Bensly, *The Missing Fragment*. It should be noted, however, that in 1826, almost fifty years before Bensly's publication, J. Palmer discovered the complete version of 4 Ezra in the Complutum manuscript (C) in the University Library in Alcalá de Heñares, Spain. The discovery was kept private until 1877. See Bergren, *Fifth Ezra*, 9f and the literature cited there.

and content to some of the biblical prophetic writings and to certain of the Sibylline Oracles. Although the full text of 6 Ezra is attested only in Latin, the existence of a Greek version was confirmed by the discovery of a small 4th century vellum Greek fragment of the work at Oxyrhynchus.[44] The Latin is almost certainly a translation of the Greek. There is no compelling reason to believe that any other language version underlay the Greek or that the Greek was translated from Latin.

The earliest certain witness to the Latin text of 6 Ezra is Gildas, a 6th century historian of Britain, who quotes 6 Ezra in his De excidio Britanniae (composed between 516 and 547 CE).[45] Ambrose may quote 6 Ezra in his Epistle 29.[46] There are also a response in the Mozarabic (Hispanic) liturgy that quotes 6 Ezra and an antiphon in the Roman liturgy that seems to reflect the text of the book.[47] The full Latin text of 6 Ezra is found in the same eight manuscripts that contain the complete Latin text of 4 Ezra.

At some point, apparently in the Latin tradition,[48] the text of 6 Ezra came to be associated with that of 4 Ezra. In fact, in certain manuscripts, 6 Ezra is attached to the end of 4 Ezra.[49] In its present form, 6 Ezra is anonymous.

5 Ezra (2 Esdras 1-2) is a short tractate again concerned largely with eschatological matters. It survives only in Latin.

The earliest witnesses to the text of 5 Ezra are the pseudo-Augustinian De altercatione ecclesiae et synagogae and the anonymous Acta Silvestri, both of which probably date to the 5th century.[50] 5 Ezra is quoted extensively in both the Roman and Mozarabic liturgies, many elements of which probably go back at least to the 5th century. 5 Ezra, like 4 Ezra, seems to be known by the anonymous author-compiler of the Inventiones Nominum (7th century or earlier). The full Latin text of 5 Ezra occurs in the same eight manuscripts that contain complete Latin versions of 4 and 6 Ezra. Also, 5 Ezra 1:1-2:20 appears independently of 4 and 6 Ezra at the end of a 13th century Bible manuscript (K) from Chesnay, France.

At some point in its history of transmission, 5 Ezra became associated with,

---

[44] Hunt, *Oxyrhynchus Papyri* 7, 11-15. The fragment contains 6 Ezra 15:57-59.

[45] For the Latin citations of 6 Ezra, see M.R. James' introduction to Bensly, *The Fourth Book of Ezra*, xxxviii-xliii.

[46] ib xlii-xliii.

[47] For the Mozarabic liturgy, see Brou-Vives, *Antifonario visigotico*, 126f (= 6 Ezra 15:8-9). For the Roman, see Marbach, *Carmina scripturarum*, 538 (cf 6 Ezra 16:53).

[48] It is often claimed that 6 Ezra was written as an 'appendix' to a Greek version of 4 Ezra. Two points, however, make this unlikely. First, no other translation of the Greek text of 4 Ezra besides the Latin has 6 Ezra. Second, a study of the Oxyrhynchus Greek fragment of 6 Ezra 15:57-59 by Hunt (*Oxyrhynchus Papyri* 7, 11-15) indicated that, given the pagination of the fragment, it is improbable that the copy of 6 Ezra to which the fragment belonged was preceded by a work as long as 4 Ezra.

[49] For details, see below.

[50] For the Latin citations of 5 Ezra, see James' introduction to Bensly, *The Fourth Book*, xxxviii-xliii and Bergren, *Fifth Ezra*, chaps. 2-3.

and in some cases connected to the end of, a Latin corpus that seems by then already to have consisted of 4/6 Ezra.[51] At a later stage of revision, 5 Ezra was moved to the beginning of the corpus, resulting in the sequence 5/4/6 Ezra that occurs in editions of the Vulgate and in many Latin manuscripts.

Because editions of the Vulgate, based on the example of certain manuscripts, conflate these three works into one text unit, often labeled '2 Esdras', this practice and terminology have been taken over in most modern translations of the 'apocrypha'. This practice is in many ways unfortunate because it tends to blur the distinctions between the three separate works. In this study, the term '2 Esdras' is used only to refer to the three works as they appear in connection with one another in their history of transmission.

For each work – 4, 5 and 6 Ezra – the earliest witness to the full Latin text is a two-volume Bible manuscript (S) from St. Germain de Prés that is dated by a scribal note to 821/22 CE. Thus, in each case, we must assume a substantial period of transmission between the presumed time of composition of the work and its earliest full attestation in Latin. During this period, not only did the texts of the three works become associated (and probably modified in the process), but each text underwent a process of editorial recension that was, in some cases, quite dramatic.

THE PROCESS OF ASSOCIATION OF 4, 5 AND 6 EZRA

Only one source prior to the St. Germain manuscript shows a knowledge of any two components of 2 Esdras in association with one another: the Inventiones Nominum, which cites in close connection material that seems to derive from 4 and 5 Ezra.[52] Although this work is known at the earliest in manuscripts of the 8th century, E.A. Lowe judged one of these manuscripts, on paleographical grounds, to derive from 'an exemplar of high antiquity'.[53] Thus it seems that by the 7th century, if not much earlier, the Latin texts of 4 and 5 Ezra were associated with one another.

Several other observations of a slightly more conjectural nature can be brought to bear on the question of the association of the three works. First, the quotations of 6 Ezra by Gildas are prefaced by the words 'Hear, besides, what

---

[51] The basis for the inference that the association of 4 and 6 Ezra occurred first is that, in every independent manuscript, 6 Ezra follows immediately upon 4 Ezra, whereas 5 Ezra occurs sometimes after these two, sometimes before, and once (in S) before but separated from 4 Ezra by a section of 1 Esdras. There is no reason to think that 6 and 5 Ezra were connected before their association with 4 Ezra.

[52] Pericope 49 of the St. Gall manuscript, for example, states 'There are two Ezra's: one is the prophet, son of Chusi [cf 5 Ezra 1:4], to whom the Lord spoke from a bush as to Moses [cf 4 Ezra 14:1-7], and who renewed by memory the holy scriptures that Nebuchadnezzar burned [cf 4 Ezra 14].' See Bergren, *Fifth Ezra*, 76-78 for further details.

[53] Lowe, *Codices Latini* 7, no. 911.

the blessed prophet Ezra, library (bibliotheca) of the law, has threatened...'[54]
This reference may reflect a knowledge of the episode related in 4 Ezra 14 and
may indicate that 4 and 6 Ezra were associated by the time of Gildas. Furthermore, Gildas quotes 6 Ezra in the context of other 'canonical prophets' of the
Hebrew Bible and clearly considers it to be of equal authority to them; it could
reasonably be conjectured that this status accrued to 6 Ezra only in its connection with 4 Ezra.

Likewise, the citations of 5 Ezra in the 5th century *De altercatione ecclesiae
et synagogae* and in the Roman and Mozarabic liturgies clearly imply that the
work is as authoritative as the other 'canonical' writings in whose context it is
quoted.[55] Again, 5 Ezra probably gained this status only in its association with 4
Ezra.[56]

On the basis of these observations, it can be argued that 5 Ezra became
associated with the text group 4/6 Ezra probably as early as 450 CE, and perhaps
even before. This means that the association between 4 and 6 Ezra, which was
clearly earlier, can reasonably be pushed back at least to 400 CE.

Another factor to be considered here is the manner in which the three works
are arranged and titled in the eight surviving significant manuscripts.[57] These
manuscripts exhibit a similar stemmatic arrangement for each of the three parts
of the 2 Esdras corpus:

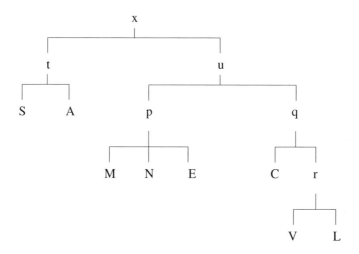

---

[54] Gildas, De excidio Britanniae 60.1 (Winterbottom, *Gildas*, 48, 115).

[55] Bergren, *Fifth Ezra*, chaps. 2-3.

[56] It is noteworthy that every manuscript in which any part of the 2 Esdras corpus is attested is
biblical, and that many citations of its three constituents also assume their 'scriptural' character.
The corpus seems to have been widely regarded as authoritative.

[57] For detailed discussion, see Bergren, *Fifth Ezra*, 39-58.

In the St. Germain manuscript (S), 4, 5 and 6 Ezra are placed with Ezra-Nehemiah among the Hebrew biblical writings: Ezra-Nehemiah (entitled '1 Ezra'); 1 Esdras 3:1- 5:3 (untitled); 5 Ezra ('2 Ezra'); 1 Esdras 1:1-2:15 ('3 Ezra'); 4 Ezra ('4 Ezra'); and 6 Ezra ('5 Ezra'). The Amiens manuscript (A), which is related textually to S, contains *only* five writings, all attributed to 'Ezra': Ezra-Nehemiah ('1 Ezra'); 1 Esdras ('2 Ezra'); 5 Ezra ('3 Ezra'); 4 Ezra ('4 Ezra'); and 6 Ezra ('5 Ezra'). In the Alcalà manuscript (C), 2 Esdras again appears with Ezra-Nehemiah in the midst of the Hebrew biblical writings: Ezra ('1 Ezra'); Nehemiah ('2 Ezra'); 4 Ezra ('3 Ezra'); and 6 and 5 Ezra ('4 Ezra'; 6 and 5 Ezra are separated only by a large initial letter beginning 5 Ezra).[58]

The other two manuscripts of Spanish origin are related textually to C. The Avila manuscript (V) originally had 2 Esdras at the end of the manuscript, after the New Testament and 1 Esdras in the following sequence: 1 Esdras ('3 Ezra'; Ezra and Nehemiah, which come earlier, are labeled '1' and '2 Ezra'); 4 Ezra 3:1-13:56 ('4 Ezra'); 4 Ezra 13:56-end/6 Ezra/5 Ezra ('5 Ezra') (with no textual break indicated between 4 and 6 Ezra; a clear break between 6 and 5 Ezra). At a later time, the codex was rearranged so that the 1 and 2 Esdras materials were moved from the end of the manuscript to a position among the Hebrew biblical writings, following Ezra and Nehemiah.

In the León Bible (L), 2 Esdras stands toward the end of the manuscript, after the New Testament, in the following order: 4 and 6 Ezra (with no numeration and no break between them); then 5 Ezra (no numeration, but clearly marked as a separate book).

The three other significant manuscripts, besides being closely related textually, are of approximately the same age and come from the same geographical region. The Les Cordeliers manuscript (M) places 2 Esdras with Ezra-Nehemiah among the Hebrew biblical books: Ezra-Nehemiah and 1 Esdras 3:1-5:3 ('1 Esdras'); 4/6/5 Ezra ('2 Esdras'), written with no indication of a major break between the texts. The Belgian Bible (N) places 2 Esdras with the Hebrew biblical material, but separates it from Ezra-Nehemiah ('1 Esdras'): 4/6/5 Ezra ('2 Esdras'), again written with no sign of break between the texts. The Echternach Bible (E) again places 2 Esdras among the Hebrew biblical books in connection with Ezra-Nehemiah: Ezra-Nehemiah ('1 Ezra'); 4/6/5 Ezra ('2 Ezra'). There is no break between 4 and 6 Ezra, but a minor division is indicated between 6 and 5 Ezra.

Several important points emerge from these data. First, it is clear that the division and titling of the three components of 2 Esdras vary according to the textual stemma of the manuscripts. Mss M, N and E, which share a hyparchetype, are the only manuscripts that read 4/6/5 Ezra as one book and label it '2 Esdras'. The stemmatic situation indicates that both the connection of the text and the title are secondary. Mss V and L, which also share a hyparchetype, connect the end of 4 Ezra directly with 6 Ezra, but separate 5 Ezra. Again, the

---

[58] '3 and 4 Ezra' receive a special introduction in this manuscript.

stemma indicates the connection to be secondary. In fact, the manuscript stemma suggests that the separation of the three components of 2 Esdras in the forms in which they are known to modern scholarship (viz., 4, 5 and 6 Ezra), a division present in some form in mss S, A and C, was original to the Latin text tradition of the corpus. With time, the individual components of the corpus tended to become merged, but in different ways.

No such general statement can be made regarding the 'original' numeration of the Latin 'Ezra' books, however, since the numeration varies so dramatically in the manuscripts.

Another point with regard to the process of association of 4, 5, and 6 Ezra is that almost certainly the end of 4 Ezra, and possibly also the beginning of 6 Ezra, was modified when or after the two books became connected. Virtually every version of 4 Ezra besides the Latin features an ending in which are described Ezra's assumption to heaven, his transcription of 4 Ezra, and his continuing function as a heavenly scribe.[59] The Latin version lacks all of this, ending with Ezra still on the earth. Presuming that the Latin translation of the Greek originally had the longer ending, it seems reasonable to postulate that it was excised when 6 Ezra became connected to the end of 4 Ezra, in order to allow the seer to continue prophesying in an earthbound setting.

Also, it is often observed that the present text of 6 Ezra begins rather abruptly, without ever giving the name of a prophet or a context for prophecy. It seems possible that part of the original beginning of 6 Ezra, which might have contained these elements, was removed when it was connected with 4 Ezra, perhaps to afford a smoother transition between the two.[60] Indeed, when the two works are read together, 4 Ezra provides both the name of the seer and a prophetic context. As noted above, the present text of 6 Ezra is anonymous, and nowhere mentions the name Ezra.

A final consideration under this rubric concerns the circumstances surrounding and the reasons for the association of the three works. For the connection of 4 and 6 Ezra, which seems to have occurred first, it is difficult to identify a rationale. The question is complicated, of course, by the uncertainty regarding the original beginning of 6 Ezra. It is true that both works are concerned with predicting eschatological events and with exhorting their audiences, but this hardly seems sufficient cause for linking them. 6 Ezra does not seem to show a knowledge of 4 Ezra. If 'Ezra' originally was designated explicitly as the seer of 6 Ezra, the association is easier to explain, but this is impossible to verify. In theory, the connection could also have occurred by chance: 6 Ezra might have followed 4 Ezra in some collection or manuscript, and the association might have become traditional.

The textual connection of 4 and 6 Ezra could have occurred at almost any

---

[59] See Violet, *Die Esra-Apokalypse*, 428-32. Both manuscripts of the Arabic2 text, however, end at 14:44, somewhat before the Latin ending.

[60] Unfortunately, the evidence of the Greek fragment of 6 Ezra, while tending to confirm the originally independent character of the work, leaves it uncertain whether in Greek the book had a longer beginning than it now has in Latin; see Hunt, *Oxyrhynchus Papyri*, 13.

time between 120 CE (the earliest possible date for both 4 and 6 Ezra to have been translated into Latin) and 400 CE (presuming that the connection was made before 5 Ezra came to be associated with the unit).

Regarding the (apparently) later association of 5 Ezra with the 4/6 Ezra corpus, there is slightly more evidence on which to proceed. First, both 4 and 5 Ezra are clearly, in their original forms, attributed to an 'Ezra'. Second, it seems probable to me that the author of 5 Ezra knew 4 Ezra. The two share many themes and images, including portrayal of Jerusalem or Israel as a 'mother', emphasis on resurrection and use of similar language to describe the pre-resurrection state, depiction of Ezra as a prophet and visionary seer, description of a people coming from the east, a vision of a 'son/servant of God' on Mt. Zion with a surrounding multitude, and Ezra's conversation with an angelic interpreter.[61] Perhaps most importantly, the attribution of 5 Ezra to the strange figure 'Ezra the son of Chusi' (1:1) seems to make more sense when read in the context of the equally unusual 'Ezra-Salathiel' of 4 Ezra 3:1.

Furthermore, 5 Ezra can be read as a Christian 'reply' to or adaptation of 4 Ezra. Just as the potent and charismatic Jewish prophet had, in 4 Ezra, forecast many aspects of the eschaton, so he (5 Ezra might say) had also forecast the coming of Jesus and the Christians to take the place of Israel in the eschatological scenario.

Whether the actual physical association of 5 Ezra with 4/6 Ezra took place near the time of its composition or at some later period is difficult to judge. It is possible that 5 Ezra originally circulated separately from the Jewish apocalypse and that the two came into association later by virtue of their common attribution. It is also conceivable that 5 Ezra was textually connected with the 4/6 Ezra corpus from the time of its composition. It is important to note that, just as 6 Ezra was appended to 4 Ezra, so 5 Ezra was originally added to the end of the 4/6 Ezra corpus.

One other aspect of the textual association of the three works is purely speculative, but is nevertheless an intriguing possibility. It was noted above that three of the eight significant manuscripts of 2 Esdras explicitly denote a total of five Ezra books. Furthermore, in the case of one manuscript (A), these five Ezra books constitute the entire contents of the codex: it is, quite literally, an 'Ezra pentateuch'. It is conceivable that the three components of the 2 Esdras corpus were grouped together, and placed with Ezra-Nehemiah and 1 Esdras, in some codices intentionally to form an 'Ezra pentateuch'.[62]

---

[61] See also Geoltrain, 'Remarques sur la diversité'.

[62] It is important to stress that this idea is purely speculative. For example, the theory advanced by Milik, 'Problèmes de la littérature hénochique', that there was an 'Enochic pentateuch' at Qumran, has been refuted in Greenfield-Stone, 'The Enochic Pentateuch'. The fact remains, however, that the Ethiopic version of 1 Enoch can be argued to constitute an 'Enochic pentateuch', even if this cannot be proved to be deliberately modeled after the Mosaic pentateuch. Other examples of groupings of five in early Jewish literature are the Megillot and the corpus of biblical psalms. With regard to an 'Ezra pentateuch', it should be noted that Ezra and Moses are explicitly connected and compared in 4 Ezra 14 and in several rabbinic sources; see Bergren, *Fifth Ezra*, 223f n58.

THE RECENSIONAL SITUATION

Since the 1895 text edition of Bensly-James,[63] it has been recognized that each of the three parts of the 2 Esdras corpus exists in two distinct textual recensions. In each work, the two recensions divide along the lines of the same manuscripts: mss S and A consistently manifest a recension labeled by James the 'French', while the remaining mss CMNEVL show a recension that James called the 'Spanish'.[64]

This recensional situation is complicated by two factors. First, the degree of textual variation between the two recensions differs significantly in the three works. In 4 Ezra, the recensions are rather close: in chaps. 11 and 12, for example, they are identical, in both wording and word sequence, in about 93% of all cases. At the beginning of 6 Ezra, the situation is roughly similar: in 15:1-37, for example, the recensions agree in about 85% of cases. As 6 Ezra progresses, however, the recensions diverge increasingly, so that when the book is considered as a whole, only 72% of all words in the recensions are equivalent. In 5 Ezra, the divergence is even more pronounced: only 62% of the words in the two recensions are identical.

A second complicating factor is that the two recensions actually appear to differ in value in the three works. In 4 Ezra, it has been acknowledged since the time of Violet that the 'French' recension is textually superior, and that the 'Spanish' represents a secondary reworking that apparently took place in a Latin medium. In 6 Ezra, preliminary investigations by M.R. James,[65] A.S. Hunt,[66] and the present author[67] indicate a similar situation: the 'French' recension almost certainly represents more closely the earliest recoverable Latin text.

In 5 Ezra, however, the reverse situation seems to obtain. A study by the present author supports the view that, as argued by James almost a century ago, the Spanish text of 5 Ezra is superior to the French, and that the latter is a secondary reworking of the text that took place in a Latin medium.[68] (Interestingly, the methods and aims of the 'French' reviser[s] of 5 Ezra are not unlike those of the 'Spanish' reviser[s] of 6 Ezra, although there are no grounds for assuming a common agency of revision.)

This situation also has implications for the differing placement of 5 Ezra in the surviving significant manuscripts. As noted above, all the 'Spanish' manuscripts read 5 Ezra *after* the 4/6 Ezra unit, whereas both of the 'French' manu-

---

[63] See above n45.

[64] It is now recognized that these names do not necessarily identify the geographical provenance of the two recensions; nevertheless, they are retained here due to convention. For the geographical provenance of the two recensions, see further below. Especially in 4 Ezra, the 'French' recension is often called *Φ, the 'Spanish', *Ψ.

[65] James' introduction to Bensly, *The Fourth Book of Ezra*, lxiii-lxxviii.

[66] Hunt, *Oxyrhynchus Papyri* 7, 11-15.

[67] Bergren, 'Assessing the Two Recensions'.

[68] Bergren, *Fifth Ezra*, chap. 4; James' introduction to Bensly, *The Fourth Book of Ezra*, xliv-lxiii.

scripts place it *before* this unit. It seems possible that the editor(s) or reviser(s) who produced the French recension of 5 Ezra were also responsible for repositioning the book before 4/6 Ezra. This shift was presumably made because the French recension of the book opens with a lengthy genealogy of the seer (1:1-3), which would seem more appropriate at the head of a corpus of prophetic 'Ezra' writings than in the middle of it. It is also possible, however, that the repositioning took place independently of the 'French' editorial recension of 5 Ezra; the genealogy, for example, could have been added at a later stage.

Some attempt must be made to account for this complex recensional situation. It was observed above that the methods and aims of the Spanish revision of 6 Ezra are not unlike those of the French revision of 5 Ezra. On the grounds of the disparities in the recensional situation, however, it does not seem possible to understand the textual revision of 4 and 6 Ezra on the one hand, and of 5 Ezra on the other, as originating in the same milieu.

It is conceivable, however, that the Spanish revision of 4 and 6 Ezra took place at the same time, when the two books had already been connected, and that for some reason the revisional hand became heavier as it progressed toward the end of the corpus (see the comments above).[69] There are, of course, other, more complicated ways to account for the process.

It seems most logical to explain the recensional situation in 2 Esdras as a whole with one of two scenarios, neither of which is without its difficulties. First, it is possible that the Spanish revision of 4/6 Ezra and the French revision of 5 Ezra took place independently, when these two corpora had not yet become associated. Subsequently, the revised French version of 5 Ezra was prefixed to the more original French text of 4/6 Ezra, giving rise to the situation in mss S and A. Independently, the more original Spanish text of 5 Ezra was appended to the revised Spanish version of 4/6 Ezra, producing the text in mss CMNEVL.

A second scenario is that the original French text of 4/6 Ezra first underwent the Spanish revision. Then, the original Spanish version of 5 Ezra was added to the end of both the French and Spanish versions of 4/6 Ezra. The latter case would produce the version found in mss CMNEVL. Finally, the French corrector of 5 Ezra revised the book and moved it to the front of the original French 4/6 Ezra corpus, perhaps without making major revisions to 4 or 6 Ezra. This would produce the text situation in mss S and A.

The actual situation may well be even more complicated than either of these hypothetical scenarios.

Unfortunately, there is not yet any solid evidence to indicate when any of this recensional activity took place. This is because, for both 5 and 6 Ezra, the earliest definite and extended attestation of the 'secondary' recensions (the

---

[69] M.E. Stone has brought it to my attention that in the short recension of the Armenian version of the Testaments of the Twelve Patriarchs, it is always the end that is most heavily reworked. It would be interesting to pursue this idea in other works that survive in both a more original and a revised version.

'French' for 5 Ezra and the 'Spanish' for 6 Ezra) occurs in ms S itself (9th century).[70] (To my knowledge, no study that addresses this issue in 4 Ezra has yet been undertaken.[71]) Thus, there is presently no substantial evidence that can shed light on the process of recensional activity in 2 Esdras prior to the onset of the tradition of complete manuscripts in the 9th century.

Another issue that should be addressed here is whether it is possible to detect any identifiably 'Christian' influences in the processes of recension. To my knowledge, neither the secondary Spanish recension of 4 or 6 Ezra, nor the secondary French recension of 5 Ezra, contains any textual modification that is motivated in a positive direction by identifiably Christian interests. There are, however, several passages in the French recension of 5 Ezra that actually seem to indicate the reverse – that a reviser (or revisers) has attempted to suppress or adjust elements in the more original text that might appear too overtly 'Christian' to be appropriate, or genuine, in a prophecy of the 'Jewish' Ezra!

In 1:11, where the more original Spanish text reads 'Did I not destroy the town of Bethsaida because of you?', the French recension has 'I have destroyed all nations before them'. It is possible that a reviser read 'Bethsaida' as a 'Christian' element (see Matt 11:21; Mark 6:45; 8:22; Luke 9:10; 10:13; John 1:44; 12:21; the name occurs nowhere in the Jewish scriptures or Jewish apocrypha) that was out of place in an 'Ezra' writing, and modified the text for this reason.

Again, the Spanish texts of 1:32 and 1:37 refer to 'apostles' or 'emissaries' (Latin *apostoli*): 1:32 'you ... tore to pieces the bodies of the *apostoli*; 1:37 'The *apostoli* bear witness to the coming people with joy'. The French recension of 1:32 states that the bodies of the *prophets* were torn in pieces; in 1:37, it reads '*I* call to witness the gratitude of the coming people'. In both cases, it is possible that a reviser sensitive to what could seem inappropriate in a Jewish writing has modified the text.[72]

One additional 'Christian' modification to the text of 5 Ezra that is worthy of note is a long interpolation which appears between 1:32 and 1:33 in mss M, N and E. Since no other manuscript of 5 Ezra has this section, it may be assumed to have been introduced at the level of 'p', the hyparchetype of M, N and E. The interpolated section reads:

> Thus says the Lord Almighty: "Most recently you even laid your hands on me, crying out before the tribunal of the judge for him to hand me over to you. You took

---

[70] Ms S departs from its normal filiation and exhibits a 'Spanish' text of 6 Ezra in 15:59-16:32. Presumably, at some stage in the background of its transmission, a leaf of a ms was lost and recopied from a 'Spanish' ms. It should be noted here that 'p', the hyparchetype of the ms family MNE, can probably be dated in or before the 5th century, since a source from that period cites a section of 5 Ezra that is peculiar to that family. See Bergren, *Fifth Ezra*, 62-64.

[71] It has been argued, however, that a 7th century fragment of 4 Ezra attests a 'mixed' textual stage before the two recensions had separated. See de Bruyne, 'Quelques nouveaux documents'; Violet-Gressmann, *Die Apokalypsen* xix-xxi; Klijn, *Der lateinische Text*, 16.

[72] See James' introduction to Bensly, *The Fourth Book of Ezra*, xlvii, li; Bergren, *Fifth Ezra*, 206f.

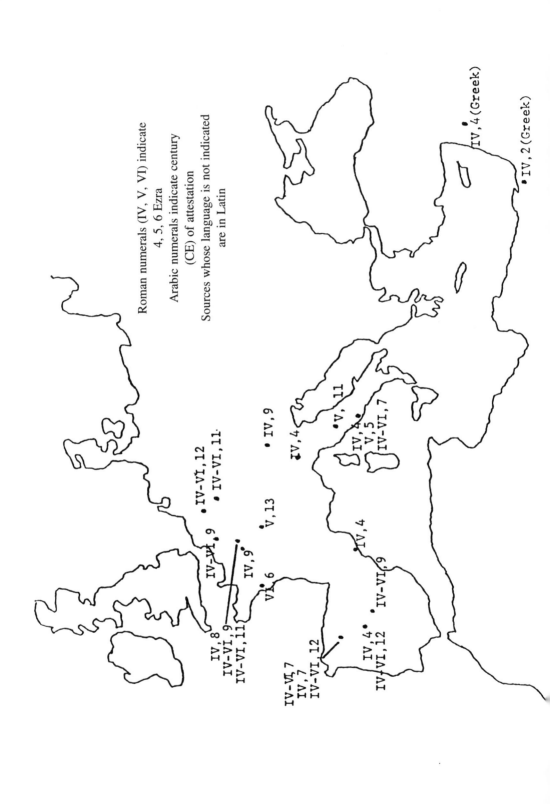

Roman numerals (IV, V, VI) indicate
4, 5, 6 Ezra

Arabic numerals indicate century
(CE) of attestation

Sources whose language is not indicated
are in Latin

IV-VI, 12
IV-VI, 11

IV, 9

IV, 4

V, 11

IV-VI, 9

V, 13

IV, 4
V, 5
IV-VI, 7

IV, 9

V, 6

IV, 8
IV-VI, 9
IV-VI, 11

IV, 4

IV-VI, 7
IV, 7
IV-VI, 12

IV, 4
IV-VI, 12
IV-VI, 9

IV, 4 (Greek)

IV, 2 (Greek)

me as an unrighteous person, not as the father who freed you from slavery, and hanging me on a tree, you handed me over to death. These are the works that you have done.

"Therefore", says the Lord, "let my father and his angels return, and let them judge between me and you, if I have not carried out the command of the father, if I have not cared for you, if I have not done what my father commanded: I shall contend with you in judgment," says the Lord.[73]

This section is intended to make the general indictment of the people of Israel in 5 Ezra more specific from a Christian point of view.

GEOGRAPHICAL CONSIDERATIONS

Finally, it will be valuable to consider the geographical evidence for the Latin transmission history of 2 Esdras. This study can be facilitated by charting the locations of all the Greek and Latin witnesses to any part of the corpus on a map (see the accompanying map).[74] It is also useful in this context to consider the geographical implications of the manuscript stemma.

As noted above, both of the 'French' manuscripts, S and A, come from the environs of Paris. It is possible that the hyparchetype of the French family, and perhaps also the 'French' reviser of 5 Ezra, can be located in this area.

The 'Spanish' manuscripts divide textually into two subgroups, CVL and MNE. Since C, V and L all come from north-central Spain, their hyparchetype might also have resided in this region. M, N and E were all copied in north, west-central Europe. This 'split' geographical situation makes it difficult to make general statements about the origin of the 'Spanish' hyparchetype or the provenance of the 'Spanish' revision of 4/6 Ezra.

Considering the locations of the primary and secondary Latin sources that cite any of the three books, one notes that the field of attestation begins in the 4th century with 4 Ezra (only) being attested strongly in both Italy (Ambrose and Jerome) and Spain (Priscillian and Vigilantius). In the 5th century, 5 Ezra is cited in a Roman source (Acta Silvestri). Moving into the 6th and 7th centuries, 4, 5 and 6 Ezra all are quoted in both the Mozarabic (Spanish) and the Roman liturgies, and 6 Ezra is cited by an (apparently) French witness (Gildas). Two early manuscript fragments of 4 Ezra come from León, Spain (7th century) and Paris (8th century).

The tradition of full manuscripts that attest the three works in conjunction begins in the 9th century with two manuscripts from around Paris (SA) and one from Spain (C). There are also two 9th century manuscript fragments of 4 Ezra, from Chartres and Munich. The 11th and 12th centuries witness one manuscript

---

[73] See Bergren ib 62-64, 131-33, 358-60. This section may be compared with some of the Armenian interpolations quoted above.

[74] Naturally, there are some witnesses whose provenance cannot be ascertained.

each from France (M), Belgium (N), and Luxembourg (E), and two from Spain (VL). There is also an 11th century quotation of 5 Ezra in an Italian liturgical piece. In the 13th century there is a French manuscript (K) that contains a segment of 5 Ezra.

These data, while only indicative, suggest that the Latin 2 Esdras was first known most extensively in the 4th century, in Italy and Spain. As time passes, northern continental European witnesses begin to appear, eventually overshadowing all other locations. Italian witnesses, so strong in the beginning, virtually disappear in the manuscript tradition after the 9th century. It is only in Spain that the corpus maintains a strong showing in both the early and later stages of the tradition.

It is tempting to speculate on the role that the Spanish thinker Priscillian and the movement that he initiated might have played in the popularity and dissemination of the 2 Esdras corpus.[75] It is well known that one of the main tenents of Priscillianism was an acceptance and use of both Jewish and Christian 'apocryphal' texts. Priscillian himself both knew 4 Ezra and defended its scriptural authority. The influence of Priscillianism was extremely strong and widespread both in Spain and in southern France. Several scholars have suggested that Priscillian and his school might have played a significant role not only in the spread of 2 Esdras but also in its recension.[76] Given the importance of apocryphal writings in Priscillianism, and the geographical data surveyed above, it seems probable that this judgment is valid in at least some measure.[77]

It can also be surmised that mounting Italian ecclesiastical opposition to the 'apocryphal' 2 Esdras might have contributed to the decline of its attestation in Italy.[78]

CONCLUSIONS

The individual components of the 2 Esdras corpus varied widely in origin, both in time, place and original language. 4 and 6 Ezra presumably were translated from Greek into Latin separately and at a relatively early date (before the 5th century). 5 Ezra is also known in Latin in the 5th century. The Latin texts of 4 and 6 Ezra probably became associated with one another by 400 CE; the reason

---

[75] On Priscillian, see Chadwick, *Priscillian*.

[76] James' introduction to Bensly, *The Fourth Book of Ezra*, xxxvi; de Bruyne, 'Quelques nouveaux documents', 46f.

[77] As de Bruyne ib pointed out, it is noteworthy that all the Spanish mss of 2 Esdras tend to mark the book as being unusual in some manner. In C, the corpus receives a special introduction, and in both V and L it was originally placed at the very end of the Bible, after the New Testament (as also in K). In fact, in L, 2 Esdras might have been copied from a different source than the rest of the manuscript. Perhaps this unusual treatment can be traced to the Priscillianist controversy.

[78] See especially Jerome's comments against the work in Contra Vigilantium 6 and in his preface to his Vulgate translation of the canonical Ezra.

for the association is unclear. Both texts were apparently altered in the process.

At some time after the association of 4 and 6 Ezra, either before or after 5 Ezra became connected to 4/6 Ezra, each of these two corpora seems to have undergone a process of editorial revision, resulting in two 'text versions' of each corpus.

5 Ezra probably became associated with 4/6 Ezra by the mid-5th century at the latest. Presumably the association was made because of the common attribution of the two corpora. It is theoretically possible that one rationale behind the association of these three 'Ezra' books, or at least one result of this association, was an effort to construct an 'Ezra pentateuch'. Unfortunately, the details of how the secondary, 'Spanish' recension of 4/6 Ezra became connected with the more original 'Spanish' text of 5 Ezra, and how the more original 'French' version of 4/6 Ezra came to be joined with the secondary 'French' recension of 5 Ezra, are obscure.

In its earliest phase, the Latin 2 Esdras corpus seems to have been known especially in Italy and Spain. As time passed, the corpus apparently increased in currency in northern continental Europe and retained its popularity in Spain, but declined in currency in Italy. The manuscript stemma suggests that the 'French' family stems from around Paris; the 'Spanish' family is split between Spain and northern Europe. It is possible that the Priscillianist movement contributed to the popularity of 2 Esdras in Spain, and perhaps also to its spread into northern Europe.

A few final comments are in order about the phenomenon of textual accretion that occurred around the 'nucleus' of 4 Ezra – i.e., about the association of 6 and 5 Ezra with that work. As noted above, 6 and 5 Ezra seem to have become connected successively to the end of 4 Ezra, with 5 Ezra being moved to the head of the entire corpus at a later time. 4 Ezra is clearly Jewish; 6 and 5 Ezra are both probably Christian; and the process of accretion almost certainly took place in a Christian context.

There are several other instances among the pseudepigrapha where similar processes of textual accretion might have taken place. Critics of the Ascension of Isaiah have traditionally held that chaps. 1-5 (with the exception of 3:13-4:22, usually labeled Christian) represent a Jewish 'core' of the book, to which chaps. 6-11, a Christian composition, were added later.[79] In the case of the Greek text of the History of the Rechabites, J.H. Charlesworth argues that the central section (chaps. 3-15) is an originally Jewish document that was supplemented with initial and final sections that are of Christian origin.[80] If these theories are correct, these two texts represent close parallels in terms of composition history to the 2 Esdras corpus.

---

[79] In opposition to this theory, see recently Acerbi, *L'Ascensione di Isaia*; and Hall, 'The *Ascension of Isaiah*'. Both authors see the work as a whole as originating in Christian prophetic circles at the beginning of the 2nd century.

[80] Charlesworth, 'History of the Rechabites'.

Chapter Four

The Legacy of Jewish Apocalypses in Early Christianity: Regional Trajectories

David Frankfurter

Introduction

The following study concerns what might be called the 'religious' context of apocalypses in early Christianity: that is, their significance as sacred texts, their meaning for sectarian self-definition, and their influence on religious communities' evolving conceptions of a sacred realm and the means of access to it.

APOCALYPSES AND APOCALYPTICISM

Jewish apocalypses appealed to early Christian communities because they reflected two models of authority essential for religious innovation in late antiquity: a model of revelatory authority that implied validity to 'new' revelations such as prophecy and that drew upon a broader Mediterranean conception of a secret (yet available) 'gnosis',[1] and a model of literary authority that grounded a community's ongoing compositional activities in the tradition of a culture hero. The 'influence' of Jewish apocalypses is thus gauged and discussed largely on the basis of these twin *concepts*, gnosis and the authority of the written text.

One may justly criticize this use of categories as imprecise, since attention to particular texts becomes somewhat overwhelmed by abstraction. Tracing the influence of abstract categories of gnosis and heavenly book is meaningful only if pursued in connection with invocations of the heroic authorities of the Bible, like Enoch and Moses, and as much as possible with references to particular books. But it is the cultural and documentary evidence which itself requires an

---

[1] My use of 'gnosis' as a quality of apocalypticism rather than of a specific Christian ideology is informed most immediately by Gruenwald, 'Knowledge and Vision', although it has been similarly approached from other quadrants. Compare, e.g., Daniélou's 'esoteric knowledge bearing on celestial and infernal places, the names of angels, [and] the divine hypostases' ('Judéo-christianisme', 139) and the Messina Colloquium's 'knowledge of the divine mysteries reserved for an élite' (Bianchi, *Origini*, xxvi). See also Wilson, 'Gnosis' and Rudolph, '"Gnosis" and "Gnosticism"'.

abstract definition of apocalypticism to gain meaningful analysis: as we will see in both Asia Minor and Egypt, the domestication of apocalypses in non-literate cultures often involved precisely the *shift* of the notion of 'apocalypse' as revelatory axis, from book to prophetic holy man or to the otherworldly sect itself. Similarly, without a broader understanding of the *ways* in which Jewish apocalypses were meaningful to their readers it would be difficult to view the reception of the Jewish apocalypse among Egyptian intellectual conventicles in continuity with Egypt's own revelatory books. Thus to restrict one's analysis of 'influence' to use of particular books would exclude the most vital aspects of early Christian 'apocalypticism'.

Two additional methodological caveats must be raised before examining the cultures themselves. Both concern the historical reification of a picture of Christians 'using' Jewish apocalypses. The first issue, aptly broached in the introduction to this volume, regards the notion of scripture itself: did use of Jewish apocalypses differ significantly from use of biblical literature more broadly? It seems clear that in the first three centuries there was not such a distinction, although apocalyptic texts were often viewed as more esoteric or as more reflective of heavenly wisdom than the more commonly revered Torah, Writings, and Prophets (cf. 4 Ezra 14:45-47). And even in the fourth century and thereafter, when ecclesiarchs like Athanasius of Alexandria developed canons explicitly excluding biblical apocrypha we should be careful about assuming the uniform assimilation of such canons, especially in non-literate environments where expansions of biblical lore such as apocalypses and apocryphal acts were read aloud or epitomized in sermons. In sixth-century Egypt, for example, John of Paralos warned that 'if simple people pay attention to [apocryphal writings] in the villages and towns of Egypt while certain "zealots" listen to them, they might think that the words [in these books] are wise'.[2] And we know that in medieval Ireland, where an enormous corpus of biblical and New Testament apocrypha developed, 'there prevailed no clear and immediate mental distinction between "canonical" and "uncanonical" biblical texts'.[3]

The second caveat concerns 'Jewish' and 'Christian' as exclusive categories of texts in antiquity. If Jean Daniélou's extensive description of 'Jewish' Christianity demonstrates anything historically, it is that in late antiquity the lines between 'Jew' and 'Christian' were on the whole fuzzy, especially among those communities devoted to cultivating a gnosis of the heavenly world through apocalypses.[4] The evidence for apocalyptic traditions in Egypt and Asia Minor, for example, demonstrates that it was through the metamophosis of individual

---

[2] John of Paralos, Homily Against Heretical Books 49 (Vienna K 9831ᵛa; ed Van Lantschoot, 'Fragments') 1.304.

[3] Dumville, 'Biblical Apocrypha', 333; cf McNamara, *Apocrypha*, 5. On the fifth-century east see Sozomen, Hist. eccl. 7.19.

[4] Daniélou, *Jewish Christianity*. Significant historical discussions of 'Jewish Christianity' have been pursued by Kraft, 'Jewish Christianity' and 'Jewish Heritage', Murray, 'Jews, Hebrews'and Segal, 'Jewish Christianity'.

communities dedicated to prophecy and apocalyptic gnosis, not through inter-religious exchange, that Jewish texts were 'christianized' and that christianized sects continued to issue revelatory literature in the names of biblical heroes. A historical model of evolving communities can better explain phenomena like the Testament of Abraham or the Testaments of the Twelve Patriarchs, or religious groups like the Elchasaites, than a model whereby texts or people are 'converted' to the new religion.[5] Thus in this study we will endeavor to con-strue the question of 'legacy' in the broadest possible terms to avoid the meth-odologically unsound implication that a 'Jewish' text was 'taken over by Chris-tians', or that a 'Christian' movement was 'influenced' by 'Jewish texts'.

A REGIONAL APPROACH TO THE USE OF APOCALYPSES

Since the focus is the religious use of apocalypses, a regional approach to early Christianities makes better historical sense than one that attempts to generalize about movements spread across the Mediterranean world (e.g. Gnosticism, Montanism, Manichaeism).[6] Religions and religious diversity reflect by neces-sity their geographical, demographic, and economic location; and the transmis-sion and the use of apocalypses is largely dependent upon indigenous traditions about sacred texts and oracles, prophecy and charisma, and such socio-econom-ic factors as typically give rise to millennialist sectarianism.

But having established the priority of locale in studying texts' transmissions, why cover exclusively Egypt and Asia Minor? Certainly apocalyptic texts cir-culated in Lyons, Rome, Carthage and Cyrene, Athens, Palestine, Syria, and other points east. However, our data for Christian use of Jewish apocalypses in these latter regions consists entirely of highly idiosyncratic patristic citations and hypothetical provenances (e.g. the Christian redaction of the Testament of the Twelve Patriarchs). Egypt alone provides a rich balance of manuscript finds, explicit patristic references, the continuous composition of apocrypha, and other literary remains, altogether reflecting a culture steeped in 'apoc-alypticism'.

Asia Minor, on the other hand, while barren of manuscript remains and murky in regard to the Jewish background of local Christianities, offers unique evidence from local Christian sources for a widespread and long-lasting 'apoc-alyptic' movement, the 'New Prophecy', which extended into the third century from indubitably first-century roots. Thus the question of whether Jewish apoc-alyptic texts contributed to this movement is of great importance for this vol-

---

[5] Cf Koester, 'Intention', 271f; Kraft, 'Jewish Heritage', 177-88; id, 'Recensional Problem', 135-7; De Jonge, 'Testaments...: Christian and Jewish'. On the religious identity of the Elchasaites see Baumgarten, 'Book of Elkesai', 223 and F.S. Jones, review of Luttikhuizen, *The Revelation of Elchasai* in *JAC* 30 (1987) 208.

[6] Cf Koester, 'Intention', 273-7; and Frankfurter, 'Cult'. A similar theme has been sounded by BeDuhn, 'Cross-Cultural Unity'.

ume's endeavor; it is also of considerable comparative relevance for other places in the early Christian world that saw upsurges of millennialism, like Carthage, but which otherwise provide little data for observing the use of apocalypses.[7] A third region where Christians' profound veneration for Jewish apocalypses can be closely observed, the Babylonian Jewish-Christian world of the Elchasaites and their renegade disciple Mani, has been already covered in the Introduction to this volume.[8] Finally, a fifth-century ascetic sect in the west often cited as devoted to apocryphal literature, the followers of Priscillian of Avila, seems rather to have confined its extra-canonical studies to New Testament apocrypha, whose radically ascetic teachings tended to undergird the Priscillianists' own inclinations.[9]

Apocalypticism in Asia Minor

INTRODUCTION

Scholars have been hard-pressed to account for the pronounced millennialist tendency in Roman Asia Minor without resorting to the typical ethnic slurs of the Christian apologists. The ecstasy of Phrygian priests described by several ancient tourists does not explain the rise of prophetic and millennialist movements in the first and second centuries CE, as Hippolytus and Eusebius imply it should by referring to prophetic activity there as 'the Phrygian heresy'.[10] However, Sherman Johnson has discerned in the early second-century correspondence of Pliny, governor of Bithynia, with the emperor Trajan 'an understanding that in Anatolia there was a latent hostility to the empire that might emerge in popular movements'.[11]

The literature of Christianity in Asia Minor suggests that this 'latent hostility' expressed itself in a series of religious movements both strongly sectarian and vividly other-worldly. The Book of Revelation from the second half of the first century and the witnesses to 'New Prophecy' at the end of the second century represent the principal data for a type of Christianity emphasizing visionary prophets and sectarian world-renunciation that was in continuous activity for at least a century.[12] Scholars have also perceived in the early second-century let-

---

[7] The Martyrdom of Perpetua will be discussed in the section on Asia Minor as an extension of Anatolian New Prophecy, even though the text was clearly generated in Carthage.

[8] See especially Gruenwald, 'Manichaeism'; Stroumsa, 'Esotericism'; Koenen, 'Manichaean Apocalypticism'; Reeves, Jewish Lore.

[9] See Chadwick, Priscillian of Avila, 23-25, 77-84, 209-12.

[10] Hippolytus, Refutation of All Heresies 8.19 (= Heine, Oracles, § 32); Eusebius, Hist. eccl. 5.16.7 (Heine, ib § 23); 5.18.1 (Heine, ib § 24). See criticisms by Frend, 'Montanism', 531f; Powell, 'Tertullianists', 40f, 46-48; Fox, Pagans, 405.

[11] Johnson, 'Asia Minor', 96.

[12] The term 'Montanist' is here dispensed with as polemical and historically misleading, and replaced with the self-reference of the devotees.

ters of Ignatius to Anatolian churches that religious leadership there was based on a kind of prophetic charisma (e.g. Phld. 7.1-2);[13] in the early second-century Pastoral Epistles (1, 2 Timothy, Titus) an earnest polemic against an ascetic and anti-hierarchical Christian movement (e.g. 1 Tim 4:1-3; 5:3);[14] and, from a separate but linked quarter, in the deutero-Pauline 2 Thessalonians (second half of the first century), an active millennialist expectation (2:2b), circulation of literary propaganda to promote these views (2:2a), and sectarian sentiments so violent as to suggest intra-Christian schism (1:4-10).[15] The range of witnesses to the 'New Prophecy' that swept the Roman world from Phrygia by the end of the second century extend from its contemporaneous North African apologist Tertullian to the various detractors that Eusebius collected, and ultimately to the sensationally hostile lore in Epiphanius' Panarion. Finally, the religious situation reflected in the documents for Christianity in Asia Minor would also seem to provide the best context for the Ascension of Isaiah, which exalts a kind of visionary charismatic leadership much as the Book of Revelation does (3:31; 6-11).[16]

PROPHETIC SECTS AND LITERARY COMPOSITION

That religious situation has been generally reconstructed to consist of 'guilds' or 'schools' of prophets – ecstatic visionary seers – who mediated between a vividly-sensed heavenly world and congregations of devotees. The leaders of 'New Prophecy' consisted largely of women – Ammia, Maximilla, Priscilla – but came also to include several men as prophets (Quadratus, Theodotus, Montanus) and as principal apologists, like the North African author Tertullian. The activities of these prophets, which seem to have commenced already by the beginning of the second century,[17] included not only revelations of an incipient millennium but claims to incarnate the very spirit of Christ; they preached strict purification and heavenly rewards for martyrdom.[18] Likewise from approximately a century earlier, the Book of Revelation reflects a similar millennialism: eschatological imminence (22:10-12, 20, etc.), strict purification (14:4-5),[19] and heavenly rewards for martyrdom (2:10-11; 6:9-11; 7:14; etc.). In

---

[13] See Schüssler Fiorenza, 'Apokalypsis' 142-4.

[14] See in general MacDonald, *Legend*, chaps. 3-4.

[15] I here follow the interpretive principle that the more vehement the polemic the historically closer the polemicists (or, 'the closer you are the harder you fight'), since it is proximity that leads to anxiety over difference. See Simmel, *Conflict* and Coser, *Functions*, 67-72.

[16] See esp. Hall, *'Ascension'*; cf Himmelfarb, 'Experience', 98f.

[17] The Anatolian prophets mentioned in the Anonymous source (Eusebius, Hist. eccl. 5.16.16-17.4 = Heine, *Oracles* § 23) extend over the entire second century. See Calder, 'Philadelphia', 329f.

[18] Oracles collected in Heine ib § 1-14. For a convincing reconstruction of the original form of beliefs see Powell, 'Tertullianists', 43f.

[19] See A.Y. Collins, *Crisis*, 129-31.

the milieu of Revelation prophetic charisma signifies (at least in the author's case) that one is the mouthpiece for the Christ-angel (1:9-18; 2:1, 8, etc.). But it is striking to find in the 'letters' to Ephesus, Pergamum, and Thyatira (Revelation 2) a heated rivalry among three different prophetic guilds: the 'Nicolatians' (2:6, 15), the followers of a woman prophet ('Jezebel', 2:20), and the author, John, who evidently retains adherents in Philadelphia and Laodicea (3:7-21).[20]

A similar scenario of bitter rivalry among prophetic guilds lies behind the Ascension of Isaiah, so Robert Hall has reconstructed from its final Christian redaction (3:13-31; 6):

> ... an early Christian prophetic school which periodically gathered from various early Christian communities to form an outpost of heaven in which senior prophets imparted the gift of prophecy by laying on of hands and offered instructions to refine the technique and prophetic sensitivity of their juniors. Although the author's school participated with other early Christians in charismatic worship, it distinguished itself from them in experiencing heavenly trips to see God.[21]

In the text, Hall infers, 'the author's group appears as a small prophetic minority alienated from a rival prophetic group to which it formerly belonged' and which is cryptically reflected in the 'false prophets' (under the figure Belkira) who gain the confidence of officials and have Isaiah executed (Ascension of Isaiah 5).[22] The point of contention and schism, according to Hall, is the authenticity of a particular vision of Christ's descent (Ascension of Isaiah 10; cf 3:13; 5:1).

The type of situation reigning behind these two texts is not unusual in religions emphasizing charismatic leadership, since the usual friction among sectarian cliques becomes intensified due to the unstable absolutism of charismatic leadership.[23] At the very least it suggests that 'prophecy' – charismatic leadership with a sectarian tendency that could become millennialist – was part of the pluralistic religious landscape of Asia Minor.[24] It is impossible to say whether such prophetic piety continued as a distinctive aspect of rural Anatolian *Judaism*; although one should note that both the Book of Revelation and the Ascension of Isaiah reflect self-definitions strongly rooted in Israelite prophetic heritage (Rev 4:5-9; 11:3-6; Asc. Is. 2:11-16). That prophets should be so established as to be organized in guilds or schools would also suggest a strong resistance to hierarchical leadership in the region, indeed, a critique of

---

[20] Schüssler Fiorenza, 'Apokalypsis', 144-46.

[21] Hall, *'Ascension'*, 294.

[22]. ib 297.

[23] Sociology shows a tendency towards schism in charismatic and millennialist movements; see on religious schism Stark-Bainbridge, *Future*, 101-7; Simmel, *Conflict*; as well as the general observations on conflict among early Christian prophets in Aune, *Prophecy*, 204f.

[24] Cf Fox, *Pagans*, 405f. The time-span involved in Anatolian Christian prophecy would militate against a socio-economic explanation of 'New Prophecy' that depends only on late second-century factors, such as proposed by Williams, 'Origins'.

such leadership as 'worldly' (cf. Asc. Is. 3:21-31), which is likely the situation underlying the Pastoral Epistles and certainly a principal aspect of the controversy over the 'New Prophecy' of the later second century.[25] Because it fits so well into this historical and religious context I place the Ascension of Isaiah here among documents of Anatolian Christianity.[26]

Very much like the Book of Revelation the Ascension of Isaiah reflects a 'prophecy', an ecstatic discourse, whose entire symbolic world is drawn from that of Jewish apocalyptic literature: ascent to heaven, vivid descriptions of heavenly places and inhabitants, close attention to angelic liturgy as a practice to be imitated by righteous humans, and a consistent message that heaven is where the righteous belong. Does this inextricable relationship between prophetic leadership and apocalyptic symbolism imply the historical influence of pseudepigraphic apocalypses? Or, conversely, should we suppose that apocalyptic *traditions* of heavenly ascent and vision constituted a collective repository for religious expression for sects of a prophetic, millennialist, or generally 'gnostic' orientation--that is, *independently* of the apocalypses themselves?[27] The flexibility of such oral traditions would, for example, explain the early and important use of apocalyptic imagery and ideology to frame martyrdoms as a kind of ascent to heaven, such as one finds in the Book of Revelation, Ignatius's Epistle to the Romans, the Martyrdom of Perpetua, the letters of Cyprian, and the Apocalypse of Elijah.[28]

The latter alternative may best explain the Book of Revelation: as Schüssler Fiorenza has noted, 'Early Christian prophecy is expressed in apocalyptic form and early Christian apocalyptic is carried on by early Christian prophets.'[29] Indeed, the very word *apokalypsis* in the earliest Christian texts 'denotes a visionary ecstatic experience similar to prophecy' rather than a literary presentation of esoteric knowledge.[30] It is evidently a principal aspect of this apocalyptic prophecy as it extends from the first through the second centuries that authority lies not in citations of texts (like Jude) or in literary framing (like Jewish pseudepigrapha) but rather in the 'charisma' of the prophet: both her

---

[25] Cf Calder, 'Philadelphia', 328 and Trevett, 'Apocalypse', 319-21, 325.

[26] While similarly recognizing the importance of a prophetic Christian milieu Norelli, *Ascension*, 75f, 95-99 now proposes an Antiochene provenance on the basis of similarities with Ignatius's letters *to* (!) Tralles and Smyrna.

[27] Cf Schlüssler Fiorenza, 'Phenomenon', 299-301 on the patterns and motifs that would have influenced an early Christian prophet's speech. A third alternative traces the symbolic sources of these texts to the (Jewish or Christian) liturgy, which presumably might exert a hypnotic or psychedelic effect upon someone already prone to extasy: Rowland, *Open Heaven*, 395. Unfortunately this explains neither the nature of these liturgies nor why certain groups experienced the liturgy this way and others did not.

[28] See Fischel, 'Martyr and Prophet' and Frankfurter, *Elijah*, 147-51.

[29] Schlüssler Fiorenza, 'Apokalypsis', 149.

[30] ib 151.

dynamic presentation and the intensity of local devotion to her.[31] Both charismatic factors may be functions of her acquaintance and adroitness with apocalyptic discourse, but not necessarily familiarity with apocalypses themselves.

EVIDENCE FOR JEWISH APOCALYPTIC LITERATURE

Then is there evidence for the circulation of apocalypses in Asia Minor in the first and second century? As much evidence for Jewish socio-economic life as, for example, the Sardis synagogue provides, that for Jewish apocalypses (or any other Jewish texts) is almost non-existent.[32] We ought to take the references to angel-veneration and calendrical purity in Paul's and his disciples' letters to Anatolian congregations (Gal 4:8-10; Col 2:16-18) as typical of early Judaism rather than indicative of some sectarian or syncretistic piety.[33] But 1 Timothy's disapproving reference to 'myths and endless genealogies that promote ἐκζητή-σεις' (1:4; cf Tit 1:14), coming as it does from a region prone to prophets well-versed in visionary discourse, may refer to the circulation of Jewish apocalypses like those of Enoch or Adam and Eve.[34]

One reason to infer the influence of apocalyptic *texts*, not simply sectarian traditions, may be the very literary activity that the Asia Minor movements prompted. Sherman Johnson has inferred from the Roman author Lucian's images of Christians 'that one of the most noticeable activities of Christians, apart from their sharing of goods and ministry to the martyrs, is the writing of books and exposition of scriptures'.[35] While the marked oral tendencies of Revelation tend not to suggest a highly literary milieu,[36] the prophets and apologists of 'New Prophecy' had issued a veritable library of oracles, including explanations for the resurgence of prophecy, by the end of the second century.[37]

As evidence for 'New Prophecy's' use of apocalypses it is often believed that the movement drew on the Book of Revelation itself.[38] Yet this conclusion relies largely upon a disputed oracle: that the heavenly Jerusalem was to de-

---

[31] On the phenomenology of early Christian prophecy see Aune, *Prophecy*, 195-98.

[32] See review of archaeological and epigraphical evidence in Trebilco, *Jewish Communities*.

[33] Johnson, 'Asia Minor', 102f reflects the traditional standpoint of syncretistic Judaism. On the re-evaluation of Jewish piety on the basis of 'magical' corpora see the Introduction to Schiffman-Swartz, *Incantation Texts*, 11-62. On Jewish angelological influence on native cults in Asia Minor see Sheppard, 'Pagan Cults'.

[34] Cf Rudolph, *Gnosis*, 277; Gruenwald, *Apocalyptic*, 22-25.

[35] Johnson, 'Asia Minor', 90.

[36] Cf Barr, 'Apocalypse of John'.

[37] Anonymous source in Eusebius, Hist. eccl. 5.16.17; 17.1-5 (Heine, *Oracles* 23); Hippolytus, Refutatio 8.19 (Heine ib § 32). Powell, 'Tertullianists', 50 places the 'Montanist' literary stage as *subsequent to* the original prophets' activities.

[38] E.g. Groh, 'Utterance and Exegesis', 77 n18; Trevett, 'Apocalypse, Ignatius, Montanism', 323-5; and Aune, *Prophecy*, 313.

scend in the small Phrygian town of Pepouza. This 'oracle' should rather be interpreted either as a parody of Revelation 22 attributed to the 'new prophets' by Epiphanius as a way of trivializing them, or as a confused report of the heaven-*like* ecstatic reality claimed by participants in this town. In neither case does the oracle provide certain influence from Revelation.[39]

Still it would seem likely, even if unmentioned in the extant testimonies, that literate millennialists would have known Jewish apocalyptic literature, much of which gave foundation to assertions of 'prophetic' status and the importance of otherworldly mediation. Jerome, for example, recalls a tract of Montanus describing how the patriarchs and prophets spoke in ecstasy – a revaluation of biblical figures typical to apocalyptic genres.[40]

The Martyrdom of Perpetua and Felicitas (202 CE), which reflects the importation of 'New Prophecy' to North African Christianity, opens with a defense of 'new' revelations that specifically associates them with ancient revelations and visions:

> The deeds recounted about the faith in ancient times were a proof of God's favour and achieved the spiritual strengthening of men as well; and they were set forth in writing precisely that honour might be rendered to God and comfort to men by the recollection of the past through the written word. Should not then more recent examples be set down that contribute equally to both ends? for indeed these too will one day become ancient and needful for the ages to come, even though in our own day they may enjoy less prestige because of the prior claim of antiquity... "For in the last days, God declares, I will pour out my Spirit upon all flesh, and their sons and daughters shall prophesy..." [Ac 2:17; Joel 2:28]. So too we hold in honour and acknowledge not only new prophecies but new visions as well, according to the promise... Thus no one of weak or despairing faith may think that supernatural grace was present only among men of ancient times, either in the grace of martyrdom or of visions.[41]

The Martyrdom's introduction is self-consciously literary: what follows is a new *book* of revelation. Indeed, in its evocation of the 'ancients" revelations

---

[39] Epiphanius, Panarion 49.1 (Heine, *Oracles*, § 11) on which see Fox, *Pagans*, 405. The second-century opponent of New Prophecy, Apollonius, is quoted as saying that Montanus 'named [ὀνο-μάσας] Pepouza and Tymion "Jerusalem"' (*apud* Eusebius, Hist. eccl. 5.18.2 = Heine, ib § 24) – indicating, in the words of Powell, 'the re-creation of the highly organized but Spirit-directed primitive Church', or more likely, a religious sect's typical demarcation of its own sacred space according to mythical ideals. See Powell, 'Tertullianists', 43-46, quote p44. On the evidence for a particular village (seemingly Pepouza) as the center of the New Prophecy see Calder, 'The New Jerusalem', 421-5.

[40] Jerome, Commentary on Ephesians 2.3 (Heine, *Oracles*, § 108). Cf Gruenwald, *Apocalyptic*, 22-25. It may be suggested that for a millennialist movement putting great emphasis on prophecy and charismatic leadership the most accessible models for those roles would be biblical נביאים rather than apocalyptic seers; and thus its literature would promote these models even while participating in a culture that knew apocalyptic texts. This seems to be the case with Revelation, which depends most vividly on the visionary models of Isaiah and Ezekiel.

[41] Martyrdom of Perpetua and Felicitas 1.1-5, tr Musurillo, *Acts*, 107.

this text deliberately attempts to reformulate Jewish apocalyptic literature. Not surprisingly, the composition of the ensuing ascent and vision narratives attributed to these Carthaginian martyrs reflects a deep acquaintance with Jewish apocalyptic traditions, from the language of rapture to the depiction of God.[42] The Martyrdom of Perpetua and Felicitas therefore represents the continuity and use, not only of apocalyptic *traditions* (e.g. of gnosis and otherworldly identity), but also of the textual self-consciousness of Jewish apocalypses described earlier: they are the accounts of the revelations by which God rewarded the *ancients*. One could plausibly make the argument against silence that tracts similar to this one from North Africa were already being prepared in Asia Minor by the end of the second century.

The most secure evidence for sectarian Christian use of Jewish apocalyptic literature in Roman Asia Minor is the Ascension of Isaiah, according to the provenance I have advanced here for it.[43] Most scholars have seen the extant text as a Christian reworking of a Jewish legend of the prophet Isaiah's martyrdom; and most assume that this legend was an existing text before Christian reworking.[44] But the putative Jewish *Vorlage* (1:1-3:12; 5:1b-16) is itself so sectarian and so committed to a prophetic self-definition that more than one scholar has suggested the Qumran Essenes as this 'text's' provenance.[45] Thus it would seem that the Christian redaction did not so much overhaul and correct a muted Jewish legend as nuance and clarify a sectarian document astoundingly close in ideology to the redactors' own milieu.[46] By drawing the putative *Vorlage* closer in sentiment to the Christian redaction we can sense a situation probably closer to historical realities than previous models of Christian redaction: that is, a fairly unbroken line within sectarian prophetic groups between 'Jewish' and 'Christian' stages. If we dispense with the Ascension of Isaiah's hypothetical *Vorlage* altogether, as do Burkitt and Müller, in favor of traditions and fragments worked into an originally Christian text, then this 'continuity' scenario emerges even more clearly. For without a *Vorlage* one is left with a community thoroughly steeped in a sectarian Jewish identity grounded in esoteric traditions of prophets.

[42] See Daniélou, *Latin Christianity*, 59-62, and Rowland, *The Open Heaven*, 396-402.

[43] *Pace* T. Orlandi, who has recently suggested an Egyptian provenance: 'Gli Apocrifi copti', and 'Coptic Literature', 58.

[44] See Kraft, 'Jewish Heritage', 184; Charlesworth, 'Self-Definition', 41-46; Knibb, 'Martyrdom', 147-49; and Schürer, *History* 3, 335-41. Although Schürer, 337 asserts that 'the Jewishness of the *Martyrdom of Isaiah* can scarcely be questioned' because of its similarity to other prophets' legends of the Greco-Roman period, D. Müller, 'Ascension of Isaiah', 604 has recently taken the restrained view 'that the work takes up *traditions already in existence* and makes them serve its purpose' (emphasis mine). This view essentially restores that of Burkitt, *Apocalypses*, 45f, 72. See Knibb, ib 148 for a discussion of theories of a Jewish *Grundlage*.

[45] Flusser, '*Ascensio Isaiae*'. On the respect accorded this hypothesis, see Schürer, *History* 3, 338 n6, and Nickelsburg, *Jewish Literature*, 145.

[46] *Pace* Charlesworth, 'Self-Definition', 46.

Thus at the same time as Asia Minor provides evidence of almost unbroken millennialist activity over the first and second centuries led by actual 'guilds' of prophets, female and male, the region offers little evidence for the influence of Jewish apocalypses *per se*. One assumes their circulation generally as part of the literature of early Judaism; but even in the composition of the Book of Revelation one can account for apocalyptic images, patterns, symbols, and the general tendency towards otherworldly gnosis without recourse to intertextuality.[47]

THE BYZANTINE LEGACY OF THE ASCENSION OF ISAIAH

Attributing the compilation of the Ascension of Isaiah to an Anatolian provenance may help explain this document's unique appropriation by the Bogomils, a sect that arose in the Balkans in the early tenth century and that was already well ensconced in rural Asia Minor by the end of the tenth century. The sect's rigid dualism of flesh and spirit, God and Satanael, heavenly and lower worlds, seems to have had a political dimension: the explicit rejection, by predominantly Slavic adherents, of the Byzantine church's authority and with it the hegemony of Bulgar landowners.[48]

The central 'myth' of Bogomilism accounted for the world's state according to the fall of Satanael, an angel thrown down to earth for refusing to worship Adam. Satanael subsequently created earth and bodies – becoming in effect the lord of this lower world. To bolster this myth, it was once thought, the Bogomils themselves produced a large body of biblical pseudepigrapha promoting or giving substance to dualism. But in an important 1950 review of the literature on Slavonic pseudepigrapha Émile Turdeanu demonstrated instead that Bogomil scribes and apologists had in fact only drawn upon extant pseudepigrapha that contained speculations on the origin of Satan.[49] 3 Baruch, 2 Enoch, and the Assumption of Moses were actually Jewish in origin; yet the existence of often several Slavonic recensions testifies to their earlier circulation in Slavic Christianity and, therefore, availability to Bogomils. The contribution of such texts (as well as of canonical Christian documents like the Gospel of John) to Bogomil thinking can be seen in an apocalyptic document composed within Bogomil circles before the end of the eleventh century: the Interrogatio Iohannis. This

---

[47] Aune's extensive review of possible intertextual links in Revelation ('Intertextuality') results in only general statements about use of apocalyptic traditions. Perhaps also to be included under Anatolian prophetic literature is 6 Ezra (2 Esdras 15-16), an anonymous discourse on imminent judgment with a particular obsession with 'Babylon' and images of prostitutes, and including a discourse against Asia Minor (15:46-63).

[48] On social and political interpretations of Bogomil ideology see Runciman, *The Medieval Manichee*, 63-69; Loos, *Dualist Heresy*, 43-46, 54-59; and especially Erbstösser, *Heretics*, 43-59.

[49] Turdeanu, 'Apocryphes bogomiles'.

text, constructed according to the 'revelation dialogue' genre well-known from Nag Hammadi literature, reveals the origin of the enmity between God and Satan, the construction of the world and bodies by Satan, Satan's secret activity behind well-known figures like John the Baptist, and the Last Judgment. It has been shown to have made explicit use of Jewish and Christian apocalypses transmitted along Byzantine missionary routes.[50] In a time and region of political and ecclesiastical turmoil, so one would plausibly conclude, the Bogomils' resort to and composition of apocryphal literature represented an attempt to establish authority for a direct gnosis of cosmic secrets restricted to the sect and demarcating the Bogomil 'sacred' against the Byzantine world.

The Ascension of Isaiah itself seems to have functioned centrally in Bogomil ideology. For example, the Interrogatio Iohannis, which relies on a seven-heaven structure both to dramatize cosmogonic events vertically and to denote absolute separation between this world and God's heaven,[51] would seem to reflect the influence from the Ascension of Isaiah, whose *particular* emphasis on a seven-heaven cosmology makes it distinctive in the history of apocalyptic literature and which circulated widely in Slavonic. A more certain witness to the text's popularity among Bogomils appears in the work of the twelfth-century Byzantine heresiographer Euthymius Zigabenus, who reports in the late twelfth century that a sect otherwise answering the description of Bogomils made use of 'the abominable pseudepigraphon the Vision of Isaiah'.[52] And fourteenth-century inquisitional transcripts from Pamiers, France, record an oral legend about someone who ascended through seven heavens, noting as he went the greater brilliance of the angels of each heaven and mistakenly worshiping the lord of each level.[53] This latter testimony offers insight into the domestication of (Jewish) apocalypses at the popular, oral level.

But even more significantly for our understanding of the christianization of Jewish apocalypses, Turdeanu has shown that one recension of the manuscripts of Ascension of Isaiah, represented both in Latin (Lat2) and in Slavonic (Po), reflects actual Bogomil editing.[54] For example, in keeping with an ideology that rejected Hebrew tradition, this Bogomil Ascension of Isaiah eliminates references to biblical patriarchs in heaven (9:7-9, 28); and likewise, in keeping with an ideology that viewed the cross as the devil's work, the robes in the seventh

---

[50] See Bozóky, *Livre secret*, especially 142f (use of 2 Enoch) and 210-7 on its relationship with apocryphal literature. An annotated translation has been published by Wakefield-Evans, *Heresies*, 458-65, 773-6.

[51] Cf Bozóky, *Livre secret*, 113f.

[52] Euthymius Zigabenus, *Confutatio et Eversio...* (*PG* 131:44A), cit. Turdeanu, 'Vision d'Isaïe', 151.

[53] Vat. lat. 4030, ed von Döllinger, *Beiträge* 2, 166f, tr in Wakefield-Evans, *Heresies*, 456-8.

[54] Turdeanu, 'Apocryphes bogomiles, 213-8, and id, 'Vision d'Isaïe', 160-64. Cf A. Vaillant, 'Un apocryphe pseudo-bogomile: La Vision d'Isaïe', *Revue des études slaves* 42 (1963) 109-21, and the discussion by Knibb, 'Martyrdom and Ascension of Isaiah', 145f.

heaven are not preserved for those who 'believe in his cross' but rather those who 'believe in the word of which I have spoken' (9:26).[55]

In this case one can accurately speak of a Christian sect's dynamic 'use' of a pseudepigraphon with potential Jewish origins. On the one hand the Ascension of Isaiah functioned clearly as a proof-text, scriptural witness to a world-view that Bogomils were actively promoting from Asia Minor as far as southern France. And yet on the other hand one can perceive the legacy of the apocalypse in the Bogomils' profound commitment to the *type* of literature represented in the Ascension of Isaiah and the Interrogatio Iohannis (such that they would revise the former and compose the latter): texts that offered the secrets of the nature of the cosmos, its creation, fall, and salvation, all presented as esoteric revelations from heavenly beings to legendary figures already endowed with authority by the dominant culture. The commitment to esoteric revelations that, in fact, *reversed* the world-view of the dominant culture (iconoclasm, rejection of the crucifix, rejection of 'true Israel' claims of church and empire by demonizing the Old Testament, etc.) gave Bogomils the assurance of being 'true' *cognoscenti* over against the corrupt (and in their view actively Satanic) Byzantine church. The revelatory text becomes in this case the locus of sectarian conviction and rejection of the world. What is notable is that Bogomilism in Bulgaria as well as in Asia Minor was a rural movement of disenfranchised peasants, not a speculative trend among urban intelligentsia (as it became in spreading from Constantinople to Italy).[56] Perhaps one might see in this fact the unique charisma of the revelatory text in largely non-literate cultures that are dominated economically and culturally by a literate elite. This is a situation also typical of Roman Egypt.

CONCLUSIONS

The evidence from Asia Minor tends to challenge our presuppositions about 'Christian use of Jewish apocalypses' in several ways. Whereas little to no evidence exists for the actual circulation of particular Jewish apocalypses, the extant Christian texts – Revelation, Ascension of Isaiah, and the witnesses to the 'New Prophecy' – suggest the existence of a thriving lore about the biblical prophets and their powers, a lore that had been embraced as self-defining by otherworldly sects by the end of the first century CE. The nature of these texts, indeed, would suggest, far from a Christian 'importation' of Jewish texts, instead a multifaceted 'prophetic sectarianism' that continued with fairly consistent identity and impulse from Jewish into Christian matrices.

[55] Cf Turdeanu, 'Vision d'Isaïe', 160-62.
[56] On Bogomils in Asia Minor (called the *Phundagiogitae*) see Loos, *Dualist Heresy*, 67-77 on the early eleventh-century testimony of Euthymius of Acmonia.

'Apocalypticism' in Asia Minor therefore functions initially on the basis of an *oral* literature of prophets, their powers and visions. According to the evidence of Revelation, Ascension of Isaiah, and the oracle texts of the 'New Prophecy', it would seem that the oral literature is only *subsequently* compiled in books in the context of internecine disputes among the prophetic sects. Such disputes are typical of such otherworldly social groups when they attempt to maintain themselves over several generations. Remarkably, none of the extant evidence suggests that disputes arose around Christian identity.[57] Rather, the very impulse to compose propaganda for these Christian sects seems to consist essentially in an appeal to biblical models of prophetic authority.

The evidence of the Bogomil movement also shows a dialectic between the composition of apocrypha and a rich oral literature. Yet the redacting of the Ascension of Isaiah also demonstrates, in its attention to detail, a developed scribal institution in the service of sectarian self-definition (a phenomenon that develops only in the latter period of 'New Prophecy'). The Bogomil sect's reverence for biblical apocrypha, especially the Ascension of Isaiah, in spite of their ideological rejection of the Old Testament (as it was by then deemed), shows both the continuing appeal of this literature in rural Byzantium and the continuing notion of these materials as secret and authoritative revelations of heavenly truths.

Egyptian Apocalypticism (1): Gnosis and Holy Books[58]

Across a diverse network of Christianities that included Alexandrian Gnostics, proto-monastic anchorites, millennialist movements, and monasteries, Egypt became a crucible of apocalyptic writing in the Roman and Byzantine period. The vast troves of Jewish, Christian, Hermetic and Gnostic, and native priestly literature unearthed in Egypt display a singular fascination with prophecy, revelation, and other types of esoteric knowledge, and a particular devotion to the revelatory *text* – the *book* of oracles, the *narrative* of how some privileged figure won access to the supernatural realm. This Egyptian fascination with heavenly revelations and their literature may be attributed to a number of cultural factors: the proclivities and traditions of native Egyptian priestly literature,

---

[57] The popular interpretation of Rev 2:9 that infers conflict with a local Jewish community tends to contradict itself, since it requires that *Ioudaious* must mean, literally, 'Jews' even though John is thereby identifying himself as Jewish and as the true synagogue (so Charles, *Revelation* 1, 56f; A.Y. Collins, *Crisis*, 85f; Hemer, *Letters*, 65-67). It makes better historical sense to take the whole conflict as internecine 'Jewish' Christian, reflecting typical early Christian debate over the Jewish identity of Jesus-believers (cf 2 Cor 11:22; Gal 2:14; Rev 2:20 on purity laws; etc). See my 'Jews or not?'

[58] I am indebted to Birger Pearson for consultation on this section, and to Stephen Emmel and David Brakke on the next section.

the diverse Judaisms of Alexandria and the *chōra*, a diverse and quite fractious assortment of Christianities in Alexandria and *chōra*, the development of a dynamic scribal institution in Christian monasticism, and particularly ruthless economic exploitation during the Roman period that reached acute proportions in the mid-third century and contributed to the urgency of oracles and religious sectarianism manifest in this period.

Such factors motivated diverse Christian groups to explore ideas of revelation, gnosis, authority, and eso- and exoteric textuality in many different media: pseudepigrapha according to biblical, Christian, and broader Greco-Roman authorities; oracles; millennialism; charisma and sainthood; iconography; and new literary genres like the martyrology.

As in Asia Minor the trajectory of apocalypticism in Egypt largely involves a *continuity*, in Egyptian Christianity, of a literary process of apocalyptic composition and redaction already practiced among Jewish circles since the Hellenistic period. And it is likely that the motivations behind Christian apocalypticism also developed from Jewish apocalypticism: (a) to define and *locate* revelation and authority (particularly vital in Christian and Gnostic milieux); and (b) to define a group as (or in a relationship with) a living 'Israel', focusing charisma upon biblical heroes and identity rather than gospel figures.

JUDAISM IN EGYPT

Since Egypt's sands have yielded more documentary information on the Roman empire than other Mediterranean regions, one would expect to know comparatively more about Egyptian Judaism with respect to apocalypses than we do about Anatolian Judaism. But in fact the data, albeit reflecting a thriving and important Jewry from the Persian period through 116 CE, have little about distinctive ideological trends in Egyptian Judaism of the Roman period. The evidence for Egyptian Judaism of the Roman period shows, more than anything else, diversity: a diversity that utterly belies the old scholarly distinction of a 'Torah-observant Pharisaic orthodoxy' versus 'allegorizing Hellenizers'.[59]

The pursuit of a gnosis akin to that represented in apocalypses appears in at least two circles of Alexandrian Judaism, represented by the first-century CE text the Wisdom of Solomon and by the author Philo. Wisdom expresses a special interest in afterlife details (integrating vividly Egyptian images of judgment into its scenario – 4:20-5:1), in attaining divine knowledge through the infusion of heavenly Wisdom (chap. 9), and in gaining specific knowledge of such typical apocalyptic subjects as:

---

[59] See Pearson, 'Christians and Jews', 207-9; id, 'Earliest Christianity', 145-49; and id, 'Friedländer Revisited'. Barnard, 'Judaism in Egypt' offers an earnest but sociologically naive picture of two opposing communities.

...the structure of the world and the activity of the elements; the beginning and end
and middle of times, the alternations of the solstices and the changes of the seasons,
the cycles of the year and the constellations of the stars, the natures of animals and
the tempers of wild animals, the powers of spirits and the thoughts of human beings,
the varieties of plants and the virtues of roots; ...both what is secret and what is
manifest. (7:17-21 [NRSV])

This list is identical to the 'lists of revealed things' often proffered in apocalypses as the components of heavenly wisdom.[60]

Philo's allegorical approach to scripture, aiming at a transcendent comprehension of God through symbolic interpretations of biblical narratives and figures, is often compared to apocalyptic re-tellings of biblical stories. While not
generalizing 'apocalypticism' to include Philo himself, we might infer that his
particular interests in penetrating scripture for more transcendent meaning, his
exaltation of biblical figures like Seth, Melchizedek, Joseph, and Moses as
divine types, and the general goal of perceiving the divine *Logos* through these
figures probably extended themes that were viewed in more esoteric context
within apocalyptic communities.

A distinctive aspect of Egyptian Jewish apocalyptic literature is its evident
interest in non-Jewish and native Egyptian traditions. The Third Sibylline Oracle, dating from the Ptolemaic period, shows familiarity with native Egyptian
royal propaganda in its invocation of a 'King from the Sun' (652-56).[61] The
Testament of Abraham, generally viewed as Jewish in origin although preserved in Christian redactions, makes considerable use of Egyptian afterlife
mythology.[62] The Book of the Secrets of Enoch, an apocalypse dated roughly to
the early Roman period, seems to invoke an Egyptian cosmogonic motif in one
of its revelations.[63] Such literary experimentations with indigenous traditions
suggest that the literary endeavors themselves represented ways of defining
Jewish knowledge and revelation in a multicultural context.

Egyptian Jewish apocalypses like 2 Enoch, 'apocalyptic' works like the
Third Sibylline Oracle and Wisdom of Solomon, and the writings of Philo offer
various reflections of the gnosis typical of Jewish apocalypticism in general.
But whether these works represent solitary authors, 'schools', or religious sects
is quite hard to judge. L.W. Barnard once argued that the Epistle of Barnabas
could be used as evidence for at least one constituency of Alexandrian Jews (a
member of which, christianized, wrote the document); and interestingly, Barnabas stresses the gaining of a *gnosis* or esoteric wisdom similar to that of the
apocalypses (2.3-4; 5.4; 18.1; 19.1; etc.).[64] Birger Pearson has gone further,

---

[60] Cf Stone, 'Lists of Revealed Things'; Gruenwald, *Apocalyptic*, 3-16.

[61] Collins, *Sibylline Oracles*, 41-44.

[62] James, *Testament of Abraham*, 55-58, 70-76; Delcor, *Testament d'Abraham*, 57-69; Nickelsburg,
'Eschatology'.

[63] N. Forbes and R. H. Charles in *APOT* 2, 426; Nickelsburg, *Jewish Literature*, 188. On the source
of the cosmogonic egg motif see Lefébure, 'L'oeuf'.

[64] Barnard, 'Judaism in Egypt', 46-51.

noting Philo's own subtle polemics against radical inversions of biblical ideas and arguing that the authors of such 'out-of-control' exegeses must have been circles of proto-Gnostic Jews.[65] In both cases we see the silhouettes of the *kind of sects or conventicles that studied and wrote apocalypses.* The putative milieu of Barnabas, as well as the radical Jewish exegetes Pearson views beyond the writings of Philo, all seem to have contributed to the growth of an intellectual and Gnostic Christianity already in the first century.

But it is likely that these Alexandrian trends and conventicles only tell half the story of Egyptian Judaism's diverse literature and piety. The signal event in the Roman period for Egyptian Judaism was the pan-Mediterranean war of 116-17 CE, sparked by messianic rumors in Cyrene, North Africa, and fanned by local millennialist fervor across to Egypt and Asia Minor. Insofar as the majority of Alexandrian and Egyptian Jews joined the uprising enthusiastically, destroying Egyptian temples and ultimately suffering virtual extermination, one might expect that Egyptian Judaism held a particular interest in eschatology and a particular tendency towards millennialist activity.[66] Now, Wisdom of Solomon, 2 Enoch, the third Sibylline Oracle, and Philo himself place little emphasis on cataclysmic or millennialist eschatology. But sectarian works like 3 Maccabees, which exalts martyrdom and curses other Jews, and the fifth Sibylline Oracle (which curses Memphis, the religious 'capitol' of Egypt – ll.60-92, 179-86) suggest communities prone to messianic oracles and willing to write propaganda for a millennialist uprising.[67] The execration of Memphis in Sibylline Oracle 5, for example, may correspond to an apparent massing of Jewish forces there in 116, presumably to destroy major Egyptian shrines.[68]

The immediate fomenters of messianic revolt in 116 evidently consisted of zealots from Palestine, refugees from the Jewish revolt, who incited rural Jews to attack their Egyptian neighbors. These Egyptian Jews themselves may have been primed for such fanaticism since the onset of Roman rule, which had created tense economic and ethnic relations throughout Egypt.[69] For example, a letter from the Emperor Claudius to Alexandrine Jews (P. London 1912; 38 CE) warns the community 'not to introduce or invite Jews who sail down to Alexandria from Syria or Egypt', implying that these outlying regions were hotbeds of insurgency already in the beginning of the first century.[70] This picture of an epichoric Egyptian Judaism primed by prophecies and oracles to a state of millennialist fervor might also explain the 'Egyptian false prophet' who ap-

---

[65] Pearson, 'Friedländer Revisited'.

[66] On the messianic character of the revolt see Fuks, 'Aspects of the Jewish Revolt' and especially Hengel, 'Messianische Hoffnung'.

[67] Hengel, 'Messianische Hoffnung', 668-74; cf Collins, *Athens and Jerusalem*, 102-11, 120-28.

[68] Cf CPJ 439, and on the iconoclastic aims of the Jewish forces see Fuks, 'The Jewish Revolt in Egypt', 156-58.

[69] Josephus, J.W. 7.409-21; see Kasher, *Jews in Hellenistic and Roman Egypt*, 25-27.

[70] P. Lond. 1912, ll.96-98, in Bell, *Jews and Christians*, 25; see discussion ib 17f.

peared in Judea ca. 52-60 CE, who quickly gained an enormous following, and who even after his brutal demise achieved legendary status in terms of his regional affiliation.[71] In light of the other evidence one is tempted to see in this story evidence of Egyptian Jewish prophets 'spilling over' into Palestine, perhaps (at least in this case) wielding Exodus imagery as an extension of his Egyptian provenance.[72]

Certainly since ethnic relations merely worsened in the second half of the century (and particularly following 70 CE) it is reasonable to assume that millennialist propaganda was circulating abundantly in the decades preceding 116. Yet this propaganda undoubtedly came more in the form of unattributed prophecies and oracles, such as we find in the fifth Sibylline Oracle, than literary apocalypses. Perhaps these differently oriented types of 'apocalyptic' literature – oracular/millennialist and literary/gnosis-oriented – should lead us to separate a 'speculative apocalypticism' evident in much Alexandrian literature, from a 'millennialist prophecy' much like that of Asia Minor Christianity. As the prophetic materials circulated, gained popularity and a modicum of authority in their own right, their scribes began to contribute literary grounding and attribution, in both scripture and pseudepigraphic genres. Most importantly, these fragmentary oracles and prophecies, issued in an Egyptian Jewish milieu, could also be collected and edited only later in a Christian milieu. The Apocalypse of Elijah, 6 Ezra, and the fifth Sibylline Oracle are only three examples of conglomerate prophetic texts many of whose sections could be viewed as Jewish.

EGYPTIAN PRIESTLY 'APOCALYPTICISM'

The apocalyptic endeavors of Egyptian Christians also continued Egyptian priestly traditions of sacred books, culture heroes, and a kind of gnosis gained through oracles and books. Indeed, the Egyptologist Gaston Maspero proposed at the turn of the century 'that the Jewish apocalypses [from Egypt] that were adapted or imitated by Christians were themselves preceded by rudimentary sorts of apocalypses composed by Pagans, some in Greek, others in the native language of Egypt'.[73] Multiple papyrological discoveries of this century have proved Maspero's notion.

The priestly culture of Egypt largely concerned itself with maintaining the

---

[71] Josephus, J.W. 2.261-63; Ant. 20.169-72; Acts 21:38. See Gray, *Prophetic Figures*, 116-18, for a contemporary analysis of his activities, and Kasher, *Jews in Hellenistic and Roman Egypt*, 26, for his context in Egyptian Judaism.

[72] Both Socrates and John of Nikiu report a Jewish millennialist movement in Crete, ca. 435 CE, led by a prophet claiming to be Moses. Convincing his enormous following to give up their possessions, he promised to lead them across the sea to the holy land. A large number apparently drowned, including the 'Moses'. See Socrates, Eccl. hist. 38; John of Nikiu, Chronicle 86.

[73] Maspero, review of Steindorff, *Apokalypse des Elias*, in *Journal des savants* (1899) 43.

authority of old texts and rituals whose contents the gods themselves had endowed with perennial efficacy and whose 'wisdom' was expected to function with equal authority in any social, political, or environmental situation.[74] The main extant examples of this phenomenon are the Demotic Chronicle, the Oracle of the Lamb to Bocchoris, and the Oracle of the Potter, all composed during the Ptolemaic period out of priestly concern for the status of the kingship.[75] The Demotic Chronicle, from the early Hellenistic period, consists of brief, enigmatic oracles ('Left will be exchanged for right', 'The widow of Busiris, her descendant was received') that were apparently delivered at the temple of Harsaphes at Herakleopolis, each of which is followed by commentary applying the oracle generally to events contemporaneous with the scribe.[76] Behind this endeavor stood a priestly circle engaged in studying past oracles as revealed literature, recopying them with interpretations, and presumably altering these interpretations over time. Indeed, the attitude toward past oracle 'texts' in the Demotic Chronicle has been cogently compared to that of *pesher* at Qumran, where biblical passages were studied as a priori references to events contemporaneous with the Essenes.[77]

The Oracle of the Lamb to Bocchoris and the Oracle of the Potter consist of prophetic tableaux of times of woe very much like the apocalyptic discourses in 4 Ezra 5:1-13, 7:26-44, and Mark 13. Such tableaux in fact constitute an archaic Egyptian literary form used in kingship propaganda to show the immanent chaos of an Egypt without or between kings – or, in Late and Greco-Roman periods, the chaos preceding the accession of an ideal king.[78] But both of these oracle texts actually belong to the ancient Egyptian genre *Königsnovelle*, whose central or frame narrative concerns a legendary pharaoh encountering and resolving some catastrophe.[79] While the *Königsnovelle* had become quite popular by itself, informing such late antique romances as Pseudo-Callisthenes' Life of Alexander, it also served as frame-narrative for oracles and discourses. Its function was then to retroject the oracle itself into the distant past, such that its symbols might *predict* the authors' times – much like Jewish apocalyptic *vaticinia ex eventu*. The *Königsnovelle* thus gave the archaic oracles of woe a 'revealed' or apocalyptic aspect: predictions of future woes to past kings as occurring after their reigns would implicitly apply to the current situation.[80]

---

[74] See Smith, 'Wisdom and Apocalyptic'.

[75] Dem. Chron.: Spiegelberg, *Demotische Chronik*; Or. of the Lamb: Zauzich, 'Das Lamm des Bokchoris'; Or. of the Potter: Koenen, 'Prophezeiungen' and 'Bemerkungen'.

[76] See McCown, 'Apocalyptic Literature', 387-92; Johnson, 'Historical Source' and 'Anti-Greek Tract'.

[77] Daumas, 'Littérature prophétique et exégétique'.

[78] See Weill, *La fin du moyen empire*, 22-145; Doresse, 'Visions méditerranéennes'; Assmann, 'Königsdogma und Heilserwartung'; Frankfurter, *Elijah*, chap 7.

[79] A. Hermann, *Ägyptische Königsnovelle*; Braun, *History and Romance*; Koenen, 'The Dream of Nektanebos', 172f.

[80] So Smith, 'Wisdom and Apocalyptic.'

With Egyptian priestly literature it is important to consider the temple context for compositional and editorial activity. Both the Oracle of the Lamb and
Oracle of the Potter derive from the priesthood of Khnum, since their oracular
personae represent aspects of Khnum, a potter and a lamb or ram.[81] Indeed, as
Ludwig Koenen has intricately demonstrated, the two texts were subtly connected and subject to the same kind of oracular exegesis as the Demotic Chronicle.[82] Both were composed during the mid-second century BCE when, following
the wars with the Seleucids and increasingly incompetent Ptolemaic rule, the
Greek rulers began to provoke disapproval among certain priesthoods and even
revolution in the Thebaid.[83] The Oracle of the Lamb – ostensibly delivered in
the early eighth century BCE – characterizes Egypt as bound for nine hundred
years of social and cosmic breakdown, to end with the rule of 'the one of the 55
[years?]'. But in about 130 BCE some priests of Khnum apparently applied this
quasi-messianic oracle to a living figure, one Harsiesis, as propaganda for his
claim to rid Egypt of Greeks and other foreigners and ascend the throne of
Egypt. We can infer the composition of this latter propaganda for Harsiesis
because the first version of the Oracle of the Potter was evidently composed
soon afterwards, denigrating Harsiesis as a demonic foreigner and as a mere
'two-year [ruler]' (indeed, Harsiesis' revolt was quelled in 129 BCE).[84] Subsequently, in response to continuing tension and anxiety about Ptolemaic rule
and the status of the native kingship, a further version of the Oracle of the
Potter set the messianic Pharaoh off in the distant future: 'The one who is ours
of the fifty-five years will bring the evils to the Greeks that the Lamb announced to Bacharis.'[85]

As in the case of the Demotic Chronicle, the evidence of these native documents from the Ptolemaic period demonstrates a professional reverence for the
revelatory authority of oracles such that the same oracles (or a linked series of
oracles from the same god or temple) might be continually applied to local
circumstances. But the evidence also shows a self-consciousness surrounding
the preservation of these oracles: the use of the frame narrative to retroject the
revelatory episode into legendary time, thus to imbue it with the authority of a
legendary king, and the meticulously interpolated commentary that kept the
whole *text* relevant even into the second and third centuries CE when the extant
manuscripts were copied. This native Egyptian institution devoted to the copying and editing of revelatory texts indeed fleshes out Maspero's proposal, and it

---

[81] The Oracle of the Lamb was actually meant to correspond to a well-known legend that during the
reign of Pharaoh Bocchoris (ca. 717-712 BCE) 'a lamb spoke', as if these were the words it spoke
(Manetho, frags. 64 and 65, in Waddell, *Manetho*, 164f). Koenen, 'Supplementary Note', 10 n9, 11
n12 has asserted that Manetho must be referring to the text of the Oracle of the Lamb itself.
[82] Koenen, *opera cit.*
[83] See Préaux, 'Esquisse'; Alliot, 'La thébaïde'.
[84] Or. Pot. ms P[2] (P. Rainer G 19 813) 19-20, ed Koenen, 'Prophezeiungen', 202.
[85] Or. Pot. ms P[3] (P. Oxy 2332) 31-34, ed Koenen, 'Prophezeiungen', 203.

does suggest a possible context for later Christian authorship of apocalyptic literature. That is, it suggests that alongside the diverse Egyptian Judaisms responsible for apocalypses and Sibylline Oracles one must consider developments in the Egyptian priestly scribal institutions as a source of Egyptian Christian apocalypticism.[86]

Abundant papyrological evidence that includes the manuscripts of the Oracle of the Lamb and the Oracle of the Potter testifies to the continuation (in Greek and Egyptian) of such institutions throughout the third century CE, as well as the continuation of typical priestly genres in Coptic thereafter.[87] Podemann Sørensen has further proposed that the Greek and Demotic 'magical' papyri reflect a tendency towards divination and vision unprecedented in earlier priestly ritual spells yet parallel to the growth of just this kind of 'apocalyptic' oracle literature.[88] And Fowden has shown the continuity of such priestly 'revelatory' interests in the form of Hermeticism, a religious-intellectual movement that maintained a body of revelatory literature attributed pseudepigraphically to the god Thoth-Hermes.[89] This literature, while composed in Greek, was steeped in the real and idealized lore of Egyptian priests and continued many of the traditional literary forms of the temple scriptoria. For example, the Perfect Discourse in the Hermetic tractate Asclepius contains a tableau of chaos in Egypt so close to those of the Oracles of the Lamb and the Potter that it was clearly composed by someone versed in the traditional temple literature.[90]   With Hermetic literature we in fact move closer historically and culturally to the milieux that spawned Christianity. For example, many scholars have pointed to Hermeticism as a background to Gnosticism; and a link of some sort is demonstrated by the inclusion of Hermetic or Hermetic-Gnostic tracts in the Nag Hammadi library (Discourse on the Eighth and Ninth, Asclepius), as well as by the knowledge of Egyptian priestly themes reflected in several Gnostic texts (Gospel of Truth, Eugnostos, Apocalypse of Adam).[91] Indeed, Frederik Wisse has suggested that it is precisely 'early monastic Hermetic circles' that would have been most interested in Jewish apocryphal works and that would have subsequently transmitted them to Gnostic sects.[92]

It would therefore seem that Christian apocalyptic writing involved not only Greco-Egyptians inspired by the power and authority of Jewish apocalypses but

---

[86] On analogous concepts of 'revelation' in Egyptan priestly tradition, see Shirun-Grumach, 'On "Revelation"'.

[87] See Frankfurter, *Elijah*, 185-94.

[88] Sørensen, 'Native Reactions'.

[89] See Fowden, *The Egyptian Hermes*; Kákosy, 'Hermes and Egypt', 258-61.

[90] Mahé, *Hermès* 2, 72-97, 111-113.

[91] On Hermetic-Gnostic continuities see Fowden, *Egyptian Hermes*, 113-15, 172f. On Egyptian-Gnostic continuities in general see Motte, 'L'hiéroglyphe', 111-16. Important studies of general continuity include Kákosy, 'Gnosis'; Parrott, 'Gnosticism' and id, 'The 13 Kingdoms'.

[92] Discussion of Session One of the Yale Conference, see Layton, *Rediscovery* 2, 512f.

also members of the Egyptian priesthood familiar with native concepts of revelation and sacred book, with forms of oracular and revelatory writing, and with
presenting ancient ideas in the new genres of the Greco-Roman world. It would
be this sort of milieu, for example, that would translate into Coptic the traditional Egyptian sagas of Persian invasion, using biblical symbols,[93] or that
would appropriate Enoch to mask the god Thoth as originator of writing and
divine scribe.[94]

One can certainly see the participation of Egyptian priests in the pompous
intertextuality advertised in the Gnostic texts. The Gospel of the Egyptians
presents itself as 'The [holy] book [of the Egyptians] about the great invisible
[Spirit, ...]' (III.40.12).[95] The Discourse on the Eighth and Ninth contains the
admonition to 'write this book for the temple at Diospolis in hieroglyphic
characters, entitling it 'The Eighth Reveals the Ninth' ... It is proper to write
this book on steles of turquoise ... And write an oath in the book, lest those who
read the book bring the language into abuse' (VI.61.19-22, 28-29, 62.22-26).
On the Origin of the World refers in passing to such lost (or imaginary) volumes as 'the Archangelic (Book) of the Prophet Moses', 'the first Account of
Oraia' (II.102), 'the Configurations of the Fate of Heaven That Is Beneath the
Twelve' (II.107).[96] These types of literary references were typical of Egyptian
priestly literature, whose covert purpose was to bolster the authority of the
temples by mystifying the text: e.g. the Demotic Story of Setne-Khamwas, in
which the protagonist seeks an all-powerful Book of Thoth under the Nile, or
pretentious allusions to secret priestly tomes in the Greek Magical Papyri.[97]
While certainly inheriting Egyptian scribal tradition, this overt intertextuality in
Gnostic scribal milieux may also explain the attraction of Jewish apocalypses to
Gnostics: they provided another realm of textual authority imbued with the
added charisma of biblical heroes, a mysterious God, and an internationally
renowned people.

GNOSTICISM AS HEIR TO JEWISH APOCALYPSES[98]

Religious Continuities Between Jewish Apocalypticism and Gnosticism. Gnosticism itself has deep roots in Jewish apocalypticism. Even if it did not develop
out of the very Jewish enclaves that produced apocalyptic literature, as Grant

---

[93] See Jansen, *Coptic Story.*

[94] See Fodor, 'Origins', 340f, and below 187-9 on the development of the Enoch tradition in Coptic
Christianity.

[95] Unless otherwise noted, all translations of Nag Hammadi texts are taken from *NHL*, 3rd ed.

[96] See Pearson, 'Jewish Sources', 448f.

[97] E.g. *PGM* IV.154, 3007; V.96; XIII.933-79. *PGM* IV.885 and XIII.229-34 offer temple scenarios
comparable to that of Discourse on the Eighth and Ninth. See in general Betz, 'Formation of
Authoritative Tradition'.

[98] The following section generalizes across Gnostic sects while focusing as much as the data allow

and Pearson have argued, Gnosticism and its texts demonstrate obvious influence from Jewish apocalyptic literature and its general ideas of gnosis and the heavenly book.[99] The self-conscious textuality of Gnostic literature may itself be attributed largely to Egyptian priestly tradition, on the basis of parallels with Hermetic literature and magical papyri. However, one can certainly imagine the *attraction* that Jewish apocalypses obviously held for Gnostics who revered the book in this way: an aura of authority due to the renown of the figures and the importance of Judaism, the apparent antiquity of the revelations, and the distinctiveness of the cosmology and the genre.

A product of the same kind of intellectual conventicles found among Alexandrian Jews and priestly Hermeticists, Gnosticism placed extraordinary emphasis on mental activity that ranged from the apprehension of mystical truths (e.g. Gospel of Thomas, Gospel of the Egyptians) to the cognitive awareness of cosmological secrets (e.g. Gospel of Truth, Apocryphon of John); at stake was a reward of no less than salvation from an evil world. Thus the idea of 'gnosis' became vastly nuanced; and by the second-century systems of Valentinus and Marcus the concept of 'gnosis' pertained to particular *sets* of cosmological truths.

Like apocalypses, many Gnostic revelatory texts appeal to the authoritative tradition of legendary seers. Two such authorities in fact derive from Jewish apocalyptic tradition: the Apocalypse of Adam (NHC V, 5) not only bears the pseudonym but shares actual material with other Adam pseudepigrapha;[100] Pistis Sophia attributes two other Gnostic tractates, the Books of Jeu, to Enoch 'when [Jesus] spoke with him from the tree of Knowledge and from the Tree of Life' (3.134).[101] Yet one also sees a distinctively Hellenistic ecumenism in other attributions: the allegorical 'Allogenes' (NHC XI, 3), the exotically eastern Zoroaster (NHC VIII, 1),[102] and the Greco-Roman prophet Marsanes (NHC X, 1).[103] In Christian Gnosticism the predominant shift in authority from archaic seers – Enoch, Moses, Ezra – to gospel figures like Mary, Thomas, James, and

---

upon developments within Egypt (including Alexandria). It should be remembered that the evolution of Gnosticism owes much to religious trends in Syria (Thomas and Johannine traditions) and Rome (Valentinians); however, the speed at which Syrian traditions entered Egypt (Gospel of Thomas: P. Oxy 1; P. Oxy 655; Gospel of John: P. Rylands 457; Manichaean texts) militates against dividing Syrian and Egyptian Gnosticism too strongly.

[99] Grant, *Gnosticism*, 22-38; Pearson, 'Jewish Sources', 478-80; cf id, 'Friedländer Revisited', and 'Jewish Elements'. See also on the predominance of the Jewish apocalyptic legacy in Gnosticism: Rudolph, *Gnosis*, 277-82; Quispel, 'Judaism'; MacRae, 'Apocalyptic Eschatology', 317-9; and Stroumsa, *Another Seed*, 18, cf 9-11.

[100] Perkins, 'Apocalypse of Adam', 386f; Pearson, 'Jewish Sources', 445f.

[101] Ed and tr Schmidt-MacDermot, *Pistis Sophia*, 349. See Pearson, 'Jewish Sources', 449.

[102] Note the 'Book of Zoroaster' cited in the Apocryphon of John II.19.6-10, on which see Pearson, 'Jewish Sources', 447f.

[103] Pearson connects this pseudonym with a reference in Epiphanius' Panarion to a 'Marsianus' who was known to have gone up to heaven for three days (40.7.6; Pearson in *NHL*, 460). On 'pagan' apocalypses see Doresse, 'Les apocalypses'.

Paul may have asserted the particular authority of those revelations that began with Jesus's post-resurrection appearances: in opposition to other Christians they claimed continuing appearances, while in opposition to those who revered Enoch they claimed that a new age of revelatory access had begun with Christ.

The literature of Gnosticism ascribes a degree of authority beyond that of apocalypses to those who own and read the texts. The sacred book itself is a guarantee of sectarian boundaries, for the revelations distinguish sharply between insiders and outsiders, and only one who has access to the text can be an insider. Furthermore, the Gnostic sect claims unique access to revelation through the 'living authority' represented in the text. Pagels has found this Gnostic claim to direct revelation epitomized in their preference for the Dialogue genre (e.g. Dialogue of the Savior, Gospel of Thomas, Apocryphon of James), which subordinates such visionary motifs as ascent and heavenly description to the direct encounter of the divine mediator Christ and the select apostles, drawn out in a discussion of heavenly secrets:[104]

> [The disciples'] recognition of the risen Christ has ceased to be the climax of the account. Instead it becomes only the frame for further revelations. This frame, however artificial, is more than a literary cliché: it places the revelations that follow where gnostics think they belong – in the context of visionary experiences.
> ... What is essential is the claim this [literary] stereotype conveys – the claim to have access to continuing revelation through visions.[105]

It would certainly appear that the symposium-like discussions and discourses between heavenly teacher and disciples that are found in Gnostic dialogues (as well as Hermetic materials) reflect in exalted form the very social milieux of these sects, which seem to have involved an overwhelming emphasis on the master-disciple relationship.[106] Thus the Jewish apocalypses' systematic and anachronistic retellings of biblical legend to frame heavenly revelations seem to evolve, through the Gnostic dialogue, into an appropriation of gospel figures as types for masters and disciples in the second and later centuries.

The master-disciple emphasis of Gnostic texts may also continue the very scribal *Sitz im Leben* apparent behind some Jewish apocalypses.[107] In the period following the destruction of Jerusalem and the council of Yavneh such 'esoteric wisdom' circles as these apocalypses reflect could well have found themselves increasingly adrift from Judaism's own moorings. Kurt Rudolph traces Gnostic sects to just such alienated milieux:

> To use modern terms, to all appearances they were rootless intellectuals with no political influence, who had a more or less philosophical and, above all, mythological culture, which won adherents from the plebeian classes... [T]hey probably adopt-

---

[104] Cf Perkins, *Gnostic Dialogue*, 19-73.
[105] Pagels, 'Visions', 419f.
[106] See Fowden, *Egyptian Hermes*, 187-91; Rudolph, *Gnosis*, 213f.
[107] Cf 4 Ezra 14:24-26, 46-47; 2 Bar 5:5-7.

ed as a starting point the position of the Jewish wisdom teachers, who formed a kind of 'scribal' or 'lay-intellectualism'.[108]

Responses to this rootlessness involved not only a profound yearning for other-worldly identity and absolute transcendence, but also, inevitably, the attempt to establish a secure locus of authority that might transcend all ostensible author-ities to which the 'world' adhered. As paradigms for this kind of secure author-ity Egyptian religion provided the romanticized image of priestly secrets and books of Thoth, and Judaism provided apocalypses.

Mission and Book. The Gnostic sects' devotion to missionary activity might also provide a context for looking to such prior secret holy books as models.[109] As missionaries of new religions tended to travel along well-known routes, through communities familiar with the prominent religions and their authorities and books, providing a hitherto unknown apocryphon would gain authority for the missionary's message. The epistolary introduction to the Apocryphon of James reflects such a use of 'secret books' to ground the oral revelation of a missionary:

> Since you asked that I send you a secret book which was revealed to me and Peter by the Lord, I could not turn you away or gainsay(?) you; but [I have written] it in the Hebrew alphabet and sent it to you alone. But since you are a minister of the salvation of the saints, endeavor earnestly and take care not to rehearse this text to many – this that the Savior did not wish to tell to all of us, his twelve disciples. But blessed will they be who will be saved through the faith of this discourse.
> I also sent you, ten months ago, another secret book which the Savior had revealed to me... [Ap. Jas. (NHC I, 2) 1.8-32]

Beneath the overt 'orality' stressed in the ensuing dialogue format of Apoc-ryphon of James and many other Gnostic documents, there is an insistence on the *books* of revelation that could guarantee the timeless truth of the message over many different cities.

Self-Definition. The Gnostic message singled out the discerning reader of the text from the rest of humanity. To designate their transcendent status Gnostics borrowed terms of self-definition from Jewish sectarian tradition: 'elect', 'saints', 'sons of light', alongside more arcane labels like 'perfect' or 'seed'.[110] While it would be incorrect to infer the influence of apocalyptic *texts* from the use of these terms, the larger context in which these terms were used suggests the legacy of a Jewish community that revered apocalyptic texts and certainly offers an ideological context for the later reception of Jewish apocalypses. Many Jewish apocalypses do give an elevated, even potentially heavenly status to their readers: the one who holds (and presumably comprehends) the Book of

---

[108] Rudolph, *Gnosis*, 209.
[109] Cf Rudolph, *Gnosis*, 217f.
[110] See Pearson, 'Jewish Elements', 156-8.

Daniel is akin to 'the wise among the people' (11:33) and even to 'the people of the holy ones of the Most High' (7:27);[111] 4 Ezra casts the reader of virtually any apocryphon as 'the wise among your people', privileged by innately deep gnosis to understand the divine revelations deeper than the Bible (14:46-47); the Epistle of Enoch promises that when certain people

> ...write out all my words exactly in their languages, and do not alter or omit anything from my words, but write out everything exactly, everything which I testified about them before – then I know another mystery, that books will be given to the righteous and wise which will be the source of joy and truth and much wisdom. And books will be given to them, and they will believe in them and rejoice over them; and all the righteous who have learnt from them all the ways of truth shall be glad.[112]

The common term of self-definition in these Jewish texts is 'wise [*maskîl*]', which carried an elevated status vis-à-vis the rest of Israel and humanity. Such promises of a quasi-heavenly status to readers (and copiers) of apocalypses would seem to prepare the way for Gnostic self-definition, which likewise revolved around access to and comprehension of otherworldly truths.[113]

Liturgy. A further link between Jewish apocalypses and Gnostic religion that would provide a context for the apocalypses' transmission among Gnostics appears in the extensive liturgies produced in Gnostic texts. The Gospel of the Egyptians (NHC III, 2; IV, 2) combines a series of hymns with a recitation of cosmogony, all culminating in an ecstatic baptismal chant (III.66-67). The two Books of Jeu begin as revelations of the 'living Jesus' to the apostles, but quickly become rituals of ascent to the other world, involving hymn and gesture. Pistis Sophia is punctuated with hymns throughout. Liturgy in Gnosticism functioned vividly as a means of ascent, transformation, and ultimately participation with the other world.[114]

Certainly the interest Judaism had long expressed in the heavenly nature of liturgy had parallels in other Mediterranean cultures and subcultures such as Greek Orphism and Neoplatonic theurgy.[115] Indeed, texts like the Gospel of the Egyptians and the Hermetic Discourse on the Eighth and Ninth reflect a perfect synthesis of these various traditions. But the notion of including liturgy *as part of* a revelatory text, as the readers' or conventicles' means of participating in the revelations, seems rooted in Jewish apocalyptic tradition. The Apocalypse

---

[111] Cf Collins, *Apocalyptic Vision*, 167-70.

[112] 1 Enoch 104:11-13, tr M.A. Knibb in Sparks, *Apocryphal Old Testament*, 313. The books mentioned seem to be related to the 'tablets of heaven and ...the writing of the holy ones' that Enoch has already claimed to have read (103:2-3).

[113] Cf Himmelfarb, 'Revelation and Rapture', who deduces the message from a variety of early apocalypses that the image of the righteous one involves a cosmic status akin to that of the angels.

[114] Cf Rudolph, *Gnosis*, 220-5.

[115] Cf Plato, Republic 10.617b. See in general Dornseiff, *Alphabet*, 11-16, 35-60, 81f; LeClerq, 'Alphabet vocalique'; Miller, 'Nonsense', 482-6; and Johnston, *Hekate Soteira*, 90-110.

of Abraham and the Qumran Sabbath Songs, while neither circulated in Egypt, express a basic idea in apocalyptic literature: that an earthly seer's assimilation to the heavenly world depended on his joining the ranks of that world in their preternatural hymns. Ascent, transformation, ecstatic experience, and song were considered integrally connected.[116] These ideas and images were particularly available to Egyptian Christians with the importation of the Book of Revelation and the Ascension of Isaiah in the second and third centuries.[117] But the importance of the heavenly liturgy seems also to have informed such Egyptian Jewish apocalypses as 2 Enoch (8-9) and the Apocalypse of Zephaniah (8). It is important to note that, while liturgies are a mere component of the apocalypses, Gnostic texts like the Gospel of the Egyptians and the Books of Jeu are essentially liturgical handbooks. This observation would confirm the Gnostic texts' tendency to 'focus in' on the process of revelation and otherworldliness to the exclusion of narrative context and structure. Thus we might well see the Jewish apocalypses' idealization of heavenly liturgy as a principal contribution to Gnostic literature and ritual, and the Gnostics' emphasis on secret liturgies as a context for studying apocalypses.

Literary Continuities Between Jewish Apocalypses and Gnostic Texts. Gnostic literature can be generally divided according to two major forms: the dialogue and the discourse. In the latter, an otherworldly mediator figure 'reveals' esoteric truths in a sustained monologue; in the dialogue, one or several human auditors procure esoteric truths by addressing questions to an otherworldly mediator, who has either descended to the auditors or met them in heaven. Both literary forms can easily be derived from forms integral to the Jewish apocalypse: in the Book of the Watchers (1 Enoch 1-36), 3 Baruch, and 4 Ezra the seers gain heavenly knowledge through questions directed to *angeli interpretes*, while Daniel and 2 Baruch (55-74) have the angels deliver revelations in sustained discourses.[118]

The literary differences between Jewish apocalypses and Gnostic revelatory texts are significant, however. The Jewish apocalypses were consciously written as extensions and unveilings of biblical traditions. The revelation dialogues and discourses were components within the larger frame that retold, say, the story of Ezra's reconciliation to the destruction of Jerusalem or Enoch's astounding privilege of seeing the heavenly temple and the corners of heaven. The Gnostic texts focus upon the revelatory scene itself, reducing the frame

---

[116] Apocalypse of Abraham 18; 4QShirShabb, on which see Newsom, *Sacrifice*. See in general Himmelfarb, 'Heavenly Ascent', 91-93. Philo seems to describe such Jewish 'angelic liturgies' taking place in early Roman Egypt: On the Contemplative Life 83-88.

[117] Revelation: P. Mich. 130 (late 2nd cent.), on which see Roberts, *Manuscript*, 21f. Fourth-century Coptic mss of The Ascension of Isaiah (see below 186 n250) suggest its importation by the end of the third century from Asia Minor (according to provenance discussed above 134f, 138).

[118] See Koester, 'One Jesus', 196-98; Pearson, 'Jewish Sources', 478.

narrative to the minimum sufficient to ground the revelation in some authoritative tradition (gospel lore, Egyptian temple secrets, or ascents to heaven).[119]
Apocalypses thus particularly influenced Gnostic literature in providing the
literary prototypes for secret revelatory scenes.[120]

Beyond these important formal links between the Gnostic revelatory texts
and those of Jewish apocalypses there may also be a correspondence in literary
self-conception, as witnessed in the use of genre-titles. One quickly notes the
frequency of the title 'apocalypse' in the extensive Gnostic library of Nag
Hammadi: indeed, 'apocalypse' appears somewhat more frequently than 'gospel' or 'apocryphon' in the library's range of titles.[121] Would this fact imply the
conscious use of Jewish apocalypses as a model? Morton Smith has noted that
ἀποκάλυψις came into currency as a genre title only in the second century CE,
and was applied only retrospectively to Jewish pseudepigrapha.[122] The Gnostic
materials themselves come from a period of increasing self-consciousness about
literary genre: Nag Hammadi Codex V, from the mid-fourth century, is an
anthology of texts all labeled 'apocalypse', bespeaking some self-conscious
organization according to that title; Synesius of Cyrene complains about the
circulation of so-called 'apocalypses' in late fourth-century Alexandria (Ep.
54); and even in the third century Porphyry describes 'sectarians [*hairetikoi*]'
who 'produced *apokalypseis* by Zoroaster and Zostrianos and Nicotheus and
Allogenes and Messus and other people of the kind'.[123]. It would seem that the
designation 'apocalypse' reflected a particularly late antique attitude toward
certain texts (and especially towards their promotion), rather than typical content or structure: as Philipp Vielhauer has noted, the titles appended to Gnostic
tractates 'should not be understood in the traditional sense as literary characterizations' but rather in the approximate sense of 'the *Revelation* or *Good News*
of the redeeming Gnosis'.[124] Even beyond Gnostic literature we can see titles
such as 'gospel', 'apocryphon', and 'apocalypse' applied often merely as bibli-
ographical conveniences for the organization of collections and canon lists
(such as the Stichometry of Nicephorus and the Catalogue of Sixty Books). The
Nag Hammadi library reflects a growing fascination with the idea of a literary
'apocalypse'; but this fascination should not be attributed to the legacy of
Jewish apocalypses so much as to broader Mediterranean trends in labeling
texts and organizing libraries.

The general contours of the Jewish apocalyptic legacy are most evident in the

---

[119] See Fallon, 'Gnostic Apocalypses', 136.

[120] Apart from the influence of apocalypses it is important to recognize the use of Hermetic and
Greek philosophical literary forms in the construction of discourses and dialogues.

[121] *NHC* V, 2-5, VII, 3; cf VII, 5: the appended title reads 'Three Steles of Seth', but the text opens
as 'Apocalypse of Dositheus'. See Janssens, 'Apocalypses', 69-75, especially 72.

[122] M. Smith, 'On the History', 18f.

[123] Porphyry, Life of Plotinus 16, ed and tr A.H. Armstrong, *Plotinus* 1 (LCL, 1966) 44f.

[124] Vielhauer, 'Apocalyptic in Early Christianity' (1965 ed) 599.

structure and *interests* of Gnostic texts, as Fallon's phenomenological approach to the literature shows.[125] Following a scheme developed for the contributors to the Semeia volume *Apocalypse: The Morphology of a Genre*, Fallon finds two general categories in Gnostic literature: 'otherworldly revelations' that do and do not include an actual otherworldly tour or ascent narrative, plus a third category of revelatory texts that lack an account of the revealer's appearance or departure.[126] These categories are then subdivided into the predominant Gnostic revelatory genres of discourses and dialogues.

1. *Otherworldly Revelation with Otherworldly Journey*
   a) *Discourses:* Paraphrase of Shem (VII, 1); Marsanes (X, 1)[127] Allogenes (XI, 3)[128]
   b) *Dialogues:* Zostrianos (VIII, 1); Apocalypse of Paul (V, 2)

2. *Otherworldly Revelation without Otherworldly Journey*
   a) *Discourses:* Apocalypse of Adam (V, 5); (Second) Apocalypse of James (V, 4); Melchizedek (IX, 1)
   b) *Dialogues:* Sophia of Jesus Christ (III, 4; BG 8502); Apocryphon of John (II, 1; III, 1; IV, 1; BG 8502); Gospel of Mary (BG 8502); Hypostasis of the Archons (II, 4); (First) Apocalypse of James (V, 3); Apocalypse of Peter (VII, 3); Letter of Peter to Philip (VIII, 2); Pistis Sophia

3. *Otherworldly Revelations without Literary Account of Revelation*
   a) *Discourses:* Thunder, Perfect Mind (VI, 2); The Concept of Our Great Power (VI, 4); The Second Treatise of the Great Seth (VII, 2); Trimorphic Protennoia (XIII, 1)
   b) *Dialogues:* Book of Thomas the Contender (II, 7); Dialogue of the Savior (III, 5); First and Second Books of Jeu

One can see that virtually the entirety of the extant Gnostic literary corpus fits effortlessly under rubrics that stress revelation, indicating that the revelation of otherworldly truths was a *basic function of Gnostic literature*. Fallon's overview suggests that Gnostic literature derived from Jewish apocalyptic literature both structurally and thematically.[129] And closer examinations of the structure and details of some Gnostic revelation accounts disclose a real compositional debt to Jewish apocalypses.

---

[125] Fallon, 'Gnostic Apocalypses', 123-58; cf Casadio, 'Patterns of Vision', 395-401.

[126] I have reversed the order of these two categories from Fallon's presentation.

[127] Fallon does not include this text in his scheme. On Marsanes' use of heavenly travel, see Janssens, 'Apocalypses', 74, and Pearson in Robinson, *Nag Hammadi Library*, 460.

[128] Fallon, 'Gnostic Apocalypses', 127 places Allogenes among otherworldly revelations without otherworldly journeys because the critical journey does not occur at the beginning of the text. The otherworldly journey (57.27-69.20), however, conforms closely to Jewish apocalyptic models and therefore should be emphasized in classifying the text.

[129] Note that Fallon's classification cannot be said to have any historical value, e.g., as stages in the evolution from apocalyptic retellings of the Bible to Gnostic revelatory tracts.

The narrative in the Apocalypse of Adam (V, 5) stays so close to the archaic Jewish genre of Testament that for many scholars the text signals 'a transitional stage in an evolution from Jewish to gnostic apocalyptic'.[130] A traditional preface that introduces the text as 'the revelation which Adam taught his son Seth in the seven hundredth year', is evidently intended to trigger the audience's associations with testament literature. The author uses the concept of antediluvian prophecy very much in the way of Jewish apocalypses, as enigmatic predictions of events the readers know have already taken place. Apocalypse of Adam's threefold periodization of mythical time indeed echoes other apocryphal Adam literature (e.g. Adam and Eve 49:2-50:2).[131]

A movement in authorial interests towards Gnosticism appears in a) the exclusive interest in the origins of races and the culminating descent of the Illuminator (Apoc. Ad. 3-6;[132] cf Gen 9-19); and b) an esoteric orientation in the conclusion of the frame narrative: 'These are the revelations which Adam made known to Seth his son, and his son taught his *seed* about them. This is the *secret knowledge* of Adam which he imparted to Seth, ...' (8:16-17a).[133] In addition, the revelation serves as an overt guarantee for the ritual of baptism (8:9-11, 17b), an atypical motif in Jewish apocalyptic literature.[134]

The tractate Allogenes also reflects influence of Jewish apocalyptic compositional traditions. The first part, delivered as a discourse from Allogenes ('stranger') to his son Messos, inherits its literary style from the apocalyptic Testament even while these characters seem to function allegorically: 'Now after I heard these things, my son [Messos, I was] afraid, ... And then, my son Messos, the all-glorious One, Youel, spoke to me again ... And [I] turned to myself [and] saw the light that [surrounded] me ...'[135] As in Jewish (and Christian) testamentary literature, Allogenes' discourse consists of his recollection of a *past* revelatory experience, whose basic teachings he transmits to Messos. And while the extant manuscript merely hints that Allogenes' revelations were gained directly during some otherworldly encounter, the second section of the text proceeds to describe such an encounter, a heavenly ascent, in detail.

Allogenes' ascent follows a typically apocalyptic pattern: he prepares himself (57.29-39; cf 4 Ezra 5:20-22), he receives a visit from a heavenly mediator (58.7-27), he is transfigured and 'taken up to a holy place whose likenesss cannot be revealed in the world' (58.27-33), he participates in a heavenly liturgy (58.34-38), he encounters heavenly beings and is reassured that 'although it

---

[130] MacRae in *NHL*, 277. See Fallon, 'Gnostic Apocalypses', 126f; Pearson, 'Jewish Sources', 470-4; and especially Perkins, 'Apocalypse of Adam', 382-95.

[131] Cf Josephus, Ant. 1.2.3. See in general Perkins, 'Apocalypse of Adam', 385-9.

[132] Chapter numbers refer to those assigned by MacRae in *OTP* 1, 712-19.

[133] Translation of MacRae in *OTP* 1.719.

[134] Cf Böhlig-Labib, *Koptisch-gnostische Apokalypsen*, 95; MacRae, 'Apocalypse of Adam', 577.

[135] NHC XI.49.38-50.1; 50.17-20; 52.8-10. On the allegorical function of the narrative figures see A. Wire in *NHL*, 490.

is impossible for you to stand, fear nothing' (59.1-19; cf Apocalypse of Abraham 17), and there he gains gnosis, 'a revelation of the Indivisible One and the One who is at rest' (60.35-37 and following). While the heavenly revelation itself is Gnostic, the stages of ascent were evidently meant to evoke the readers' or audiences' respect for traditional Jewish apocalyptic ascent narratives (1 Enoch 14; 71; 2 Enoch 1; 3-42; Apocalypse of Abraham 16-17).[136]

A third example of obvious influence from Jewish apocalypses is the Apocryphon of John. Pearson and, in this volume, VanderKam have demonstrated that the Apocryphon of John's recounting of Gen 6:1-5 (Ap. John 29.16-30.11) as part of an exegetical discourse on antediluvian history conforms so closely to its retelling in 1 Enoch 6-8 that direct dependence on the latter must be assumed.[137] The composition of the frame narrative appears to draw explicitly on apocalyptic motifs. The text focuses immediately upon the situation of the *dramatis personae*: John, son of Zebedee, is despondent because of Christ's departure. Taunted by a Pharisee, he retreats to the desert; and in anguish he apostrophically addresses a series of questions about Christ's nature and the fate of the apostles (II.1.5-29). It is at this point, when John is alone in the desert, asking questions, that theophany occurs:

> Straightway, [while I was contemplating these things,] behold the [heavens opened and] the whole creation [which is] below heaven shone and [the world] was shaken. [I was afraid, and behold I] saw in the light [a youth who stood] by me. [II.1.30-2.2][138]

The heavenly mediator's initial words console John; then he delivers a discourse on cosmogony, which is notably based in biblical scripture (II.2.16-22.9); and then there begins a dialogue between the mediator and John on the Gnostic interpretation of biblical history before the flood (II.22.10-31.25). The text closes with an admonition to preserve the revelations:

> "I have completed everything for you in your hearing. And I have said everything to you that you might write them down and give them secretly to your fellow spirits, for this is the mystery of the immovable race."
> And the savior presented these things to him that he might write them down and keep them secure. And he said to him, "Cursed be everyone who will exchange these things for a gift or for food or for drink or for clothing or for any other such thing." ... And he went to his fellow disciples and related to them what the savior had told him. [II.31.27-32.5]

According to what literary model could this narrative have been composed? Koester has argued that the Gnostic revelation scenario exemplified in the Apocryphon of John bears little or no relationship to early gospel traditions of

---

[136] *Pace* Wire, who derives the ascent from a Hermetic tradition reflected in Corpus Hermeticum 1.24-26 (ib 490). The Hermetic parallel is strained, and 'heavenly ascent' is not typical of Hermetic tradition.

[137] Pearson, 'Jewish Sources', 453-5; VanderKam above 70-72.

[138] Note that lacunae in ms NHC II, 1 are filled on the basis of IV, 1 (cf. III, 1 and BG 8502, 2).

Christ's appearances, and instead 'continue[s] the Jewish genre of "apocalyps-es"'.[139] Indeed, the closest literary parallel to the Apocryphon of John's narra-tive scheme seems to be 4 Ezra. 4 Ezra begins in similar fashion by describing the protagonist's anguish (destruction of Jerusalem, 3:1-3), his prayer of apos-trophic questions (3:4-36), the appearance of the mediator (Uriel, 4:1-4, trans-formed into the 'Lord', 14:3), and then a series of visions and dialogues that gradually reveal to Ezra the nature of the divine plan (4:5-14:22). Before each vision Ezra prepares himself through protracted solitude and weeping (e.g. 5:19-22; 9:23-28). The text concludes with an admonition to record its revela-tions in books:

> [The angel, "Lord"] answered me and said, "Go and gather the people, and tell them not to seek you for forty days. But prepare for yourself many writing tablets, and take with you Sarea, Dabria, Selemia, Ethanus, and Asiel – these five, who are trained to write rapidly; and you shall come here, and I will light in your heart the lamp of understanding, which shall not be put out until what you are about to write is finished. And when you have finished, some things you shall make public, and some you shall deliver in secret to the wise; tomorrow at this hour you shall begin to write." [14:23-26 NRSV]

The final verses describe the completion of these instructions and the striking separation between the twenty-four books for everyone and seventy books only for 'the wise among your people' (14:27-48).[140]

A comparison of 4 Ezra and the Apocryphon of John shows important litera-ry parallels in the genesis of the vision itself, the form of revelation, and the concluding admonition to record it in books. The main differences are theolog-ical: the specific theodicy of 4 Ezra, the Gnostic world-view of the Apocryphon of John. While one could hardly propose direct literary influence from the former upon the latter, it seems evident that the author of the Apocryphon of John has framed its specific Gnostic ideology using a Jewish apocalyptic *tradi-tion* of revelation accounts that is best represented in 4 Ezra.[141] The extent of the narrative parallels, that is, demonstrates the extent of the Jewish apocalyptic legacy.

The Nag Hammadi tractate Zostrianos seems to inherit the same apocalyptic frame narrative: initial questions (VIII.2.24-3.13), preparatory despondent state (3.23-28), angelophany that commences with rebuke and consolation (3.28-4.19), and angelic transformation of the seer (6.17-7.22), concluding with an account of the transcription of the revelations (129.26-130.4).[142] But the tremen-dous length of this text signals the degree to which the genre apocalypse has

---

[139] Koester, 'One Jesus', 194-96.

[140] See Stone, *Fourth Ezra*, 439.

[141] *Pace* B. Layton, *Gnostic Scriptures* (1987 ed) 24, who derives the frame-narrative from chris-tianized apocryphal acts.

[142] Zostrianos's direct inheritance of Jewish apocalyptic literary tradition extends to the vocabulary of ascent, as Scopello, 'Apocalypse of Zostrianos' has shown with parallels from the *Egyptian* Jewish apocalypse 2 Enoch.

been appropriated and subordinated to the broader Gnostic ideology; and likewise the pseudonym 'Zostrianos', which is used throughout the text's dialogues, indicates the authors' or editors' desire to ground the revelations in Greco-Roman traditions of authority other than Jewish. Resembling the Jewish appeal to Sibylline tradition in the Sibylline Oracles, the ecumenical intentions of the pseudonym Zostrianos are evident in the title: 'Zostrianos, Oracles of Truth of Zostrianos, God of Truth, Teachings of Zoroaster' (132.6-10).

Like both Zostrianos and the Apocryphon of John, the Apocalypse of Paul appropriates the model of the Jewish apocalypse within a new tradition of authority, that of the Christian apostle. Its composition should also be seen in the context of other Christian compositions (in non-Gnostic Christian quarters) that cast traditional apocalypses under the pseudonym of a Christian hero: e.g. the Apocalypses of Philip and of Peter. The Apocalypse of Paul actually reflects influences more from the Jewish tradition of ascent narratives (including the Ascension of Isaiah) than from the Gnostic tradition of discourses and dialogues because of its exclusive focus upon the cosmology that Paul beholds as he ascends to a tenth heaven: the author describes the angels and their functions for each heaven. However, in contrast to apocalyptic tour narratives, the Apocalypse of Paul clearly emphasizes the *restrictiveness* of the first seven heavens: guarded by 'toll-collectors [τελώνης]' they are generally closed to humans who are not, like Paul, endowed with passwords and signs (NHC V.5.19-23; 23.18-28). This ascent motif became particularly prominent in Gnostic and other Christian literature of Egyptian provenance, probably because of its origins in Egyptian mortuary literature.[143]

Indeed, the vertical cosmology of Enochic tradition serves to underline the very restrictiveness the Apocalypse of Paul wants to attribute to the celestial powers; for whereas a ten-heaven cosmology appears also in 2 Enoch (^{J}22), in the Apocalypse of Paul the top three heavens are the 'true' ones available only to the Gnostic (23.29-24.8). The image of God in the seventh heaven, 'an old man ... [whose garment] was white' and whose throne is 'brighter than the sun by [seven] times' (22.25-30), is obviously drawn closely upon Jewish apocalyptic descriptions (e.g. Dan 7:9); yet in the Apocalypse of Paul this figure acts as principal obstacle to the gnosis gained in the higher heavens.

In these ways the Apocalypse of Paul represents the most traditional use of Jewish apocalyptic tradition even while inverting the value of Jewish apocalyptic cosmology and grounding the text's authority in Christian legend.

Conclusions: Gnostic Use of Jewish Apocalypses. The Gnostic literature examined here demonstrates the thorough influence of Jewish apocalyptic literature,

---

[143] Cf Apoc. El. 1:8-12; 1, 2 Jeu; Irenaeus, Against Heresies 1.21.5; Origen, Against Celsus 6.31. In general see Rudolph, *Gnosis*, 171-75; Himmelfarb, 'Heavenly Ascent', 80-85; Frankfurter, *Elijah*, 35-37. On its roots in Egyptian mortuary literature see Kákosy, 'Gnosis', 241-3.

its goals in revealing heavenly secrets, and its compositional forms, as well as specific motifs from the Enochic tradition. But this influence should not be taken merely in the sense of one religion's use of another's texts. The presence of Gnostic biblical pseudepigrapha with no or little Christian editing (especially the Apocalypse of Adam) and the cogent scholarly proposition of a Jewish proto-Gnosticism should demonstrate that in the Roman period the actual lines between the communities that produced the Enoch literature and those that produced Gnostic texts were probably quite vague, if existing at all. The Gnostic texts probably represent the evolution of communities rather than the importation of others' texts. Moreover, allusions to biblical apocrypha in the writings of the Alexandrian fathers Clement, Origen, and Didymus the Blind suggest that Gnostics constituted only one of a number of lines of development from an originally Jewish Alexandrian 'apocalypticism'.[144]

It could be argued that in the period between 117 CE, when much of Egyptian Jewry was destroyed, and the early fourth century, when a Jewish community is again represented in papyri, only those 'neo-apocalyptic' or 'proto-Gnostic' sects that no longer identified themselves as Jews were composing texts. One could then assume a strict line between an 'orthodox' Jewish apocalyptic community and a 'heterodox' and 'post-Jewish' proto-Gnostic community, where only the latter survived after 117. However, it is doubtful that Egyptian and Roman forces would gauge 'Jewishness' by the nature of exegesis and so distinguish between Jews and non-Jews in the massacres of 117, and equally doubtful that a certain type or degree of exegesis might place a sect pointedly 'outside' Judaism in Alexandria.[145] One can distinguish Gnostic from apocalyptic readings of biblical scripture in terms of a transvaluation or inversion of Torah and its narrative themes and figures; but one cannot extrapolate from these transvaluations to establish which authors were inside and which outside 'Judaism', especially in Alexandria.[146]

The evidence discussed here must therefore illustrate a *continuum* in the use of apocalypses during the first, second, and third centuries CE. In this regard it makes less sense to speak of a Gnostic apocalypse's use of books of Enoch (which proceeded in the same way that other Egyptian Jewish apocalypses used Enoch) than to speak of a Gnostic apocalypse's overt use of apocalyptic frame narrative and ascent motifs. In this way one can actually view the reification of a *genre* 'apocalypse'.

---

[144] On Clement see James, *Lost Apocrypha*, 90f. On Origen see his Commentary on John 2:31; Commentary on Matthew 13:57; 27:9; On First Principles 2.3.6; and in general Ruwet, 'Les apocryphes'. On Didymus the Blind see Lührmann, 'Pseudepigraphen'.

[145] See the remarks by Pearson, 'Jewish Sources', 479f.

[146] Cf Pearson, 'Jewish Elements'.

Egyptian Apocalypticism (2): Millennialist Groups and Holy Men

Ever since research into Jewish apocrypha became popular a century ago, Egyptian monasteries and, in some cases, Egyptian archeology have yielded some of the greatest manuscript troves. Important and occasionally sole manuscripts of the Apocalypses of Enoch, Elijah, Zephaniah, the Testaments of Abraham, Isaac, Jacob, and Job, and the Ascension of Isaiah, among others, all originated in Egyptian monasteries and tombs. These facts imply at the very least a pronounced interest on the part of the monastic scriptoria in preserving such materials and maintaining them prominently alongside biblical, New Testament, and eventually martyrological texts. Where Alexandrian Gnostic literature reflected a tendency to 'move beyond' its Jewish prototypes – to establish a Gnostic literary tradition of 'living' witnesses to the heavenly secrets – the Egyptian monastic corpus betrays an archaistic 'return' to the accomplishments of the biblical models and heroes, ultimately to ground in biblical legend the distinctive piety of the Egyptian anchorites as well as a profound, institutional interest in the kind of knowledge dispensed by angels. We turn therefore to the ascetic and monastic sources with the question, how did the *Jewish* apocalypses fit into the religion of the monasteries?

Whereas the manuscripts themselves derive from scribes living anytime between the fourth and the tenth centuries, the distinctive piety that employed them must be understood in the context of religious trends and developments of the third through fifth centuries, when a loose 'movement' of charismatic anchorites coalesced into a monastic*ism*. Specifically, we find the *fifth-century* fascination with (originally Jewish) apocalypses of biblical heroes to be clearly rooted in the claims and reputations of desert anchorites and in a popular apocalyptic sectarianism of the *third and early fourth centuries*. The latter probably took a number of forms: texts read publicly and subsequently retold;[147] apocalyptic oracular fragments uttered during prophetic performances; and a general acquaintance among the sparse Christian population with an apocalyptic cosmology and eschatology, which later texts show to have articulated comprehensibly the wild activities of the martyrs.

Ultimately, it may be suggested, both the charismatic prophets of the desert and the 'popular apocalypticism' must have evolved from movements within upper Egyptian Jewry before its near-extermination in 117 CE (presumably such movements would explain the Egyptian Jews' enthusiasm to join a Cyrenaican messianic wave at that time). But there are presently no data with which to nuance these suppositions.[148]

---

[147] On the public reading of apocalyptic texts see Shaw, 'Perpetua', 33 referring to Augustine, Sermon 280.1.1, and Arabic Life of Shenoute, ed and tr in Amélineau, *Monuments*, 334.

[148] One may confidently ascribe part of this 'apocalyptic' culture to the contribution of Manichaean missions to the corpus of Jewish apocalypses and apocalyptic fragments circulating in upper Egypt. Yet the Manichaeans' profound reverence for the Jewish apocalyptic tradition would only have contributed to a rural Egyptian culture already steeped in such materials. Cf Griggs, *Early Egyptian Christianity*, 96f.

There is also no direct proof of Egyptian Christians' *use* of Jewish apocalypses in the *chōra* before the earliest extant manuscripts in the late fourth century. Obviously we must assume the texts' continuity and importance in order to explain their existence in Greek and Coptic manuscripts of this later period. Therefore this section will proceed by discussing a number of early Christian documents that suggest, through their traditional attitudes toward Jewish apocalyptic gnosis and apocalyptic authority or access, the general or immediate *influence* of Jewish apocalypses of the Enochic (ascent) type. For the third and fourth centuries the historian must be satisfied with an amorphous and implicit 'presence' of these texts until more and earlier manuscripts are discovered.

APOCALYPTIC MOVEMENTS IN THE THIRD CENTURY

Certain evidence for the popular sectarian use of *an* apocalypse comes from the region of Arsinoë, in the Fayyum, in the early 260's CE. An account of a millennialist movement there prefaces Dionysius of Alexandria's treatise on the Book of Revelation, which attempts to rescue Revelation from millennialist interpretations.[149]

Such interpretations had evidently become so popular in upper Egypt that the Arsinoïte bishop, Nepos, had written a learned *apologia* for the literalist use of the Book of Revelation. It is this tract against which Dionysius aims his critique. However, the exegetical debate between competing approaches to Revelation seems to mask a broad regional *movement* of collective millennialist expectation, a social type that anthropologists often find in transitional societies, attracting the poor and economically liminal and spreading over a broad area in the form of rumors of imminent millennium. Dionysius alludes to the fact that the idea 'that Christ's kingdom will be here on earth ... had long been widely held' in the district of Arsinoë, and that this expectation evidently appealed to 'our simpler brethren'. The movement's leaders 'persuade them to expect in the Kingdom of God what is trifling and mortal and like the present'.[150] That is, there was widespread anticipation of an imminent millennium, inspired by several charismatic leaders.

Two notable aspects of this Arsinoïte movement appear in Dionysius' report: the use of Revelation itself and the circumscribed literacy of the followers of the movement. The singular importance of the Book of Revelation here parallels, in a social sphere, its singular importance for the composition of two other Egyptian-Christian documents of the third century, the Apocalypse of Paul and

---

[149] Eusebius, Hist. eccl. 7.24, on which see Maier, *Johannesoffenbarung* 87-96, and Frankfurter, *Elijah*, chap 10.

[150] Dionysius, *apud* Eusebius, Hist. eccl. 7.24.4-5.

the Apocalypse of Elijah.[151] There is reason to infer the unusual appeal of Revelation in third-century Egypt on the basis of this and other evidence. And indeed, the immediate impact of this text in upper Egypt may be due to a general cultural relationship between the prophetic Christianity of Asia Minor and the nascent prophetic Christianity of upper Egypt, suggested by the early presence of other texts from Asia Minor: the Ascension of Isaiah, Melito of Sardis's Paschal Homily, and, as some have suggested, the Epistula Apostolorum.[152]

But from a historical viewpoint Revelation may no more have been the unique inspiration in Arsinoë than it was for the Apocalypse of Paul and the Apocalypse of Elijah. In this case Revelation would most likely have crystalized a far richer apocalyptic lore such as we have inferred for Asia Minor. It is notable, for example, that while the exegetical debate between Dionysius and Nepos expresses itself through written tracts, Dionysius describes his own encounter with enthusiasts in Arsinoë in terms emphasizing *oral* exchange. Thus one cannot assume from his description that millennialist piety in Arsinoë is closely tied to the *text* of Revelation. More likely it was based on images and fragments of the text that were told, memorized, improvised, and reformulated in popular prophecy.[153] Thus Dionysius's evidence for Revelation's influence in Arsinoë in fact invites us to reassess what we mean by an apocalypse's influence – or by apocalypticism in general.

Dionysius gives no evidence for the use of other, Jewish apocalypses in Arsinoë. But his language does suggest that, for a predominantly non-literate culture like rural Roman Egypt's, the vivid textuality of Jewish apocalypses may have been replaced by an oral, prophetic apocalypt*icism* much like that in Asia Minor. Building on a number of different sources from the third through fifth centuries, we might reconstruct this apocalypticism as having involved an almost cultic reverence for the heroic seers of biblical tradition and a popular conception of the heavenly tableaux detailed in the classic apocalypses, the supernatural powers that might be unleashed from heaven, and the privilege of access to such heavenly secrets as might be bestowed upon certain holy figures of 'these times'. Thus according to the twin aspects of Jewish apocalypticism presented at the beginning of this study, gnosis and authoritative access, rural Egyptian-Christian apocalypticism maintained the orientation towards the for-

---

[151] See Charlesworth-Mueller, *New Testament Apocrypha*, 34-36, 39-40, and Frankfurter, *Elijah*, 37f, 276.

[152] See Orlandi, 'Coptic Literature', 58. The Epistula Apostolorum may derive equally from Asia Minor, where its account of the descent of Christ (chap 13) reflects that in the Ascension of Isaiah 10 (see also Pearson, 'Earliest Christianity', 149 n93), or from Egypt itself, which seems to have provided some of the text's visionary imagery and whose early Gnosticisms would have provided a suitable opponent for the text's polemics (see Muller, 'Epistula Apostolorum', 251; on Egyptian motifs compare Epistula Apostulorum 16:3-5 with Apoc.El. 3:2-4, with Frankfurter, *Elijah*, 231f).

[153] Note the terms of discourse used by Dionysius in Eusebius, Hist. eccl. 7.24.7-8. In general see Frankfurter, *Elijah*, 273-5.

mer while (we shall see) substituting oral charismatic leadership for the traditional textuality of the latter.

Where Dionysius's report of the Arsinoïte movement offers only the skeleton
of such an apocalypticism, a virtually contemporaneous text that draws on
Revelation to develop an image of imminent millennium gives it more substance. The Apocalypse of Elijah is, for all intents and purposes, the transcript
of a prophecy delivered orally to some group claiming, in some degree, privileged access to heavenly secrets and status. The text's orality parallels the
apparent orality of the Arsinoïte movement as well as documentary data on
Egyptian society of the period.[154] The self-definition of the audience, which can
be inferred from the terms of second-person address in the text ('saints', 'wise
men', 'priests'), suggests a sect whose polarizing boundaries against the world
are understood according to sectarian ideology reminiscent of some Jewish
apocalyptic texts. To what extent does a prophetic 'apocalypse' under the authority of Elijah participate in a literary culture of apocalyptic texts?[155]

One can easily comprehend the Apocalypse of Elijah's use of stock biblical
phrases, terms, and formulas in a time and culture where scripture itself was, on
the whole, an oral phenomenon, recited or read aloud.[156] And from the audience's perspective the integrity of recited 'scripture' lay more in the sound of
the language, the familiarity of the imagery, and the charisma of the speaker
than in its conformity to a *textus receptus*, as is clear in this early fourth-century
description of an Egyptian martyr's 'reading' of scripture:

> ... Like some treasury of discourses [he could recite], now a text from the Law and
> the Prophets, now from the Writings, and other times a gospel or apostolic text... :
> standing before a large assembly in a church he recited certain parts of holy scrip-
> ture. While I could only hear his voice I thought that someone was reading aloud
> [*anaginōskein*], as is the custom in the meetings, but when I came closer I saw at
> once what was going on: all the others stood with clear eyes in a circle around him;
> and he, using only his mind's eye, spoke plainly, without flourish, like some prophet,
> overcoming many of them in their strong bodies.[157]

It is likely that in early Christian Egypt apocalyptic texts had entered the same
medium: stock phrases, images, oracles, traditions inherited, for example, from
Enochic tradition, but combined in liturgical performance with little or impre-

---

[154] See Youtie, 'AGRAMMATOS' and 'HYPOGRAPHEUS'; and Harris, *Ancient Literacy*, 276-
81. Compare now the convincing argument for a democratization of the *idea* of literacy and books
by Hopkins, 'Conquest by Book'.

[155] See Frankfurter, *Elijah*, 31-39.

[156] See in general Balogh, 'Voces Paginarum'; Bardy, 'Les premiers temps', 209; Graham, *Beyond
the Written Word*, chap 11; Harris, *Ancient Literacy*, 35f, 125f, 224-6, 231f, 304f; Achtemeier,
'*Omne verbum sonat*'.

[157] Eusebius, Martyrs of Palestine [Grk] 13.7, 8, (Bardy, *Eusèbe de Césarée*, 169-72). A sixth- or
seventh-century hermit named Elijah is commemorated in the Egyptian (Jacobite) Synaxarium for
memorizing thirty books of the Bible and being able to recite the entire Psalter (17 Kihak, ed and tr
in Basset, *Synaxaire*, 475f).

cise regard to 'original' attribution.[158] In the Apocalypse of Elijah this 'oral' legacy best explains the vague influence of the Book of Revelation, 1 John 2:15-17, and various biblical prophetic formulae in the beginning of the document as appeals to an authoritative 'biblical-ese':

> The word of the Lord came to me thus: [Son of Man, (Ach)] Say to this people, why do you sin and add sin to your sins, angering the Lord God who created you? Do not love the world, nor what is in the world, for the pride of the world and its destruction are of the devil. Remember that the Lord [of Glory (Ach)] who created everything had mercy on you, so that he might rescue us from the captivity of this age. [Apoc.El. 1:1-3][159]
> Such an oral legacy would also explain the following sectarian description of heavenly ascent:

Remember that he has prepared for you [pl.] thrones and crowns in heaven. For everyone who will obey me [/his voice (Sa)] will receive thrones and crowns.

> Among those who are mine, says the Lord, I will write my name upon their foreheads and seal their right hands. They will not be hungry, nor will they thirst, nor will the Lawless One have power over them, nor will the Thrones hinder them, but they will go with the angels to my city. But as for those who sin [they will be shamed (Ach)], they will not pass by the Thrones, but the Thrones of death will seize them and exert power over them, because the angels do not trust them, and they have estranged themselves from his dwelling places. [Apoc. El. 1:8-12]

As an indirect synthesis of diverse apocalyptic cosmologies, this ascent account has more in common with contemporaneous Gnostic instructions for ascent than any specific Jewish text, suggesting that images from such texts had entered a popular lore, to be drawn upon in speculative, liturgical, or in this case prophetic situations.[160]

Such a 'popularized' apocalypticism would hardly have been independent of texts; but it would perhaps be more appropriate to imagine such texts along the lines of the unattributed oracles and 'apocalyptic' fragments that lie behind the Sibylline texts than to assume the circulation of entire literary works. At least one manuscript of the Apocalypse of Elijah evidently circulated in incomplete form.[161] The evidence of contemporaneous temple oracles shows that small or fragmentary texts did function and circulate independently in upper Egypt during the Roman period.[162] Indeed, it is likely that a fourth-century fragment of 6 Ezra (15:57-59), P. Oxy VII.1010, would reflect this kind of literary culture,

---

[158] Compare the theory of pseudepigraphy advanced by Aland, 'Problem of Anonymity', esp 43-45.
[159] All translations of the Apocalypse of Elijah are my own, giving priority to the Sahidic recension while noting variations in the Achmimic.
[160] See above, n143.
[161] P. Chester Beatty 2018, p20, on which see Pietersma et al, *Apocalypse of Elijah* 6, 88. I suspect the same of B.M. 7594 (designated Sa²), the colophon to which consists of the Apocalypse of Elijah written in Greek script but in Sahidic Coptic (see Schmidt, 'Kolophon').
[162] E.g. P. Oxy 2554; PSI 760 (CPJ 520); P. Stanford G93bv (in Shelton, 'Astrological Prediction', 209-13); P. Tebt. Tait 13 (in Tait, *Papyri from Tebtunis*, 45-48).

since by itself (or even accompanied by some additional verses) it would resemble a typical oracle of doom from Egyptian, Jewish, or Christian pens.[163]

Both the Apocalypse of Elijah and Dionysius's report of the Arsinoïte millennialists, therefore, describe a Christian culture in third-century Egypt where
the oral transmission and 'prophetic' performance of scripture (including apocalyptic texts) had popularized apocalyptic ideology, that is, an enthusiasm for
heavenly gnosis as well as for the now-prophetic channels by which it might be
gained. And during the latter half of the third century, when economic catastrophe, imperial religious edicts, and inter-sectarian schism produced high tension
among the small congregations in the *chōra*, this apocalyptic ideology provided
the fertile soil for millennialist movements.[164] Thus, in spite of our lack of
evidence for *specific* Jewish apocalypses in circulation in the third century, we
can reconstruct an 'apocalypticism', undoubtedly rooted in prior Jewish tendencies, that had evidently taken on a life of its own and that would ultimately
explain the special Coptic interest in preserving and writing apocalypses under
biblical names.

One form in which millennialist apocalypticism expressed itself in Egypt, as
in Asia Minor and North Africa, was the ideology of martyrdom. The Martyrdom of Perpetua, from early third-century Carthage (discussed above as a document of the 'New Prophecy', but a text with wide circulation and appeal in
antiquity), demonstrates how the ideologies of Jewish apocalyptic literature
might be 'lived out' in small conventicles dedicated to actualizing an otherworldly status; and Cyprian, reflecting a similar culture, regards living martyrs
as the authoritative channels to the heavenly world.[165] The Apocalypse of Elijah
likewise regards the full attainment of otherworldly identity, described in the
terminology of apocalyptic 'ascent', as the achievement not merely of separation but also of gruesome martyrdom.[166]

The extreme behavior of the Christian martyr-sects certainly reflects an ideology based in Jewish apocalyptic traditions of righteous sufferers and the
heavenly favors they earned.[167] Where the Apocalypse of Elijah provides a
glimpse into the apocalyptic propaganda used to exhort martyrs, a scene from
Eusebius' eyewitness report of Egyptian martyrs in Palestine suggests the deep
influence this propaganda had on the minds of enthusiasts:

> ... [T]he governor [Firmilian] tried the Egyptians, and proved them by every kind of
> torture; and he brought forward the first of them into the midst, and asked him what
> was his name; but instead of his real name he heard from them the name of a
> prophet. Also the rest of the Egyptians who were with him, instead of those names
> which their fathers had given them after the name of some idol, had taken for
> themselves the names of the prophets, such as these – Elias, Jeremiah, Isaiah, Sam-

---

[163] cf Hunt, *Oxyrhynchus Papyri* 7, 13.
[164] Frankfurter, *Elijah*, 265-98.
[165] ib 145-51. See e.g. Cyprian, Ep. 31.2; 37.1.3.
[166] Frankfurter, *Elijah*, chap 6.
[167] See especially Nickelsburg, *Resurrection*, 93-111.

uel, Daniel. And when the judge heard from the same martyrs some such name as
these, he did not perceive the force of what they said, and asked them again what was
the city to which they belonged. He then gave a reply similar to the former, and said,
Jerusalem is my city[-] ... Jerusalem which is above is free.[168]

The martyrs' names, that is, signify their roles both as sufferers and as participants in the heavenly realm (for so the biblical prophets were revered at this
time). Their invocation of a heavenly Jerusalem echoes the Jewish apocalyptic
tradition of the heavenly temple compound, central to Qumran and Enochic
literature as well as to Ezekiel, and continuing as a motif in later apocalyptic
texts like Sefer Zerubbabel. While hardly unique to Revelation, apocalyptic
speculations about a heavenly or eschatological Jerusalem did achieve great
popularity in Christian cosmological and eschatological tradition.[169] Of course
by the late third or early fourth centuries one need not attribute the Egyptian
martyrs' fantasy to Jewish texts; but one can indeed posit a quite vital apocalyptic 'tradition' in Egypt as the basis for that sense of gnosis which led to
such conviction about the heavenly Jerusalem.

The evidence of the third century thus allows the following conclusions
about Jewish apocalypses in the Egyptian *chōra*:

(1) With the demise of Egyptian Jewry in 117 CE literary apocalypticism in
Egypt became the inheritance of literate Christian or Gnostic groups that themselves had come to claim biblical seers or the apocalyptic model of gnosis as
authoritative. The Gnostic literature expresses just this kind of continuity of the
apocalyptic literary endeavor. Likewise the earliest Christian manuscript remains from the Egyptian cities reflect the prominence of apocalyptic texts:
Revelation, 6 Ezra, 1 Enoch, 2 Baruch, and – represented in a striking seven
manuscripts – the Shepherd of Hermas.[170] One would assume that the popular
recognition and acceptance of the themes in these texts would be predicated
upon some familiarity with Jewish apocalypses.

(2) But in the *chōra*, where Christian sects were also forming within the
non-literate and semi-literate majority, the legacy of apocalypticism was oral by
necessity. This apocalyptic *lore* may perhaps be traced to those Jewish conventicles and sects in Upper Egypt whose communication with Palestine and dissemination of messianic propaganda in the late first century CE contributed to
Egyptian Jews' enthusiastic participation in the Cyrenaican revolt of 116-17.
But in the later second and third centuries we may attribute this lore especially
to the importation and public reading of apocalyptic literature both Jewish and
Christian, which quickly led to the fragmentary dissemination and performance
of biblical and pseudo-biblical texts before non-literate audiences, and ultimately to a kind of ecstatic improvisation of biblical prophecy by charismatic figures who assumed the *personae* of seers from the biblical tradition. This oral

---

[168] Eusebius, Martyrs in Palestine [Syr.] 11.8, tr Cureton, *History of the Martyrs*, 40.
[169] Cf esp. Apoc. Paul 23-30. In general see Wilken, *The Land Called Holy*, chaps 3-4.
[170] Roberts, *Manuscript*, 11, 22, 63.

culture of scripture and oracle explains the distance from specific apocalypses and yet the enthusiastic invocation of apocalyptic motifs in the Arsinoïte millennialist movement, the language and rhetorical form of the Apocalypse of Elijah, and the ideology and self-defining symbols of Egyptian martyrs. It is important, therefore, to conceive 'literary influence' in a general rather than immediately intertextual sense, for upper Egypt was a culture of sparse literacy and a fluid sense of scriptural authority.

APOCALYPSES AND SECTARIANISM IN THE FOURTH CENTURY

There are possible links between the martyrdom ideology of the Apocalypse of Elijah in the third century and that of the Melitian movement in the fourth century, which broke away from the Alexandrian church leadership over the status of Christian leaders who had gone into hiding or even sacrificed during the persecution of 303-306.[171] The Apocalypse of Elijah portrays an explicit eschatological hierarchy between those who flee into the desert and those who 'endure': the fugitives 'will not be in the kingdom of the Christ like those who have endured' (4:27) – i.e., endured torture and execution. These sentiments place the milieu of the Apocalypse of Elijah at a radical remove from those Alexandrian ecclesiastical milieux of the third century where flight was favored. Among Christian fugitives from martyrdom were, in fact, the bishops Dionysius and Peter.[172]

In the fourth century, when the question of the status of Christian leaders who had 'lapsed' under persecution became a major source of contention for the newly legitimate religion, it is interesting to find the battle lines still drawn along Alexandrian-rural cultural divisions. Those rallying under bishop Melitius of Lycopolis to condemn the lapsed consisted to a large extent of Copticspeaking Egyptians from the *chōra*, while it was Alexandrian ecclesiarchs who sought to reintegrate the lapsed and who vehemently opposed the widening schism of the Melitians.[173] The Melitians themselves actually assumed the new identity 'Church of the Martyrs' with autonomous monasteries and even, if Athanasius of Alexandria is precise in his ascription, their own reliquary practices with the corpses of martyrs.[174]

Although it is safest to postulate no more than an ideological link between

---

[171] See Frankfurter, *Elijah*, 152-54.

[172] Eusebius, Hist. eccl. 6.40 (Dionysius); Vivian, *St. Peter of Alexandria*, 15-40; Nicholson, 'Flight from Persecution'.

[173] Bell, *Jews and Christians*, 38-99; Martin, 'Athanase et les mélitiens'; Vivian, *St. Peter of Alexandria*, 36-38; Griggs, *Early Egyptian Christianity*, 121-30. See Wipszycka's cautions ('Le nationalisme') on assuming too strict an Alexandrian-epichoric dichotomy in the Melitian schism. In general on debates over the 'lapsed' see Martin, 'La réconciliation'.

[174] Athanasius, Life of Antony 90; Festal Letter 41 (369 CE), ed Lefort, *S. Athanase* 1, 23-26, 62-64.

the milieu of the Apocalypse of Elijah and that of the Melitians, such a link does allow for the possible continuity of actual millennialist sectarian formations between the third and the fourth century. The existence of such sects, however, would not interest us if it were not for a list of apocryphal texts allegedly promoted among the 'Melitians' that Athanasius includes in his Festal Letter 39 (367 CE):[175]

> [The category of apocrypha] is an invention of heretics, who write these books whenever they want and then grant and bestow on them dates, so that, by publishing them as if they were ancient, they might have a pretext for deceiving the simple folk... Who has made the simple folk believe that those books belong to Enoch even though no Scriptures existed before Moses? On what basis will they say there is an apocryphal book of Isaiah? He preaches openly on the high mountain and says, "These words are not hidden or in a dark land" (Isa 45:19). How could Moses have an apocryphal book? He is the one who published Deuteronomy with heaven and earth as witnesses (Deut 4:26; 30:19)...
> I have not written these things as if I were teaching, for I have not attained such a rank. Rather, because I heard that the heretics, particularly the wretched Melitians, were boasting about the books that they call apocryphal, I thus have informed you of everything that I heard from my father (Bishop Alexander of Alexandria), as if I were with you and you with me in a single house, i.e., the church of the living God, the pillar and strength of truth.[176]

In his defense of a fixed canon of scripture Athanasius thus gives evidence that 'Melitians' – it is uncertain whether Athanasius means by this term a self-defined group – read and actively promoted the authority of Enochic, Isaianic, and Mosaic pseudepigrapha. One might tentatively assume that the texts to which he alludes correspond to the extant Ascension of Isaiah,[177] portions of the 1 Enoch corpus, and any of a vast amount of known Moses pseudepigrapha.[178] Athanasius therefore provides a rare and important witness to Christian use of (ostensibly, though not certainly) Jewish apocalypses.

Three important points arise from the context in which Athanasius places these texts. First, Athanasius does not attack these texts on their specific contents, as later Coptic authorities do with Gnostic materials.[179] Rather, he excludes them on precisely the grounds for which apocalypses were most valued:

---

[175] Athanasius, Festal Letter 39, ib 15-22 (ascription to 'Melitians' on 17, 21), with Coquin, 'Les lettres festales'. Discussion of this text is greatly indebted to Brakke, 'Canon Formation'.

[176] Athanasius, Festal Letter 39, ed Lefort, *S. Athanase* 1, 20-21; tr in Brakke, *Athanasius.*

[177] Athanasius's testimony here is supported by two fourth-century Coptic manuscript fragments of the Ascension of Isaiah (see below, 186) and the witness of Didymus the Blind (see Lührmann, 'Pseudepigraphen', 233-9).

[178] On the range of Moses pseudepigrapha known to have existed in antiquity see James, *Lost Apocrypha*, 42-51; Denis, *Introduction*, 128-41; Charlesworth, *Pseudepigrapha and Modern Research*, 159-66. The circulation and/or composition of such texts in Egypt may be witnessed by a fragment of a Coptic vision, P. Berlin Königl. Museen 3212, whose seer Leipoldt believes to be Moses (Leipoldt, *Ägyptische Urkunden* 1, 171f, no. 181).

[179] Compare e.g. Young, 'Milieu of Nag Hammadi'; and Johnson, 'Coptic Reactions'.

as preternatural authorities, empowered through their very apocryphal nature. It is not as a collection of doctrines or arguments that the 'Melitians' valued these texts, Athanasius implies, but as secret repositories of ancient teaching and gnosis. To ascribe this type of supernatural authority to texts as the 'Melitians' seem to do would link this group, indeed, with Alexandrian Gnostic attitudes, as discussed above, p142ff. Yet Athanasius himself elsewhere makes a distinction between these 'Melitian' heretics and so-called 'Teachers', whose intellectualism and emphasis on instructor-disciple *paideia* could imply a broad range of Christian groups, from the circles of Clement and Arius to Valentinian and Sethian Gnostics.[180] We already know that biblical apocrypha were read and critiqued, often abundantly, in these circles according to both the Gnostic materials and the testimonies of Clement, Origen, and Didymus the Blind.[181] So if Athanasius here picks out 'Melitians' alone for promulgating apocrypha they would represent a second secure Christian constituency in which Jewish apocalypses were read and, presumably, biblical pseudepigrapha were still composed.

Secondly, as part of a polemic against those texts favored by a censured sect, Athanasius's brief list significantly excludes *New Testament* apocrypha. Although not themselves included in Athanasius's canon of approved books, the Apocalypses of Peter and Paul were gaining considerable importance as edifying works in Egyptian Christianity; the Epistula Apostolorum was circulating as additional armory against certain Christian heterodoxies; and from heterodox quarters there was a sizable promulgation of apocrypha based in Christian legend, such as the Pistis Sophia, the Apocryphon of John, the Gospel of Philip, and the Dialogue of the Saviour. In the fifth century abbot Shenoute registered his vociferous opposition to certain Gnostic texts as 'apocryphal books' but nowhere discriminates against biblical pseudepigrapha (some of which were being collected in his own monastery).[182] It is therefore quite significant that Athanasius specifies the 'Melitians'' concerns as based upon the revelations of biblical figures. This tendency would seem to link the sect with a stream of epichoric Christianity, to be discussed in more detail in the next section, that ascribed the potential for 'continuing revelation' and heavenly gnosis not only to Christian figures, as did many Alexandrian Gnostics, but most importantly to biblical figures. This stream of Christianity, perhaps following Egyptian priestly scribal tradition, put great importance on the antiquity of biblical figures in guaranteeing their revelations. In a paraphrase of Athanasius's letter cited in the Bohairic Life of Pachomius the accusation is summarized: 'They have fabricated for themselves what are called apocryphal books, claiming for them antiquity and giving them the names of saints.'[183] Figures like Enoch, Isaiah,

---

[180] Brakke, 'Canon Formation'.
[181] See references above n144.
[182] See Orlandi, 'A Catechesis'.
[183] Athanasius *apud* Bohairic Life of Pachomius 189, tr Veilleux, *Pachomian Koinonia* 1, 231.

and Moses had particular authority because they were 'the saints'.

Thirdly, we learn from Athanasius's letter that it is the circulation of these biblical apocalypses among a rival Christian constituency that has largely contributed to Athanasius's desire to define a scriptural canon. Thus at one dimension the exclusion of texts favored by the 'Melitians' would merely symbolize the exclusion of the 'Melitians' themselves. But Athanasius describes his proposed canon in terms evoking the same supernatural and authoritative claims as are implied in apocalyptic literature: his choice of texts constitutes 'those believed to be divine books' and 'the springs of salvation, so that someone who thirsts may be satisfied by the words they contain. In these books alone the teaching of piety is proclaimed'. It is 'the Scripture inspired by God to instruct us'.[184]

So, at another dimension, Athanasius is attempting to circumscribe access to heavenly secrets and gnosis in competition with a field of texts--the Jewish and Christian biblical apocalypses – that would have claimed this kind of access in particular. In Athanasius's scheme it is the 'canon' that should provide mediation with the divine voice and heavenly wisdom; those who seek other paths are 'heretics'.[185] This aspect of the festal letter also implies that the 'Melitians' read the Enochic, Isaianic, and Mosaic apocalypses ascribed to them as more than simply edifying supplements to the Bible, but rather as visionary literature that provided access to heavenly secrets unavailable in biblical narrative. Coincidentally, Melitians of some sort may have been responsible for the promulgation of apocrypha in the sixth century also, for John of Paralos's Homily Against Heretical Books mentions σπουδαῖοι in the Egyptian countryside who revered texts like 'The Teachings of Adam' and the 'Investiture of Michael', while the Synaxarium describes heated battles with Melitians in the same period and region.[186]

Whoever the 'Melitians' of Athanasius's polemic were, their self-definition probably revolved to a certain degree around martyrdom as an exalted and visionary act, for the historical Melitians did consider themselves 'the Church of the Martyrs' and Athanasius himself associates so-called 'Melitians' with pronounced veneration of martyrs' relics.[187] A link with the third-century milieu of the Apocalypse of Elijah, suggested by the latter's rigorist attitude towards martyrdom, would now be corroborated by the Apocalypse of Elijah's use of biblical figures such as Enoch and Elijah as paradigms for martyrdom and also by its image of martyrdom as the paradigm for visionary ascent.[188] But whereas the Apocalypse of Elijah casts martyrdom as demonstrably an act and sign of

---

[184] Athanasius, Festal Letter 39, ed Lefort, S. Athanase 1, 18f, 21, tr Brakke, Athanasius.

[185] These observations are drawn largely from Brakke, 'Canon Formation'.

[186] John of Paralos, Homily Against Heretical Books 49 (Vienna K 9831ᵛa), ed van Lantschoot, 'Fragments coptes', 304; cf Evelyn-White, Monasteries 2, 248f.

[187] See above, n174.

[188] See Frankfurter, 'Cult of the Martyrs'.

the eschaton, Athanasius's references to 'Melitians' include no such millennialist sentiments.[189]

Between the third- and fourth-century evidence we gain important insight into the continuation of Christian milieux in which Jewish apocalypses were valued for their presentation of visionary potential, for their exaltation of biblical figures (the 'saints'), and, in the case of Isaiah (and perhaps at this point Enoch), for their equation of visionary mediation and martyrdom. In addition, Athanasius's testimony gives us documentary evidence for the specific circulation of Enochic and Mosaic texts and, undoubtedly, the Ascension of Isaiah, among certain Christians of the mid-fourth century.

ANCHORITIC CHARISMA, THIRD THROUGH FIFTH CENTURIES

> We also saw another old man in the desert of Antinoë, the metropolis of the Thebaid, called Elias. By now he would be a hundred years old. People said that the spirit of the prophet Elijah rested on him. He was famous for having spent seventy years in the terrible desert... Every day he worked many miracles and did not cease healing the sick.[190]

As Peter Brown put it, 'The "man of God", the "righteous man", had a *revelatory* quality about him. The known presence of righteous men in Israel had the effect of bringing God himself back from exile in the hearts of those who doubted his abiding presence in a darkening world.'[191]

The vital catalyst in the transition of local cultures to Christianity was the phenomenon of the rural holy man in his diverse charismatic functions.[192] But it is in the *drama* of the holy man's charisma – his gestures, teachings, prophecies, warnings, and demeanor – that we may see the continuation of that 'biblical' prophetism reconstructed for the third century: the ecstatic reciter and the martyr-prophets witnessed by Eusebius as well as the author of the Apocalypse of Elijah. As Brown views it, 'strong millennial hopes flickered around the persons of the holy men and around the walled monasteries of the Nile. For his region Abba Apollon was "like some new prophet and apostle dwelling in our own generation"'.[193] This 'prophetic' aspect of anchorites might appear to contradict that silence and humility for which hermits are generally renowned, an

---

[189] A story that John of Paralos opposed 'sectarians who took communion twenty times a day', implying Melitians of some sort, suggests that their piety involved the cultivation of ritual states of high purity and an otherworldly identity (Jacobite Synaxarium, tr Basset, 'Synaxaire', 488; Evelyn-White, *Monasteries* 2, 249 n3). This piety would seem to recreate that of martyrs even if it did not involve millennialist attitudes.

[190] Historia monachorum in aegypto 7, ed Festugière, *Historia monachorum*, 45f, tr Russell, *Lives of the Desert Fathers*, 69.

[191] Brown, 'The Saint As Exemplar', 5.

[192] See Brown, *The Making of Late Antiquity* and 'The Rise and Function'.

[193] Brown, 'The Saint as Exemplar', 11, with Historia monachorum 7.8.

image that the best known literature promoted strenuously.[194] But an attentive reading of Egyptian monastic literature discloses a picture of holy men who interact dynamically with their audiences and gain reputations for visions, prophecy, heavenly mediumship, and angelic status, gaining a charisma, indeed, that ultimately had to be reined in by Alexandrian church authorities.[195]

Not only were Egyptian holy men viewed in the guise of prophets, but the fifth-century abbot Shenoute acquired the actual designation 'prophet' along with the reputation for continual communication with the biblical prophets.[196] With their charisma established through visionary claims and rumors, the very instructions offered by anchorites to local suppliants were perceived as from angelic revelation. Figures like Antony, John of Lycopolis, and Theon of Oxyrhynchus were popularly credited with powers of prophecy and clairvoyance, often of political and social content.[197] Shenoute, supposed to have talked regularly with Jeremiah and Ezekiel, is able to sink an island of pagans with a strike of his rod, while his contemporary Macarius of Tkōw brought down fire from heaven on a local temple.[198] This prophetic function may indeed be one of the earliest aspects of the anchorite movement, since a similar charismatic status stands behind the composition of the third-century Apocalypse of Elijah, a conglomerate of political and social woe-oracles; and one is tempted to connect these prophetic holy men that emerge in fifth-century literature with those shadowy Jewish figures who promulgated anti-Egyptian oracles in the *chōra* in 116 CE.

We can see the legacy of Jewish apocalyptic literature in both the character of the visions and the notion that the *living* holy man speaks from heaven itself. In this predominantly non-literate rural society the revelatory *text* has been replaced by a revelatory *voice* – indeed, often under the same heroic name as the legendary seers of apocalypses: Elijah, Enoch, Daniel, Isaiah, Ezekiel, Abraham. Instead of reading (or hearing the texts of) oracles and eschatological tracts, early fourth-century Egyptian peasants could visit John of Lycopolis or, in the following case, Antony:

> Once while [Antony] sat working, he went into ecstasy, so to speak, and he groaned a great deal during the spectacle. Then turning to his companions after a while, he moaned as he trembled; and then he prayed and bending his knees he remained that way for a long time. When he rose the old man was weeping. Those with him now began to tremble, and greatly frightened, they begged to learn from him what it was. And they pressed him a great deal until, being forced, he spoke. And so with much groaning he said, "My children, it is better for you to die before the things in the

---

[194] Athanasius, Life of Antony 3; Jerome, Life of Paul.

[195] See Leipoldt, *Schenute von Atripe*, 53-58; Williams, 'The *Life of Antony*'; Regnault, *La vie quotidienne*, chap 16.

[196] See Bell, *Life of Shenoute*, 93 n1.

[197] Athanasius, Life of Antony 82; Historia monachorum 1.1-11, 64; 6.

[198] Besa, Life of Shenoute 85-86; Pseudo-Dioscorus of Alexandria, Panegyric on Macarius of Tkôw V.9 (ed Johnson 1.35-37; 2.27f).

vision take place." Again they importuned him, and he said through his tears, "Wrath is about to overtake the Church, and she is about to be handed over to men who are like irrational beasts. For I saw the table of the Lord's house, and in a circle all around it stood mules kicking the things within, just like the kicking that might occur when beasts leap around rebelliously. Surely you knew," he said, "how I groaned, for I heard a voice saying, 'My altar shall be defiled.'" The old man said this, and two years later the current assault of the Arians began, ... [And] we all came to understand then that vision of these kicking mules had announced in advance to Antony what the Arians now do senselessly, like beasts.[199]

Visions. Scholars of earliest monastic literature have underlined the prominence of such visions in hagiography as the means of access to heavenly revelation and as heralds of any type of personal or institutional change.[200] With the development of the hagiographical tradition the lavish description of a leader's visionary experience would become an integral component of monastic biography, an important literary development that must reflect the ongoing literary influence of apocalypses in the monasteries. But the visionary reports do not represent an exclusively literary idea; there is the implication that 'visions' of some sort were considered integral aspects of leaders' charisma during the formative stages of monasticism. Indeed, Charles Hedrick has connected the monastic visionary impulse convincingly with attitudes toward vision among contemporaneous Gnostic communities. In both monastic and Gnostic cases reputations for ongoing visionary experience were restricted to certain charismatic figures: in Gnosticism to the wisdom teacher, in anachoresis and monasticism to great anchorites and abbots like Antony, John of Lycopolis, Onnophrius, Pachomius, and Shenoute.[201] It seems likely, therefore, that the visionary traditions of both Christian monasticism and Gnosticism stand in continuity with earlier forms of apocalypticism in the *chōra*, evolving before hard-and-fast 'Gnostic'-'Orthodox' divisions began to be articulated in the fourth century.[202]

What happened in anchorites' visions? One should first note the 'popular' or cultic implication in such rumors that vertical boundaries between earthly and heavenly realms had collapsed in the environs of the holy man, rendering him like a shrine in the landscape. Furthermore, in illustration of this eruption of the sacred, anchorites and abbots enjoyed the perpetual visitations of heavenly figures, described according to traditions reverting to apocalyptic angelology. Abba Timothy tells the late fourth-century monk Paphnuti about 'a man radiant with glory' who appeared and cured his liver ailment, and four monks from

---

[199] Athanasius, Life of Antony 82 (*PG* 26:957-60), tr Gregg, *Athanasius*, 90f. Athanasius explicitly contrasts Antony's function with that of local oracles in 32-35. Compare John of Lycopolis' prophetic powers in Historia Monachorum 1.11, 64.

[200] Rousseau, 'Formation', 116; id, *Pachomius*, 61-63. See also the helpful synthesis of Egyptian monastic revelation imagery in MacDermot, *Cult of the Seer*, 102-107.

[201] Hedrick, 'Gnostic Proclivities', 84-86.

[202] See Rousseau, *Pachomius*, 20-22.

Pemje tell him about 'a man wholly of light' who brought them to an ancho-rite.[203] Antony describes his ecstatic encounters with 'the Holy Ones'.[204] In one fragmentary text Apa Hamoi receives both Gabriel and Michael.[205]

Anchorites' legends also appropriated the heavenly tour motif from Jewish (and subsequently Christian) apocalyptic literature to a degree suggesting a special reverence for these kinds of supernatural claims.[206] In describing the strange lifestyle of desert hermits, Onnophrius adds that,

> ... if they desire to see anyone, they are taken up [ἀναλαμβάνειν] into the heavenly places where they see all the saints and greet them, and their hearts are filled with light; they rejoice and are glad with God in these good things... Afterwards, they return to their bodies and they continue to feel comforted for a long time. If they travel to another world [αἰών] through the joy which they have seen, they do not even remember that this world [κόσμος] exists.[207]

The fifth-century anchorite Abba Silvanus travels to another heavenly region during a typical monastic séance:

> As Abba Silvanus was sitting with the brethren one day he was rapt in ecstasy and fell with his face to the ground. After a long time he got up and wept. The brethren besought him saying, "What is it, Father?" But he remained silent and wept. When they insisted on his speaking he said, "I was taken up [ἡρπάγην] to see the judge-ment and I saw there many of our sort coming to punishment and many seculars [τῶν κοσμικῶν] going into the kingdom."[208]

Such visionary claims also distinguished Pachomius and Shenoute, the charis-matic monastic founders of the fourth and fifth centuries. By the time of their hagiographies the apocalyptic tour had become a staple of Coptic literature, modeled closely upon the tours available to the scribe in extant apocalyptic texts.[209] But the less systematic or literary accounts of visions and tours may derive from oral traditions and reputations from these abbots' lifetimes. One ascent to heaven credited to Pachomius takes place in a liturgical setting, and its account seems to have functioned in the monastery as an etiology for his charis-matic preaching:

> Still another day, while our father Pachomius was praying somewhere alone, he fell into an ecstasy: all the brothers were in the *synaxis* and our Lord was seated on a

---

[203] Paphnuti, Life of Onnophrius, tr Vivian, *Histories of the Monks*, 8, 31; cf Amélineau, 'Voyage d'une moine', 172, 186.

[204] Athanasius, Life of Antony 35, 43.

[205] P. Bala'izah 37, in Kahle, *Bala'izah* 1, 433-35.

[206] Guillaumont, 'Les visions mystiques', 139-43; Regnault, *La vie quotidienne*, 225f.

[207] Paphnuti, Life of Onnophrius 17, tr Vivian, *Histories of the Monks*, 156.

[208] Apophthegmata patrum: Silvanus 2 (*PG* 65:408), tr Ward, *Desert Fathers*, 222. It is important to note that here the ongoing judgment of souls is situated in heaven, as in Apoc. Paul 13-18, in contrast to the tours of hell in the Lives of Pachomius and Shenoute. The 'heavenly' hell is in fact typical of Jewish apocalyptic tradition (see Himmelfarb, *Tours of Hell*, chap. 2 and p147-53).

[209] Guillaumont, 'Les visions mystiques', 142f and see below 190-5.

raised throne, speaking to them about the parables of the holy Gospel. In the vision
he saw on that day, he could hear the words He was saying, as well as their interpretation, while He was pronouncing them with His mouth. From that day on,
when our father Pachomius wished to address the word of God to the brothers, he
would occupy the place where he had seen the Lord seated and speaking to the
brothers. And if he repeated the words and their commentary which he had heard
from the Lord's mouth, great lights would come out in his words, shooting out
brilliant flashes; and all the brothers would be terribly frightened because of our
father Pachomius' words, which resembled flashing lights coming from his
mouth.[210]

Shenoute's claim to have visited hell carries rhetorical value, rendering him as a
prophet with divine knowledge of a past enemy's just deserts:

> It happened once that there was a pagan whose name was Gesios. He was very
> impious and used to blaspheme Christ, speaking profanities about him in his foolish-
> ness and his evil wickedness. When our righteous father [Shenoute] came to know of
> his profanities, he cursed him, saying: "His tongue shall be bound to the big toe of
> his foot in hell!" And this is what was done to him after he had died. My father
> testified to us and said: "I saw him in hell with his tongue bound to the big toe of his
> foot, tormented without forgiveness because of his impiety."[211]

In these anecdotes one can see how apocalyptic claims to supernatural travel
and vision might arise in particular circumstances as the typical discourse of
prophets.[212] By understanding such claims as part of the performance and folklore of charismatic figures in Coptic Egypt one can attribute some form of the
vision accounts to the figures' lifetimes without speculating about the psychological authenticity of the experiences.[213] Athanasius's account of Antony's
ascent to heaven could have had a similar basis in such claims, since in Athanasius's memory Antony had acquired a local reputation for divine knowledge
about the afterlife and judgment:

> He felt himself being carried off in thought, and the wonder was that while standing
> there he saw himself, as if he were outside himself, and as if he were being led
> through the air by certain beings. Next he saw some foul and terrible figures standing

---

[210] Life of Pachomius (Bohairic) 86, tr Veilleux, *Pachomian Koinonia* 1, 112.

[211] Besa, Life of Shenoute 88, tr Bell, *Life of Shenoute*, 67-68.

[212] See especially Leipoldt, *Schenute von Atripe*, 53-58. Leipoldt has also credited to Shenoute's
own hand a tour of hell found among Shenoutiana of the White Monastery (ib 206-8). Although
composed in first-person and in Shenoute's style the work is more properly discussed among the
Coptic apocalyptic texts below, 191-3. A fragmentary life of one Matthew the Poor calls this saint
'a holy prophet, too, in our generation like our father Apa Shenoute, the prophet of the hill of
Atripe', and thus attributes to them both the feat of causing the earth to swallow sinners: Clarendon
Press Coptic ms 61[5], 6th cent., ed and tr Winstedt, 'Coptic Saints'.

[213] For example, Shenoute himself curses an enemy in a sermon with the imprecation 'that his
tongue be bound to the toes of his foot on the day of his "necessity" [i.e. the judgment], that he be
thrown into the depths of Amenti so that the Abyss devours him' (Amélineau, *Oeuvres de Schenoudi* 1, 379). The abbot's own use of such curses would give some biographical reliability to these
particular sections of Besa. I am indebted to Stephen Emmel for this reference.

in the air, intent on holding him back so he could not pass by. When his guides combatted them, they demanded to know the reason, if he was not answerable to them... [T]hey sought an accounting of his life from the time of birth, ... Then as they leveled accusations and failed to prove them, the passage opened before him free and unobstructed. And just then he saw himself appear to come and stand with himself, and once more he was Antony, as before.[214]

While personalized as the authentic experience of Antony, this passage offers striking parallels to the 'ascent' in the Apocalypse of Elijah, where 'Thrones of death' seize sinners during eschatological ascent, and in Gnostic literature like the Books of Jeu, whose complex sets of instructions, warnings, and passwords prevent one's destruction at the hands of vicious lower angels. In subsequent demonological tradition these 'toll-collector' angels would become a component of the Byzantine cosmos;[215] but in Athanasius's time the only literary delineations of this scheme could be found in apocalyptic and Gnostic texts. While it is certainly possible that Antony had heard or read such texts, it is most likely that Antony's vision, like the hortatory 'ascent' scenarios in the Apocalypse of Elijah, is an example of a popular ascent motif widespread in Egypt, deriving most immediately in Coptic culture from apocalyptic texts.[216] The Life of Antony also records details of the motif's popular transmission: Antony later 'had a conversation with someone who visited him about the soul's passage, and its location after this life', and 'when those with him inquired and pressed him [about eschatological matters], he was compelled to speak'.[217] Thus a hermit might earn a reputation for visions and gnosis, becoming the authoritative channel for such matters in a semi-literate region.

Occasionally the anchorites themselves are transfigured as angels: like Pachomius, who shot fiery sparks from the pulpit, the anchorite Onnophrius appears to Paphnuti 'turned completely into fire and his appearance greatly frightened me'.[218] Abba Silvanus, who beheld judgment while in ecstasy (see above), was glimpsed with 'his face and body flashing like an angel', prompting a witness to fall on his face in awe.[219] Himmelfarb has pointed out the importance of such transfigurations of seers in Jewish apocalypses, in that they signify the righteous human's capability to attain heavenly knowledge and angelic fellowship.[220] It would seem that in applying identical imagery to Egyptian anchorites these legends, both oral and hagiographical, have appropriated an essential apocalyptic theme to express the charisma and heavenly channels of the holy men.

---

[214] Athanasius, Life of Antony 65 (*PG* 26:933-36), tr Gregg, *Athanasius*, 78f.

[215] cf Mango, *Byzantium*, 164f; Greenfield, *Traditions of Belief*, 16-18.

[216] See MacDermot, *Cult of the Seer*, 114f, 127-32.

[217] Athanasius, Life of Antony 66, tr Gregg, *Athanasius*, 80.

[218] Paphnuti, Life of Onnophrius 20, tr Vivian, *Histories of the Monks*, 158; cf Amélineau, 'Voyage d'un moine', 181.

[219] Apophthegmata patrum: Silvanus 12 (*PG* 65:412).

[220] Himmelfarb, 'Revelation and Rapture', 79-90.

The popular reputation of hermits for visionary powers is also evident in the hagiographical literature's attempts to mute or deny these powers. Such polemical devices suggest that the authors (and the institutions they represented) disapproved of the extent of the anchorites' charisma. Michael Williams has argued that such a muting or 'domestication' of popular, visionary charisma was a principle agenda behind Athanasius's work on Antony, which was largely designed for outsiders to the Egyptian *chōra*. Athanasius repeatedly juxtaposes Antony to precisely the Christian constituencies with which he could have been identified in his day, like Melitians (chap. 68; cf 90), Manichaean ascetics (chap. 68), and visionary prophets (especially chap. 40).[221] Even insiders' literature like Evagrius Ponticus's Chapters On Prayer advises: 'Do not cherish the desire to see sensibly angels or powers or even Christ lest you be led completely out of your wits...'[222] Evagrius here implies that ascetic activity would quite often have involved such desires (and to see Christ might implicitly involve an ascent to the throne of the highest heaven). His advice also suggests that both devotees and local people may have been familiar with such visionary accomplishments as context for an anchorite's charisma and wisdom.

The skeptical attitude toward visions expressed within monastic literature has often been taken to indicate the anchorites' humility.[223] Two passages from the Apophthegmata patrum might suggest this interpretation:

> The devil appeared to a brother disguised as an angel of light and said to him, "I am Gabriel and I have been sent to you." The brother said to him, 'See if it is not someone else to whom you have been sent; as for me, I am not worthy of it' – and immediately the devil vanished.
> It was said of an old man that while he was sitting in the cell and striving, he saw the demons visibly and he scorned them. The devil, seeing himself overcome, came to show himself to him, saying, "I, indeed, am Christ." When he saw him, the old man closed his eyes, and the devil said to him, "Why do you close your eyes? I am Christ," and the old man answered him, "I do not want to see Christ here below." When he heard these words, the devil vanished.[224]

When set against a cultural background of charismatic, visionary anchorites as has so far been reconstructed, these apophthegms seem to carry a polemical tone – that is, *against* the claims and popular reputations of Egyptian anchorites as beholders of angels of light and of Christ himself. The polemic itself provides further evidence that such claims and reputations existed, indeed to such an extent that an author saw fit to criticize them. One might well imagine the disapproval of an ecclesiastical outsider confronted with the popular terms of veneration used towards two Theban anchorites: 'I salute the sweetness of your

---

[221] Williams, 'The *Life of Antony*'; cf Grant, 'Manichees and Christians', 438f.

[222] Evagrius Ponticus, On Prayer 115, tr Bamberger, *Evagrius Ponticus*, 74.

[223] Guillaumont, 'Les visions mystiques', 137; Regnault, *La vie quotidienne*, 226-30.

[224] Apophthegmata patrum (anonymous), ed Nau, 'Histoires des solitaires', p206 nos. 310, 312, tr Ward, *Desert Fathers*, p50 nos. 178, 180.

piety and your saintliness and your angel. Moreover I worship the prints of your revered and holy feet...'[225]

Names and Avatars of the 'Saints'. Perhaps the most vivid legacy of Jewish apocalyptic literature in anchoritic culture lies in the appropriation of the very names and figures that apocalypses had established as heavenly seers. The Greek and Coptic evidence discloses an intense fascination with biblical figures that ranged from cultic reverence to a belief in their continuing activity whether in visions or in the form of holy men. One must also remember that naming in late antiquity held considerable significance for one's character, fortune, and relative access to cosmic power, particularly when the name was assumed in the context of initiatory ritual (like anointment or baptism). More than a consecrated identity, one gained virtually 'a guide and companion, who could act almost as an ideogram for one's own soul'.[226] By the early fourth century, when Eusebius witnesses the trials of Egyptians in Palestine, and continuing through the records of anchorites in the fifth and sixth centuries, one finds a preponderance of biblical *prophets'* names among Egyptian Christians: Daniel, Ezekiel, Isaiah, Elisha, and especially Elijah.[227] The popularity of this kind of self-definition – a real claim to the *natures* of the prophets – suggests that it was the visionary powers attributed to these figures that mattered to the anchorites, not simply the recollection of Hebraic past. Even in the sixth century a monk was drawing a

---

[225] Cairo ostracon 46304.38, ed and tr Crum, *Monastery of Epiphanius* 2, 37, 182; cf note *ad loc* p182. The reference to the anchorites' 'angel' seems to recall a tradition reflected in the third-century Egyptian Apocalypse of Paul: 'Each of the [heavenly] saints has his own angel who helps him and sings a hymn, and the one does not leave the other' (49, tr Duensing and De Santos Otero, in Hennecke-Schneemelcher, *New Testament Apocrypha,* [2]2.739). On the Apophthegmata patrum as outsiders' literature see Brown, *Power and Persuasion,* 71-75.

[226] Brown, 'The Saint as Exemplar', 13. Harnack, *Mission* 1, 422-6 may be correct in seeing Christian name-changes as gaining popularity only in the late third century. On the religious significance attributed to names in late antique Egypt, see also the debate between Bagnall, 'Religious Conversion', 1080 and Wipszycka, 'La valeur de l'onomastique', 176f, and in general Horsley, 'Name Change'.

[227] Cf Harnack, *Mission* 1, 427, 429 n3, noticing the concentration *in Egypt* of such names (although in the context of an ecclesiastical conference they are overshadowed by Greek names). On the significance of biblical heroes in popular Coptic Christianity, see Kropp, *Zaubertexte* 3, 180-82. A distinctive Coptic veneration of biblical heroes' names can also be seen in lists of Hebrew patriarchs' and prophets' names preserved in two manuscripts in the Monastery of St. Macarius (see Evelyn-White, *Monasteries* 1, 20, 22, 68; Pl. IIb). A similar list of Hebrew figures from Abel and Enoch to David seems to inspire a woman's ritual acclamation of the martyr in The Martyrdom of Saint Victor the General (BM ms Oriental 7022, fol. 24a-b, tr Budge, *Coptic Martyrdoms,* 294f). In the same text it is mentioned that 'the angels are wont to utter the names of saints coupled with [their own] names' (fol. 12b, tr Budge ib 274). One finds such lists of biblical heroes also in Christian and monastic graffiti: e.g. on the outer wall of the Abydos Memnonion, 'John, Enoch, Jacob, Isaac' (Perdrizet-Lefebvre, *Les graffites grecs,* no. 491).

large following in the region of Scetis when he claimed to be transmitting mysteries that he had received from the prophet Habakkuk.[228]

Three typical incidences of the name Enoch may suggest some relationship between the apocalyptic figure and the bearer of the name as his avatar. While in one case the name seems to belong neutrally to the captain of a Nile boat (P. Jonathan Bird 36.2), in another it seems to reflect the important scribal functions of its bearer, a monk in the monastery of Apollos (Cairo S. R. 3733.12).[229] But the renowned presence of one Apa Enoch near the Theban monastery of St. Epiphanius would certainly suggest a popular interest in appropriating the visionary powers of legend and translating the 'presence' of the literary figure Enoch from books (of which we have several manuscripts) to the ascetic drama occurring in the desert.[230]

Of course, one cannot impute too much meaning to every bearer of a biblical name. But the heroic namesakes of monks continued to be items of interest and speculation in the monastic environment, as in the discourse [eusaji] Onnophrius heard in a monastery in Upper Egypt:

> ... [T]hese divine and perfect elders who lived in the manner of angels of God ... [spoke] a discourse on Elijah the Tishbite – that at the moment when he had the most power in God of any sort, he was in the desert. Similarly John the Baptist, whom nobody could imitate, lived in the desert without showing himself in Jerusalem.[231]

This discourse gives some indication of the particular importance of Elijah as a model for attaining power among Egyptian anchorites. It seems that to 'be' an Elijah meant that one became (in the world of popular Egyptian Christianity) a channel for Elianic powers and divine oracles as well as the recipient of heavenly revelations.[232] The author of the Historia monachorum meets an anchorite who channelled the spirit of Elijah and thereby performed miracles for the local people and pilgrims.[233] Charismatic monastic leaders from Antony to Shenoute and Makarios of Tkōw are perceived by their immediate disciples as endowed with the prophetic powers of Elijah.[234] It is in this context of the charismatic

---

[228] Synaxarium: 19 Kihak, ed and tr Basset, 'Synaxaire', 487, and tr Forget, *Synaxarium Alexandrinum*, 251.

[229] P. Jonathan Byrd 36.2, ll. 7-8, ed Warga, 'Coptic Letter', 79f. Cairo S. R. 3733.12, ed MacCoull, 'Apa Apollos Monastery', 42f (no. 16).

[230] See Crum, *Monastery of Epiphanius* 1, 138.

[231] Paphnouti, Life of Onnophrius 11, ed and tr Amélineau, 'Voyage d'un moine', 175. Cf Vivian, *Histories of the Monks*, 152.

[232] Frankfurter, *Elijah*, 65-77.

[233] Historia monachorum 7.1-2, ed Festugière, *Historia monachorum*, 45f.

[234] Frankfurter, *Elijah*, 66-69. A similar charismatic typology may have accounted for the Pachomian successor Apa Theodore: his 'reputation for piety had spread throughout Egypt. Many sick and possessed persons used to be brought to him that he might heal them through his gift of the grace of the Lord, who in former times had glorified his servant Elisha ...[ ]' (Life of Pachomius, Bo 151, tr Veilleux, *Pachomian Koinonia* 1, 214).

model that the extended eschatological discourse called the Apocalypse of Elijah probably came to be attributed to Elijah, since apart from the title it lacks any literary frame narrating a vision of the biblical Elijah. The text's earliest scribes either knew it to have been delivered by an 'Elianic' prophet of the desert or considered it the type of discourse an Elijah *redivivus* might offer.[235] The concept of a 'living' Elianic power and revelation that developed in the desert of the fourth and fifth centuries may also have been related to actual literary apocalypses in the name of Elijah, such as Origen and Didymus the Blind seem to have known in Alexandria, or to a 'folklore' of the prophet's tours and secrets transmitted by mouth.[236] We may therefore take the charismatic model of Elijah in its fourth and fifth-century context among anchorites as indeed an 'apocalyptic' figure: people viewed 'Elijahs' as privy to heavenly scenes, in fellowship with angels, and spokesmen for heaven.

It is also within the context of this fascination with biblical paradigms for charisma and vision that we should understand the abundant Egyptian Christian materials on Melchizedek. A figure of extensive lore in early Judaism, by the early Christian period Melchizedek had already become a heavenly double for the archangel Michael at Qumran (11QMelch), for Christ among the audience of Hebrews (5:5-6; 7), and for the spirit of God among others.[237] Thus it is of particular interest to find in fourth- or fifth-century Egypt not only the mention of a 'Melchizedekian sect' (according to Epiphanius) and a Gnostic treatise on Melchizedek from Nag Hammadi (NHC IX, 1),[238] but also the following discussion with an anchorite:

> Abba Daniel told of another great old man who dwelt in lower Egypt, who in his simplicity, said that Melchizedek was the son of God. When blessed Cyril, Archbishop of Alexandria, was told about this he sent someone to him. Learning that the old man was a worker of miracles and that all he asked of God was revealed to him, and that it was because of his simplicity that he had given utterance to this saying, using guile the Archbishop said to him, "Abba, I think that Melchizedek is the son of God, while a contrary thought says to me, no, that he is simply a man, high-priest of God. Since I am thus plagued, I have sent someone to you that you may pray God to reveal to you what he is." Confident of his gift, the old man said without hesitation, "Give me three days, I will ask God about this matter and I will tell you who he is." So he withdrew and prayed to God about this question. Coming three days later he said to the blessed Cyril that Melchizedek was a man. The archbishop said to him, "How do you know, Abba?" He replied, "God has shown me all the patriarchs in such a way

---

[235] Frankfurter, *Elijah*, 75-77.

[236] Origen, Commentary on Matthew 27:9, 23.37 (see Stone-Strugnell, *Books of Elijah*, 64-65); Didymus, Commentary on Ecclesiastes 3:16, 92.5 (see Gronewald, *Didymos der Blinde* 2, 130f; Krebber, *Didymos der Blinde* 4, 160; Lührmann, 'Pseudepigraphen', 246). And see in general Frankfurter, *Elijah*, 39-44, 54-57.

[237] De Jonge – van der Woude, '11Q Melchizedek'; Delcor, 'Melchizedek'; and Robinson, 'Apocryphal Story'.

[238] See Pearson, 'Figure of Melchizedek; Helderman, 'Melchisedek'.

that each one, from Adam to Melchizedek, passed before me. Therefore be sure that it is so.'' Then the old man withdrew, having preached to himself that Melchizedek was a man. Then the blessed Cyril rejoiced greatly.[239]

One notices in this account that the 'debate' over Melchizedek's nature takes place in the context of the encounter of an Alexandrian ecclesiarch and a rural charismatic figure renowned both for miracles and access to heavenly gnosis. Another story paints an exclusively monastic scenario: 'the inhabitants of Scetis assembled together to discuss Melchizedek, and they forgot to invite Abba Copres' – who, like the 'old man' above, apparently had some special interest or expertise in this figure.[240]

Legends of Melchizedek the wild nazirite that were preserved in Coptic suggest that part of the interest in this figure may have been his character as a desert ascetic.[241] Because of its professed desire to negate worldly for heavenly things desert asceticism, like apocalyptic sects, made fertile intellectual ground for sustained speculation about heavenly powers and their relationship to earthly avatars – speculation that reached ecclesiastical crisis points throughout the second, third, and fourth centuries.[242] Like Cyril of Alexandria in the story above, a number of fourth-century church leaders came to preach against exaltations of Melchizedek as the chief heavenly mediator.[243] In the *chōra*, however, speculation on and reverence for Melchizedek fit neatly into a piety generally directed towards archangels, visions of heavenly beings, and heavenly ascent in general, which was supported textually by an ever-widening corpus of biblical pseudepigrapha with apocalyptic and angelological themes.[244]

The prophetic charisma of Egyptian anchorites of approximately the third through fifth centuries seems to continue the legacy of Jewish apocalyptic literature in early Egyptian Christianity. Following the scheme that apocalypses represented models for supernatural gnosis and for authoritative access to that gnosis, one can plausibly view these ascetic figures as 'living' representations of apocalyptic gnosis and authority in a culture of sparse literacy. The cultural link between prophetic anchorites and the literary tradition of Jewish apocalypses seems to be furthermore corroborated by the anchorites' names, the very pseudonyms promoted in apocalyptic literature. One might therefore conclude that the ideology of Jewish apocalyptic tradition became 'democratized' or domesticated in the world of the Egyptian *chōra*. The principles of visionary authority that derive from Jewish apocalyptic tradition were well rooted in the

---

[239] Apophthegmata patrum: Daniel 8 (*PG* 65:160), tr Ward, *Desert Fathers*, 54.

[240] Apophthegmata patrum: Copres 3 (*PG* 65:252), tr Ward, *Desert Fathers*, 118.

[241] See Robinson, 'Apocryphal Story', 35-37.

[242] See Clark, 'New Perspectives'.

[243] See esp. Bardy, 'Melchisédech' and Evelyn-White, *Monasteries* 2, 115-17. Note also the presence of Melchizedek in Coptic iconography: Grabar, *Martyrium* 2, 217f.

[244] As cogently argued by Helderman, 'Melchisedek', 408-15.

culture of rural Christianity. To use a category developed by Robert Murray to nuance the old concept 'Jewish-Christianity', rural Egyptian Christianity had a 'Hebraistic' basis, insofar as the paradigms for charisma, social identity, and eschatology were rooted archaistically in biblical legend, its prophets, supernatural channels, and accomplishments, while the participants themselves had no relationship to Judaism.[245]

MONASTIC SCRIPTORIA, FOURTH THROUGH SEVENTH CENTURIES

The evidence of the Egyptian anchorites at the very least implies that 'apocalypticism' functioned in a popular or charismatic dimension between the period before 116 CE, when Egyptian Jewish apocalypses were composed and apocalyptic oracles circulated, and the early fourth century, when the manuscript record for the monastic scriptoria discloses a concerted devotion to apocalyptic texts. The preceding reconstruction of a culture in which apocalyptic motifs and ideology were meaningful and 'realized' therefore provides a context for the historical *transmission* of Jewish apocalyptic literature in the centuries before literary evidence gives immediate documentation to its popularity. The religion of the desert anchorites that we have reviewed was itself continuous with that of the monasteries, since anchorites themselves became monastic leaders and monasteries promoted anchoritic asceticism. Thus it is all the more understandable that Coptic monks would actually have preserved Jewish apocalyptic literature despite Athanasius's attempt to exclude it in 367.[246]

What we see at this point in Egypt is a kind of 'institutionalized' Christian apocalypticism, defining itself according to pseudonyms, cosmologies, and apocalyptic motifs that had been rendered popular or authoritative in the Jewish apocalypses, and ultimately transforming apocalypticism itself into an indigenous system of discourse for the definition of authority and power. One finds apocalyptic influence throughout Coptic literature: in the festival encomia on martyrs, in the enormous literature on the archangel Michael (much still unpublished), and as a distinctive aspect of monastic life (as we have already seen in monastic hagiography). Coptic liturgical spells (generally for protection and for gaining oracles) often were constructed with traditional Jewish imagery of heavenly ascent, angelology, and temple.[247] Shenoute drew on apocalyptic images of holy war and the heavenly hosts to exhort his monks in their battles

---

[245] Murray, 'Jews, Hebrews', 205f.

[246] See esp Orlandi, 'Gli apocrifi copti', 57-61, 63-66. On methodological issues concerning Christian scribes' preservation of Jewish texts see R. Kraft, 'Recensional Problem', 135-37.

[247] E.g. Cairo inv. 49547, ed and tr Saint-Paul Girard, 'Un fragment'; ET and comm. by D. Frankfurter in Meyer-Smith, *Ancient Christian Magic*, 226-8 no. 113. Also the Coptic amulet edited by Drescher, 'Coptic Amulet'.

with demons.[248] And the iconography of Coptic chapels displays a unique devotion to visions of heaven and judgment.[249]

The most important literary evidence for this monastic apocalyptic institution can be divided into three categories: (1) the collection and redaction of apocalyptic manuscripts inherited from pre-117 Judaism or composed in the second or third centuries, *as well as* the continuing composition of new apocalypses attributed to biblical heroes; (2) the traditionalizing of apocalyptic visions in monastic hagiography; and (3) the development of the genre martyrology as a new form of apocalypse.

Manuscripts. One can easily understand the importance given to biblical pseudepigrapha in Coptic scriptoria: even beyond their revelations of heavenly matters they provided accessible and relevant narratives about the Hebrew 'saints', the perennially sacred models for Egyptian monks. Apocalyptic texts in the names of biblical prophets, for example, may have been preserved in connection with the self-understanding of anchorites: the Apocalypse of Zephaniah, preserved in both Achmimic and Sahidic manuscripts from the fourth century, and the Ascension of Isaiah (often taken to have a Jewish *Grundlage*), which is extant in two fourth-century Coptic texts and at least one fifth-century Greek manuscript.[250] A third-century Christian prophetic discourse examined here in detail was probably preserved as an 'Apocalypse of Elijah' in at least one of its four Coptic manuscripts for much the same reason, to reflect Elijah's 'living' prophecy in the form of anchorites and holy men.[251] Yet, another apocryphon of Elijah with probable Jewish origins did not survive beyond the witness of Didymus the Blind (Commentary on Eccl 3:16), suggesting that biblical pseudepigraphy could have a life of its own, to be applied even to a third-century Christian prophecy, rather than being tied to particular ancient texts in a unilinear series of redactions.

Indeed, it is highly doubtful that scribes made any distinctions between extrabiblical narratives with Jewish origins and those composed by Christians. The special veneration with which the prophet Jeremiah was viewed in early Egyptian Christianity appears both in the Lives of the Prophets, where he is rendered

---

[248] Van der Vliet, 'Chenouté', 44. In an Arabic version of the abbot's life Christ appears and promises: 'You will glorify in your monastery the Jerusalem that you have consecrated to my name, and those who hear you and obey you will be equal to angels' (ed and tr Amélineau, *Monuments*, 333).

[249] See Grabar, *Martyrium* 2, 207-35, especially p210 on biblical visions.

[250] Apocalypse of Zephaniah: Steindorff, *Apokalypse des Elias*. Ascension of Isaiah: Lefort, 'Coptica Lovaniensia', 24-30 Pl. IVa; id, 'Fragments d'apocryphes', 7-10 Pl. II; Lacau, 'Fragments'; Grenfell-Hunt, *Amherst Papyri* 1, 1-22; cf P. Oxy XVII.2069, which includes a reference to a seven-heaven ascent; and see Acerbi, *Serra Lignea*, esp. 38-53 on circulation in Egypt.

[251] The title 'Apocalypse of Elijah' appears only in Berlin, Staatl. Museen, Abt. P. 1862 + Paris, BN copte 135, ms p44 (ed Steindorff, *Apokalypse des Elias*, 106f). See in general Frankfurter, *Elijah*, 65-74.

in the guise of an Egyptian holy man, and in the traditions of the fourth-century anchorite Bishōi, whose interest in Jeremiah's prophecies won him the special appearance of the prophet himself and thereafter the reputation of being 'of Jeremiah'.[252] Thus it is unsurprising to find a Coptic Jeremiah apocryphon preserved in a seventh century manuscript.[253]

The scribes' equanimity about texts of Jewish and Christian background is most clear in the Testaments of Abraham, Isaac, and Jacob. Whatever the origin of Testament of Abraham, it was read and copied with great interest through the early monastic period, often in conjunction with other apocalyptic testaments: P. Cologne 3221 (fifth century) preserves it along with the Testament of Adam and the Testament of Job. In a world dominated by extravagant angelology, biblical models for asceticism, and visionary charisma, texts like the Testament of Abraham that combined these features would have functioned essentially as proof-texts for ascetic or liturgical realities. It is significant that by the Byzantine period (Vat. copt. 61, tenth century) scribes had seen fit to extend Testament of Abraham into a series with Testaments of Isaac and Jacob. In this case, apparently, an 'inherited' text like Testament of Abraham (or, as we shall see, the Jewish Enoch corpus) could be viewed not only as a repository of gnosis but also as inspiration for an ongoing literary endeavor.[254]

The continued copying of books of Enoch may have a context different from that of Coptic apocrypha in the names of prophets and post-diluvian patriarchs.[255] There is sparse evidence for anchorites' 'being' Enoch or channels for the prophet. However, in iconographic and literary sources he appears as the heavenly scribe, with a quasi-angelic role in the judgment. Excavations of two Byzantine (ca. tenth century) monasteries have disclosed chapels with images of 'Enoch the Scribe', holding a tome identified as 'The Book of Life'; and in one case Enoch is presiding over a judgment scene.[256] A seventh or eighth-century healing spell invokes Enoch in this same capacity of eschatological scribe rather than as revealer: 'Enoch the scribe, don't stick your pen into your ink until Michael comes from heaven and heals my eye!'[257] An encomium 'On the Four Bodiless Creatures' (Pierpont Morgan M612; ninth century) reveals his origins and ongoing function at the throne of God:

> [Enoch speaks:] "I rejoice today since God transformed me and gave me the pen-holder of salvation and the tomes which were in the hand of the angel Mefriel, scribe

---

[252] Torrey, *Lives of the Prophets*, 9f, 49-52. On Apa Bishōi see Evelyn-White, *Monasteries* 2, 113.

[253] Kuhn, 'Coptic Jeremiah Apocryphon'.

[254] On P. Col. 3221 see Römer-Thissen, 'P. Köln inv. nr. 3221', 33-35. On Vatican copt. 61 see MacRae, 'Coptic Testament of Abraham', 327, 339.

[255] On Enoch's various roles in early Christianity see Adler, 'Enoch', 273-5.

[256] Tebtunis: Walters, 'Christian Paintings', 201-202, Pl. XXVI; Saqqara: Quibell, *Excavations at Saqqara* 2, Pls. LV-LVI; 4, 134f, Pl. XXIV.

[257] Anastasi 29528, Hall *Coptic and Greek Texts*, 148f, corr. and tr Kropp, *Zaubertexte* 2, 66f, ET Pearson, 'Pierpont Morgan Fragments', 245.

of old. I copied them in six days and six nights according to the eons of light. After that the Lord issued a command to a cherub, one of the four creatures. After he had taken me to the land of my relatives, I gave orders to my children and my relatives and was taken up to heaven again. God established me before the throne of the cherub, ...''

[Christ speaks:] 'If it were not for these four creatures, these archangels Michael and Gabriel, Mary my mother, and Enoch the scribe of righteousness, if it were not for their prayers which they pray on behalf of the human race, the latter would have been wiped out on earth because of their sins.

Because of this my Father has assigned Enoch, the scribe of righteousness, to the creature with the human face. Whenever a human being sins ... one of the creatures, the human-faced one, cries out and urges Enoch the scribe of righteousness, ''Do not hurry to write down the sins of the children of humankind, but be patient and I will call the archangel Michael ... Restrain yourself a little, O Enoch, and I will call Gabriel ... O you have have pleased God and have been transformed and taken up in the eons of light, be tolerant ... [God gave] you the spiritual penholder so that you might take into account the weakness of people of flesh and blood.''[258]

The origins of this tradition of 'Enoch the Scribe' lie already in the Book of the Watchers (cf. 1 Enoch 12:4, etc.), just as his transfiguration in the above homily ultimately derives from the Similitudes of Enoch (1 Enoch 71). But it is clear that by the Coptic period Enoch had also inherited the role of the Egyptian god Thoth in the latter's dual capacities of scribal culture-hero and scribe of the judgment. Whatever the antiquity of the Enochic 'enthronement' myth assumed in the latter encomium, it clearly serves as background to the articulation of Enoch's *ongoing* heavenly function and power over the recording of sins.

Enoch's special significance as eschatological scribe in Egyptian monasticism is also evident in two important apocryphal texts from the Coptic period (ca. seventh century). Two fragmentary manuscripts, apparently additional apocalypses of Enoch, discuss his role in the judgment and emphasize the power of Enoch's pen to determine afterlife.[259] These manuscripts imply that Coptic monks maintained an Enochic 'tradition' of apocalyptic composition, interpreting it to reflect their own interests in Enoch as eschatological scribe.

One of the manuscripts of 1 Enoch itself also suggests a popular understanding of Enoch's eschatological-juridical function. This manuscript, a Greek codex (Cairo 10759; fifth-sixth centuries), assumes importance because of its archeological context: it was buried with the corpse of a monk. Along with a large portion of the Book of the Watchers the codex includes sections of the Gospel and the Apocalypse of Peter. The placement of the codex suggests some correspondence between the anticipated afterlife of the deceased and themes

---

[258] Homily 4.11, 27, ed and tr Wansinck, *Homiletica* 1, p33f (text), vol 2 p30, 34f (tr). The Pierpont Morgan Homilies are part of an enormous corpus of Coptic encomia attributed to John Chrysostom.
[259] Pierpont Morgan Copt. Theol. 3, fol. 1-9, in Pearson, 'Pierpont Morgan Fragments', 227-83; Cairo 48085, ed Munier, 'Mélanges', Latin tr and discussion in Milik, *Books of Enoch*, 103f. On Coptic developments of the figure of Enoch see Milik ib 100-105; Pearson, ib 236-9, 244-8.

contained in the texts themselves. Nickelsburg has speculated that the common theme is eschatological revelation:

> The *Gospel of Peter* refers to the dead to whom Christ preached between his death and resurrection, and it features a sensational narrative about Jesus' resurrection (35-42). The other texts deal with the realm of the dead, the judgment, and the hope of the righteous. Such concerns were eminently appropriate in a book laid in a Christian grave, and it would appear that the codex was compiled for this purpose. Two relevant extracts from Petrine texts, perhaps copied for the purpose, were supplemented with a part from extant Enochic text and laid in the grave, following the old Egyptian custom of burying a copy of the Book of the Dead.[260]

Thus we might attribute at least one of the Christian copies of 1 Enoch to the particular Egyptian monastic interest in Enoch as scribe of the judgment. The other (P. Chester Beatty 12 + P. Michigan 5552) contains the Epistle of Enoch, the story of Noah's birth, along with Melito's Homily on the Passion, an Ezekiel apocryphon, and a lost brief text that must have begun the codex.[261] While it is difficult to discern common themes in the contents of this codex, one can recognize the prophetic character of the Epistle's woes and exhortations, as well as the first-person claims to 'have read the tablets of heaven and ... seen the writing of authority; [and] learned that which was written upon them and graven thereon concerning you' (103:2; ms p8), as conducive to a culture of charismatic anchorites claiming heavenly authority for their 'prophecies'.

In contrast to P. Cairo 10759 and P. Chester Beatty 12, both of which show the independent circulation of particular Enoch books, fragments of two Greek codices from the late fourth century suggest a continuing regard for an integrated Enochic literary corpus such as ultimately developed in the Ethiopic tradition. P. Oxyrhynchus XVII.2069 consists of five fragments, of which three belong to a codex of the Enochic Dream Visions and two to another codex containing (at least) the Astronomical Book of Enoch, according to the reconstruction of J.T. Milik.[262] That the fragments were deposited together may imply that codices containing Enoch's revelations were regarded as part of a corpus, 'the Books of Enoch' as Athanasius castigated them in 367.

The use of 4 Ezra among Egyptian monks is evident in both a sixth/eighth-century fragment of the text itself (P. Berlin Kgl. Mus. 9096) and a brief list of texts from the Apocrypha inscribed on an ostracon (BP 1069).[263] Since there is no reason for assuming that the fragment contained significantly more of 4

---

[260] Nickelsburg, 'Two Enochic Manuscripts', 254, *pace* Milik, *Books of Enoch*, 71. On the inclusion of mortuary texts in traditional Egyptian burials during the Greco-Roman period see now Allen, 'Funerary Texts', 43.

[261] See Bonner, *Last Chapters of Enoch*, 3-12; Milik, *Books of Enoch*, 75f; and Nickelsburg, 'Two Enochic Manuscripts', 255-9.

[262] Milik, 'Fragments grecs', 343.

[263] P. Berlin Kgl. Mus. 9096, ed and tr Leipoldt-Violet, 'Ein saïdisches Bruchstück'; Ostracon BP 1069, ed Crum, *Monastery of Epiphanius* 1, 197.

Ezra, it is interesting to note the part of the text contained on this fragment: 4
Ez 13:29-46 forms a portion of the eschatological interpretation of Ezra's sixth
vision, describing the restoration of the tribes of Israel at Mount Zion and the
judgment of the Gentile nations. It is hardly surprising to find such exclusively
Jewish eschatology in Egyptian Christianity, considering the prominence of
Jewish traditions in this culture that emphasize Jerusalem and Palestine as
dominant loci.[264]

With a late-fourth-century leaf from what was probably the entirety of 2
Baruch in Greek (P. Oxy III.403) we can see the extent of Jewish apocalypses
imported to Egypt, even those with concerns more for the Jewish Temple than
for the cosmos at large. As with the Greek fragments of Enoch from Oxyrhynchus, the leaf from 2 Baruch would not necessarily derive from a monastic
setting; but given the diversity of such settings, the restriction of literacy, and
the sectarian and monastic social contexts for apocalypses in the late fourth
century, the likeliest source for these texts was probably monasticism of some
sort.[265]

Hagiography. The presence or absence of Jewish apocalypses in the manuscript
record could not by itself reflect the extent to which Jewish apocalypses and
apocalyptic tradition influenced Egyptian Christianity. We have seen that one
method of continuing or updating the apocalyptic tradition beyond those texts
that were inherited from Judaism was to compose 'new' apocrypha within the
archaic pseudonyms. Another was to sow the literary elements and ideology of
apocalypses into new literary genres, thus broadening or domesticating the
concept of 'apocalypse' in Egyptian monastic experience. It is, therefore, within
the context of scribal function that we should examine the apocalyptic 'tours'
ascribed to such figureheads of Egyptian monasticism as Pachomius and Shenoute in their hagiographies.[266] While traditions about their revelatory powers
probably go back to reputations during their lifetimes or even to their own
self-conceptions as saints, hagiography itself involved a complex of literary
influences and techniques that must be understood in the context of the monastic scriptorium.

In the Bohairic Life Pachomius is described twice as taken away to view hell
(88, 103) and later as ascending to view the eschatological cities of the saints
(114). The second vision of hell (103), describing a dark region with a pillar
around which the damned circle, is unusual from a literary point of view and
may derive from Pachomius's own imagination or experience. The other two

---

[264] Cf Apoc.El. 2:39-40, on which see Frankfurter, *Elijah*, 226-8, and in general R.L. Wilken, 'The
Restoration of Israel'. Note on the other hand T. Job 28:7, where Job turns out to be king of Egypt.
[265] On urban monasticism see Goehring, 'The Encroaching Desert'.
[266] Compare similar tours in hagiographies of Macarius and the Syrian Marcus collected in Mac-
Dermot, *Cult of the Seer*, 551-5.

narratives use Pauline language to characterize rapture: e.g. 'Was it in the body that he was carried away, was it out of the body? – God knows that he was carried away.'[267] In these two cases the hagiographer proceeds to describe the various regions of infernal and heavenly worlds according to schemes explicitly derived from topography ('north ... southwest') and urban life ('constructions, monuments, ... fruit trees, vineyards'). Thus in one dimension the scribe is certainly proposing an explicit typology with the Paul of 2 Corinthians 12; and whereas the apostle's original vision is described with little content, we know that by the end of the third century an Egyptian Christian had composed an Apocalypse of Paul that fleshed it out with particular details of hell (Apocalypse of Paul 30-42) and of the urban aspects of heaven (22-30). This text drew from an apocalyptic tradition of tours of hell and heaven that was still thriving in Egypt: as Himmelfarb has demonstrated, the structure of the material in the Apocalypse of Paul ultimately derived from 1 Enoch 17-36 but its most immediate prototype was the Apocalypse of Zephaniah, an apparently Jewish text of the late second-temple period.[268]

It would be plausible to regard Pachomius' visions as a sort of précis of the Apocalypse of Paul if this were the only apocalypse available in Egypt by the time when the Pachomian Life was composed. Yet the manuscript discoveries make it certain that the Apocalypse of Paul hardly replaced its Jewish prototypes in the monastic world: both the Book of the Watchers and the Apocalypse of Zephaniah, among other traditional apocalyptic 'tour' narratives, were still being read and copied. So in another dimension the visionary tours in the Life of Pachomius reflect a conscious intertextuality that went beyond the comparatively new Apocalypse of Paul and that related Pachomius, like other early anchorites, to traditions of *biblical* heroes' revelations of heaven and hell.[269] Even while plundering the Apocalypse of Paul most directly for description, the author of the Pachomian Life understood the significance of writing a Pachomian 'apocalypse' within the *tradition* of Jewish apocalypses.[270]

The literature that surrounds Shenoute of Atripe includes apocalyptic passages that, like the Pachomian materials above, are closely modelled upon pre-existing apocalyptic literature. Ms 82 of the published Shenoute corpus consists of a vision of hell in the abbot's own style.[271] While cleaving to the tradition of the Apocalypse of Zephaniah and the Apocalypse of Paul in its

---

[267] Tr Veilleux, *Pachomian Koinonia* 1, 113.

[268] Himmelfarb, *Tours of Hell*, 169f.

[269] Crum proposed that a reference to a text entitled 'Apa Pachomius: On the End [*haê*] of the Community [*koinônia*]' in a 'Bibliography of Apa Elijah' could reflect an eschatological vision attributed to the monk (*Monastery of Epiphanius* 1, 200f; Bouriant, 'Notes de voyage', 133 no. 37).

[270] Cf MacDermot, *Cult of the Seer*, 114f and texts p553-62.

[271] Shenute no. 82 (Paris copt. 130⁵, fol. 134-36, 138), Leipoldt, *Sinuthii ... opera omnia* 4, 198-204. Stephen Emmel advises me on the basis of the Shenoute corpus as a whole that there is no good reason to ascribe this apocalyptic passage to Shenoute himself (personal communication).

emphasis on types of punishment, the text seems to reflect an immediate environment in which scripture is read aloud and clerics are impious. On these as well as stylistic grounds Johannes Leipoldt argued for Shenoute's own authorship, a compelling proposition since Shenoute's disciple and biographer Besa recalls the abbot as having claimed to 'see' a non-Christian in hell.[272] But even if it is Shenoute's own composition, Leipoldt admitted, the structure of the vision is clearly indebted to apocalypses that were available in the abbot's time. Indeed, the two Coptic manuscripts of the Apocalypse of Zephaniah were found in Shenoute's own White Monastery.[273] These facts would suggest that scribes in the White Monastery (possibly including Shenoute himself) were endeavoring to translate the apocalyptic tradition as it was represented in their library into hagiography for their abbot, who clearly endorsed this effort by his own supernatural self-conception.

This scribal exaltation of Shenoute with apocalyptic visions becomes all the more evident with the Arabic version of Besa's Life of Shenoute, produced shortly after the Arabic invasion (ca. 685-90 CE). Perhaps due to a crisis of Coptic authority under the new Muslim rule, the Arabic scribe added innumerable visions of heaven, hell, and angelic figures, plus an extensive eschatological discourse that 'predicts' the invasion of Arabs as 'Persians'.[274] As the details of encroaching chaos progress with increasing luridness, it becomes clear that the scribe has made direct use of motifs from the eschatological discourse of the Apocalypse of Elijah, especially a woe upon pregnant women forced to suckle snakes 'in that time'.[275] In fact the Apocalypse of Elijah was preserved along with the Apocalypse of Zephaniah in both manuscripts in Shenoute's White Monastery. So in both cases where apocalyptic revelations were credited to Shenoute in propaganda issued by the White Monastery we can find scribes drawing upon biblical apocrypha available in the White Monastery's own library to construct his supernatural authority as a holy man.[276]

Additional apocalyptic visions attributed to Shenoute and preserved in Ethiopic and Arabic demonstrate the abbot's continuing reputation as seer in White Monastery tradition as well as the continuing scribal interests in maintaining an apocalyptic literature under his authority.[277] As in the case of the Coptic frag-

---

[272] Leipoldt, *Schenute von Atripe*, 206-9; cf Besa, Life of Shenoute 88, above p178.

[273] Leipoldt ib 207f.

[274] Amélineau, *Monuments*, 338-46. On dating see ib, lvi-lix.

[275] Amélineau, *Monuments*, 343, compare Apoc.El. 2:35. On the influence of Apocalypse of Elijah see Rosenstiehl, *L'Apocalypse d'Élie*, 40-42, and Frankfurter, *Elijah*, 25f, 225.

[276] Cf also Paris copte 131[6] f.96[v], described by Porcher, 'Analyse des manuscrits coptes', 88f as a 'récit d'un personnage à qui un autre montre un jardin et une vigne, une église et un autel'. Stephen Emmel informs me that based on similarities with other Shenoutiana the seer is likely to be Shenoute himself and this tour may be part of the Shenoute 'Apocalypse' (ms 82) edited by Leipoldt (personal communication).

[277] Grohmann, 'Visionen Apa Schenute's'.

ment, the content of these later apocalypses included critiques of contemporaneous ecclesiastical life. Thus a fundamental purpose of apocalypses from the era of Book of the Watchers and Jubilees, to address practical religious debates in the time of the author, is maintained in Coptic tradition throughout the Byzantine period.

Martyrology. It has often been observed that the 'genre' of martyrology evolved out of Jewish apocalyptic texts and motifs, a process particularly evident in such early Christian texts as the Book of Revelation, the Martyrdom of Perpetua, and the Martyrdom and Ascension of Isaiah.[278] Yet by the fourth century, with its profusion of Christian martyrological literature, one finds that the literary models used to promote a martyr's authority had diversified into numerous genres: court protocols, military and athletic descriptions, and the highly stereotyped encomia.

In Egyptian monastic literature especially there is a pronounced attention to heavenly ascent and tours as an integral component of the martyrology; and the details of these apocalyptic sections must reflect the scribes' modeling of these narratives upon apocalyptic literature.[279] In this way the revelatory authority of the ancient biblical hero, for which Jewish apocalypses gave literary foundation, has shifted: first to the 'living' prophets of the desert, then to monastic leaders in their institutional legends, and now to certain martyrs, who themselves might still grant revelations and favors from heaven to supplicants who attend their shrines. And whereas in Jewish apocalyptic literature the descriptions of heavenly wonders – those secrets bequeathed from heaven to mankind in book form – were made accessible to gnosis for an interested conventicle, similar descriptions of heavenly wonders in martyrologies (which were composed for public reading at festivals) would now serve the promotion of the physical cult.[280]

The two most vivid examples of apocalyptic visions or tours as central aspects of Coptic martyrologies occur in the Martyrdom of St. Victor the General and the Martyrdom of SS. Paese and Thekla, which originated at some point in the spate of martyrological composition that followed the fourth century.[281]

It is at the end of the third of four lurid torture accounts that 'the heart of Apa

---

[278] See early studies by Riddle, 'From Apocalypse to Martyrology', and Fischel, 'Martyr and Prophet.'

[279] See MacDermot, *Cult of the Seer*, 183f, 193-95.

[280] See Baumeister, *Martyr invictus*, 172-83.

[281] Coptic martyrologies are notoriously difficult to date; it is also not easy to infer *Vorlagen* from their texts. The probable Greek original to the Martyrdom of Victor may place it in the fifth or sixth century; while the Martyrdom of Paêse and Thekla, dependent as it is on a living cult of St. Victor, must have arisen considerably later. On Martyrdom of Victor see Delehaye, 'Les martyrs d'Égypte', 131. See other examples of Coptic martyrological visions and tours translated in MacDermot, *Cult of the Seer*, 626-56.

Victor was carried up into the heights of heaven, and [the angels] instructed him concerning the kingdom of heaven, and concerning the city of the righteous, and the saints saluted him'. He is greeted by Abel, Zachariah, and the Archangel Michael; he is compared to 'the three holy' children from the story of Daniel; and Michael promises him an imminent ascent: 'Thy throne shall be stablished in heaven ... [and] when thou shalt lift thy hands up to heaven they shall take the form of the seal of heaven, and they shall give light within the veil, before the altar of sacrifice.' Victor is then returned to torture.[282]

The 'apocalypse' of Paêse takes place after he is jailed: 'At midnight the angel of the Lord came to him, and set the holy Apa Paêse upon his shining wings, and took him to heaven and showed him the holy city, the heavenly Jerusalem; and all the saints come out to meet him ...' The urban imagery of heaven is then focused upon one particular house, whose numbers and concentric arrangement of pillars and thrones are described in minute detail – a recollection of both Ezekiel and the Book of the Watchers (1 Enoch 14). This heavenly palace, it turns out, belongs to the newly enthroned Apa Victor. With the description of the palace the voice turns from third to first person – 'And I, Paêse, saw ...' – recalling a classical apocalyptic motif and conceivably implying a prior apocalypse. The apocalyptic section then reveals a) how saints like Victor can help a soul at judgment if that soul has supported the saint's shrine during life, and b) the existence of a palace in the heavenly city equivalent to Victor's, ready to receive the ascended Paêse and his siblings, even while 'your bodies shall be in a single shrine on earth'.[283]

The visions serve the express purpose of promoting the authority of particular saints as heavenly mediators and regional 'saviors'. Whereas the ascent language of the Martyrdom of Victor bears echoes of Jewish apocalyptic symbolism of the heavenly temple, the celestial imagery in the 'apocalypse' of Paêse is drawn from the late antique picture of the 'holy city', and not from such esoteric priestly images of divine architecture as 1 Enoch or Ezekiel offer. The length and vividness of the description of heavenly Jerusalem must have been intended to strike listeners with an absolute contrast to the rural environment of Byzantine Egypt.[284]

A parenetical section in the middle of this 'apocalypse', promising the saint's help at death for anyone who aids the shrine in one of a number of ways, becomes a standard motif of hagiographical literature by the later Coptic period, and it demonstrates the overtly didactic function to which scribes could devote the apocalyptic vision. It is interesting to note that this promise of

---

[282] B.M. Ms Oriental 7022, fol. 12b-13a, tr Budge, *Coptic Martyrdoms*, 274f.

[283] Pierpont Morgan Codex M 591, T.28, fols. 77ᵛ ii-81ʳ i, ed and tr Reymond-Barns, *Four Martyrdoms*, text 67-70, tr 174-78. Cf Monastery of Macarius text XXI, frag. 5 (Codex Tisch. XXIV, 39), ed and tr Evelyn-White, *Monasteries* 1, 118.

[284] Compare the realities of fourth-century rural life outlined by Bagnall, *Egypt in Late Antiquity*, 110-14.

heavenly favors for anyone patronizing the cult has parallels in the Testament of Isaac and a Coptic encomium on the prophet Elijah, once again illustrating the abiding importance of biblical figures as living 'saints' in the sacred landscape of late antique Egypt.[285]

The Coptic martyrologies, far from representing any immediate knowledge of the Jewish apocalyptic prototypes, reflect the thorough assimilation of an 'apocalypticism' in the scribal world of Coptic Christianity. The oft-invoked imagery of the celestial city lies closer to the Apocalypse of Paul than to Jewish visions of the heavenly temple; details of the soul's departure from the body and its judgment, two contexts in with the saint can aid the patron, reflect indigenous Egyptian conceptions of eschatology; and even the attention to biblical 'saints' at this point reflects their popularization in shrines and in Coptic Christian literature rather than sources in Jewish pseudepigraphic apocalypses. One may therefore speak of an 'apocalypticism' characteristic of Coptic Christianity, indeed even a 'biblical' or 'Hebraistic' apocalypticism; but that apocalypticism has become thoroughly Coptic in literature, symbolism, and function.

'APOCALYPTICISM' IN COPTIC EGYPT

From manuscript discoveries, Coptic literature, and evidence for religious movements and attitudes we have seen that Jewish 'apocalypticism' – the emphasis on revelatory authority and heavenly gnosis – came to be assimilated into Coptic Christianity for several purposes. The concept of seer in Jewish apocalypses, inherited as it was from both prophetic and sapiential traditions, was already being invoked by the third century to express local attitudes about holy men, 'living saints', as seers and visionary prophets. The particular degree of authority that apocalyptic tradition endowed upon seers would answer indigenous needs and anxieties about the whereabouts of true holiness and true revelation such as Peter Brown has described.[286]

Apocalyptic motifs and literary forms also provided a context for the articulation of traditional mortuary ideas in a Christian culture. Thus the professional interest of Egyptian temple scribes in describing stages of afterlife might continue in new terms (Enoch the Scribe, Abaddon and Tartarouchos the angels of death) as well as old ones (the 'West' as the land of the dead, the weighing

---

[285] T. Isaac 6.16-22; encomium on Elijah in Budge, 'Fragments of a Coptic Version', 369, 394; on the history of the text see Evelyn-White, *Monasteries* 1, 71. See the other versions in MacDermot, *Cult of the Seer*, 679-82, and Apocalypse of Sedrach 16:3.
[286] See especially *The Making of Late Antiquity*.

of souls) as a project of monastic scriptoria.[287] If the Testament of Abraham was indeed first composed by (Egyptian) Jews, then we might see in it an early synthesis of these traditional ideas, a biblical frame-story employed to give a popular Egyptian conception of the process of death.[288]

In general the Jewish apocalypses established a cosmology in which there could be articulated the power that was popularly available through liturgy and spells, the intercession offered by monks and anchorites, and the cult of deceased saints. Because of its general idea that divine and human boundaries could be breached, apocalyptic ideology conveyed a notion of power that was popularly *accessible*, albeit awesome and removed.[289]

Egyptian Apocalypticism: Conclusions

TWO KINDS OF APOCALYPTICISM

In surveying Egyptian Judaism as the source of Jewish apocalypses in Egypt we saw evidence for two kinds of apocalypticism: one that was urban and literate, devoted to apocalypses as sacred books and to achieving a gnosis through the collecting and interpretation of such books; another that was part of a broader eschatological hope, seeking information and certainty to correspond to a sense of the last days, and appealing to a popular and orally-based social world. The first, which we may denote as 'speculative apocalypticism', probably organized itself in conventicles; the second, 'millennialist prophecy', probably was organized concentrically around holy men, self-proclaimed prophets, and the few literati who might proclaim scripture or the Book of Revelation as 'living' words to popular audiences already in some fervor. Of course it is always tendentious to construct such cultural dichotomies, and it is important to assume considerable overlap. Yet we have seen a spate of evidence for these kinds of apocalyptic piety reaching back before 116 CE. The important aspect of these two apocalypticisms for the study of 'Christian use of Jewish apocalypses' is that they reflect two *continuous social worlds*, from Judaism into Christianity, that extend from before 116 through the fourth century and thereafter.

We may follow 'speculative apocalypticism' as a context for the promulgation of Jewish apocalypses at least through the diverse Gnostic, Hermetic-Gnostic, and Alexandrian intellectual circles in the fourth and fifth centuries. In

---

[287] See in general Budge, 'Egyptian Mythology', lxi-lxxii; Piankoff, 'La descente aux enfers'; Doresse, *Des hiéroglyphes à la croix*, 45-56; Zandee, *Death as an Enemy*, 303-42 (although Zandee's assertions about the impact of canonical Christian materials verge on the confessional); MacDermot, *Cult of the Seer*, 108-78; and Baumeister, *Martyr invictus*, 51-86.

[288] Cf Nickelsburg, 'Eschatology', 32-39.

[289] On the apocalyptic idea of breaching boundaries see now Himmelfarb, *Ascent to Heaven*, 69-71.

our review of the native Egyptian context we noted the legacy of an indigenous quasi-apocalyptic literary tradition as an influence on Hermeticism and Gnosticism, as well as the distinctively literary impetus towards 'gnosis', a gnosis that intrinsically involved a purified 'priestly' life. For these groups the Jewish apocalypses constituted primarily *books* of divine wisdom. And we have seen the Jewish apocalypses' historical influence on these groups both in the citations of Alexandrian scholars like Clement and Didymus, and in the compositions of certain Gnostic texts. Presumably, as Alexandrian authorities reined in such diversity increasingly over the fourth and fifth centuries, such eclectically oriented conventicles and individuals found more receptive milieux in certain monasteries of the *chôra*.

The millennialist impulse in upper Egyptian Judaism probably changed with the demise of that Judaism and with the increasing influence of native oracular forms, which grounded eschatological messages in the indigenous expressions of Egypt (the latter phenomenon being most evident in certain Sibylline oracles and in the second chapter of the Apocalypse of Elijah). And yet a reverence for *biblical* heroes as paradigms for charisma, oracular and prophetic speech, and religious action (like martyrdom) seems to have distinguished upper Egyptian Christianity far more than that in Alexandria and its nodal cities. Out of this Christianity, for example, rose holy men who presented themselves – and gained reputations – as biblical prophets *redivivi*. It was this type of apocalypticism, reaching its apex of fervor during the second half of the third century, that fed into the diverse movements of 'Melitians' of subsequent centuries as well as into certain basic forms of Egyptian monastic piety: the importance ascribed to visions, the power in names, and the omnipotence of the biblical paradigm. We have seen the influence of Jewish apocalypses in this millennialist-prophetic apocalypticism not only in their very preservation in manuscripts (by the 'Melitians' opposed by Athanasius and by monastic scribes themselves), but also in the continuity of the 'Jewish' apocalyptic literary tradition in such forms as new apocrypha composed under the old names (e.g. the Coptic Enoch and Moses apocrypha, the Testaments of Isaac and Jacob), old apocalyptic motifs presented in the hagiography for new holy men and martyrs (Lives of Pachomius and Shenoute, Martyrdoms of St. Victor and Paêse), and even an expansion of the tradition of apocalyptic angelology with new speculations (the Pierpont Morgan homily 'On the Four Bodiless Creatures').

There were, of course, important overlaps between these two apocalypticisms. For one, the discrepancy in literacy between the two cultures would allow literate Alexandrian scribal circles devoted to revelations of all types to gather and edit as literature the fragmentary oracles, prophecies, and other texts issued in the *chôra*. Examples might include the Sibylline Oracles; the Apocalypse of Elijah, which both Origen and Didymus the Blind seem to have encountered in Alexandria; and the Hermetic Asclepius tractate, which was preserved in Coptic as part of the Nag Hammadi Gnostic library. It is significant that all three examples represent *syntheses* of native Egyptian tradition and the authoritative ideology of their scribes (Jewish-Christian or, in the latter case, Hermetic-Gnostic), suggesting that the issuing of oracles and prophecies in the *chôra* functioned as a form of native revelation from an early point.[290]

A second overlap may be due to Egyptian influence itself. In texts and iconography the antediluvian patriarch Enoch, installed as eternal scribe of the judgment, also acquires the status of culture-hero of the monastic scriptorium (and, in some traditions, of Egypt itself),[291] precisely the role the Egyptian scribal god Thoth held for the scriptoria of the native priesthood. In this way the scriptorium of the monastic culture is heir to the same native scribal traditions as the conventicles of Hermetic and Gnostic groups, in which we have already seen the legacy of Egyptian priestly ideals.

A third overlap would consist of the notion of the 'living' authority or revealer as it existed in Gnosticism and in the epichoric cult of the holy man-prophet. In both cases the traditional conceit of apocalypses, that the revelations of the ancient seer are accessible only via the text itself, allegedly preserved over the generations, has been supplanted by the notion that revelations and direct encounters with *angeli interpretes* are contemporary realities, whether as biblical prophets *redivivi* in the *chôra* or, as Pagels has shown, the continuing mediation of a revealer Christ for the Gnostic heirs to his true disciples.[292]

APOCALYPSES AND SCRIPTURE IN EGYPTIAN CHRISTIANITY

It is certainly clear that Athanasius's attempt to restrict the canon of Egyptian Christians in 367 CE had an impact on the respect accorded the Jewish apocalypses in Egypt, since the manuscripts of Jewish apocalypses preserved in Greek and Coptic clearly pale in quantity next to those of biblical and New Testament scripture. After the fourth century such literature circulated and fascinated in the periphery of Christian reading. Of course, apocalyptic literature had always contributed to its own peripheral status simply through its claim to secret and direct access to heavenly wisdom and to an access explicitly surpassing that available to the multitude with its canonical texts. The literature is intrinsically resistant to its own popularizing; even Jude's explicit invocation of apocalyptic literature arises in a milieu given to strong boundaries against the world. For this reason one tends to find apocalypses most valued among *sects*, which define themselves in terms of greater holiness, more intimate congress

---

[290] Note that the Oracle of the Potter and other native oracles were also circulating in fragmentary manuscripts during the second and third centuries CE, the period of the compilation of some Sibylline oracles and the composition of both the Apocalypse of Elijah and the Perfect Discourse. Cf Frankfurter, *Elijah*, 185-94.

[291] See Fodor, 'Origins', 340f.

[292] Pagels, 'Visions'.

with a heavenly world, and a greater and more vital gnosis into the secrets of that world than what is popularly pursued outside.

And yet apocalypses were read, copied, preserved, and composed in monasteries throughout the history of Coptic Egypt. It would, of course, be meaningless to regard monastic culture as itself sectarian, even though many of the defining aspects of sectarian Christianity continued to be cultivated in monastic settings. Rather, we may attribute the continuing value of apocalypses largely to the bibliophilia of the monastic scriptorium and, to a lesser extent, the great holiness with which the non-literate 'folk' outside the monasteries tended to regard the written words of any biblical figure. The monastic scribal endeavor might almost be called folkloristic in its wide-ranging collection of apophthegmata, stories of martyrs, protective and healing spells, and, most importantly, legendary materials about biblical and New Testament figures.[293] That so much of this material obviously derives from the immediate world of Coptic folk Christianity with its popular tales of martyrs and saints must reflect ongoing communication between the cultures within and without the monastery, and therefore a strong motivation to 'collect' lore relevant to the monks' piety and life. Under these circumstances the preservation of Jewish apocalyptic texts can be understood as part of the broader scribal endeavor of copying and editing texts relevant to the revered saints of Coptic monastic and 'folk' piety. It was the desire for edifying literature about the saints, moreover, that explains how the monastic scriptorium might preserve, undifferentiated, texts that we know to be originally Jewish (e.g. 1 Enoch, 4 Ezra), texts with probable Jewish origins (e.g. Testament of Abraham, Apocalypse of Zephaniah), and texts that quite obviously derived from Christian scribes (Apocalypse of Elijah, Testaments of Isaac and Jacob, the Coptic Enoch apocrypha). Preservation, editing, and composition were all part of the same 'collecting' endeavor of the monastic scriptorium.

Of course, at various times and for various reasons (e.g. ecclesiastical conflict, political turmoil, new charismatic figures), monks and their popular audiences might acquire a particular longing for the 'deeper' meaning of biblical narrative and for gnosis into scriptural or heavenly secrets. Such circumstances might create a context for the acquisition of, composition of, or greater attention to an apocalyptic text framed as the revelation of a biblical hero. Certainly by the sixth or seventh centuries a biblical pseudepigraphon could easily be a Christian composition. And because it tends to arise in particular social situations like conflict, this kind of longing for gnosis or claim to gnosis through ancient or recent apocalyptic texts seems to have typified sectarian groups in

---

[293] See Evelyn-White, *Monasteries*, contents to vol. 1, and bibliographies of smaller monastic libraries (ca. sixth century) in Bouriant, 'Notes de voyage', and ostracon BP 1069 in Crum, *Monastery of Epiphanius* 1, 197f. For a monastic collection of ritual spells (exorcism, protection, healing) see ms Anastasy 9, Pleyte-Boeser, *Manuscrits coptes*, 439-78; tr and notes in Kropp, *Zaubertexte* 2, 161-75, XLV-XLVI.

Egyptian monastic history. As Athanasius opposed 'Melitians' with their Jewish apocalyptic tracts in the mid-fourth century, so John of Paralos, a sixth-
century monk obsessed with eliminating 'heretical' books, castigated a sect in
his own day that was promoting 'The Investiture of Michael', 'The *Kerygma* of
John', 'The Jubilation of the Apostles', 'The Teachings of Adam', and 'The
Counsel of the Savior.'[294]

But even in this case we can see signs that apocryphal literature had much
broader appeal in John's region of Scetis than simply to sectarians. All but 'The
Teachings of Adam' are really apocrypha of the New Testament, a genus of
literature that seems to have irritated monastic leaders particularly. Yet John's
homily does not attack apocrypha per se. Rather, he criticizes a desire that is
evidently popular among folk and monks to comprehend the genesis of the
angels in connection with the creation of the world, one of the oldest and most
basic motivations in apocalypticism (cf Jubilees 2):

> For what concerns the creation of these holy angelic armies nobody has written
> anything on this subject. In this period in effect the intellect of people was not perfect
> in the glory of God. The blessed Moses thus wrote nothing on this subject; he
> certainly could have, but he knew that the intellect of people was not perfect and,
> regarding this issue [of the creation of the angelic hierarchies], he did not speak
> about them but treated only the creation of the world. As for the things pronounced
> before the six days, on the subject of the creation of heavenly powers, he did not
> speak on it.[295]

The homily implies by its very argument that the attraction of apocryphal books
that answer these questions extends beyond a particular sect and probably into
John's own monastery. Thus it is all the more interesting to find that their
substance is circulating orally among the 'folk [*haplous*] of the cities and towns
of Egypt'. They 'pay attention [*meleta*]' to the books and 'think that the words
of these books ... are truthful things'.[296] Thus we can see that even beyond the
distinctive claims to gnosis of sectarian groups, apocalyptic texts – including in
this case a pseudepigraphon of Adam – served a popular yearning to understand
facets of the cosmos and a desire to hear popular ideas undergirded by a written
text.

---

[294] John of Paralos, Homily Against Heretical Books 48 (Vienna K 9831ʳb), ed van Lantschoot,
'Fragments coptes', 303. The sect is probably some form of Melitians, as mentioned above; see
Evelyn-White, *Monasteries* 2, 248f.

[295] John of Paralos, Homily Against Heretical Books 57 (Vienna K 9835ᵛ), ed and tr van Lantschoot ib 312, 324.

[296] John of Paralos, Homily Against Heretical Books 49 (Vienna K 9831ᵛa), ed van Lantschoot ib
304.

Chapter Five

The Apocalyptic Survey of History Adapted by Christians: Daniel's Prophecy of 70 Weeks

William Adler

Introduction

Studies of apocalyptic literature have often observed that historical surveys, a vital element of many Jewish apocalypses, are largely absent in their Christian counterparts. But this feature of the Jewish apocalypse did not disappear. Sweeping surveys of the past based on some older Jewish apocalyptic scheme found a home in other genres, in particular Christian apologetic and historiography.[1]

One apocalyptic text that proved especially amenable to adaptation by Christian historians was Dan 9:24-27, the apocalypse of 70 weeks. Eusebius' Ecclesiastical History reports that during the reign of the Emperor Septimius Severus, a certain Judas, otherwise unknown, composed a chronicle in the form of a commentary on Dan 9:24-27. In his regrettably condensed summary of the work, Eusebius says very little about the actual contents of the work. But he does offer an opinion about the historical conditions that provoked it. The author of the chronicle, which ceased with the tenth year of Severus, was convinced that the 'much talked of coming of the Antichrist was then already near (ἤδη τότε πλησιάζειν)'. Eusebius, who was known to oppose speculation like this, offers what may well be the first documented psycho-social explanation of the apocalyptic mentality. 'The persecution which was then stirred up against us', he says, 'disturbed the minds of the many (τὰς τῶν πολλῶν ἀνατεταράχει διανοίας).'[2] Judas was simply caught up in the hysteria.

Judas' chronicle marks the first attested case in which Daniel's apocalypse of 70 weeks underpinned a Christian chronicle. Many such works pursuing the same end were to follow. Shortly after Judas, the universal chronicler Julius

---

[1] See Vielhauer-Strecker, 'Apocalyptic', 560 (cf chap. 1 n6); also A.Y. Collins, 'The Early Christian Apocalypses', 67.
[2] Eusebius, Hist. eccl. 6.7.1 (tr Oulton).

Africanus (ca. 160-240) claimed to find in Daniel's apocalyptic vision an un-ambiguous foreshadowing of Christ's advent. 'I am shocked', he writes after an extensive chronological analysis of Daniel 9, 'at the Jews who say that the Messiah has not arrived, and the Marcionites who say that there was no pre-diction of him in the prophecies.'[3] In the fourth century, Eusebius, no less intrigued than his predecessors by the vision, subjected the passage to a detailed analysis in four separate works. Indeed, Eusebius' identification of central fig-ures in the vision exercised a profound influence on his overall understanding of sacred history.[4]

Daniel's apocalypse of 70 weeks was one of several chronological schemes that Christian historiography inherited from Jewish tradition. The interest de-voted to the passage is hardly surprising. Because the canonical authority of Daniel was not contested, Christian historians could ponder the meaning of these verses without fear of incurring the suspicion that recourse to other apoc-alyptic works might arouse. Cast in the form of a historical survey generally free of the metaphysical speculation of many other Jewish apocalypses, Da-niel's vision of 70 weeks offered a theory of history that Christian chroniclers found quite congenial to their own: namely, that events preceding the end of the age could be periodized according to a providentially determined plan.

The real *floruit* of interpretation of Daniel 9 does not occur until the third and fourth centuries, when eschatological fervor in the early Church was already waning. As a result, Eusebius and the other Christian historians who increasing-ly dominated the discussion of these verses tended to eschew the future prom-ises of the vision in favor of a more retrospective messianic understanding. But despite this orientation, it is still possible to recover from their testimony par-tially submerged vestiges of earlier strata in Jewish and Christian interpretation. Our chief interest in this chapter is to illustrate how Daniel's vision, a classic example of the apocalyptic historical survey, underwent continuous adaptation and reinterpretation in Jewish and Christian exegesis and historiography.

Daniel's 70 Weeks and the 'Apocalyptic View of History'

In the section immediately preceding the apocalypse of 70 weeks (9:3-20), Daniel beseeches God with a prayer common in the liturgy of the synagogues.[5] Describing God as 'keeper of the covenant' (9:4), it confesses his majesty and righteousness, attributes the sufferings of his people to their trangressions

---

[3] Excerpt in George Syncellus, Ecloga Chronographica 393.25-27 (ed. Mosshammer). The trans-lation is mine.

[4] See below p237f.

[5] For other examples of prayers preceding visionary experiences and interpretation in the Jewish apocalypses, see also 1 Enoch 84:2-6, 4 Ezra, *passim*. For discussion, see Vielhauer-Strecker, 'Apocalyptic', 548f.

against the Law, and pleads with God for forgiveness. The ensuing vision, however, is oddly unresponsive to the prayer. In the first place, it is given in answer, not to a confession of sins, but rather in order to provide illumination and guidance to the question that the seer had earlier posed (9:2,22): namely, the meaning of God's promise to Jeremiah that after 70 years of captivity, the king of Babylon would be punished, his land made desolate, and the people of Israel restored to their own land (cf. Jer 25:11-12; 29:10). Moreover, after the prayer is offered, Gabriel states that the divine response explicating the meaning of Jeremiah's prophecy had already been issued 'at the beginning of your supplications' (9:23). It is as if to say that the plan of redemption had been decreed independently of Daniel's supplications for forgiveness.

Because of this contrast, it has been often suggested that the prayer of confession was a secondary editorial addition.[6] Whether or not this is true, the present canonical shape of the passage, as Collins has written, 'neatly highlights a fundamental difference between the apocalyptic view of history and the traditional Deuteronomic theology.'[7]

HISTORY AS REVEALED WISDOM

Daniel was not the only work of post-exilic biblical literature to seek for the meaning of Jeremiah's prophecy.[8] But only in Daniel was the explanation offered to supply 'understanding and wisdom' (9:22) after the seer had pored over the meaning of the prophecy 'in the books' (9:2). Although mysterious, Jeremiah's prophecy must contain a meaning, accessible only to the seer, that could be decoded through what Russell has called 'allegorical arithmetic'.[9]

In the vision itself, Gabriel informs the seer that the 70 years of Jeremiah's prophecy should be understood as '70 weeks of years', that is, 490 years. During this period of 70 heptads, the historical drama would unfold in precisely segmented epochs. The first seven weeks (49 years) would encompass the era 'from the going forth of the word to restore and build Jerusalem to the coming of an anointed one, a prince'. Over the course of the succeeding 62 weeks (434 years) the city would be rebuilt, 'but in a troubled time'. The final week would inaugurate the endtimes, a period of turbulence leading up to the moment when the 'decreed end is poured out on the desolator' and the final restoration takes place.

---

[6] For discussion of this problem, see Lacocque, 'Liturgical Prayer'; also Jones, 'Prayer', and the secondary literature cited there.

[7] Collins, *Apocalyptic Imagination*, 86-87. For discussion of the 'apocalyptic view of history', see Dexinger, *Henochs Zehnwochenapokalypse*, 64-70; Davies, 'Apocalyptic and Historiography'; Hall, *Revealed Histories*, 61-121.

[8] Cf Ezra 1:1; 2 Chron 36:21-23; Zech 1:12-17.

[9] See Russell, *Method and Message*, 195; also, Koch, 'Die mysteriösen Zahlen', 439-41.

Daniel's periodization of Israelite history into year-weeks was, of course, an artificial construct. The 434 years (62 'weeks') that the vision assigns to the period from the accession of Cyrus to the death of Onias III exceed the actual span of time by some 70 years.[10] But the chronology of the vision was not simply an idiosyncratic attempt by the author to update Jeremiah's prophecy. A precedent for reinterpreting the years of Jeremiah's prophecy as 'sabbatical years' had been established already in 2 Chron 36:21. Moreover, overestimates of the chronology of the post-exilic period very similar to Daniel's permeate Hellenistic Jewish chronography. Although it would probably be extreme to suggest that Dan 9:24-27 represents a chronographic 'school', the author appears to be drawing, as Schürer has commented, on 'some current view on the matter'.[11] Like other Jewish apocalyptic seers, Daniel was 'versed in every branch of wisdom' (1:4), of which chronography was one important facet.[12]

THE CURRENT CRISIS AS THE FOREORDAINED CULMINATION OF HISTORY

Although interpreters, both ancient and modern, often disagreed as to the identity of the principal figures of the apocalypse, they recognized that the seer's language demanded chronological and historical specificity on the part of its interpreters. Indeed, its apparent precision proved to be one of its most compelling features. Through his visions, Josephus remarks, Daniel 'not only prophesied future events, as did the other prophets, but ...he also determined the time (καιρὸν ὥριζεν) of their accomplishment'.[13] As a result, much subsequent interpretion of the passage consisted of identifying historically the main actors in Daniel's apocalypse.

While repeated reinterpretation contributed to the blurring of the original Maccabean context, a few ancient writers still managed to grasp the vision's

---

[10] See Schürer, *Geschichte* 3, 267.

[11] ib, ib. Schürer calls particular attention to a fragment from the early third-century Hellenistic Jewish chronographer Demetrius (in Clement, Stromata 1.21.141). From his own time (222 BCE) to the captivity of Israel, Demetrius reckons 573 years (= 795 BCE). Demetrius' chronology exceeds the actual duration of time by a little over 70 years. On the other hand, Beckwith, 'Daniel 9' suggests that the date may be the result of a scribal 'correction', the purpose of which was to ensure that Demetrius' chronology would make the 490 years of Daniel's vision end with the death of Onias. For a critique of Schürer, see also Laato, 'The Seventy Yearweeks', esp 214, 216f.

[12] For discussion of this feature of Daniel in relationship to the other apocalyptic literature, see von Rad, *Old Testament Theology*, 2, 306-308. For discussion of the chronological significance of the 70 weeks, see Grelot, 'Soixante-dix semaines'.

[13] Josephus, Ant. 10.267; unless otherwise noted, all English translations are based on the LCL edition. As Hartman, 'Functions' points out, Dan 9:24-27 is in fact one of the few apocalyptic texts that definitively answers what is supposedly an indispensable feature of apocalyptic literature: the eschatological question 'How Long?'

original intent.[14] One of them, the pagan anti-Christian polemicist Porphyry, recognized that the key to determining the date of the passage was to locate the point at which Daniel was no longer narrating the past, but rather was speaking about the future.[15] For although the backdrop of the vision is the reign of Darius the Mede, certain telltale signs divulged the real historical standpoint of the seer. The crisis of his own age was the one about which he furnished the most detailed information, and it was this crisis that immediately preceded the end times. After that, as D.S. Russell writes, the seer was walking by 'faith, not by sight'.[16]

The immediate crisis that calls forth the vision is Antiochus Epiphanes' ('the coming prince') alliance with Hellenizing Jews and his 'abomination of desolation' against the temple (9:27; cf. 1 Macc 1:54). But although the seer is contemporary with the events described, he abstracts himself from the current crisis through pseudonymity. The use of such a literary device was not simply to inspire confidence in the credibility of the prediction. By projecting his identity into the past, the seer wished to present a view of history that was predetermined and non-contingent. The numerically defined epochs of Daniel 9 are fixed and irrevocable (cf. Dan 9:24 [MT] נֶחְתַּךְ; [Theod.] συνετμήθησαν), and historical figures in Daniel's vision are little more than actors with a necessary role to play in the fulfillment of a divine plan. Since the crisis that inspired Daniel's vision concerned the temple cult, the seer's historical survey of the 70 year-weeks was defined accordingly. Unlike the schematization of history according to the succession of world empires found in the other two historical surveys in Daniel (Dan 2:36-45; 7:1-28), the epochal events of the 70 weeks involve mainly the city, the priesthood and the temple. Thus, the 'anointed prince' of 9:25 whose coming marks the end of the first seven weeks in all likelihood refers to the Zadokite high priest Jeshua, who returned to Jerusalem in the year of Cyrus' edict permitting the rebuilding of the temple. And the 'cutting off of the anointed one' in v26 refers to the death of Onias III, with whom the legitimate sacerdotal succession ceased in 171 BCE.

By showing that the course of history was moving inexorably towards its culmination in the present crisis, after which comes the final restoration, the overall effect of the vision was to endow current events with a broader meaning and a psychological immediacy. It was this feature of the vision that invited constant reinterpretation. No other apocalyptic vision was subject to more historical analysis and reevaluation.

---

[14] See e.g. Julius Hilarianus, Libellus de mundi duratione 14 (PL 13, 1104); Josephus, Ant. 10.276.50.

[15] Excerpt in Jerome's prologue to his Commentary on Daniel (ed Glorie) 771.5-7: 'denique quidquid usque ad Antiochum dixerit ueram historiam continere, siquid autem ultra opinatus sit, quae futura nescierit esse mentitum.'

[16] Russell, *Method and Message*, 198.

The 70 Weeks of Years in Jewish Chronography of the Second Temple Period

THE OLD GREEK RENDERING OF DAN 9:24-27

An early attempt to update the chronology of the 70 year-weeks in the light of the subsequent events of Hasmonean history appears in the Old Greek (OG) translation of Daniel. It is well known that the translation's deviation from 'Hebraica veritas' was at least partly to blame for the early Church's subsequent replacement of it with the version of 'Theodotion'.[17] Although there are many conceivable explanations as to why the OG exercised such seeming latitude in the translation of Dan 9:24-27, one of the motives was to shape the wording to correspond as closely as possible with recent events as the translator(s) understood them.[18]

In the Hebrew version of the passage, 'heptads' uniformly refer to year-weeks. By contrast, the Greek translators use the corresponding Greek term ἑβδομάδη only sporadically. Where they do employ this word, they appear to understand an actual seven-day week.[19] Elsewhere, the translators have abandoned the idea of 'year-weeks' in favor of straightforward reckoning in years, which they render either by the Greek word καιροί or ἔτη. Thus, the OG version of the relevant portion of vv 26 and 27 is the following: '(26a): And after seven and 70 and 62 (καὶ μετὰ ἑπτὰ καὶ ἑβδομήκοντα καὶ ἑξήκοντα δύο; cf. MT: ושנים ששים שבעים ואחרי), an anointing will be taken away and it will not be... (27) And at the completion of times (συντέλειαν καιρῶν), and after seven and 70 periods (καιρούς) and 62 years (ἔτη) up to the time of the completion of the war, the desolation will be taken away in the strengthening of the covenant for many weeks (πολλὰς ἑβδομάδας).'[20] In this highly paraphrastic rendering of the 70 heptads, only 139 years have been assigned to the duration of the city and sanctuary.

---

[17] So Jerome, Commentary on Daniel 1.4.5a (881.818-28). The OG of Daniel survives in only two mss and in the Syrohexapla. The Old Greek is given alongside Theodotion in Ziegler's edition. The designation 'Theodotion' is a somewhat misleading term that conceals the complexity of the development of this version; 'Theodotionic' readings are attested before Theodotion. For discussion of the Greek texts of Daniel, see Grelot, 'Les versions grecques'; Hartman – Di Lella, *The Book of Daniel*, 76-84.

[18] For discussion of the theological interests of the Old Greek text of Dan 9:24-27, see Bludau, *Die alexandrinische Übersetzung*, 104-130; also Swete, *Introduction*, 43f.

[19] Cf 9:24 ἑβδομήκοντα ἑβδομάδες; 9:27 ἐν τῷ τέλει τῆς ἑβδομάδος. That the translators understood the term as an actual week is implied by their version of 9:27, where they render the Hebrew אחד שבוע with the Greek 'πολλὰς ἑβδομάδας'. The translator here has rendered the Hebrew as 'many weeks', because as elsewhere he imagines the weeks as seven-day intervals. At the same time, however, he recognizes that this duration would hardly constitute a satisfactory chronology for the purification of the temple and reconstruction of the city.

[20] For the meaning of καιροί as years, see also Dan 12:7.

[21] Montgomery, *Daniel*, 380.

The 'sad mess' created by the OG translation of the 70 year-weeks may be the result, as Montgomery has suggested, of confusing the Hebrew 'weeks' with the identical word 'seventy'.[21] There is, however, a distinctive historical viewpoint informing this interpretation. Fraidl has offered the plausible suggestion that the chronology of 139 years is reckoned according to the Seleucid era.[22] According to 1 Macc 1:10, Antiochus Epiphanes acceded to power in 137 of this era. From this chronological perspective, the translators' 139 years refer to the period of Seleucid rule preceding Antiochus' inauguration of measures against Jerusalem, the priesthood and the temple cult. One gets a clear sense of the historical vantage point of the translators in their interpretation of the final eschatological year-week. In the Hebrew version, the vision foretells that during the last half of this year-week, there would come an end to Antiochus' sacrilege against the temple. This may be the only part of the vision in which the seer expresses a genuine future hope. But the wording of the OG implies that in the eyes of the translators the final week had already been realized in the temple reforms instituted by Judas – reforms apparently still fresh in their minds.[23]

One of the notable features of the Hebrew text of Daniel's apocalypse of 70 weeks is its absence of a messianic expectation. The 'two anointed ones' in Dan 9:25-26 are simply historical figures in the succession of Jewish high priests, Jeshua and Onias III. The OG translation also takes the minimalist view, perhaps even more so than the Hebrew:

9:24: OG: εὐφρᾶναι ἅγιον ἁγίων
MT: למשח קדש קדשים
9:25: OG: κὰ οἰκοδομήσεις Ιερουσαλημ πόλιν κυρίῳ
MT: ולבנות ירושלם עד משיח נגיד
9:26: OG: ἀποσταθήσεται χρῖσμα καὶ οὐκ ἔσται
MT: יברת משיח ואין לו
9:26b: OG: καὶ βασιλεία ἐθνῶν φθερεῖ τὴν πόλιν καὶ τό ἅγιον μετὰ τοῦ χριστοῦ
MT: והעיר וההקדש ישחית עם נגיד הבא

At v24, the word εὐφρᾶναι in all likelihood translates through metathesis לשמח instead of למשח. The expression ἅγιον ἁγίων is a literal rendering of the Hebrew and could refer either to an individual or the sanctuary.[24] At v25,

---

[22] Fraidl, *Die Exegese*, 6-8. See also Bludau, *Die alexandrinische Übersetzung*, 120-23; Montgomery, *Daniel*, 395. Arguing against this suggestion is Jeansonne, *Old Greek Translation*, 127.

[23] At v27, the Old Greek states that at 'the end of times, and after the 77 periods and 62 years up to the time of the conclusion of the war, the desolation will be taken away in the strengthening of the covenant for many weeks'. Fraidl, *Die Exegese*, 9 suggests that by the word διαθήκη (9:27), the translators understood the agreement that Hasideans concluded with the Hasmonean leadership (cf 1 Macc 2:27-48). For an opposing view, see Jeansonne, *Old Greek Translation*, 129f.

[24] Since the expression appears with εὐφρᾶναι ('to gladden'), Bludau, *Die alexandrinische Übersetzung*, 107 and Fraidl, *Die Exegese*, 6 maintain that ἅγιον ἁγίων must refer to an individual, either Daniel himself or the highpriest. However, the following verse refers to the rebuilding of Jerusalem, and v26 speaks of the destruction of the sanctuary (τὸ ἅγιον).

where the MT has 'an anointed one, a prince', the OG gives simply 'to the Lord'. This contrasts with the later translators, who consistently speak of some future anointed individual.[25] The OG translation of v26 reveals the same 'non-messianic' tendency. Whereas the Hebrew and some of the later versions refer to the cutting off of an 'anointed one', the OG speaks instead only of the removal of 'anointing'. Whether or not this reflects the Hebrew word, מְשֻׁחַ, the translators clearly did not envisage here the removal of a messianic figure, but rather the cessation of a ritual function or office. Verse 27 contains the only clear allusion to the removal of an 'anointed one'. Construing the Hebrew עַם as 'with', the translators render the expression עַם נָגִיד as μετὰ τοῦ χριστοῦ. Presumably, this is in reference to the murder of the high priest Onias III.

In general, it may be said that the lexical choices of the OG reveal an orientation that is historical and retrospective, focusing far more on the cessation and Maccabean restoration of sacerdotal functions than on the coming of the eschatological age or a future 'anointed one'. This perspective is sharply at variance with the later development. As we shall see, Christian commentators had their own reasons for extracting messianic content from the passage. And intensifying apocalyptic fervor, ignited by the turbulent events in Jewish history preceding the destruction of Jerusalem, revitalized the eschatological dimension of the prophecy.

DANIEL 9 IN JEWISH 'APOCALYPTIC CHRONOGRAPHY'

Although chronological and messianic schemes similar to Daniel's 70 year-weeks are pervasive in the Jewish literature of the second temple period, very little survives that is in any way comparable to the fully developed verse-by-verse commentaries on the passage found in later Christian interpreters. The authors of these works rarely quote directly from the relevant passage in Daniel, and the periodization of the 70 weeks typically does not conform to the Daniel-ic pattern of periodization into seven and 62 weeks, plus one. For this reason it is difficult to ascertain whether the use of parallel chronological devices in apocalyptic[26] and sectarian[27] literature implies direct influence from Daniel 9 or

---

[25] See below at n93.

[26] For chronological schemes bearing a possible relationship to Daniel's 70 heptads, see, for example, As. Mos. 10:12, and especially the shepherd-vision of 1 Enoch's animal apocalypse (1 Enoch 89:59-90:25; see also the 70 generations in 1 Enoch 10). Although the shepherd-vision contains certain similarities with Daniel's vision of 70 weeks, it is in all likelihood independent of and possibly earlier than it. Here Enoch has a vision of 70 shepherds symbolizing the 70 angels who are commissioned to rule over Israel for a specific period of time correlated with the number of angels exercising dominion (12 + 23 + 23 + 12). Like Daniel 9, the vision of 70 shepherds is cast in the form of an allegorical historical survey, commencing either with Babylonian or Assyrian domination and culminating with the Maccabean revolt and the advent of the eschatological age. For discussion of apocalyptic use of 70-week schemes, see Fraidl, *Die Exegese*, 11-18, 27-29; Russell, *Method and Message*, 195-202; Beckwith, 'Daniel 9'; Beale, *The Use of Daniel*, 83-85, 310.

[27] In the introduction to the Damascus Document, the author attempts to sanctify his community's

simply independent use of a popular apocalyptic formulation. But it is clear from the testimony of both Josephus and the Jewish chronicle Seder Olam that the process of updating and reinterpreting Daniel's vision of 70 weeks persisted in Judaism up to and even after the destruction of the temple in 70.

Insofar as the periodization of Daniel's 70 heptads was marked by the investiture, succession, and 'cutting off of the anointed', it is to be expected that continuing reassessment of the 70 heptads by Jewish interpreters sometimes focused on a perceived disruption in or pollution of the office of the high priest. One example of this appears in a notoriously cryptic section of the Greek Testament of Levi. After a lurid description of the abasement of the office, the author forecasts 70 weeks during which the priesthood will be profaned. Given its representation as a testament from Levi to his sons, one should not be surprised to find the author attributing his knowledge to the 'writing of Enoch', the latter a popular figure of apocalyptic and scribal authority in Judaism of the time.[28]

It is regrettable that the Qumran Aramaic fragments do not include this portion of the testament. For the Greek recension of the work has been left in a sad state of disrepair by Christian reworking. The author states at 16:1 that he has learned 'that for 70 weeks you shall go astray, and profane the priesthood and pollute the priesthood'. As if to imply that Levi has already detailed the chronology of 70 weeks, the following chapter commences with the words, 'Whereas you have heard concerning the 70 weeks'. But the intervening material, which shows evidence of extensive Christian interpolation, contains no discussion of the 70 weeks chronology. Instead, it mainly epitomizes the polemic against the priesthood in chap. 14 and 15. To add to the confusion, the rest of chap. 17 offers a timetable of the corruptions of the Jerusalem priesthood, based on a garbled and fragmentary sequence of seven (or possibly ten) jubilees

---

history and expected eschatological triumph by weaving into the narrative a chronology probably derived from Ezek 4:4-6 and Dan 9:24-27. The introduction of that document describes how 'in the epoch of wrath', God visited his people '390 years after he had given them into the hands of Nebuchadnezzar and raised up a godly community in their midst'. The work then recounts a period of groping for 20 years until God raised up a 'Teacher of Righteousness to lead them in the way of His heart'. After the teacher's death, another 40 years are to elapse 'until the consuming of all the men of war who returned with the man of falsehood'. The 390 years is apparently based on Ezek 4:4-6, where Ezekiel is instructed to lie on his left side to bear the punishment of Israel. If one estimates the age of the Teacher of Righteousness at death as 40, this would yield a total of 490 years, in conformity with the 70 year weeks of Daniel 9. See Bruce, *Biblical Exegesis*, 59f; Russell, *Method and Message*, 199f; Martens, *Das Buch Daniel*, 84-90; Talmon, *Jewish Civilization*, 254-56; Hahn, 'Josephus und die Eschatologie', 172-75. For the use of schemes similar to the 70 heptads in other Qumran texts, see most recently, Dimant, 'The Seventy Weeks Chronology'; also, Milik, *The Books of Enoch*, 248-58; Beckwith, 'Significance of the Calendar', 167-179; Huggins, 'Book of Periods'.

[28] T. Levi 14:1; 16:1.

whose relationship to the 70 weeks is uncertain.[29] Although the manifest difficulties of the preserved text make it virtually impossible to determine the historical referents or the extent of dependence on Dan 9:24-27, it is clear that the
author of the Testament of Levi found in the chronology of 70 weeks a way to
vent bitter indignation against the transgressions of the Hasmonean high priesthood and to express his expectation of the appearance of a new and purified
messianic priesthood.[30]

Traces of this continuous reapplication of Daniel 9 also survive in Josephus'
several chronological schemes for the chronology and high-priestly succession
of the second temple period. The wide divergence of these systems from one
another has led to a general assumption that Josephus must have gotten them
from different sources. Detailed analysis of these schemes by I. Lévy and later
A. Ehrhardt has shown persuasively that several of these chronological schemes
are vestiges of an early and ongoing tradition of what Lévy calls 'chronologie
apocalyptique' based on the disruption in the succession of the 'anointing' after
the 62 weeks (434 years) of Daniel's vision.[31]

As Ehrhardt suggests, this tradition of reinterpretation of Daniel's prophecy
may explain, for example, Josephus' conflicting chronologies of the succession
of the Jewish high priests after Alcimus.[32] In the 12th book of his Antiquities,
Josephus states that after the death of Alcimus, 'the people gave the high
priesthood to Judas... And (Judas) held the high priesthood for three years when
he died'.[33] In the 13th book, Josephus then records that Jonathan 'put on the
high-priestly robe four years after the death of Judas Maccabeus, this being four
years after the death of his brother Judas--for there had been no high priest
during this time'.[34] As Ehrhardt and others have noted, this tradition contradicts
the succession of the high priests that Josephus records in the 20th book of the
Antiquities. Here Josephus is entirely silent about Judas' term as high priest,
stating instead that after holding the office of high priest for three years, Alci-

---

[29] For various attempts to resolve the textual problems of this section of the Testament of Levi, see
De Jonge, *Testaments*, 40-42; Hultgård, *L'eschatologie* 2, 117-121; Becker, *Untersuchungen*,
283-8; Beckwith, 'Significance of the Calendar', 173-79. The (Ps-) Ezekiel document from Qumran
(4Q384-90) also records a polemic against the high priesthood possibly based on 70 heptads; it
speaks of ten jubilees, subdivided into heptads, during which the sons of Aaron transgressed.

[30] Charles, *APOT* 2, 312 *ad loc* thinks that the composition of this passsage is demonstrably later
than the rest of this section and dates from the years 70-50 BCE. He suggests that the author's
characterization of the priesthood's corruption most closely fits the rule of Alexander Jannaeus. On
the other hand, Milik, *The Books of Enoch*, 252f dates the composition of the original Aramaic form
of the Testament of Levi earlier than the composition of Daniel, to the third or even the end of the
fourth century BCE. See also Bruce, 'Book of Daniel', 230f, and 'Biblical Exegesis', 61f.

[31] Lévy, 'Les soixante-dix semaines'; Ehrhardt, *Apostolic Succession*, 49-53. For analysis of Jo-
sephan chronological systems for the second temple period based on Dan 9:24-27, see also von
Destinon, *Chronologie*, 30f; Hölscher, *Die Quellen des Josephus*, 47, 56, 75ff.; Schürer, *Geschichte*
3, 189.

[32] Ehrhardt ib; Lévy ib.

[33] Josephus, Ant. 12.414, 434.

[34] Ant. 13.46.

mus died without leaving a successor. Only after an interregnum of seven years was Jonathan appointed to that office.[35] The same tradition is reflected in the succession of high priests recorded in 1 Maccabees. Like Josephus, 1 Maccabees records a seven-year interregnum before Jonathan's succession. In this version, Judas was unable to succeed Alcimus to the priesthood, because Alcimus had outlived him.[36]

In Ehrhardt's view, the three years of Alcimus' rule and the seven year interregnum before Jonathan's accession preserve a contemporary interpretation of the Jewish high priesthood devised by Jason of Cyrene and based on Daniel's apocalypse of 70 weeks.[37] The three years of rule that Jason credited to Alcimus were intended to confirm the prediction in Dan 9:27 that 'in the midst of the week, sacrifice and oblation shall cease'. Pursuing an eschatological purpose, this chronology saw the seven-year interregnum between 159 and 152 as the calamitous 70th heptad in Daniel's vision, after which sin would be abolished. For what Ehrhardt calls 'patriotic reasons', this list was subsequently revised to include a three-year priesthood for Judas, thereby reducing the length of Jonathan's term of office from seven to four years.[38] It is this revision that is represented in Josephus' alternate succession list.

Elsewhere, Josephus preserves chronological traditions that may reveal the same influence of Daniel 9. It is well known that Josephus consistently overestimated the duration of the era of the second temple. In the Jewish War, for example, he is about 50 years too high in his calculation of the 589-year period from the rebuilding of the temple to its capture under Vespasian.[39] In the Antiquities, he also miscalculates Aristobulus' accession by about the same number of years, asserting here that Aristobulus began his reign 481 years and three months after the 'people had come home from the Babylonian captivity'.[40] Since Aristobulus I reigned for one year, the author of this chronology must have believed that his successor, Alexander Jannaeus, began his rule 483 years after Cyrus' edict, that is the 62th heptad (7 + 62) of Daniel's vision.

Ehrhardt proposes that this interpretation must have come from Pharisaic opponents of Alexander fairly early in his reign.[41] Vigorously opposed to Jan-

---

[35] Ant. 20.237-238: 'No one succeeded him; and the city continued for seven years without a high priest. Then the descendants of the son of Asamonaios, entrusted with the rulership of the nation... resumed the tradition, appointing as high priest Jonathan, who held office for for seven years.'

[36] 1 Macc 9:54; 10:21. Here it is stated that Alcimus ascended to the priesthood in the 153rd year of the Seleucid era (159 BCE) and died in the year 160 (152 BCE).

[37] Ehrhardt, *Apostolic Succession*, 52.

[38] ib 50. For a different interpretation, see Lévy, 'Les soixante-dix semaines', 167f.

[39] See J.W. 6.270, where he assigns 639 years, 45 days to this period.

[40] Ant. 13.301: 'After their father's death, the eldest son Aristobulus saw fit to transform the government into a kingdom, which he judged the best form, and he was the first to put a diadem on his head, 481 years and three months after the time when the people were released from the Babylonian captivity and returned to their own country.' The actual duration of time was approximately 434 years.

[41] Ehrhardt, *Apostolic Succession*, 53; but cf Lévy, 'Les soixante-dix semaines', 166f.

naeus' rule, they saw his accession to the priesthood and the conversion of his rule into a kingship as portending the beginning of the eschatological woes. As it turned out, Alexander's reign extended much longer than the expected seven years (103-76 BCE). But the failure of the prophecy to be realized did not dampen efforts by others to reapply the chronology to the subsequent history of the Hasmonean priesthood. As will be seen below, Eusebius later reprises two Jewish traditions that saw both in the death of the high priest Alexander Jannaeus and Herod's murder of Hyrcanus the 'cutting off of the anointed one' and the fulfillment of the 69 year-weeks of Daniel's vision.[42]

If we may judge from Josephus' unwitting incorporation of these earlier chronological schemes associated with Daniel 9, the long and developed interpretative history of the apocalypse of 70 weeks represented for him little more than literary relics of a previous tradition. But his guarded use of Daniel 9 in connection with events with which he was more directly familiar suggests a deliberate effort on his part either to invalidate or to suppress a contemporary and competing interpretation of the passage.

Josephus and the Crisis of the Jewish War

JOSEPHUS AND DANIEL'S APOCALYPTIC HOPE

In the Antiquities, Josephus expresses the highest regard for Daniel.[43] What particularly commended him to Jewish readers, he says, were both the chronological precision and the reassuring character of his prophecy. 'Whereas the other prophets foretold disasters and were for that reason in disfavor with kings and people, Daniel was a prophet of good tidings (ἀγαθῶν) to them, so that through the auspiciousness (εὐφημίας) of his predictions, he attracted the good will of all.'[44] The specificity of his predictions and their realization in his own day affirm the role of divine providence in human affairs and dispel the error of the Epicureans.[45]

When Josephus actually describes the 'good tidings' of Daniel's predictions, however, he is conspicuously evasive. An example of this is his narration of Nebuchadnezzar's dream and Daniel's interpretation of it (Dan 2:31-45). In that dream, Nebuchadnezzar saw a stone cut out of a mountain without hands smiting an image of earthenware, iron, bronze, silver and gold. After identifying the gold of the Babylonian reign, the silver of the Median-Persian power, and the bronze of Alexander's reign, Josephus adds: 'And this power will be ended by

---

[42] See below 229-36.
[43] For discussion of Josephus' use of Daniel, see Vermes, 'Josephus' Treatment'; Bruce, 'Josephus and Daniel'.
[44] Ant. 10.268.
[45] Ant. 10.278-80.

still another, like iron, that will have dominion forever (εἰς ἅπαντα) through its iron nature.'[46] But when he comes to the symbolic meaning of the stone that crushes the iron kingdom, Josephus suddenly suspends the narrative: 'Daniel also revealed to the king the meaning of the stone, but I have not thought it proper to relate this, since I am expected to write of what is past and done and not of what is to be.'[47]

There can be little doubt that Josephus knew a more developed interpretation of Daniel 2 and that he deliberately suppressed that part of the explanation that he considered potentially offensive. From the context, it is clear that Josephus understood 'the power that will have dominion' to be Rome. To avoid an affront against his Roman readers, he therefore discreetly neglected the detail about the division of the fourth kingdom and its mixed composition of iron and clay. The symbolic significance of the stone is passed over for much the same reason. In Daniel's explication of Nebuchadnezzar's dream, the stone symbolizes the establishment of God's kingdom, which 'shall beat to pieces and grind to powder all other kingdoms, and it shall stand forever' (2:44). Sensing the obvious political overtones, Josephus carefully avoided any overt reference to an interpretation of Daniel that he knew looked forward to the 'good things' of Daniel's vision: that is, the inauguration of the eternal kingdom of God and the crushing of Rome, the kingdom of iron.[48]

It is a curious fact about Josephus that while he delights in narrating stories about portents and miracles, 'when it comes to expecting concrete extraordinary actions of divine salvation in the present, he was reluctant.'[49] This same reluctance characterizes his approach to Nebuchadnezzar's dream. The reason he proffers for not delving into the future meaning of the dream is that it is not the historian's task to play the role of the seer. 'If, however', he says, 'there is anyone who has so keen a desire for exact information that he will not stop short of inquiring more closely but wishes to learn about the uncertain things that are to come (περὶ τῶν ἀδήλων τί γενήσεται βούλεσθαι μαθεῖν), let him take the trouble to read the Book of Daniel, which he will find among the sacred writings.'[50] The phrase τῶν ἀδήλων conveys a note of much greater uncertainty than Marcus' translation as 'hidden things'. What Josephus wants to stress is the difficulty of decoding Daniel's prognostications.

In underscoring the futility of using Daniel for oracular purposes, we may suspect that Josephus' intention was to dampen the eschatological hope that Daniel offered in the face of Roman occupation. Precisely the same motive

---

[46] Ant. 10.209.

[47] Ant. 10.210.

[48] See Marcus' note *ad loc* in the LCL edition; Vermes, 'Josephus' Treatment', 155, 165; Bruce, 'Josephus and Daniel', 159-60. On the identification of Rome with the kingdom of iron, see Exod. Rab. 35:5.

[49] Hartman, 'Functions', 6.

[50] Ant. 10.210.

underlies Josephus' highly cautious handling of Daniel's apocalypse of 70 weeks. Here too Josephus was troubled by the appeal that anti-Roman Jewish political factions were making to what Josephus considered the 'ambiguous oracle' of Daniel 9.

JOSEPHUS' 'AMBIGUOUS ORACLE'

Josephus' record of events in the Jewish War preceding the destruction of the temple adheres so closely to Daniel's prediction about the pollution of the temple that it is difficult to imagine that his own narrative was not influenced by it.[51] When, for example, the buffoon Phanni ben Samuel was elected as high priest, Josephus expresses bitter astonishment at the impiety of the act, characterizing it as a 'monstrous sacrilege (τὸ τηλικοῦτον ἀσέβημα)'.[52] In Josephus' view, its enormity was compounded by the fact that Ananus the younger, a legitimate candidate for the office, was still alive. With the ill-omened death of Ananus 'the high priest, captain of their salvation (τὸν ἀρχιερέα καὶ ἡγεμόνα τῆς ἰδίας σωτηρίας)', Josephus understood the 'cutting off of the anointed one' of Dan 9:26, that is the disruption and cessation of the sacerdotal succession.[53] This was the prelude to the disastrous course of events culminating with the destruction of the city and the temple.

In the light of the ostensible influence of Daniel 9 in the shaping of his narrative, it is striking that Josephus' actual allusions to the 70-weeks apocalypse in the Jewish War are invariably cast in the vaguest of terms. In one passage, he cites an 'ancient saying of inspired men (τις παλαιὸς λόγος ἀνδρῶν ἐνθέων) that the city would be taken and the sanctuary burnt to the ground by the right of war, whensoever it should be visited by sedition and native hands should be the first to defile God's sacred monuments'.[54] Insofar as the Zealots lent themselves as instruments of the accomplishment of this saying, Josephus suggests that the profanation and destruction of the sanctuary by the Jews themselves was a true sign that the saying was coming to pass. Modern commentators have suggested that Josephus' 'ancient saying' is an allusion to Dan 9:24-27.[55] But if this is true, the reference is highly muted. What is equally notable is Josephus' presentation of the 'ancient saying' in the terms of the Greek oracle. As Louis Feldman has recently noted, Josephus' character-

---

[51] See Bruce, 'Josephus and Daniel', 153-59; Fraidl, *Die Exegese*, 21-23.

[52] J.W. 4.157.

[53] J.W. 4.318: 'I should not be wrong in saying that the capture of the city began with the death of Ananus; and that the overthrow of the wall and the downfall of the Jewish state dated from the day on which the Jews beheld their high priest, the captain of their salvation, butchered in the heart of Jerusalem.'

[54] J.W. 4.388.

[55] Bruce, 'Josephus and Daniel', 155; Fraidl, *Die Exegese*, 21. See also Gaston, *No Stone on Another*, 461f.

ization of this 'ancient saying' corresponds to a kind of Greek oracle which conditioned its fulfillment on the accomplishment of some prior action.[56]

The same tendencies mark Josephus' treatment of Daniel's vision in the sixth book of the Jewish War. Here he refers vaguely to 'the records of the ancient prophets, and the oracle which threatens this poor city, and is even now come true. For they foretold that it would be taken whensoever one should begin to slaughter his own countryman. And is not the city and the whole temple filled with your corpses?'[57] Shortly thereafter, Josephus speaks again of an oracle that spoke darkly of events coming to pass in his own age. The single thing, he says, that incited the Jews to war against Rome was an erroneous interpretation of an 'ambiguous oracle announcing that at that time a man from their country would become ruler of the world'. While acknowledging that the view propagated by 'many of their scholars' favored an identification of the 'coming prince' with someone of their own race, Josephus was certain that they had gone astray. The coming prince 'in reality signified the sovereignty of Vespasian, who was proclaimed Emperor on Jewish soil'. As Bruce has pointed out, the ruler 'at that time' appears to refer to the expected advent of the 'coming prince' in Dan 9:26.[58]

These allusions to Daniel are assuredly oblique, probably intentionally so. Readers nonetheless would have readily understood from Josephus' characterization the disastrous consequences for those who presumed to find in these oracles solace for their false hopes. In the years that elapsed between the composition of the War and the Antiquities, Josephus seems to have moderated his views about Daniel's vision. But his position about the oracular uses of Daniel 9 remained essentially unchanged.

Bowing to the older interpretation of Dan 9:24-27 and 12:11-13, Josephus acknowledges in the Antiquities that Daniel's predictions about a war against the Jewish nation and the despoiling of the temple for three years had already been realized in the time of Antiochus Epiphanes. 'These misfortunes', he says, 'our nation did in fact come to experience under Antiochus Epiphanes, just as Daniel many years before saw and wrote that they would happen.' He insists, however, that Daniel's foretelling of the destruction of the city and the sanctuary were not entirely fulfilled until the fall of Jerusalem to the Romans.[59]

But despite his earlier assurance that Daniel surpassed the other prophets in

---

[56] Feldman, 'Prophets and Prophecy', 414f. The parallel that Feldman mentions is the oracle that told Agamemnon that Troy would be taken when the Achaeans would quarrel.

[57] J.W. 6.109-110.

[58] J.W. 6.312-13. See Bruce, 'Josephus and Daniel', 155. Bruce also suggests that when Josephus states in J.W. 6.311 that 'the Jews reduced the temple to a square, although they had it recorded that the city and the sanctuary would be taken when the temple should be four-square', he may have been thinking of Dan 9:25: 'It shall be built with square and water-channel.' See also Hahn, 'Josephus és a Bellum Judaicum'; id, 'Josephus und die Eschatologie', 170-72, 176-78; Strobel, *Ursprung*, 417; Str-B 4/2, 998.

[59] Cf Ant. 10.276.

chronological exactitude, Josephus fails to demonstrate how Daniel's 70 weeks terminated with the Roman conquest.[60] In his narration of the fulfillment of Daniel's vision in his day, Josephus speaks only of the calamities that befell the Jews: the destruction of the temple and the city of Jerusalem. Since Josephus conveniently omits the destruction of the desolator foretold in v27, readers not familiar with Daniel 9 might even have inferred from him that Daniel foretold the triumph of Rome. One is also struck by his cryptic paraphrase of relevant portions of the vision. In an apparent allusion to Dan 9:26, he states: 'In the same manner, Daniel also wrote about the empire of the Romans and that it (?) would be laid waste (ἐρημωθήσεται) by them (?).'[61] An excerpt from John Chrysostom has imposed some clarity on the text by inserting the phrase: 'Jerusalem would be taken by them and the temple laid waste.'[62] But without this explanatory gloss, the antecedent of ἐρημωθήσεται is unclear. The passage, Delphic in its double-edged ambiguity, could also be read to mean that Rome would be laid waste by the Jews.[63] As in the case of the vision of the stone from a mountain, we must suppose that Josephus was presenting here a truncated and sanitized version of what must have been a far more optimistic reading of Daniel's apocalypse of 70 weeks.

The events of 70 thus served to widen deep fault lines in the Jewish interpretation of Daniel 9. With the impending fall of the city and the temple, apocalyptic Judaism, fueled by anti-Roman sentiment, was certain that the catastrophes wrought by Rome were only a prelude to the 'good things to come'. Josephus was willing to acknowledge that the destruction of the temple and the city were clear and objectifiable vindications of Daniel's prophetic insight. But Daniel's accuracy could be rationally tested only with the benefit of historical hindsight. Anticipating the 'good tidings' of this ambiguous vision was outside the pale.

Although the delay of the messianic age after 70 may have strengthened Josephus' position for a time, the Bar Kochba revolt at least momentarily incited another round of feverish speculation about the imminent fulfillment of the 70 weeks.[64] At the same time, however, the two catastrophes must have abetted the kind of warning against such speculation that we find attributed to Rabbi Eliezer ben Hyrcanus. Israel's repentance, he says, not a fixed apoc-

---

[60] This is particularly striking since Dan 9:24-27 is the only one of Daniel's predictions that would allow for the chronological precision that Josephus praises as the hallmark of Daniel's prophecy. In other predictions, Daniel speaks of periods of time leading up to the end (7:25, 8:14, 9:27, 12:11), without specifying a *terminus a quo*.

[61] Ant. 10.276.

[62] See Marcus' note to Ant. 10.276 in the LCL translation.

[63] See Montgomery, *Daniel*, 396f; Braverman, *Jerome's Commentary*, 110.

[64] Thus, Jerome refers to one line of Jewish exegesis that attempted to update the 70-weeks chronology to include the final destruction of Jerusalem by Hadrian; see his Commentary on Daniel 3.9.24. For post-70 Jewish use of Daniel 9, see Beckwith, 'Daniel 9', 529-39; Gaston, *No Stone on Another*, 462-64; Str-B 4/2, 1006-1011.

alyptic plan, is the precondition for the final redemption.[65] The interpretation of Daniel 9 found in the second-century rabbinic chronicle Seder Olam reinforced the latter opinion. It retains as a kind of chronological artifact the *terminus ad quem* of the 490 years as the destruction of the temple, but without, it would seem, suggesting anything about the messianic age to follow.[66]

The '70 Weeks' in Christian Exegesis

EARLY TREATMENT OF THE PROPHECY

Unlike the great volume of commentary later produced on these verses, the first two centuries witnessed comparatively little attested Christian interest in the vision of 70 weeks. The handful of writers who do comment on the passage make little effort to fix the 70 weeks chronologically. And their interpretation is governed either by allegory or eschatology. Thus, Irenaeus, one of the few writers to comment on v27, discerned a connection between Paul's 'man of lawlessness' (2 Thess 2:3-4) and the 3 1/2 years of the desolation of Jerusalem by the 'desolator' of Dan 9:27.[67] But from the end of the second century, there emerges an opposing view that was inclined to see the events of v27 as having already been accomplished in Christ's ministry and the subsequent calamities that afflicted the Jewish people.

The roots of this historicizing approach to Daniel's vision of 70 weeks are already visible in the treatment of the 'desolating sacrilege' in the synoptic apocalypse of Mark and its later redactions. In the Markan form of the tradition, Jesus warns that when 'you see the desolating sacrilege (τὸ βδέλυγμα τῆς ἐρημώσεως; see Dan 9:27; 12:11) standing (ἑστηκότα) where it ought not – let him who reads understand – then let those who are in Judea flee to the mountains' (13:14).[68] It has been suggested that the literary prototype from which Mark fashioned this discourse was a Jewish apocalypse of around the year 40. The precipitating crisis that ignited eschatological expectation was the emperor Caligula's attempt to erect a statue of himself in the Jerusalem temple – for the Jewish apocalyticist a sure sign of the imminent end.[69] In the process

---

[65] b. Sanh. 97a-97b.

[66] For discussion of the chronology of Seder Olam, see Montgomery, *Daniel*, 397; Fraidl, *Die Exegese*, 122-124.

[67] Irenaeus, Against Heresies 5.25.4 For the relationship of 2 Thess 2:3-4 to Dan 9:27, see Montgomery, *Daniel*, 396. Another possible reference to the vision is Barn. 16:6, which interprets v27 as an allegory of the spiritual temple.

[68] See also Matt 24:15, which makes the Danielic origin of the image explicit.54

[69] For Mark's possible use of an older Jewish apocalypse, see Vielhauer-Strecker, 'Apocalyptic in Early Christianity', 581. One piece of evidence commonly adduced in favor of the identification of the desolating sacrilege with Caligula is Mark's ungrammatical use of a masculine participial form (ἑστηκότα) to modify the neuter noun βδέλυγμα.

of reorienting this material for a post-70 perspective, the evangelist has imbued it with a different understanding. Although the sacrilege against the temple still represents one of several critical stages in the eschatological plan, the destruction of the temple is for Mark already a thing of the past, and hence no longer an immediate prelude to the parousia. Indeed, the discourse concludes with an explicit warning against exact prognostications (13:32).[70] Luke takes this process one step farther. In place of Mark's vivid apocalyptic imagery of a 'desolating sacrilege', Luke 21:9 substitutes a factual and retrospective account of 'Jerusalem surrounded by armies', its inhabitants 'fallen by the edge of the sword' – for Luke, events already past. Moreover, it forms part of a polemical discourse by Jesus about events 'which must first take place', but after which 'the end will not follow immediately'. In this way, as Conzelmann has noted, Lukan eschatology is 'lifted out of any historical context, and is removed from all events which take place within history'.[71]

HISTORICIZING INTERPRETATIONS OF DANIEL 9
AFTER THE FIRST CENTURY

As will be seen below, the Theodotionic version of Daniel that came to be favored in the early Church partly contributed to the increasing popularity of the retrospective messianic/historical treatment of Daniel 9.[72] The other reason for the reorientation had to do with dissatisfaction with future-oriented interpretations of Daniel 9. Jerome typifies the outlook of many later interpreters when he insists that the chronological specificity of the passage demanded a degree of precision that could not tolerate ahistorical readings of the text, whether allegorical or eschatological. Normally a voluble allegorist, Origen, he writes, could find very little to say about Daniel 9 because he was frustrated by its unavoidable historical and chronological content. 'He had no leeway for allegorical interpretation, in which one may argue without constraint, but rather was restricted to matters of historical fact.'[73] Jerome applies a similar criticism to Apollinarius' future apocalyptic orientation to the text. In choosing to commence the 490 years from the birth of Christ, Apollinarius had determined that the rebuilding of the temple would occur in the year 482, to be succeeded by

---

[70] On this subject, see most recently U. Müller, 'Apocalyptic Currents', 297-306.

[71] Conzelmann, *Theology of St. Luke*, 128; cf 134. Dodd, 'The Fall of Jerusalem' has maintained, however, that we need not assume that Luke was editing Mark to conform to the fall of Jerusalem in 70. Luke's account of the capture of the city could have been fashioned entirely from biblical models, and not recent historical events as he knew them. Dodd suggests that the prototype for Luke's account of Jerusalem's destruction was not Antiochus' defilement of the temple, but rather Nebuchadnezzar's sack of Jerusalem. See also Hartman, *Prophecy Interpreted*, 230f; Daube, *New Testament*, 418-37.

[72] See below 223f.

[73] Jerome, Commentary on Daniel 3.9.24 (880.475-79), tr Archer.

the cataclysmic events of the final week. For Apollinarius, the 70 weeks were sequential and uninterrupted, and the final eschatological week thus could not be chronologically dissociated from the preceding 69. As Jerome saw it, such an approach risked transforming interpreters into seers. 'By breaking away from the stream of the past and directing his longing towards the future', Jerome complains, Apollinarius 'very unsafely ventured an opinion concerning matters so obscure. If by any chance those of future generations should not see these predictions of his fulfilled at the time he set, then they will be forced to seek for some other solution and to convict the teacher himself of erroneous interpretation.'[74]

It is true that in the third and the fourth centuries the eschatological/teleological and the messianic/historical interpretations continued to coexist, however uneasily.[75] The resultant interpretations, too numerous to describe here, were so contradictory that in his summary of them Jerome mainly restated the conflicting positions, leaving it to the 'reader's judgment as to whose explanation ought to be followed'.[76] Occasionally a single writer might be found espousing diverging positions. In Against Celsus, Origen, for example, unexpectedly reprises the older eschatological interpretation first espoused by Irenaeus, linking the Antichrist to Dan 9:27. By contrast, in his Commentary on Matthew, he proposes that the heptads of the prophecy should be taken as units of 70 years each and that its chronology encompassed the 4900 years from the creation of Adam up until the end of the first century and the close of the apostolic period.[77]

Even commentators who did not actively endorse the eschatological interpretation of Daniel 9 still managed to absorb and domesticate earlier exegetical traditions. As Strobel has suggested, a deeply held belief in early Christian apocalypticism understood the eschatological 70th week as the 70 years of the church between Christ's ascension and his expected return.[78] This expectation, which evidently influenced the dating of the close of the apostolic period in around the year 100, did receive partial confirmation from the events occurring in Judea in the year 70. But the failure of the prophecy fully to be consummated required constant reinterpretation of the pertinent passages.[79] Vestiges of the tradition survive into the fourth century, now all but purged of their future eschatological content. Although Eusebius, no friend of Christian chiliasm, ac-

---

[74] Jerome, Commentary on Daniel 3.9.24 (878.422-27). See also Augustine, Epistle 197 (ed Goldbacher, CSEL 57). In this epistle, Augustine warns Hesychius against attempting to refer the 70 weeks to Christ's second coming on the grounds that Christ himself cautioned against making exact eschatological predictions.

[75] For discussion, see Strobel, Ursprung, 421.

[76] Jerome, Commentary on Daniel 3.9.24a (865.140-43). Jerome does, however, occasionally offer criticisms of the various interpretations that he presents.

[77] Origen, Against Celsus 6.46 (669); Commentary on Matthew, ser. 40 (ed Klostermann, GCS 38²) 80.15-18 (on Matt 24:15-18).

[78] Strobel, Ursprung, 420.

[79] ib 420f.

knowledges the existence of this interpretation in his Eclogae Propheticae, in
the highly denatured version of the tradition that he reports, the 70 years represented by the last week of Daniel's prophecy are only a chapter in the history of
the Church: the apostolic period culminating with the death of John. Viewed
retrospectively, the events that occurred during that time – Vespasian's siege of
Jerusalem and the destruction of the temple – constitute for Eusebius convincing proof of the fulfillment of Daniel's prophecy. But these are events of the
distant past, which if anything only serve to dampen eschatological expectation.[80]

Another popular compromise position was to defer the final eschatological
week to some time in the future. Hippolytus, whose interpretation of Dan 9:27
was probably influenced by Irenaeus', refined the tradition by referring Daniel's segmentation of the week to the period of Elijah and Enoch, and the
period of Antichrist. But this week was not continuous with the first 69. When
Daniel 'spoke of the one week', Hippolytus writes, 'he was referring to the last
week at the culmination of the whole universe (ἐπὶ τῷ τέρματι τοῦ σύμπαν-
τος κόσμου) that will come in the end times'.[81] 'After the 62 weeks have been
completed and Christ has arrived, and the gospel has been proclaimed everywhere, and when the times have been depleted, one week, the last week, will be
left. In that week, Elijah and Enoch will appear, and in the middle of the week,
there will appear the "abomination of the desolation", the Antichrist who
proclaims destruction to the universe. With his arrival, offering and oblation
will be taken away, which is now offered everywhere by the nations to God.'[82]

A predictable outcome of the Christological/historical perspective that came
to dominate Christian intepretation from the third century was the intensifica-
tion of conflict with the prevailing non-messianic exegesis of these verses in
post-70 Judaism. Indeed, much of the commentary on Dan 9:24-27 is marked
by its polemic anti-Jewish flavor. Jerome, on uncertain authority, goes so far as
to suggest that the interpretation of Dan 9:26 by the Jews of his time was
guided by anti-Christian animus. While allowing that the death of the 'anointed
one' predicted in v26 may have referred to Christ, the 'Hebrews', he says, took
the words ול ןיאו to mean that 'the kingdom of the Jews will not be his'.[83] In

---

[80] Eusebius, Eclogae Propheticae 3 (PG 23.1189-91): 'I know another interpretation offered to
explain the week "that confirms the covenant for many". This tradition takes this week for a week
divided into ten parts and demonstrates that the entire period of the apostles lasted for 70 years.
During that time, the proclamation of the New Testament was no longer confirmed for one nation,
but for many nations over the whole earth. Indeed, the historical records demonstrate that John, the
disciple of Christ, lived for another 70 years after Christ's ascension.'

[81] On the Antichrist 43 (ed Achelis).

[82] Commentary on Daniel 4.35 (ed Bonwetsch-Achelis). Hippolytus understands Elijah and Enoch
as the two witnesses of Rev 11:3 who have authority to prophesy for 1260 days. See also (Ps-)
Cyprian, De pascha computus 14 (ed Hartel).

[83] Jerome, Commentary on Daniel 3.9.24 (887.579-83). For discussion, see J. Braverman, Jerome's
Commentary, 103-112.

opposing the manifest messianic meaning of Daniel 9, Eusebius states, the Jews willfully misrepresented these verses by insisting that the events forecast in the prophecy had not yet been realized. For Eusebius, the aftermath of Jesus' ministry and the desperate conditions of the Jews prove that they could no longer look to the future for the completion of the prophecy; everything in it had already been fulfilled.[84]

The other consequence of this transformation affected the practical function of the prophecy. It is clear from the history of Jewish and Christian interpretation of Daniel 9 that part of its psychological impact was in promising some immediate resolution of and hence emotional relief from a current crisis. But once it was established that the outcome of the prophecy was known and realized in the epochal events of the first centuries, its value as consolation in a current crisis was blunted.

This change in attitude lay behind a gradual change in Christian exegesis from the beginning of the third century. To be sure, vestiges of the eschatological hope remain. In his commentary on Daniel, Judas could still find in Daniel's vision a solution to the persecutions of his own day. But his interpretation of Daniel 9 stands out as a rare attempt to tie a contemporary crisis to the culminating last week of the prophecy. Indeed, with his dismissive psychologizing explanation of Judas' efforts, Eusebius later almost seems to take pleasure in deflating this way of approaching the passage.[85] In the light of this, it is not surprising that the passage often turns up in literature quite removed from its original apocalyptic genre. As we shall see, Eusebius treats Daniel 9 in a variety of historical/apologetic works, and Clement cites the passage to prove a familiar, but non-apocalyptic article of Christian polemic: the newness of the Greeks.[86] At the same time, exegesis of the passage becomes for the most part the province of historians and chronographers. Valuing the passage mainly as a source of objective chronological and historical information about the past, their exposition sometimes tends to an almost compulsive over-refinement.

A good illustration of this appears in the historical writing of the Christian polymath Julius Africanus. In his chronicle, Africanus refers to an entire treatise that he devoted to the passage, entitled 'On the Weeks and this Prophecy (περὶ ἑβδομάδων καὶ τῆσδε τῆς προφητείας)'.[87] Although the work is not

---

[84] 'Though we are now nearly a thousand years from the date of the prophecy, they admit no sign of the fulfillment of what was written, although the Unction has been abolished... and their sanctuary and the former inhabitants destroyed and utterly brought to naught in the flood of the completed war, and strangest thing of all even now to be seen, I mean, the abomination of desolation still standing in the one holy place, concerning which our Lord and Savior said what I have quoted' (Demonstratio evangelica 8.2.127, ed Heikel). Unless otherwise specified, the translation of Eusebius' Demonstratio is from Ferrar, *The Proof of the Gospel*.

[85] See above p201.

[86] See below 224-6, 227-36.

[87] Quoted in George Syncellus, 393.23-24 (ed Mosshammer). Although there is no way to know for certain, it is possible that Africanus' work on Daniel 9 is the same as the 'opuscula Africani' proscribed as 'apocrypha' in the decree of (Ps-) Gelasius 7.4 (ed von Dobschütz) 12 (l. 310).

preserved, we can infer from the surviving fragments of Africanus' universal chronicle that Dan 9:24-27 was a subject of consuming interest to him.[88] What is most notable about Africanus' exposition of these verses is that although his chronicle was predicated on millennialist principles, he gives scant attention to the future eschatological dimension of the vision.[89] Yes, he says, the final week might have been intended to be dissociated chronologically from the preceding 69. But he offers this only as an afterthought, in order to explain why it is that nearly 200 years after Christ's death 'nothing out of the ordinary has been recorded in the interim (οὐδὲν ἐν μέσῳ παράδοξον ἱστόρηται)'.[90]

The interpretation that Africanus prefers and to which he devotes the most analysis is to find the fulfillment of the passage entirely in the person of Christ. Even apart from chronology, the contents of Daniel's promise alone, he says, are sufficient to establish its self-evident messianic significance. Before Christ's advent, Africanus writes, the words of the prophecy existed in expectation only. But 'at the time of the Saviour, or after him, sins are done away and transgressions ended; and by this remission of sins iniquities are blotted out by a propitiation together with unrighteousness, eternal righteousness is published beyond that of the law, visions and prophecies (last) until John, and the Holy of Holies is anointed'. Any explanation of Daniel's 70-weeks chronology must, therefore, presuppose the unmistakable messianic thrust of the verses. The only *terminus a quo* that for Africanus would, with some manipulation, assure the desired chronological result is the date of Artaxerxes' order to Nehemiah to rebuild the city.[91] Any other starting point – for example, the date of Cyrus' edict or the angel's proclamation to Daniel – must be ruled out as producing chronological absurdities.

---

[88] Excerpts from his treatment of Dan 9:24-27 are preserved in Syncellus, 391.22-393.24. See also Eusebius, Demonstratio evangelica 8.2.46-54; Eclogae Propheticae 3.46 (PG 22.1176-80); Jerome, Commentary on Daniel 3.9.24 (865.145-869.223).

[89] Africanus' chronicle presupposed the Jewish/Christian belief that the world would run its course in 6000 years. He dated Christ's birth in the middle of the sixth millennium. For discussion, see Gelzer, *Sextus Julius Africanus* 1, 24-26.

[90] Syncellus, 393.4-5. Apollinarius must have picked up on this suggestion when he states that Africanus treated the final week as a future eschatological week (in Jerome, Commentary on Daniel 3.9.24 [880.460]).

[91] Africanus actually calculates only 475 years from the 20th year of Artaxerxes until Christ's advent. To explain the remaining 15 years, he proposes that the 490 years are lunar years, which if converted to solar years would come to 475 (in Syncellus, 392.7-17).

The χριστὸς ἡγούμενος and the Adaptation of a Jewish Exegetical Tradition

THE THEODOTIONIC RENDERING OF DAN 9:25

In tracing the chronology of the 70 year-weeks from the time of Artaxerxes, Africanus, like the majority of Christian exegetes, entirely ignored its period-ization into seven and 62 weeks. Although Eusebius would later rebuke Africa-nus for his disregard of the chronological divisions, he was at least partially justified by the version of Daniel that Africanus and most other Greek com-mentators knew and cited: Theodotion.

In the Masoretic version of Dan 9:25, the events predicted to occur at the end of the first seven weeks – the restoration and rebuilding of Jerusalem, and the coming of the משיח נגיד were clearly distinguished from the 'cutting off of the anointed one' after 62 weeks (v26). By delimiting the first seven weeks from the subsequent 62, the Masoretic version thereby discouraged a single mess-ianic interpretation of the verses. By contrast, Theodotion's translation, the one almost universally used in the Greek-speaking Church, encouraged a rather different understanding: 'From the going forth of the commandment until Christ the prince, there shall be seven weeks and 62 weeks.'[92] In blurring the chronological demarcation between the first seven weeks and the ensuing 62 weeks, his translation enabled the seven weeks of v25 to be construed together with the subsequent 62.

The impact of this rendering on Christian exegesis was profound. It offered chronographers an additional 49 years to fill up the interim period between the 'going forth of the word' and Christ's advent. At the same time, it allowed interpreters to impose a single messianic interpretation on the χριστὸς ἡγού-μενος of v25 and the events of v26. Neither the Vulgate nor the Syriac text, nor the other Greek versions did much to dispel the impression. To the contrary, their renderings, even more than Theodotion, encouraged interpreters to assume that the 69 weeks formed a single block of time and that vv 25 and 26 referred to the same 'anointed one'.[93] As a result, Christian interpreters only rarely saw the implications of sharply distinguishing, as the Hebrew text did, between the two periods.

There are a few exceptional cases, however, in which the exposition of Dan

---

[92] Against this, cf Dan 9:26 (MT): 'From the time that the word went out to restore and rebuild Jerusalem until the time of an anointed prince, there shall be seven weeks; and... after the 62 weeks, an anointed one shall be cut off and shall have nothing.'

[93] For קדש קדשים (v. 24), ἡγιασμένον ἡγιασμένων (Aquila); 'Messiah, the holy of holies' (Syriac). For עד משיח נגיד (v25), 'to the coming of Messiah-King' (syriac); 'ad Christum ducem' (Vulgate). For יכרת משיח (v26), 'the Messiah will be killed' (Syriac); 'occidetur Christum' (Vul-gate). Jerome also followed Theodotion in treating the seven and 62 weeks as a single period. For discussion, see Montgomery, *Daniel*, 375f, 399.

9:25-26 by Christian expositors presupposes the version found in the Masoretic punctuation of the text.[94] The significance of this minority tradition is that by dissociating the 'χριστὸς ἡγούμενος' of v25 from the anointing described in v26, its adherents deviated from the dominant Christological interpretation of Dan 9:25-26. Moreover, the periodization into seven and 62 heptads produced a chronology falling far short of the chronology required by their own Christological interpretation of this passage. What is equally notable is that the earliest and best-known exponents of this interpretation – Clement, Hippolytus and Eusebius – had at most a superficial familiarity with Hebrew and do not reveal any direct familiarity with the Hebrew version of Daniel reflected in the Masoretic tradition. Like the majority of early Christian commentaries, they continue to cite the popularly used Theodotionic form of Daniel, even though their interpretation departs from it. The tradition that they represent is thus worth examining at some length, insofar as it points to a partially submerged Jewish tradition of interpretation that survived in a Christianized form well into the third and the fourth centuries.

CLEMENT'S STROMATA

The earliest attested appearance of this interpretation is the first book of the Stromata of Clement of Alexandria. In this section of the Stromata, Clement is concerned not with messianic or eschatological matters, but rather with a commonplace of Christian apologetic writing: chronological proof for the antiquity of the Jews and the late and derivative character of Greek civilization. In the midst of an extended discussion of Jewish chronology and history, Clement cites the Theodotionic version of Dan 9:24-27 for the purpose of establishing a chronology of Jewish history from the Babylonian captivity.[95]

As the *terminus ad quem* of the first seven heptads of the prophecy, Clement must have assumed the completion of the second temple. For he asserts that the fulfillment of the 49 years coincided with the rebuilding of the temple (ὁ ναός), even though the text of Dan 9:25 that he cites speaks only of the restoration of the city after seven weeks. Confirmation for this chronology, he says, is found in the Book of Ezra. Since this latter work speaks expressly of the completion of the temple during the reign of Darius, the 49 years of the prophecy represent for him the period from Cyrus' restoration of the Jews up to the sixth year of Darius' reign.[96] The *terminus ad quem* of the 62 weeks of 'calm' is the coming

---

[94] For a discussion see Beckwith, 'Daniel 9', 540f; Montgomery ib 379f.

[95] Clement, Stromata 1.21.125.1-6 (ed, tr Mondésert-Caster). The variants of Clement's text of Dan 9:24-27 from Theodotion are mostly minor. However, at v27, Clement gives a double reading.

[96] Cf Ezra 6:15. Since Clement assigns 30 years to Cyrus and 19 years to Cambyses, Fraidl, *Die Exegese*, 32 suggests that the *terminus ad quem* of the 49 years is actually the second year of the reign of Darius, at which time the laying of the foundations of the temple commenced (cf Ezra 3:8).

of Christ in the flesh, followed by the final week, encompassing Nero's erection of an 'abomination' in Jerusalem and Vespasian's destruction of the temple.[97]

Clement's original chronology, as Fraidl has noted, inaugurates a new stage in Christian exegesis of Daniel 9.[98] If Clement held out some eschatological hope for the future completion of the 70 weeks, he says nothing here about it. His orientation to the passage is strictly historical. Moreover, by establishing a chronology of the 70 weeks that comprehended both Christ's advent as well as the destruction of the temple, he is the first to posit what becomes conventional in later interpretations: a presumed hiatus between the first 69 weeks, and the final week.

Perhaps most significant is his interpretation of the 'messianic' content of the vision. Like most Christian commentators, Clement understands the 'holy of holies' of v24 as foreshadowing Christ. However, he makes the beginning of the reign of the 'anointed one, a prince' contemporary with the rebuilding of the temple after seven weeks. After this 'all of Judea was at peace, and free from warfare' for 62 weeks. In casting the χριστὸς ἡγούμενος of Dan 9:25 as a figure distinct from the anointed one expected after the ensuing 62 weeks, Clement's interpretation of v25 presupposes the Masoretic syntax of the verse.[99] While not expressly identifying the χριστὸς ἡγούνενος, it is antecedently likely that Clement had in mind Jeshua, the first of the post-exilic high priests. The context of the passage suggests as much, and later representatives of the same exegetical tradition explicitly identify the χριστὸς ἡγούμενος with either Jeshua or the whole succession of the post-exilic Jewish high priesthood.[100]

Beckwith has maintained that, since Clement was probably unable to consult the Hebrew himself, his non-messianic interpretation of v25 was suggested to him by his Jewish contemporaries in Alexandria. In Beckwith's opinion, the period after the Bar Kochba revolt saw a disillusioned Judaism reacting to recent events by promoting a non-messianic interpretation of Dan 9:25. Reflected in the Masoretic version of this passage, this interpretation envisaged two chronologically distinct anointed ones. Although Clement's Christianized version of the prophecy was messianic in its overall perspective, Beckwith suggests that for some reason he was willing to accept this Jewish identification of the anointed one of v25 as a figure distinct from the anointed one of v26.[101]

It is more probable, however, that this section of the Stromata, conspicuously different in character from the rest of the material in the same chapter, was adapted from an earlier source. The detailed exegetical treatment of Daniel 9 is

---

[97] Stromata 1.21.126.3. Clement does not describe what Nero's abomination was.
[98] Fraidl, *Die Exegese*, 30.
[99] Stromata 1.21.126.1. See Fraidl ib 34.
[100] See below 228f.
[101] Beckwith, 'Daniel 9', 541. Beckwith suggests that this Jewish interpretation understood the anointed one of v25 as Jeshua the son of Jozadak; the cutting off of the anointed one in v26 was a priestly figure of the first century, either Ananus or Phanni.

irrelevant to the strictly chronological interests of this chapter. Moreover, the abbreviated chronology of Persian and Hellenistic history assumed by this interpretation entirely undermines the chronology of this period that Clement hopes to establish in the rest of the chapter.[102] Adolf Schlatter, who has called attention to the Jewish-Christian character of the source, traces the source to a fragmentarily preserved Jewish-Christian chronicle composed in the tenth year of Antoninus Pius.[103] Although his identification of the author as Judas, the last Jewish-Christian bishop of Jerusalem, is highly conjectural, it is clear that Clement's interpretation shows the unmistakable imprint of a Jewish exegetical tradition that exerted continued subsequent influence on Hippolytus and Eusebius.

HIPPOLYTUS' SEGMENTATION OF THE 70 YEAR-WEEKS

Shortly after the appearance of the Stromata, Hippolytus the Christian chronicler and commentator championed a similar interpretation of the apocalypse of weeks in his fragmentarily preserved commentary on Daniel. Even while citing Theodotionic Daniel, Hippolytus, like Clement before him, strictly divided the first seven weeks from the following 62 (διεῖλεν αὐτὰς εἰς δύο). Reasoning that Daniel must have experienced the vision in the 21st year of the captivity, Hippolytus then construes the 49 years as the time remaining to complete the 70 years of captivity spoken of by Jeremiah. As Hippolytus recognizes, this chronology required a non-messianic identification of the χριστὸς ἡγούμενος of v25. 'Until the anointed one, the prince', Hippolytus writes, 'shall be seven weeks, which makes 49 years... Now of what "anointed one" does he speak, other than Jeshua son of Jozadak, who returned with his people, and in the 70th year with the rebuilding of the temple brought an offering according to the Law?' Evidently dissatisfied with his own non-messianic reading of v25, Hippolytus then attempts to Christianize the χριστὸς ἡγούμενος by casting Jeshua as a prefigurement of Jesus, the perfect Messiah and high priest.[104] Here one

---

[102] A point grasped by Jerome, Commentary on Daniel 3.9.24 (880.465-74). From Cyrus to the end of the Macedonian period, Clement reckons 547 years.

[103] Schlatter, Chronograph, 1-14. What Schlatter believes (5-6) mark the source as 'Jewish-Christian' are the formulas of scriptural citation, e.g. πεπλήρωται τὰ ὑπὸ Δανιήλ; καθὼς εἶπεν ὁ προφήτης. At Stromata 1.21.126.1, the Greek text reads: καὶ οὕτως ἐγένετο χριστὸς βασιλεὺς Ἰουδαίων ἡγούμενος. The words βασιλεὺς Ἰουδαίων are ungrammatical and missing in the Theodotionic text of the prophecy. Schlatter (4) believes these words are a gloss either by Clement or a later scribe. The translation of the passage in ANF 2, 329 is certainly misleading: 'and thus Christ became king of the Jews'.

[104] Hippolytus, Commentary on Daniel 4.30 (266.5-14, ed Bonwetsch-Achelis). The messianic typology of Jeshua-Jesus may also have been encouraged by the post-exilic association of Jeshua with the coming of the messianic age. In Zech 3:5-10, the prophet has a vision of the high-priest Jeshua standing before the angel of God. After rebuking Satan for accusing Jeshua, the Lord gives Jeshua authority over the temple and pledges that the messianic age is drawing near.

may assume that Hippolytus, like Clement before him, has drawn upon an older Jewish exegetical tradition about the χριστὸς ἡγούμενος, infusing it through typology with messianic content.

From the fragments of his commentary that survive, it is difficult to ascertain the sources of Hippolytus' interpretation or its relationship with Clement. Nor can we know how Hippolytus managed to make the 62 weeks (434 years) fill up the entire period from the restoration to Christ's advent. Indeed, Jerome later complained that by his own reckoning, the period from Cyrus to Christ's advent exceeded 434 years by 126 years.[105] However, another representative of the same tradition, Eusebius of Caesarea, provides a much clearer answer to this question.

Eusebius' Interpretation of Daniel's Vision

DANIEL 9 IN EUSEBIUS' DEMONSTRATIO EVANGELICA

Eusebius' most exhaustive analysis of Daniel's apocalypse of 70 weeks appears in the eighth book of his Demonstratio evangelica.[106] The section is distinguished both by the author's detailed acquaintance with the history of the post-exilic high priesthood and his attention to philological detail. While generally adhering to the widely known version of Theodotion, Eusebius comments upon and occasionally prefers to it the alternate readings of Aquila and Symmachus. In one case, he even claims to know the original Hebrew text of Daniel, probably through the good offices of Origen's Hexapla.[107]

Displaying here the erudition for which he had earned such high renown, Eusebius offers three opposing interpretations of the vision, one of which is extracted from his predecessor Julius Africanus. The respectful criticism that Eusebius offers of Africanus sets the tone for the whole section. In Eusebius' view, Africanus' inattention to the tripartite periodization of the prophecy was the single most objectionable feature of his interpretation. 'The prophecy does not make the division of the 70 weeks without an object or haphazard', Eusebius writes. '...I do not think that anyone who regards these as the words of God can suppose that these statements have no object, or are scattered without the divine attention.' To Africanus' flawed interpretation, Eusebius prefers two other 'theories' that in his own opinion give a more 'accurate solution (ἀκριβῆ λύσιν)' to the problem.[108]

---

[105] Commentary on Daniel 9.3.24 (877.409-413). 'The dates do not agree at all... (T)he total from the beginning of the reign of Cyrus king of the Persians until the advent of the Savior will be 560 years.'

[106] See Eusebius, Dem. evang. 8.2. Eusebius also treats Daniel 9 in his Hist. eccl. 1.6.11; Eclogae Propheticae 3.45-46 (PG 22.1176-92); Chronological Canons 160a (ed Helm).

[107] Dem. evang. 8.2.11 (383c).

[108] ib 8.2.58 (391c).

In line with the apologetic aims of the Demonstratio, Eusebius contends that the promise made by Gabriel to Daniel foretold how after a predetermined time God would withdraw from the old covenant and dissolve the Jewish priesthood and the temple cult. A new covenant would be introduced to supersede the old Mosaic one. Given this perspective and his well-documented opposition to millennialism, it is not surprising that for Eusebius the promise of the prophecy was entirely realized in the person of Christ. Eschewing the eschatological interpretation of the final week popular among earlier commentators, he assigns the first half of this week to the 3 1/2 years of Christ's ministry. The second half embraces the 3 1/2 (!) years of Christ's post-resurrection appearances to the disciples, during which time he 'confirmed the covenant with the many' (cf. Dan 9:27).[109]

Eusebius' explanation of the 'abomination of the desolation' of v27 is guided by the same perspective. Up until Christ's death, both the Temple and the Holy of Holies were presided over by 'some divine presence (τινα θεοῦ δύνα- μιν)'.[110] But from the moment that the curtain of the temple was torn, the sacrifice and libation were taken away and the temple became a profane place, stripped of its atoning power. Although the physical temple may have survived for a time after Christ's death, the first visible manifestations of its profanation occurred immediately after the crucifixion with Pilate's erection of images of Caesar in the temple.[111] Once the divine presence had receded, the catastrophes visited on the Jews in 70 and 135 by the Romans were inevitable.

It is all the more striking, then, that despite his overall messianic perspective, Eusebius sometimes wavers in his identification of 'anointed' figures in the passage customarily identified with Christ. He seriously entertains the possibility, for example, that the words 'to anoint the most Holy' might be connected with the Jewish high priest. Aquila's translation seemed to suggest it, and only the high priest was known by this title. But after permitting himself to be tempted by the idea, he immediately dismisses it on the grounds that nowhere in Scripture is the high priest called 'most holy'. 'My opinion', he says, is that in this passage, 'only the only-begotten word of God is meant, who is properly and truly worthy of that name.'[112]

The high priest, however, is often called χριστός in Scripture. And thus Eusebius allows that, according to 'another meaning or interpretation', 'the anointed one, the governor' (χριστὸς ἡγούμενος) in v25 bears a more probable connection with the post-exilic Jewish high priesthood. The χριστὸς ἡγούμενος refers not merely to Jeshua, but rather to the entire succession of post-exilic Jewish high priests. Only this office combined sacerdotal and royal prerogatives. The 'catalogue of the high priests', he says, 'governed the people

---

[109] ib 8.2.107 (400b).
[110] ib 8.2.113 (401b).
[111] ib 8.2.122-124 (403ab), quoting from Josephus, Ant. 18.3.1; J.W. 2.9.2; Philo, Legatio 38.
[112] Dem. evang. 8.2.40 (388a).

after the prophecy and the return from Babylon, whom Scripture commonly calls anointed ones... They were the only governors of the nation beginning with Jeshua, son of Jozadak, the Great priest, after the return from Babylon, and up to the date of the coming of our Savior Jesus Christ.'[113] From this assumption, Eusebius then sets himself the task of demonstrating that the disruption of the high-priestly line marked the termination of the prophecy's second phase, the 62 weeks.

ALEXANDER JANNAEUS AND THE END OF THE χριστὸς ἡγούμενος

According to Eusebius' second 'theory', the 'going forth of the word' commences with Cyrus' restoration of the Jews in the first year of his reign. The scriptural basis for this chronology is the report of the Jews in John 2:20 that the temple required 46 years to be restored. On the basis of 1 Ezra 1:1-3, Eusebius takes as the prophecy's *terminus a quo* the first year of Cyrus, the 'first to issue the command to rebuild the Jerusalem, according to the book of Ezra'. From this event up to the sixth year of Darius, 46 years elapsed.[114] But Eusebius notices that this chronology falls three years short of the desired 49 years. The missing three years are then accounted for by a statement that he attributes to Josephus, according to which the outer arrangement of the temple required an additional three years for completion.[115]

The event that signals the conclusion of the next 62 weeks is the death of the high priest Alexander Jannaeus (103-76 BCE). During this period, Eusebius says, 'the high priests ruled, who I believe are called in the prophecy "anointed ones" and "governors"'. The chief significance of Alexander's death for Eusebius is that it dissolves the incorporation of royal and priestly privilege into a single office. 'When the last of them, the high priest Alexander died, the Jewish nation was left without a king or leader, so that their kingdom came to a woman.'[116] Alexandra's accession to rule instead of Alexander's sons thus abolished the political authority of the high-priestly line.

Although the originality and boldness of this interpretation and its attention to detail have been praised by modern scholars, it must be asked whether and to

---

[113] ib 8.2.58-59 (391cd).

[114] Cf Ezra 6:15. 'Cyrus reigned for 31 years and handed his rule to his son Cambyses. His reign lasted nine years, and Darius gained power. Again after Cyrus... he commanded that Jerusalem be rebuilt. And this was in fact the sixth year of his rule, which was the 46th year from Cyrus, when the rebuilding of the temple was completed.'

[115] This is apparently a reference to Ant. 11.107. Josephus states that the building of the temple extended from the second year to its rededication in the ninth year of Darius. However, contrary to Eusebius' assertion, he does not make a distinction here between the completion of the inner and outer temple precincts. In Ag. Ap. 1.154, Josephus gives another chronology, stating here that the temple was completed in the second year of Darius.

[116] Dem. evang. 8.2.75 (394b).

what extent Eusebius was drawing on earlier sources.[117] Like the explanations of Hippolytus and Clement, it presupposed a periodization of the prophecy not forthcoming from the cited version of Theodotion. By Eusebius' own calculations the critical point in the chronology of the first 69 weeks, the death of Alexander Jannaeus, occurred over a century before Christ's ministry, which for him represents the final week of the 70-weeks vision.[118] Eusebius does not take credit for formulating the theory, and it is unlikely that Eusebius would have poured so much effort into devising a chronology that so poorly served his own stated purpose of demonstrating the messianic meaning of Daniel's prophecy. Indeed, Eusebius must have recognized its inadequacies, for he immediately discards it in favor of another theory more congenial to his interests.

Possible dependence on an earlier Jewish tradition has often been suggested. F.F. Bruce proposes that in connecting the χριστὸς ἡγούμενος with the post-exilic succession of high priests, Eusebius was enlarging upon an older Jewish tradition that in 'its original form... identified the "anointed one" with the Zadokite priesthood of post-exilic times from Jeshua to Onias III'.[119] Predicated on the same idea, Eusebius' second explanation has simply continued the succession down to the time of Alexander Jannaeus. For his part, A. Ehrhardt has offered an ingenious argument tracing this chronology to an ongoing tradition of Jewish interpretation of Dan 9:24-27 dating to the Hasmonean period.

As Ehrhardt suggests, there is reason to suppose that the catalogue of high priests that constitutes the chronology of Eusebius' 62 weeks belongs to an extract taken from an earlier source. Containing only 17 names, it is 'seriously defective' in comparison with the more detailed list of 21 post-exilic high priests that Eusebius offers in his chronicle.[120] Ehrhardt believes that while the immediate inspiration for Eusebius' second 'anonymous' theory was Hippolytus, the antecedents of the χριστὸς ἡγούμενος theory predate Josephus. As we have seen, Josephus' dating of Aristobulus' accession 481 years after the return from captivity is apparently a remnant of Jewish chronography based on Daniel's apocalypse of 70 weeks.[121]

Since it assumed only seven years for Alexander's rule, Ehrhardt contends that this chronology must have originated early in his reign. When Alexander's rule turned out to last longer than the anticipated seven years, the prophecy was extended to include the entire duration of the Hasmonean priesthood. Eusebius'

---

[117] Cf Gelzer, *Sextus Julius Africanus* 2, 173: 'eine höchst sonderbare Erklärung von dem χριστὸς ἡγούμενος'; E. Schwartz, *Königslisten*, 29 n1: 'Dass Eusebius den χριστὸς ἡγούμενος richtig verstanden hat, bestreitet die Wissenschaft nicht mehr, aber die Kirche hat es stets bestritten. Seine Exegese ist, wo er sich frei bewegen kann, musterhaft.' Montgomery, *Daniel*, 392 calls Eusebius' decision to date the prophecy from the first year of Cyrus 'bold'.

[118] It is 104 years from the 175th Olympiad in which year Eusebius put the death of Alexander, up to 201.4, the year of the beginning of Jesus' ministry.

[119] Bruce, *Biblical Exegesis*, 61.

[120] Ehrhardt, *Apostolic Succession*, 55f.

[121] Cf Ant. 13.11.301. See above 211f.

second theory, tracing the end of the 69 weeks to Alexander's death, represents one such attempt at extending the chronology.[122] After recounting the death of Alexander, the explanation appends to it the subsequent course of Hasmonean history: Pompey's 'desolating sacrilege' in the holy places, the accession to power of Herod, the 'coming prince', and his final destruction of the Mosaic high priesthood.[123] Although the chronology of events is muddled at this point, this theory must have seen in these events confirmation of the events predicted to occur in the final eschatological 'week'. The exegetical and chronological details of Eusebius' second theory thus create a strong likelihood that its roots are to be found in Jewish 'apocalyptic chronography' of the first century BCE.

EUSEBIUS' 'THIRD THEORY' AND HEROD'S CESSATION OF PRIESTLY UNCTION

Because of its exegetical niceties and its attention to the periodization of the prophecy, Eusebius was happy to include the above explanation as a theory that was at least preferable to Africanus'. But while not stating his objections outright, Eusebius seems to have sensed its chief shortcoming: it required a long hiatus between the abolition of the anointing after the first 69 weeks and the last week of the prophecy, the ministry of Christ and his post-resurrection association with his disciples. He thus offers to replace it with 'another way' to approach Daniel 9. More congenial to his purposes, this 'third theory' extended the 69 weeks up to the accession of Herod and Augustus, thereby bringing the chronology into closer proximity with Christ's birth and ministry.

The formulation of this third theory proceeds from a detailed and ingenious analysis of the wording of Daniel's prophecy. When Daniel (9:2) refers to the 70 years of Jeremiah's prophecy, Eusebius first notices that the prophet does not speak of 70 years of captivity, but rather of '70 years for the accomplishment of the desolation of Jerusalem (εἰς συμπλήρωσιν ἐρημώσεως Ἱερουσαλήμ)'. Thus, when the angel spoke of the 'going forth of the word ...and the building of Jerusalem', he must have been referring to the rebuilding of Jerusalem and the temple, not Cyrus' restoration of the Jews from captivity. On the basis of Zech 1:7,12, Eusebius concludes that the 70 years of Jerusalem's desolation were completed with the rebuilding of the temple in the second year of Darius, at which time the chronology of the 70 weeks commences.

After establishing that the second year of Darius corresponds with the 66th Olympiad, Eusebius then determines that the 483 years of the prophecy would extend 121 Olympiads up to the 186th Olympiad. 'Around this time', Augustus the Roman emperor acquired 'the kingdom of Egypt and the rest of the world' in the 15th year of his reign.[124] The critical incident in the fulfilment of the 69

---

[122] Ehrhardt, *Apostolic Succession*, 59.
[123] Dem. evang. 8.2.77-79 (394d).
[124] Dem. evang. 8.2.87 (396c).

weeks occurred when Herod, appointed by Augustus as ruler of Judea, abrogated the genealogical high priesthood and 'conferred the office ...on obscure and unknown men'. Herod's haphazard appointment of high priests and his removal of the high-priestly garments thus 'make it clear to all that this was the fulfilment of the oracle, which said: "And after the seven and 62 weeks the unction shall be cast out, and there is no judgment in it."'

What is above all clear is that like Eusebius' second 'theory', the controlling exegetical principle of this explanation was not messianic, but sacerdotal. 'The anointed one shall be cast out after the completion of the said weeks', he writes. 'Who can this be but the governor and ruler of the high priestly line?'[125] The details of this explanation invite the conclusion that in its pre-Christian form Eusebius' 'third theory' was another specimen of pre-70 Jewish apocalyptic chronography. Formulated by opponents of Herod, it saw his abuse of the high-priestly office as confirmation of Daniel's prophecy and a sign of the imminence of the final eschatological week.

HEROD, THE 'COMING PRINCE' AND GEN 49:10

Dan 9:26b refers to a 'coming prince (Theod.: τῷ ἡγουμένῳ τῷ ἐρχομένῳ)' who with his supporters will destroy the city and the sanctuary. In its original form, the coming prince in all likelihood referred to Antiochus Epiphanes and his desecration of the temple. Over the course of time, the figure was variously understood as Vespasian, Hadrian, Pompey, Agrippa, or even the returning Jesus.[126] Eusebius himself represents another school of interpretation. He identifies the 'coming prince' as Herod the Great and views his accession to power as the realization of Jacob's oracle in Gen 49:10. Like the other elements of Eusebius' treatment of Dan 9:24-27, this tradition also has much earlier Jewish/ Christian roots.

As we have noted, in the War, Josephus, apparently in reference to Dan 9:26b, refers to an oracle 'announcing that at that time a man from their country would become ruler of the world'. While acknowledging that it was customary to identify this figure with 'someone of their own race', Josephus propagates the view that the oracle 'in reality signified the sovereignty of Vespasian, who was proclaimed Emperor on Jewish soil'.[127] A Slavonic addition to Josephus elaborates upon this by noting that 'some understood that this meant Herod; others the crucified miracle-worker; others again, Vespasian'.[128] In another Slavonic addition, a story is told of a secret debate conducted among Jewish priests

---

[125] Quoting here from Aquila.
[126] See Montgomery, *Daniel*, 383.
[127] J.W. 6.310-13.
[128] See Bruce, 'Josephus and Daniel', 162 n28.

about the meaning of Herod's ascendancy to the rule of Judea.[129] The question discussed is whether Herod's accession fulfilled the terms of two oracles: Jacob's blessing of Judah in Gen 49:10 and Dan 9:24-27.

A priest named Jonathan first insists that Herod could not be the Messiah, because he was foreign-born and oppressed the Jewish nation. He acknowledges, however, that from one perspective Herod might be the one mentioned in Jacob's oracle in Gen 49:10, 'there shall not want a ruler from Judah until he comes unto whom it is given up; for him do the Gentiles hope.' The sense of this is that as long as the Jews lived under native rulers, the prophecy was incomplete. But when Herod assumed the throne, Jewish sovereignty was forfeited and a foreign-born king was installed as king. Nevertheless, Ananus is adamant that Herod cannot be the one predicted in the oracle: 'Is this man the hope for the Gentiles? For we hate his misdeeds.'

The debate then adverts to Herod's role in the fulfilment of Daniel's apocalypse of 70 weeks. A second priest Ananus recalls that when Herod was besieging Jerusalem he could hardly believe that 'God would permit him to rule over us'. But Ananus urges his companions to recall the words of Daniel's prophecy predicting the desolation of the city after 70 weeks of years. When they had counted the years, they determined that there were but 34 years left in order to fulfil the 490 years. Here again the discussion turns on the question as to whether Herod could in any way have been the messianic figure predicted in Dan 9:24-27. While conceding that the 490 years were nearing their completion, Jonathan denies that Herod can possibly be the holy one predicted in Dan 9:24. 'The number of the years are even as we have said. But the Holy of Holies, where is He? For this Herod he (Daniel) cannot call the Holy One.'[130]

Although there is no need to enter here into a discussion about the historical value of the Slavonic Josephus, Herod's connection with the oracle of Gen 49:10 is independently attested.[131] In his discussion of the Herodians, for example, Epiphanius reports that this little known Jewish party saw Herod's non-Jewish background as proof that with his accession to the rule of Judea, the Messiah had arrived. They were won over to this belief by the 'literal wording' of Gen 49:10:

> This was because Herod was the son of an Antipater of Ashkelon... So Herod, a gentile, was reigning as king. Now the crown had been handed down in succession from Judah and David and the rulers or patriarchs of Judah's line <had failed> but the crown had gone to a gentile. Thus, to the notion of misguided persons, the

---

[129] An English translation of this addition can be found in Thackeray's appendix to his LCL translation of Josephus' J.W., books 4-7, 636-38 (replacing J.W. 1.364-370).

[130] The reference to the remaining 34 years is unclear. As Thackeray observes (638), it cannot refer to the remaining 34 years in Herod's rule after his capture of Jerusalem in 37 BCE, because the debate occurs five years after his accession.

[131] For arguments in favor of the antiquity and authenticity of these traditions, see Eisler, ΙΗΣΟΥΣ ΒΑΣΙΛΕΥΣ 1, 348-60, esp 350-52.

mistaken belief that he was Christ seemed reasonable in consequence of the wording
I have quoted, "There shall not fail a ruler from Judah till he come for whom it is
prepared" – as though they had taken it <to mean>, "It was 'prepared' for this ruler.
The rulers from Judah have failed and this one is not descended from Judah – indeed
not a descendant of Israel at all. But the <role> of Christ was 'prepared' for someone
like this."[132]

In both Epiphanius and the Slavonic addition, the application of Gen 49:10 to
Herod assumes his birth from an Ashkelonite father and Arab mother. Christian
writers who ascribe this ignoble lineage to Herod could not have gotten it from
either Josephus or Nicolaus of Damascus, neither of whom represent Herod in
this way.[133] Although the reliability and source of the story has been questioned,
the tradition is at least as old as the early second century.[134] In his Dialogue
with Trypho, Justin Martyr refers somewhat obliquely to a Jewish tradition that
saw the accession of the Ashkelonite Herod as realization of Jacob's prophecy.[135] For his part, Eusebius traces the report about Herod's ignoble Ashkelonite
roots to his predecessor, Julius Africanus.[136]

It is not unreasonable to suppose that the reports of both Africanus and
Justin, both of whom were of Palestinian origin, reflect a Jewish or Jewish/
Christian tradition dating to the first century. Africanus claims to have received
it from a tradition handed down by 'those who give accurate information concerning Herod of Ashkelon'. Since he links it to information that he had received about Jesus' genealogy from the δεσπόσυνοι, 'the human relatives of
the Savior', it is commonly believed that the source that he has used is a
Jewish-Christian work dating from the late first or early second century.[137] The
impulse behind this complex of traditions seems clear: a pro-Herodian propaganda campaign that inspired Jews and later Jewish Christians to extensive

---

[132] Epiphanius, Panarion 1.20.1.6 (tr Williams). Numerous other Christian sources describe the
Herodians as a group claiming Herod's messiahship. For the sources, see Rowley, 'The Herodians',
14-16.

[133] The former says he was an Idumean; the latter, descended from one of the Jewish families who
returned from Babylon; cf Ant. 14.9. It is perhaps of interest, however, that Photius, Bibliotheca
76.53a (ed, tr Henry) includes the tradition about Herod's heritage from an Ashkelonite temple-
slave and an Arab mother as part of his précis of Josephus' Antiquities.

[134] See Gelzer, Sextus Julius Africanus 1, 258-65, who considers the tradition historical and traces it
to Justus of Tiberias; also Heer, Die Stammbäume Jesu, 21-23. For the opposing view, see Schürer,
History 1, 234 n3. Schalit, 'Die frühchristliche Überlieferung' considers the tradition a piece of
Jewish polemic against Herod.

[135] Justin Martyr, Dialogue with Trypho 52.

[136] Hist. eccl. 1.7.11.

[137] See Gelzer, Sextus Julius Africanus 1, 259; Bauckham, Jude, 355-63. This is further confirmed
by a scribal gloss (in the margin of Codex Laurentianus plut. 69 cod. 20) to Josephus' narrative of
Herod's birth (Ant. 14.7.3); it attributes to James 'the brother of God' the statement that Herod's
Ashkelonite heritage fulfilled Judah's oracle; see Niese, Flavii Iosephi Opera 1, xv.

discussion about Herod's role in the fulfillment of messianic prophecy.[138]

Africanus' report makes it clear that in the hands of the Jewish Christians, the tradition about Herod's Ashkelonite background was further proof of his ignoble character. But once infused with Christian content, the tradition of Herod's foreign background and his relationship to Gen 49:10 and Dan 9:24-27 decisively influenced the development of one stream in Christian interpretation of Daniel's apocalypse of weeks. In an apparent allusion to it in his Commentary on Matthew, Origen acknowledges that some interpreters of Dan 9:26 identified the 'coming prince' with Christ. But if Christ had been meant, Daniel would certainly have used the appropriate messianic title to refer to him. The figure should instead be identified either as Herod or as Agrippa (the latter, he says, on the authority of a 'Jewish history'). In either case, it was with one of these foreign rulers that the oracle of Jacob was fulfilled.[139]

Eusebius enlarges on the tradition at much greater length. Jacob's oracle to Judah foretold the cessation of the princes and governors of the Jewish nation; Daniel's prophecy foreshadowed the end of their successors, 'the prophets and the priests, who were of old their chief ornament'.[140] Eusebius allows that the 'people of the governor who comes' may refer by extension to the Roman general and his camps. But in line with his overall interpretation of 9:25-26a, he prefers to identify the 'coming prince' with Herod and the rulers of foreign stock who succeeded him.[141] For it was Herod who was chiefly responsible for the cessation of the χριστοὶ ἡγούμενοι. 'As above he named the high priests, anointed ones and governors, saying, "Until the anointed one the governor", in the same way after their time and after their abolition there was no other "ruler to come" but the same Herod of foreign stock, and the others who ruled the nation in order after them... [Herod] destroyed the whole nation, now upsetting the established order of the priesthood, now perverting the whole people, and encouraging the city in impiety.'[142]

---

[138] For discussion, see Schlatter, *Chronograph*, 35-47. Schlatter believes that Justin and Africanus know the tradition from the early first century Jewish Christian bishop and chronographer Judas. Eisler, ΙΗΣΟΥΣ ΒΑΣΙΛΕΥΣ 1, 348-60 thinks that the story originated in the original Aramaic version of Josephus. Although little is known about Justus of Tiberias, it is tempting to trace the story to him; Justus' anti-Herodian views are well-documented. For more recent discussion of Africanus' letter, see Bauckham ib 355-64.

[139] Origen, Commentary on Matthew ser. 40 (81.9-11), on Matt 24:15-18: 'Sed et civitas et sanctum corruptum est cum superveniente postea duce populo illi, sive Herode sive Agrippa (hunc enim dicit esse historia Iudaeorum).' It is regrettable, however, that Origen fails to specify here the author of this 'Jewish history'; see also ser. 41 (82.13-15): 'Refertur ...ab his qui Iudaicam historiam conscripserunt.' For discussion, see von Harnack, *Die Kirchengeschichtliche Ertrag*, 50-52.

[140] Dem. evang. 8.2.37 (387d).

[141] For this purpose, the version of Dan 9:26 that Eusebius prefers is Aquila's: 'And the people of the governor that comes will destroy the city and the holy place.' The reason for his preference is that, unlike Theodotion, Aquila's translation clearly establishes that the agent of the city's destruction is the coming prince and his 'people'.

[142] Dem. evang. 8.2.102-103 (399bc).

The same identification of 'the coming prince' appears in Eusebius' Chronicle and the Ecclesiastical History. Following the tradition outlined above, Eusebius links Herod's dissolution of the χϱιστοὶ ἡγούμενοι with Jacob's prophecy to Judah in Gen 49:10. As long as the Jews lived under native rulers, these prophecies were incomplete. But upon his investiture by Augustus as king of Judea, Herod, 'the coming prince' of foreign stock, fulfilled the terms of both of them. Jewish sovereignty was lost and the orderly succession of the high priesthood was abrogated. 'When the kingdom of the Jews came to such a man as this the expectation of the Gentiles, in accordance with the prophecy, was already at the door, inasmuch as the succession from Moses of rulers and governors (ἀϱξάντων τε καὶ ἡγησαμένων) ceased with him.'[143] In the Jewish story about Herod's Ashkelonite heritage, Eusebius thus saw unmistakable evidence that the 'expectation of the Gentiles' was imminent.

The χϱιστοὶ ἡγούμενοι and the Formation of a Christian View of Universal History

What we have pointed to is the existence of a pre-Christian interpretation of Dan 9:24-27, whose orientation to Daniel's apocalypse was chiefly sacerdotal and eschatological. What is striking about this interpretation is its continuity. Throughout the history of the Hasmonean priesthood, some perceived degradation of the high-priestly line served to arouse interest in determining whether the first 69 year-weeks of Daniel's prophecy had been completed. In its original context, this disruption was identified with the death of Onias III. It was later associated with Alexander Jannaeus' corruption of the office, and then with the disruption caused by his death. Because Herod's rule was chronologically most proximate to Jesus' birth and ministry, Jewish Christianity adapted the tradition that saw in his murder of Hyrcanus and the ensuing chaos the determinative event defining the end of Daniel's first 69 weeks and the dawning of the eschatological week. Fundamental to this interpretation was the role that Herod's foreign-born Ashkelonite lineage played in the unfolding of the eschatological drama of Daniel 9. Already attested by the early second century, this legend was mediated to Christian commentators and chroniclers from a Palestinian Jewish Christian tradition associated with the early human family of Jesus.

In its later Christian adaptations, the eschatological orientation to these verses was replaced by the messianic perspective that came to dominate exegesis of Dan 9:24-27 from the late second century. But the vestiges of the tradition are still clearly evident, especially in the interpretation of Dan 9:25. Although the majority of Christian interpreters, following the Theodotionic text of Daniel,

---

[143] Hist. eccl. 1.6.5; see also Eusebius, Canons 160ª (242F) = Syncellus, 373.20-374.28.

identified the χριστὸς ἡγούμενος with Christ, the representatives of this minority tradition – Clement, Hippolytus and Eusebius – continued to preserve the older Jewish Christian sacerdotal interpretation of Dan 9:25. Their adherence to this tradition accounts for the exegetical anomalies that we have already described. Clement, Hippolytus and Eusebius cite Theodotionic Daniel. But their interpretation of Dan 9:25 presupposes the Hebrew text of these verses and produced a chronology that was difficult to square with their own messianic perspective. By far the most detailed forms of the tradition are found in Eusebius of Caesarea. Not only does Eusebius appeal to the tradition in several of his works; it seems to have exerted a profound influence on his conception of sacred history.

EUSEBIUS' 'CATALOGUE' OF HIGH PRIESTS AND THE SHAPING OF SACRED HISTORY

One of the works in which this older Jewish tradition has exercised such an influence is the second book of Eusebius' universal chronicle, the so-called Chronological Canons. Arranged in parallel columns, the Canons were intended among other things to establish a continuous stream of universal history from Abraham up to the time of Constantine. But in pursuing this objective, Eusebius, like Hippolytus before him, faced the task of tracing a thread of sacred history for the intertestamental period. Now in Jerome's version of Eusebius' chronicle, the distinction between sacred and secular history appeared to cease with the reign of Darius. Accordingly, when A. Schöne first published the several recensions of Eusebius' chronicle, he proposed that Eusebius introduced a hiatus in sacred history for the period from the end of the Babylonian captivity to Christ's advent; from that point 'giebt es ...für Eusebius keine gesonderte heilige und Profan-Geschichte'.[144]

More recently, E. Caspar has persuasively demonstrated that it was Jerome, not Eusebius, who imposed this unitary structure on the chronicle. In its original form, Eusebius' Canons continued to trace a separate *filum* for sacred history even for the post-exilic period.[145] What were the contents of this filum? As Caspar has shown, for the post-exilic period Eusebius conceived of sacred history as the genealogical succession of Jewish high priests from Jeshua to Hyrcanus, that is, the χριστὸς ἡγούμενος of Dan 9:25.[146] Only with Herod, the 'coming prince' of Dan 9:26, did this stream of sacred history cease. At the critical point in his chronicle, the birth of Christ, Eusebius describes the role of the high priesthood in the plan of universal history. The description summarizes Eusebius' 'third theory', boiled down to its essential points:

---

[144] Schöne, *Weltchronik*, 15f.
[145] See Caspar, *Die älteste römische Bischofsliste*, 277-287.
[146] ib 280-287.

At that time (the accession of Herod), 'an anointed one, a ruler', prophesied by Daniel, came to an end. For up to Herod, there were 'anointed ones, princes'. These were the high priests, who presided over the Jewish people, beginning with the restoration of the temple during the reign of Darius in the 65th Olympiad, and lasting to Hyrcanus in the 186th Olympiad... Herod, the son of Antipater an Ashkelonite and Cypris an Arabian woman, was entrusted with rule over the Jews by the Romans, even though it did not belong to him. In his time, when the birth of Christ was near, the genealogical succession of the high priesthood and the kingdom of the Jews were dissolved, and the Mosaic prophecy was completed, which said: 'a ruler shall not fail from Judah... (Gen 49:10).' Then Daniel says in his prophecy: 'And after seven and 62 weeks, anointing will be destroyed...' (Dan 9:26-27).[147]

It is of particular interest that from this point in Eusebius' Canons, illegitimate high priests, who abrogated Mosaic law and ruled at the pleasure of Herod and Rome, were relegated by Eusebius to the filum of secular history. In their place, Eusebius substitutes the apostles and the genealogical succession lists of the early Jerusalem episcopacy – in Eusebius' view, the legitimate successors to the ideal line of the post-exilic high priesthood.

For Eusebius, the χριστὸς ἡγούμενος of Dan 9:25 was not an individual, but rather a 'catalogue' of high priests, a διαδοχὴ ἐκ πατέρων. Understood in this way, Daniel's apocalypse of 70 weeks, mediated through a tradition of Jewish and Jewish-Christian interpretation, was the theological foundation for the idea that the temporal and genealogical succession of post-exilic high priests formed the legitimate link between the end of Old Testament history and the advent of Christ and the Church.

---

[147] In Syncellus, 373.24-374.27.

Abbreviations

AB	Anchor Bible
ABD	D.N. Freeman (ed) *Anchor Bible Dictionary*
ACW	Ancient Christian Writers
AGJU	Arbeiten zur Geschichte des antiken Judentums und des Urchristentums
AGWG	Abhandlungen der Gesellschaft der Wissenschaften zu Göttingen
ANF	Roberts-Donaldson, *The Ante-Nicene Fathers*
APOT	Charles, *Apocrypha and Pseudepigrapha of the OT*
ASTI	*Annual of the Swedish Theological Institute*
ATR	*Anglican Theological Review*
BASP	*Bulletin of the American Society of Papyrologists*
Bib	*Biblica*
BibS(F)	Biblische Studien (Freiburg 1895-)
BJRL	*Bulletin of the John Rylands Library*
BN	Bibliothèque nationale, Paris
BSO(A)S	*Bulletin of the School of Oriental (and African) Studies*
CBQ	*Catholic Biblical Quarterly*
CCL	Corpus christianorum latinorum
CH	*Church History*
CMC	Cologne Mani Codex, ed Koenen-Römer
ConBNT	Coniectanea biblica, NT
ConBOT	Coniectanea biblica, OT
CPJ	Tcherikover, *Corpus Papyrorum Iudaicorum*
CRINT	Compendia rerum judaicarum ad Novum Testamentum
CSCO	Corpus scriptorum christianorum orientalium
CSEL	Corpus scriptorum ecclesiasticorum latinorum
CSS	Cistercian Studies Series
CTSRR	College Theology Society Resources in Religion
DACL	F. Cabrol (ed) *Dictionnaire d'archéologie chrétienne et de liturgie*
DJD	Discoveries in the Judaean Desert
ed	editor(s), edition
EJL	Early Judaism and Its Literature
f	'and (single) page following'
FC	Fathers of the Church

FRLANT	Forschungen zur Religion and Literatur des Alten und Neuen Testaments
GCS	Die griechischen christlichen Schriftsteller
HSCP	*Harvard Studies in Classical Philology*
HSM	Harvard Semitic Monographs
HTR	*Harvard Theological Review*
HTS	Harvard Theological Studies
HUCA	*Hebrew Union College Annual*
HUCM	Monographs of the Hebrew Union College
HUT	Hermeneutische Untersuchungen zur Theologie
ICC	International Critical Commentary
IEJ	*Israel Exploration Journal*
Int	*Interpretation*
IOS	*Israel Oriental Studies*
JAAR	*Journal of the American Academy of Religion*
JAC	Jahrbuch für Antike und Christentum
JBL	*Journal of Biblical Literature*
JEA	*Journal of Egyptian Archaeology*
JJS	*Journal of Jewish Studies*
JQR	*Jewish Quarterly Review*
JRS	*Journal of Roman Studies*
JSJ	*Journal for the Study of Judaism*
JSNT	*Journal for the Study of the NT*
JSOT	*Journal for the Study of the Old Testament*
JSP	*Journal for the Study of the Pseudepigrapha*
JTS	*Journal of Theological Studies*
LCL	Loeb Classical Library, London / Cambridge MA
-MonSer	Monograph Series
-MS	Monograph Series
Mus	*Muséon*
NAPS	North American Patristic Society
nF	neue Folge
NHC	Nag Hammadi codex
NHL	Robinson, *The Nag Hammadi Library in English* (cited by page)
NHS	Nag Hammadi Studies
NovT	*Novum Testamentum*
NTA	Hennecke-Schneemelcher, *New Testament Apocrypha*
NTL	New Testament Library
NTS	*New Testament Studies*
OLP	Orientalia lovaniensia periodica
OTP	Charlesworth, *The Old Testament Pseudepigrapha*
P.	Papyrus
PG	J.-P. Migne, *Patrologia graeca*
PGM	K. Preisendanz (ed) *Papyri graecae magicae* 1-2. Leipzig 1928-31

PO	Patrologia orientalis
PVTG	Pseudepigrapha Veteris Testamenti graece
RB	*Revue biblique*
RBén	*Revue Bénédictine*
REJ	*Revue des études juives*
RevQ	*Revue de Qumrân*
RHR	*Revue de l'histoire des religions*
RSLR	*Revista di storia e letteratura religiosa*
RSR	*Revue de science religieuse*
SAC	Studies in Antiquity and Christianity
SBL	Society of Biblical Literature
SBLDS	SBL Dissertation Series
SBLSP	SBL Seminar Papers
SBLSCS	SBL Septuagint and Cognate Studies
SBLTT	SBL Texts and Translations
SC	Sources chrétiennes
SJLA	Studies in Judaism in Late Antiquity
SSN	Studia semitica neerlandica
Str-B	Strack-Billerbeck, *Kommentar*
STT	Semitic Texts with Translations
-Sup	Supplementa, Supplements
SVTP	Studia in Veteris Testamenti Pseudepigrapha
TextsS	Texts and Studies
TDNT	Kittel, *Theological Dictionary of the NT*
tr	translation(s), translator(s)
TRE	*Theologische Realenzyklopädie*
TU	Texte und Untersuchungen
VC	*Vigiliae christianae*
WBC	Word Biblical Commentary
WBT	Wiener Beiträge zur Theologie
WUNT	Wissenschaftliche Untersuchungen zum Neuen Testament
ZAW	*Zeitschrift für die alttestamentliche Wissenschaft*
ZDMG	*Zeitschrift der deutschen morgenländischen Gesellschaft*
ZPE	*Zeitschrift für Papyrologie und Epigraphik*

Cumulative Bibliography

Titles by the same author(s) are listed alphabetically by first noun.

Acerbi, A. *L'Ascensione di Isaia. Cristologia e profetismo in Siria nei primi decenni del II seculo* (Studia Patristica Mediolensia 17) Milan 1989
– *Serra Lignea: Studi sulla fortuna della Ascensione di Isaia*. Rome 1984
Achelis, H. – see Bonwetsch-Achelis
Achtemeier, P.J. '*Omne verbum sonat*: The New Testament and the Oral Environment of Late Western Antiquity'. *JBL* 109 (1990) 3-27
Adler, W. 'Enoch in Early Christian Literature', in P. Achtemeier (ed) *SBLSP* (1978) 271-5
– *Time Immemorial: Archaic History and its Sources in Christian Chronography from Julius Africanus to George Syncellus* (Dumbarton Oaks Studies 26) Washington, D.C. 1989
Aland, K. 'The Problem of Anonymity and Pseudonymity in Christian Literature of the First Two Centuries'. *JTS* 12 (1961) 39-49
Allen, J.P. 'Funerary Texts and Their Meaning', in S. D'Auria *et al* (eds) *Mummies and Magic: The Funerary Arts in Ancient Egypt*. 2nd ed Boston 1992, 138-49
Alliot, M. 'La thébaïde en lutte contre les rois d'Alexandrie sous Philopator et Épiphane (216-184)'. *Revue belge de philologie et d'histoire* 29 (1951) 421-43
Amélineau, E. *Monuments pour servir à l'histoire de l'Égypte chrétienne aux IVè et Vè siècles* (Mémoires publiés par les membres de la mission archéologique française au Caire 4) Paris 1888
– 'Voyage d'un moine égyptien dans le désert'. *Recueil de travaux relatifs à la philologie et à l'archéologie égyptiennes et assyriennes* 6 (1885) 166-94
Amélineau, E. (ed) *Oeuvres de Schenoudi*. Paris 1907
Archer, G.L. (tr) *Jerome's Commentary on Daniel*. Grand Rapids 1958
J. Assmann, 'Königsdogma und Heilserwartung: Politische und kultische Chaosbeschreibung in ägyptischen Texten', in Hellholm, *Apocalypticism*, 345-77
Attridge, H.W. 'Greek and Latin Apocalypses', in Collins, *Apocalypse: Morphology*, 159-86
– 'Thomas, Acts of'. *ABD* 6, 531-4
Aune D.E. 'Intertextuality and the Genre of the Apocalypse', in E. Lovering (ed) *SBLSP* (1991) 142-60
– *Prophecy in Early Christianity and the Ancient Mediterranean World*. Grand Rapids 1983
Baehrens, W.A. (ed) *Origenes Werke* 7 (GCS 30) Leipzig 1921
Bagnall R.S. *Egypt in Late Antiquity*. Princeton 1993
– 'Religious Conversion and Onomastic Change in Early Byzantine Egypt'. *BASP* 19 (1982) 105-23
Balogh, J. '"Voces Paginarum": Beiträge zur Geschichte des lauten Lesens und Schreibens'. *Philologus* 82 (1926) 84-109, 202-40
Bamberger, J.E. *Evagrius Ponticus: The Praktikos, Chapters on Prayer* (CSS 4) Kalamazoo MI 1981
Bardtke, H. (ed) *Qumran-Probleme. Vorträge des Leipziger Symposions über Qumran-Probleme vom 9. bis 14. Oktober 1961*. Berlin 1963

Bardy, G. 'Melchisédech dans la tradition patristique'. *RB* 36 (1927) 25-45
- 'Les premiers temps du christianisme de langue copte en Égypte', in L. Vincent (ed) *Mémorial Lagrange*. Paris 1940, 203-16
Bardy, G. (ed, tr) *Eusèbe de Césarée: Histoire ecclésiastique* (SC 55) Paris 1958
Barnard, L.W. *Athenagoras: A Study in Second Century Christian Apologetic* (Théologie historique 18) Paris 1972
- 'Judaism in Egypt A.D. 70-135', in L.W. Barnard (ed) *Studies in the Apostolic Fathers and Their Background*, Oxford 1966, 41-55
Barnes, T.D. *Tertullian: A Historical and Literary Study*. Oxford 1971
Barr, D.L. 'The Apocalypse of John as Oral Enactment'. *Int* 40 (1986) 243-56
Barr, J. 'Jewish Apocalyptic in Recent Study'. *BJRL* 58 (1975) 9- 35
Basset, R. *Le Synaxaire arabe jacobite II* (PO 3) Paris 1909
Bauckham, R.J. 'Early Jewish Visions of Hell'. *JTS* 41 (1990) 355-85
- 'The Fall of the Angels as the Source of Philosophy in Hermias and Clement of Alexandria'. *VC* 39 (1985) 319-30
- 'Jude, Epistle of'. *ABD* 3, 1100-1102
- *Jude, 2 Peter*. (WBC 50) Waco 1983
- *Jude and the Relatives of Jesus in the Early Church*. Edinburgh 1990
- 'The Martyrdom of Enoch and Elijah: Jewish or Christian?' *JBL* 95 (1976) 447-58
Baumeister, T. *Martyr invictus* (Forschungen zur Volkskunde 46) Münster 1972
Baumgarten, J.M. 'The Book of Elkesai and Merkabah Mysticism'. *JSJ* 17 (1986) 212-23
Beale, G.K. *The Use of Daniel in Jewish Apocalyptic Literature and in the Revelation of St. John*. Lanham 1984
Becker, J. *Untersuchungen zur Entstehungsgeschichte der Testamente der zwölf Patriarchen*. Leiden 1970
Beckwith, R.T. 'The Significance of the Calendar for Interpreting Essene Chronology and Eschatology'. *RevQ* 38 (1980) 167-202
- 'Daniel 9 and the Date of Messiah's Coming in Essene, Hellenistic, Pharisaic, Zealot and Early Christian Computation'. *RevQ* 40 (1981) 521-42
- *The Old Testament Canon of the New Testament Church and Its Background in Early Judaism*. London / Grand Rapids 1985
Bell, D.N. *The Life of Shenoute by Besa* (CSS 73) Kalamazoo MI 1983
Bell, H.I. *Jews and Christians in Egypt*. London 1924
Bensly, R.L. *The Fourth Book of Ezra* (TextsS 3,4) Cambridge 1895
- *The Missing Fragment of the Fourth Book of Ezra*. Cambridge 1875
Bergren, T.A. 'Assessing the Two Recensions of 6 Ezra', in L. Greenspoon - O. Munnich (eds) *VIII Congress of the International Organization for Septuagint and Cognate Studies*. Atlanta, forthcoming
- *Fifth Ezra: The Text, Origin and Early History* (SBLSCS 25) Atlanta 1990
- '6 Ezra', in A.Y. Collins - M. Himmelfarb (eds) *Apocalypse* (New Testament Apocrypha) Sonoma CA, forthcoming
Berthelot, M. - Ruelle, Ch.-Ém. *Collection des anciens alchimistes grecs* 1-3. Paris 1888
Bethge, H.-G. 'On the Origin of the World', in *NHL*, 170-89
Betz, H.D. 'On the Problem of the Religio-Historical Understanding of Apocalypticism', in R. Funk (ed) *Apocalypticism* = *JTC* 6 (1969) 134-56
- 'The Formation of Authoritative Tradition in the Greek Magical Papyri', in Sanders, *Self-Definition* 3, 161-70, 236-38
Bianchi, U. (ed) *Le origini dello Gnosticismo. Colloquio di Messina 13-18 aprile 1966* (NumenSup 12) Leiden 1970
Bidawid, R.J. (ed) '4 Esdras', in *The Old Testament in Syriac According to the Peshitta Version* (part 4, fasc. 3) Leiden 1973
Black, M. *Apocalypsis Henochi Graece* (PVTG 3) Leiden 1970
- *The Book of Enoch or I Enoch: A New English Edition*. Leiden 1985

- 'The "Two Witnesses" of Rev. 11:3f. in Jewish and Christia Apocalyptic Tradition', in E. Bammel – C.K. Barrett – W.D. Davies (eds) *Donum gentilicum: New Testament Studies in Honour of David Daube*. Oxford 1978, 227-37
Blake, R. P. 'The Georgian Text of Fourth Esdras from the Athos Manuscript'. *HTR* 22 (1929) 57-105
- 'The Georgian Version of Fourth Esdras from the Jerusalem Manuscript'. *HTR* 19 (1926) 299-375
Bludau, A. *Die alexandrinische Übersetzung des Buches Daniel und ihr Verhältnis zum massorethischen Text* (BibS[F] 2, 2-3) Freiburg 1897
Bockmuehl, M.N.A. *Revelation and Mystery in Ancient Judaism and Pauline Christianity*. Tübingen 1990
Böhlig, A. – Labib, P. *Koptisch-gnostische Apokalypsen aus Codex V von Nag Hammadi im koptischen Museum zum Alt-Kairo*. Halle-Wittenberg 1963
Böhlig, A. – Wisse, F. 'The Gospel of the Egyptians', in *NHL*, 208-19
Bonner, C. *The Last Chapters of Enoch in Greek* (Studies and Documents 8) London 1937
Bonwetsch, N. 'Die apokryphen Fragen des Bartholomäus'. *Nachrichten von der Gesellschaft der Wissenschaften zu Göttingen, Phil.-hist. Klasse* (1897) 9-27
Bonwetsch, G.N.- Achelis, H. (eds) *Hippolytus Werke* 1 (GCS 1) Leipzig 1897
Bornkamm, G. 'The Acts of Thomas', in *NTA* 2 (1965 ed) 425-531
- μυστήριον, μυέω, in *TDNT* 4.802-28
Borsch, F.H. *The Son of Man in Myth and History* (NTL) Philadelphia 1967
Bouriant, U. 'Notes de voyage, 1. Catalogue de la bibliothèque du couvent d'Amba Hélias'. *Recueil de travaux relatifs à la philologie et à l'archéologie* 11 (1889) 131-38
Bousset, W. *Der Antichrist in der Überlieferung des Judentums, des Neuen Testaments und der alten Kirche*. Göttingen 1895, repr Hildesheim – Zürich - New York 1983
Box, G.H. *The Apocalypse of Ezra* (Translations of Early Documents 1) London 1917
- *The Ezra-Apocalypse*. London 1912
Bozóky, E. *Le livre secret des Cathares: Interrogatio Iohannis, Apocryphe d'origine bogomile* (Textes dossiers documents 2) Paris 1980
Brakke, D. *Athanasius and the Politics of Asceticism* (Oxford Early Christian Studies) Oxford 1995
- 'Canon Formation and Social Formation in Fourth-Century Egypt', *HTR* 87 (1994) 395-419
Braun, M. *History and Romance in Graeco-Oriental Literature*. Oxford 1938
Braverman, J. *Jerome's Commentary on Daniel: A Study of Comparative Jewish and Christian Interpretations of the Hebrew Bible* (CBQMS 7) Washington 1978
Brou, L. – Vives, J. (eds) *Antifonario visigotico mozarabe de la Catedral de León* (Monumenta Hispaniae Sacra, Series Liturgica 5,1) Barcelona-Madrid 1959
Brown P. *The Making of Late Antiquity*. Cambridge MA 1975
- *Power and Persuasion in Late Antiquity*. Madison 1992
- 'The Rise and Function of the Holy Man in Late Antiquity', in id (ed) *Society and the Holy in Late Antiquity*. London 1982, 103-52
- 'The Saint As Exemplar in Late Antiquity', in J. Hawley (ed) *Saints and Virtues*. Berkeley 1987, 3-14
Bruce, F.F. *Biblical Exegesis in the Qumran Texts*. Grand Rapids 1959
- 'Josephus and Daniel'. *ASTI* 4 (1965) 148-62
- 'The Book of Daniel and the Qumran Community', in E.E. Ellis – M. Wilcox (eds) *Neotestamentica et Semitica. Studies in Honour of M. Black*. Edinburgh 1969, 221-35
Bruyne, D. de, 'Quelques nouveaux documents pour la critique textuelle de l'Apocalypse d'Esdras'. *RBén* 32 (1920) 43-47
Buchholz, D.D. *Your Eyes Will Be Opened: A Study of the Greek (Ethiopic) Apocalypse of Peter* (SBLDS 97) Atlanta 1984
Budge, E.A.W. (ed) *Coptic Martyrdoms in the Dialect of Upper Egypt*. London 1914
- 'Egyptian Mythology in Coptic Writings', in id, *Coptic Apocrypha in the Dialect of Upper Egypt*. London 1913

– 'On the Fragments of a Coptic Version of an Encomium on Elijah the Tishbite, Attributed to Saint John Chrysostom'. *Transactions of the Society of Biblical Archaeology* 9 (1893) 355-404

Burkitt, F.C. *Jewish and Christian Apocalypses*. London 1914

Butterworth, G.W. *Origen: On First Principles*. New York 1966

Calder, W.M. 'The New Jerusalem of the Montanists', *Byzantion* 6 (1931) 421-5

– 'Philadelphia and Montanism', *BJRL* 7 (1923) 309-55

Cameron, R. – Dewey (eds. trs), A.J. *The Cologne Mani Codex: 'Concerning the Origin of his Body'* (SBLTT 15) Missoula 1979

Campenhausen, H. von, *The Formation of the Christian Bible*. Philadelphia 1972

Casadio, G. 'Patterns of Vision in Some Gnostic Tractates from Nag Hammadi', in Rassart-Ries, *Actes* 2, 395-401

Casel, O. *De philosophorum graecorum silentio mystico*. Giessen 1919

Caspar, E. *Die älteste römische Bischofsliste* (Schriften der Königsberger gelehrten Gesellschaft. Geisteswissenschaftliche Klasse 4) Berlin 1926

Chadwick, H. *Origen: Contra Celsum*. Cambridge 1965

– *Priscillian of Avila: The Occult and the Charismatic in the Early Church*. Oxford 1976

Charles, R.H. *The Book of Enoch or I Enoch*. Oxford 1912

– *A Critical and Exegetical Commentary on the Revelation of St. John* (ICC) Edinburgh 1920

– *Maṣḥafa kufâlê or The Ethiopic Version of the Hebrew Book of Jubilees*. Oxford 1895

Charles, R.H. (ed) *Apocrypha and Pseudepigrapha of the Old Testament* 1-2. Oxford 1913

Charles, R.H. – Morfill, W.R. *The Book of the Secrets of Enoch*. Oxford 1896

Charlesworth, J.H. 'Christian and Jewish Self-Definition in Light of the Christian Additions to the Apocryphal Writings', in Sanders, *Self-Definition* 2, 27-55

– 'History of the Rechabites', in id, *OTP* 2, 443-45

– *The Pseudepigrapha and Modern Research, with a Supplement* (SBLSCS 7) Chico 1981

Charlesworth, J.H. (ed) *The Old Testament Pseudepigrapha* 1-2. Garden City NY 1983-85

Charlesworth, J.H. – Mueller, J. *The New Testament Apocrypha and Pseudepigrapha: A Guide to Publications, with Excurses on Apocalypses* (ATLA Bibliography Series 17) Metuchen NJ – London 1987

Clark, E.A. 'New Perspectives on the Origenist Controversy: Human Embodiment and Ascetic Strategies'. *CH* 59 (1990) 145-62

Collins, A.Y. *Crisis and Catharsis: The Power of the Apocalypse*. Philadelphia 1984

– 'The Early Christian Apocalypses', in J.J. Collins, *Apocalypse: Morphology*, 61-103

– 'The Origin of the Designation of Jesus as "Son of Man"'. *HTR* 80 (1987) 391-407

Collins, J.J. 'Apocalyptic Eschatology as the Transcendence of Death'. *CBQ* 36 (1974) 21-43

– *The Apocalyptic Imagination*. New York 1987

– 'Apocalyptic Literature', in Kraft-Nickelsburg, *Early Judaism*, 345-70

– *The Apocalyptic Vision of the Book of Daniel* (HSM 16) Missoula 1977

– *Between Athens and Jerusalem; Jewish Identity in the Hellenistic Diaspora*. New York 1983

—— 'The Genre Apocalypse in Hellenistic Judaism', in Hellholm, *Apocalypticism*, 531-48

—— 'Introduction: Towards the Morphology of a Genre', in id, *Apocalypse: Morphology*, 1-19

—— 'The Jewish Apocalypses', in id, *Apocalypse: Morphology*, 21-49

—— 'Pseudonymity, Historical Reviews, and the Genre of the Revelation of John'. *CBQ* 39 (1977) 329-43

– *The Sibylline Oracles of Egyptian Judaism* (SBLDS 13) Missoula 1974

– 'Was the Dead Sea Sect an Apocalyptic Movement?' in Schiffman, *Archaeology and History*, 25-51

Collins, J.J. (ed) *Apocalypse: The Morphology of a Genre* (Semeia 14) Missoula 1979

Conzelmann, H. *The Theology of St. Luke*. ET New York – Evanston 1961

Coquin, R.-G. 'Les lettres festales d'Athanase (CPG 2102), Un nouveau complément: Le manuscrit IFAO copte 25'. *OLP* 15 (1984) 138-44

Coser, L. *The Functions of Social Conflict*. New York 1956

Cowley, R.W. 'The Biblical Canon of the Ethiopian Orthodox Church Today'. *Ostkirchliche Studien* 27 (1974) 318-23

Crehan, J.H. *Athenagoras, Embassy for the Christians, the Resurrection of the Dead* (ACW 23) Westminster – London 1956

Cross, F.L. – Livingstone, E.A. (eds) *The Oxford Dictionary of the Christian Church*. London 1958, 2nd ed Oxford 1974

Crum, W.E. *The Monastery of Epiphanius at Thebes* 1-2. New York 1926

Cureton, W. *History of the Martyrs of Palestine by Eusebius*. London 1861

Daniélou, J. 'Judéo-christianisme et gnose', in *Aspects du judéo-christianisme: Colloque de Strasbourg 23-25 avril 1964*. Paris 1965, 139-66

– *The Origins of Latin Christianity*. ET London 1977

– *The Theology of Jewish Christianity*. ET London 1964

– 'La typologie millénariste de la semaine dans le christianisme primitif'. *VC* 2 (1948) 1-16

Daube, D. *The New Testament and Rabbinic Judaism*. New York 1973

Daumas, F. 'Littérature prophétique et exégétique égyptienne et commentaires esséniens', in *A la rencontre de Dieu*, Le Puy 1961, 203-21

Davies, G.I. 'Apocalyptic and Historiography'. *JSOT* 5 (1978) 15-28

BeDuhn, J.D. 'The Cross-Cultural Unity of Manichaeism: Problems and Prospects' (paper presented at Society of Biblical Literature 1993 Annual Meeting, Washington DC)

Deferrari, R.J. *St. Cyprian: Treatises* (FC 36) New York 1958

Delehaye, H. 'Les martyrs d'Égypte'. *Analecta Bollandiana* 40 (1922) 5-154

Delcor, M. 'Melchizedek from Genesis to the Qumran Texts and the Epistle to the Hebrews'. *JSJ* 2 (1971) 115-35

– *Le Testament d'Abraham* (SVTP 2) Leiden 1973

Denis, A.-M. *Fragmenta Pseudepigraphorum quae supersunt Graeca* (PVTG 3) Leiden 1970

– *Introduction aux pseudépigraphes grecs de l'Ancien Testament* (SVTP 1) Leiden 1970

Depuydt, L. (gen ed) *Homiletica from the Pierpont Morgan Library* 1-2 (CSCO 524-25, Scr. coptici 43-44) Louvain 1991

Destinon, J. von, *Die Chronologie des Josephus*. Kiel 1880

Dexinger, F. *Henochs Zehnwochenapokalypse und offene Probleme der Apokalyptikforschung*. Leiden 1977

– *Sturz der Göttersöhne oder Engel vor der Sintflut? Versuch eines Neuverständnisses von Genesis 6, 2-4, unter Berücksichtigung der Religionsvergleichenden und exegesegeschichtlichen Methode* (WBT 13) Wien 1966

Dillmann, A. (ed) *Biblia Veteris Testamenti Aethiopica 5: Libri Apocryphi*. Berlin 1894

Dimant, D. 'The Seventy Weeks Chronology (Dan 9,24-27) in the Light of New Qumranic Texts', in A. S. Van der Woude (ed) *The Book of Daniel in the Light of New Findings*. Leuven 1993, 57-76

Dobschütz, E. von, *Das Decretum Gelasianum* (TU 38.4) Leipzig 1912

Dodd, C.H. 'The Fall of Jerusalem and the "Abomination of Desolation"'. *JRS* 37 (1947) 47-54

Dods, M. (tr) *The City of God by Saint Augustine*. New York 1950

Döllinger, J.J.I. von, *Beiträge zur Sektengeschichte des Mittelalters*. Munich 1890

Donahue, J.R. 'Recent Studies on the Origin of "Son of Man" in the Gospels'. *CBQ* 48 (1986) 484-98

Donfried, K.P. 'Peter'. *ABD* 5, 251-63

Doresse, J. 'Les apocalypses de Zoroastre, de Zostrien, de Nicothée', in *Coptic Studies in Honor of Walter Ewing Crum*. Boston 1950, 255-63

– *Des hiéroglyphes à la croix*. Istanbul 1960

– 'Saints coptes de haute-Égypte'. *Journal asiatique* 236 (1948) 247-70

– 'Visions méditerranéennes'. *La table ronde* 110 (1957) 29-35

Dornseiff, F. *Das Alphabet in Mystik und Magie* (ΣΤΟΙΧΕΙΑ 7) Leipzig 1925

Drescher, J. 'A Coptic Amulet', in *Coptic Studies in Honor of Walter Ewing Crum*. Boston 1950, 265-70 and Plate

Drijvers, H.J.W. *Bardaisan of Edessa* (SSN 6) Assen 1966

– *The Book of the Laws of Countries: Dialogue on Fate of Bardaisan of Edessa* (SSN 3) Assen 1965

Droge, A. *Homer or Moses? Early Christian Interpretations of the History of Culture* (HUT 26) Tubingen 1989

Dumville, D.N. 'Biblical Apocrypha and the Early Irish: A Preliminary Investigation'. *Proceedings of the Royal Irish Academy* 73C, 8 (1973) 299-338

Ehrhardt, A. *The Apostolic Succession.* London 1953

Eisler R. *ΙΗΣΟΥΣ ΒΑΣΙΛΕΥΣ ΟΥ ΒΑΣΙΛΕΥΣΑΣ* 1-2. Heidelberg 1929-30

Erbstösser, M. *Heretics in the Middle Ages.* Leipzig 1984

Evans, E. *Tertullian's Treatise on the Resurrection.* London 1960

Evelyn-White, H.G. *The Monasteries of the Wadi 'n Natrun* 1-2. New York 1926

Ewald, H.G.A. (ed) *Das vierte Ezrabuch* (AGWG 11) Göttingen 1863

Fallon, F. 'The Gnostic Apocalypses', in Collins, *Apocalypse: Morphology*, 123-47

Feldman, L.H. 'Prophets and Prophecy in Josephus'. *JTS* 41 (1990) 386-422

– *Josephus and Modern Scholarship (1937-80).* Berlin 1984

– see also Thackcray-Marcus-Feldman

Ferrar, W.J. (tr) *The Proof of the Gospel being the Demonstratio Evangelica of Eusebius of Caesarea* (SPCK Translations of Christian Literature Series 1) London – New York 1920

Festugière, A.-J. (ed) *Historia monachorum in aegypto* (Subsidia hagiographica 53) Brussels 1971

– *La Révélation d'Hermès Trismégiste* 1-4. Paris 1950-54

Fischel, H.A. 'Martyr and Prophet (A Study in Jewish Literature)'. *JQR* 37 (1947) 364-71

Flusser, D. 'The Apocryphal Book of *Ascensio Isaiae* and the Dead Sea Sect'. *IEJ* 3 (1953) 34-47

Fodor, A. 'The Origins of the Arabic Legends of the Pyramids'. *Acta Orientalia Hungaricae* 23 (1970) 335-63

Forget, J. *Synaxarium Alexandrinum* (CSCO 78, Scr. arabici 12, 3rd ser. 18) Rome 1921

Fowden, G. *The Egyptian Hermes.* Cambridge 1987

Fox, R.L. *Pagans and Christians in the Mediterranean World from the Second Century AD to the Conversion of Constantine.* London 1986 – New York 1987

Fraidl, F. *Die Exegese der siebzig Wochen Daniels in der alten und mittleren Zeit.* Graz 1883

Frankfurter, D. 'The Cult of the Martyrs in Egypt Before Constantine: The Evidence of the Coptic *Apocalypse of Elijah'. VC* 48 (1994) 25-47

– *Elijah in Upper Egypt: The Apocalypse of Elijah and Early Egyptian Christianity* (SAC 7) Minneapolis 1993

Frend, W.H.C. 'Montanism: Research and Problems'. *RSLR* 20 (1984) 521-37

Fuks, A. 'Aspects of the Jewish Revolt in A.D. 115-117'. *JRS* 51 (1961) 98-104

– 'The Jewish Revolt in Egypt (A.D. 115-117) in the Light of the Papyri'. *Aegyptus* 33 (1953) 131-58

Gaston, L. *No Stone on Another: Studies in the Significance of the Fall of Jerusalem in the Synoptic Gospels* (NovTSup 23) Leiden 1970

Gelzer, H. *Sextus Julius Africanus und die byzantinische Chronographie* 1-2. Leipzig 1898, repr New York 1964

Geoltrain, P. 'Remarques sur la diversité des pratiques discursives apocryphes: l'exemple de 5 Esdras', in P. Geoltrain – E. Junod – J.-C. Picard (eds) *Apocrypha: Le Champ des Apocryphes* (La fable apocryphe 2) Turnhout 1991, 17-30

Gildemeister, J. *Esdrae liber quartus Arabice e codice Vaticano.* Bonn 1877

Ginzberg, L. 'Some Observations on the Attitude of the Synagogue toward the Apocalyptic-eschatological Writings'. *JBL* 41 (1922) 115-36

Girard, L. Saint-Paul, 'Un fragment de liturgie magique copte sur ostrakon'. *Annales du service des antiquités de l'Égypte* 27 (1927) 62-68

Giversen, S. – Pearson, B. 'The Testimony of Truth', in *NHL*, Library, 448-59

Glorie, F. (ed) *S. Hieronymi Presbyteri Opera* 1.5 (CCL 75A) Turnhout 1964

Goehring, J.E. 'The Encroaching Desert: Literary Production and Ascetic Space in Early Christian Egypt'. *Journal of Early Christian Studies* 1 (1993) 281-96

Goldbacher, A. (ed) *S. Augustini Epistulae* (CSEL 44; 57) Vienna 1904; 1911

Goodspeed, E.J. *A History of Early Christian Literature.* rev ed R. Grant. Chicago 1966

Görgemanns, H. – Karpp, H. *Origenes Vier Bücher von den Prinzipien* (Texte zur Forschung 24) Darmstadt 1976

Grabar, A. *Martyrium: Recherches sur le culte des reliques et l'art chrétien antique* 1-2, Paris 1946

Graham, W.A. *Beyond the Written Word: Oral Aspects of Scripture in the History of Religion.* Cambridge 1987

Grant, R.M. *Gnosticism and Early Christianity.* 2nd ed New York 1966

– 'Manichees and Christians in the Third and Early Fourth Centuries', in J. Bergman – K. Drynjeff – H. Ringgren (eds) *Ex Orbe Religionum* (NumenSup 21) Leiden 1972, 430-39

Gray, R. *Prophetic Figures in Late Second Temple Jewish Palestine.* New York 1993

Greenfield, J.C. – Stone, M.E. 'The Enochic Pentateuch and the Date of the Similitudes'. *HTR* 70 (1977) 51-65

Greenfield, R.P.H. *Traditions of Belief in Late Byzantine Demonology.* Amsterdam 1988

Gregg, R.C. *Athanasius: The Life of Antony and the Letter to Marcellinus.* New York 1980

Grelot, P. 'Les versions grecques de Daniel'. *Bib* 47 (1966) 381-402

– 'Soixante-dix semaines d'années'. *Bib* 50 (1969) 169-86

Grenfell, B.P. – Hunt, A.S. *The Amherst Papyri* 1: *The Ascension of Isaiah and Other Theological Fragments.* London 1900, repr Milan 1975

Griggs, C.W. *Early Egyptian Christianity: From Its Origins to 451 C.E.* (Coptic Studies 2) Leiden 1990

Groh, D.E. 'Utterance and Exegesis: Biblical Interpretation in the Montanist Crisis', in D.E. Groh – R. Jewett (eds) *The Living Text*, Lanham MD 1985, 73-95

Grohmann, A. 'Die im äthiopischen, arabischen und koptischen erhaltenen Visionen Apa Schenute's von Atripe'. *ZDMG* 67 (1913) 187-267; 68 (1914) 1-46

Gronewald, M. *Didymos der Blinde: Kommentar zum Ecclesiastes* (Papyrologische Texte und Abhandlungen 22) Bonn 1971

Gruenwald, I. *Apocalyptic and Merkavah Mysticism* (AGJU 14) Leiden 1980

– 'Knowledge and Vision'. *IOS* 3 [1973] 63-107

– 'Manichaeism and Judaism in Light of the Cologne Mani Codex'. *ZPE* 50 (1983) 29-45

Guillaumont, A. 'Les visions mystiques dans le monachisme oriental chrétien', in id, *Aux origines du monachisme chrétien* (Spiritualité orientale 30) Bégrolles-en-Mauges 1979

Gunkel, H. *Schöpfung und Chaos in Urzeit und Endzeit.* Göttingen 1895

Hahn, I. 'Josephus und die Eschatologie von Qumran', in H. Bardtke (ed) *Qumran-Probleme. Vorträge des Leipziger Symposions* (Deutsche Akad. d. Wiss. Sekt. f. Altertumswiss. 42) Berlin 1963, 167-91

– 'Josephus és a Bellum Judaicum eschatologiai hattere' (Hungarian = 'Josephus and the Eschatological Background of the Bellum Judaicum'). *Antik Tanulmanyuk – Studia Antiqua* 8 (1961) 199-220 [English summary in Feldman, *Josephus*, 471]

Hall, H.R. (ed) *Coptic and Greek Texts of the Christian Period in the British Museum.* London 1905

Hall, R.G. 'The *Ascension of Isaiah*: Community, Situation, Date, and Place in Early Christianity'. *JBL* 109 (1990) 289-306

– *Revealed Histories: Techniques for Ancient Jewish and Christian Historiography* (JSPSup 6) Sheffield 1991

Hanson, R.P.C. *Origen's Doctrine of Tradition.* London 1954

Harris, W.V. *Ancient Literacy.* Cambridge MA 1989

Harnack, A. von, *Der kirchengeschichtliche Ertrag der exegetischen Arbeiten des Origenes* (TU 42.4) Leipzig 1919

– *The Mission and Expansion of Christianity in the First Three Centuries.* 2nd ed London 1905

Hartel, G.S. (ed) *Thasci Caecili Cypriani Opera Omnia* (CSEL 3.1) Vienna 1871

Hartman, L. *Prophecy Interpreted* (ConBNT 1) Lund 1966

—— 'The Functions of Some So-called Apocalyptic Time-tables'. *NTS* 22 (1976) 1-14

Hartman, L. – Di Lella, A.A. *The Book of Daniel. A New Translation with Introduction and Commentary* (AB 23) Garden City NY 1978

Haugg, D. *Die zwei Zeugen: Eine exegetische Studie über Apok 11,1-13.* Münster 1936

Hedrick, C.W. 'Gnostic Proclivities in the Greek *Life of Pachomius* and the *Sitz im Leben* of the Nag Hammadi Library'. *NovT* 22 (1980) 78-94

Heer, J.M. *Die Stammbäume Jesu nach Matthäus und Lukas: Ihre ursprungliche Bedeutung und Text-Gestalt und ihre Quellen* (BibS[F] 15.1) Freiburg 1910

Heikel, I. (ed) *Eusebius Werke* 6 (GCS 23) Leipzig 1913

Heine, R.E. *The Montanist Oracles and Testimonia* (NAPSMonSer 14) Macon GA 1989

Helderman, J. 'Melchisedek, Melchisedekianer und die koptische Frömmigkeit', in Rassart-Ries, *Actes* 2, 402-15

Hellholm, D. *Das Visionsbuch des Hermas als Apokalypse* (ConBOT 13.1). Lund 1980

Hellholm, D. (ed) *Apocalypticism in the Mediterranean World and the Near East*. Tübingen 1983

Helm, R. (ed) *Eusebius Werke* 7 (GCS 24³) Berlin 1984

Hemer, C.J. *The Letters to the Seven Churches of Asia in Their Local Setting* (JSNTSup 11) Sheffield 1986.

Hengel, M. *Judaism and Hellenism. Studies in their Encounter in Palestine during the Early Hellenistic Period* 1-2 (in 1 vol) London – Philadelphia 1974

– 'Messianische Hoffnung und politischer "Radikalismus" in der jüdisch-hellenistischen Diaspora', in Hellholm, *Apocalypticism*, 655-86

Hennecke, E. – Schneemelcher, W. (eds) *New Testament Apocrypha* 1-2. ET Philadelphia 1963-65; Philadelphia 1976; ET of rev ed Louisville 1991-92

Henning, W.B. 'The Book of Giants'. *BSO(A)S* 11 (1943) 52-74

Henrichs, A. 'Literary Criticism of the Cologne Mani Codex', in Layton, *Rediscovery* 2, 724-33

Henrichs, A. – Koenen, L. 'Der Kölner Mani-Kodex (P. Colon. inv. nr. 4780)'. *ZPE* 19 (1975) 1-85; 32 (1978) 87-199; 44 (1981) 201-318; 48 (1982) 1-59

Henry, R. (ed, tr) *Bibliothèque Photius*. Paris 1959

Hercher, R. (ed) *Epistolographi graeci*. Paris 1873, repr Amsterdam 1965

Hermann, A. *Die ägyptische Königsnovelle* (Leipziger Ägyptologische Studien 10) Glückstadt 1938

Himmelfarb, M. *Ascent to Heaven in Jewish and Christian Apocalypses*. New York 1993

– 'The Experience of the Visionary and Genre in the *Ascension of Isaiah* 6-11 and the *Apocalypse of Paul*'. *Semeia* 36 (1986) 97-111

– 'Heavenly Ascent and the Relationship of the Apocalypses and the *Hekhalot* Literature'. *HUCA* 59 (1988) 73-100

– 'A Report on Enoch in Rabbinic Literature', in P. Achtemeier (ed) *SBLSP* (1978) 259-69

– 'Revelation and Rapture: The Transformation of the Visionary in the Ascent Apocalypses', in J.J. Collins – J.H. Charlesworth (eds) *Mysteries and Revelations: Apocalyptic Studies Since the Uppsala Colloquium* (JSPSup 9) Sheffield 1991, 79-90

– *Tours of Hell: An Apocalyptic Form in Jewish and Christian Literature*. Philadelphia 1983

Hindley, J.C. 'Towards a Date for the Similitudes of Enoch: An Historical Approach'. *NTS* 14 (1967-68) 551-65

Hölscher, G. *Die Quellen des Josephus für die Zeit vom Exil bis zum jüdischen Kriege*. Leipzig 1904

Holl, K. (ed) *Epiphanius* 1 (GCS 25) Leipzig 1915

Hopfner, T. *Griechisch-ägyptischer Offenbarungszauber* 1-2. Frankfurt 1924, repr Amsterdam 1974-90

Hopkins, K. 'Conquest by Book', in M. Beard (ed) *Literacy in the Roman World* (Journal of Roman Archaeology Supplementary Series 3) Ann Arbor 1991, 133-58

Horsley, G.H.R. 'Name Change as an Indication of Religious Conversion in Antiquity'. *Numen* 34 (1987) 1-17

Huggins, R.V. 'A Canonical "Book of Periods" at Qumran?' *RevQ* 59 (1992) 421-36

Hultgård, A. *L'eschatologie des Testaments des Douze Patriarches* 1-2. Uppsala 1977-82

Hunt, A.S. *The Oxyrhynchus Papyri* 7. London 1910

Hutter, M. '"Halte diese Worte geheim!" – Eine Notiz zu einem apokalyptischen Gebrauch'. *Biblische Notizen* 25 (1984) 14-18

Irmscher, J. 'The Book of Elchasai', in *NTA* 2, 685-90

– 'The Pseudo-Clementines', in *NTA* 2, 532-70

James, M.R. *The Lost Apocrypha of the Old Testament*. New York 1936

– *The Testament of Abraham* (TextsS 2,2) Cambridge 1892

Jansen, H.L. *The Coptic Story of Cambyses' Invasion of Egypt* (Avhandlinger utgitt av det Norske Videntskaps-Akademi i Oslo; 2, Hist.-Filos. Klasse 1950, 2) Oslo 1950
Janssens, Y. 'Apocalypses de Nag Hammadi', in J. Lambrecht (ed) *L'Apocalypse johannique et l'apocalyptique dans le Nouveau Testament*. Gembloux 1980, 69-75
– 'Le thème de la fornication des anges', in Bianchi, *Le origini*, 488-95
Jeansonne, S.P. *The Old Greek Translation of Daniel 7-12* (CBQMS 19) Washington 1988
Jenks, G.C. *The Origins and Early Development of the Antichrist Myth* (BZNW 59) Berlin – New York 1991
Jeremias, J. *The Eucharistic Words of Jesus*. ET Oxford 1955
Johnson, D.W. 'Coptic Reactions to Gnosticism and Manichaeism'. *Mus* 100 (1987) 199-209
Johnson, D.W. (ed) *A Panegyric on Macarius, Bishop of Tkôw, Attributed to Dioscorus of Alexandria* (CSCO 415-16, Scriptores coptici 41-42) Louvain 1980
Johnson, J.H. 'The Demotic Chronicle as an Historical Source'. *Enchoria* 4 (1974) 1-17
– 'Is the Demotic Chronicle an Anti-Greek Tract?' in H.-J. Thissen - K.-Th. Zauzich (eds) *Grammata Demotika*. Würzburg 1984, 107-24
Johnson, S. 'Asia Minor and Early Christianity', in Neusner, *Christianity, Judaism* 2, 77-145
Johnston, S.I. *Hekate Soteira* (American Classical Studies 21) Atlanta 1990
Jones, B.W. 'The Prayer in Daniel IX'. *VT* 17 (1968) 488-93
Jones, F.S. 'Clementines, Pseudo-', *ABD* 1, 1061f
Jonge, M. de, *The Testaments of the Twelve Patriarchs. A Study of their Text, Composition and Origin*. Assen 1953
– 'The Testaments of the Twelve Patriarchs: Christian and Jewish', in H.J. de Jonge (ed) *Jewish Eschatology, Early Christian Christology, and the Testaments of the Twelve Patriarchs* (NovTSup 63) Leiden 1991, 233-43
Jonge, M. de – Woude, A.S. van der, '11Q Melchizedek and the New Testament'. *NTS* 12 (1966) 301-26
Kahle, P.E. (ed) *Bala'izah: Coptic Texts from Deir El-Bala'izah in Upper Egypt* 1. Oxford 1954
Kákosy, L. 'Gnosis und ägyptische Religion', in Bianchi, *Le origini*, 238-47
– 'Hermes and Egypt', in A.B. Lloyd (ed) *Studies in Pharaonic Religion and Society* (Egypt Exploration Society Occasional Publications 8) London 1992, 258-61
Kasher, A. *The Jews in Hellenistic and Roman Egypt: The Struggle for Equal Rights*. Tübingen 1985
Kaufmann, J. 'Apokalyptik', in *Encylopaedia Judaica* 2. Berlin 1928-34, 1142-54
Kippenberg, H.G. 'Ein Vergleich jüdischer, christlicher, und gnostischer Apokalyptik', in Hellholm, *Apocalypticism*, 751-68
Kittel, G. (ed) *Theological Dictionary of the New Testament* 1-10. ET G.W. Bromiley, Grand Rapids – London 1964-76
Klijn, A.F.J. *Seth in Jewish, Christian and Gnostic Literature* (NovTSup 46) Leiden 1977
Klijn, A.F.J. (ed) *Der lateinische Text der Apokalypse des Esra*. Berlin 1983
Knibb, M. 'The Date of the Parables of Enoch: A Critical Review'. *NTS* 25 (1978-79) 344-59
– *The Ethiopic Book of Enoch* 1-2. Oxford 1978
– 'Martyrdom and Ascension of Isaiah', in *OTP* 2, 143-76
Klostermann, E. – Benz, E. (eds) *Origenes Werke* 10 (GCS 40) Leipzig 1935; vol 11 (GCS 38²) Berlin 1976
Koch, K. *The Rediscovery of Apocalyptic*. Naperville 1972
—— 'Die mysteriösen Zahlen der judäischen Könige und die apokalyptischen Jahrwochen'. *VT* 28 (1978) 433-41
Koenen, L. 'Bemerkungen zum Text des Töpferorakels und zu dem Akaziensymbol'. *ZPE* 13 (1974) 313-19
– 'The Dream of Nektanebos'. *BASP* 22 (1985) 171-94
– 'Manichaean Apocalypticism at the Crossroads of Iranian, Egyptian, Jewish and Christian Thought', in L. Cirillo (ed) *Codex Manichaicus Coloniensis: Atti del simposio internazionale*. Cosenza 1986, 153-68, 285-332
– 'Die Prophezeiungen des "Töpfers"'. *ZPE* 2 (1968) 178-209

– 'A Supplementary Note on the Date of the Oracle of the Potter'. *ZPE* 54 (1984) 9-13
Koenen, L. – Römer, C. (eds, tr) *Der Kölner Mani-Kodex: Über das Werden seines Leibes* (Abh. der rheinisch-westfälischen Akad. der Wiss., Papyrologica Coloniensa 14) Opladen 1988
Koester, H. 'The Intention and Scope of Trajectories', in Koester-Robinson, *Trajectories*, 269-79
– 'One Jesus and Four Primitive Gospels', in Koester-Robinson, *Trajectories*, 158-204
Koester, H. – Robinson, J.M. (eds) *Trajectories through Early Christianity*. Philadelphia 1971
Koetschau, P. (ed) *Origenes Werke* 1 (GCS 2) Leipzig 1899; vol 2 (GCS 3) 1899; vol 5 (GCS 22) 1913
Kraft, R.A. 'The Multiform Jewish Heritage of Early Christianity', in Neusner, *Christianity, Judaism* 3, 174-99
– 'The Pseudepigrapha in Christianity', in Reeves, *Tracing the Threads*, 55-86
– 'Reassessing the "Recensional Problem" in the Testament of Abraham', in Nickelsburg, *Studies on the Testament of Abraham*, 121-37
– 'In Search of "Jewish Christianity" and its "Theology": Problems of Definition and Methodology'. *RSR* 60 (1972) 81-92
Kraft, R.A. – Nickelsburg, G.W.E. (eds) *Early Judaism and its Modern Interpreters*. Atlanta 1986
Krebber, B. *Didymos der Blinde: Kommentar zum Ecclesiastes (Tura-Papyrus)* 4. *Kommentar zu Eccl. Kap. 7-8,8*. Bonn 1972
Kropp, A. *Ausgewählte koptische Zaubertexte*. Brussels 1931
Kuhn, K.H. 'A Coptic Jeremiah Apocryphon'. *Mus* 83 (1970) 95-135, 291-350
Kümmel, W.G. *Introduction to the New Testament*. [ET of 14th German edition 1965] London 1966
Laato, A. 'The Seventy Yearweeks in the Book of Daniel'. *ZAW* 102 (1990) 212-25
Lacau, P. 'Fragments de l'Ascension d'Isaie en copte'. *Mus* 59 (1946) 453-67
Lacocque, A. 'The Liturgical Prayer in Daniel 9'. *HUCA* 47 (1976) 119-142
Lake, K. *The Apostolic Fathers* 1. Cambridge MA 1985
Lake, K. – Oulton, J.E.L. (tr) *Eusebius; The Ecclesiastical History* 1-2 (LCL) London 1938
Lantschoot, A. van, 'Fragments coptes d'une homélie de Jean de Parallos contre les livres hérétiques', in *Miscellanea Giovanni Mercati* (Studi e testi 121-26) vol 1, Vatican City 1946, 296-326
Lawlor, H.J. 'The Book of Enoch in the Egyptian Church'. *Hermathena* 30 (1904) 178-83
– 'Early Citations From the Book of Enoch'. *The Journal of Philology* 25 (1897) 164-225
Layton, B. *The Gnostic Scriptures: A New Translation with Annotations and Introductions*. Garden City NY 1987 – London 1990
Layton, B. (ed) *The Rediscovery of Gnosticism. Proceedings of the International Conference on Gnosticism at Yale, 1978* 1-2 (NumenSup 41) Leiden 1981-82
LeClerq, H. 'L'alphabet vocalique des Gnostiques', in *DACL* 1, 1268-88
Lefébure, L. 'L'oeuf dans la religion égyptienne'. *RHR* 16 (1887) 16-25
Lefort, L.Th. 'Coptica Lovaniensia: Ascension d'Isaïe'. *Mus* 51 (1938) 24-30
– 'Fragments d'apocryphes: 2. Ascension d'Isaïe'. *Mus* 52 (1939) 7-10
Lefort, L.-Th. (ed) *S. Athanase: Lettres festales et pastorales en copte* 1 (CSCO 150-51, Scr. coptici 19-20) Louvain 1955
Leipoldt, J. *Ägyptische Urkunden aus den königlichen Museen zu Berlin. Koptische Urkunden* 1. Berlin 1904
– *Schenute von Atripe und die Entstehung des national-ägyptischen Christentums* (TU 25) Leipzig 1903
Leipoldt, J. (ed) *Sinuthii archimandritae vitae et opera omnia* 1, 3-4 (CSCO 41-42 73, Scr. coptici 1-2 5) Paris 1913
Leipoldt, J. – Violet, B. 'Ein säidisches Bruchstück des vierten Esrabuches'. *Zeitschrift für ägyptische Sprache und Altertumskunde* 41 (1904) 137-40
Lévy, I. 'Les soixante-dix semaines de Daniel dans la chronologie juive'. *REJ* 51 (1906) 161-90
Lightfoot, J.B. *The Apostolic Fathers* (1891) ed and compl. by J.R. Harmer. Grand Rapids 1965
Logan, A. – Wedderburn, A. (eds) *The New Testament and Gnosis*. Edinburgh 1983
Loos, M. *Dualist Heresy in the Middle Ages*. Prague 1974

Lowe, E.A. (ed) *Codices Latini antiquiores* 1-7. Oxford 1934-71

Lührmann, D. 'Alttestamentliche Pseudepigraphen bei Didymos von Alexandrien'. *ZAW* 104 (1992) 231-49

Luttikhuizen, G.P. *The Revelation of Elchasai*. Tübingen 1985

MacCoull, L. 'The Apa Apollos Monastery of Pharoou (Aphrodito) and its Papyrus Archive'. *Mus* 106 (1993) 21-63

MacDermot, V. *The Cult of the Seer in the Ancient Middle East*. London 1971

MacDonald, D.R. *The Legend and the Apostle: The Battle for Paul in Story and Canon*. Philadelphia 1983

MacRae, G.W. 'The Apocalypse of Adam Reconsidered', in *SBLSP*, Missoula 1972, 573-9

– 'Apocalyptic Eschatology in Gnosticism', in Hellholm, *Apocalypticism*, 317-25

– 'The Coptic Testament of Abraham', in Nickelsburg, *Studies on the Testament of Abraham*, 327-40

MacRae, G.W. – Parrott, D.M. 'The Apocalypse of Adam', in *NHL*, 277-86

Mahé, J.-P. *Hermès en Haute-Égypte* 2 (Bibliothèque copte de Nag Hammadi 7) Quebec 1978-82

Maier, G. *Die Johannesoffenbarung und die Kirche* (WUNT 25) Tübingen 1981

Mango, C. *Byzantium: The Empire of New Rome*. New York 1980

Marbach, C. *Carmina scripturarum*. Hildesheim 1963

Marcus, R. – see Thackeray-Marcus-Feldman

Martens, A. *Das Buch Daniel im Lichte der Texte vom Toten Meer* (Stuttgarter Biblische Monographien) Würzburg 1971

Martin, A. 'Athanase et les mélitiens (325-335)', in C. Kannengiesser (ed) *Politique et théologie chez Athanase d'Alexandrie* (Théologie historique 27) Paris 1974, 31-61

– 'La réconciliation des *lapsi* en Égypte'. *RSLR* 22 (1986) 256-69

Martin, F. *Le livre d'Hénoch*. Paris 1906

Martínez, F.G. *Qumran and Apocalyptic: Studies on the Aramaic Texts from Qumran*. Leiden, 1992

McCown, C.C. 'Hebrew and Egyptian Apocalyptic Literature'. *HTR* 18 (1925) 357-411

McDonald, M.F. *Lactantius: The Divine Institutes Books I-VII* (FC 4) Washington 1964

McNamara, M. *The Apocrypha in the Irish Church*. Dublin 1975

Mearns, C.L. 'Dating the Similitudes of Enoch'. *NTS* 25 (1979) 360-69

Mensching, G. *Das heilige Schweigen*. Giessen 1926

Meyer, M. – Smith, R. (eds) *Ancient Christian Magic*. San Francisco 1994

Milik, J.T. *The Books of Enoch: Aramaic Fragments of Qumrân Cave 4*. Oxford 1976

– 'Fragments grecs du livre d'Hénoch (P. Oxy. XVII 2069)'. *Chronique d'Égypte* 46 (1971) 321-43

– 'Problèmes de la littérature hénochique à la lumière des fragments araméens de Qumrân'. *HTR* 64 (1971) 333-78

Miller, P.C. 'In Praise of Nonsense', in A.H. Armstrong (ed) *Classical Mediterranean Spirituality*. New York 1986, 481-505

Mondésert, C. – Caster, M. (eds, tr) *Clément d'Alexandrie, Stromate* I (SC 30) Paris 1951

Montgomery, J.A. *A Critical and Exegetical Commentary on the Book of Daniel* (ICC 22) Edinburgh 1927

Morin, D.G. (ed) *S. Hieronymi Presbyteri Opera* (CCL 78.2) Turnhout 1958

Mosshammer, A.A. (ed) *Georgii Syncelli Ecloga Chronographica*. Leipzig 1984

Motte, L. 'L'hiéroglyphe, d'Esna à l'Évangile de Vérité', in *Deuxième journée d'études coptes* (Cahiers de la bibliothèque copte 3) Louvain 1986, 111-16

Müller, C.D.G. 'Epistula Apostolorum', in *NTA* 1 (1991 ed) 249-84

– 'The Ascension of Isaiah', in *NTA* 2 (1992 ed) 603-20

Müller, K. 'Die Ansätze der Apokalyptik', in J. Maier – J. Schreiner (eds) *Literatur und Religion des Frühjudentums*. Würzburg 1973, 31-42

Müller, U. 'Apocalyptic Currents', in J. Becker (ed) *Christian Beginnings*. ET Louisville 1993, 281-329

Munier, H. 'Mélanges de littérature copte'. *Annales du service des antiquités de l'Égypte* 23 (1923) 212-15

Murray R. 'Jews, Hebrews, and Christians: Some Needed Distinctions'. *NovT* 24 (1982) 194-208

Musurillo, H. *The Acts of the Christian Martyrs: Introductions, Texts and Translations* (Oxford Early Christian Texts) Oxford 1972

Nau, F. 'Histoires des solitaires égyptiens'. *Revue de l'orient chrétien* 12 (1907) 43-69, 171-89, 393-413; 13 (1908) 47-66, 266-97; 14 (1909) 357-79; 17 (1912) 204-11, 294-301; 18 (1913) 137-46

– 'Traduction des Lettres XII et XIII de Jacques d'Édessa'. *Revue de l'orient chrétien* 10 (1905) 197-208; 258-82

Neusner, J. (ed) *Christianity, Judaism, and other Greco-Roman Cults: Studies for Morton Smith at 60* 1-4. Leiden 1972

Newsom, C.A. *Songs of the Sabbath Sacrifice: A Critical Edition* (HSM 27) Atlanta 1985

Neyrey, J. *2 Peter, Jude* (AB 37C) New York 1993

Nickelsburg, G.W.E. 'The Apocalyptic Message of 1 Enoch 92-105'. *CBQ* 39 (1977) 309-28

– 'Eschatology in the Testament of Abraham: A Study of the Judgment Scenes in the Two Recensions', in id, *Studies on the Testament of Abraham*, 29-40

– *Jewish Literature Between the Bible and the Mishnah*. Philadelphia 1987

– *Resurrection, Immortality, and Eternal Life in Intertestamental Judaism* (HTS 26) Cambridge MA 1972

– 'Two Enochic Manuscripts: Unstudied Evidence for Egyptian Christianity', in H.W. Attridge – J.J. Collins – T.H. Tobin (eds) *Of Scribes and Scrolls: Studies on the Hebrew Bible, Intertestamental Judaism, and Christian Origins presented to John Strugnell on the occasion of his sixtieth birthday* (CTSRR 5) Lanham 1990, 251-60

Nickelsburg, G.W.E. (ed) *Studies on the Testament of Abraham* (SBLSCS 6) Missoula 1976

Nicholson, O. 'Flight from Persecution as Imitation of Christ: Lactantius' Divine Institutes IV.18, 1-2'. *JTS* 40 (1989) 48-65

Niese, B. (ed) *Flavii Iosephi Opera* 1-7. Berlin 1887-94

Nock, A.D. – Festugière, A.-J. (eds) *Corpus Hermeticum* 1-4. Paris 1945-54

Norden, E. *Agnostos Theos. Untersuchungen zur Formgeschichte religiöser Rede.* Leipzig 1913

Norelle, E. *L'Ascension d'Isaïe.* Turnhout 1993

Odeberg, H. 'ΕΝΩΧ'. *TDNT* 2, 556-60

Oepke, A. 'καλύπτω, κτλ., *TDNT* 3.556-92

Orlandi, T. 'A Catechesis against Apocryphal Texts by Shenute and the Gnostic Texts of Nag Hammadi'. *HTR* 75 (1982) 85-95

– 'Coptic Literature', in Pearson-Goehring, *Roots*, 51-81

– 'Gli Apocrifi copti'. *Augustinianum* 23 (1983) 57-71

Osburn, C.D. '1 Enoch 80:2-8 (67:5-7) and Jude 12-13'. *CBQ* 47 (1985) 296-303

– 'The Christological Use of I Enoch i.9 in Jude 14, 15'. *NTS* 23 (1976-77) 334-41

Oulton – see Lake-Oulton

Pagels, E. 'Visions, Appearances, and Apostolic Authority: Gnostic and Orthodox Traditions', in U. Bianchi *et al* (eds) *Gnosis: Festschrift für Hans Jonas.* Göttingen 1978, 415-30

Palmer, A. *The Seventh Century in the West-Syrian Chronicles.* Liverpool 1993

Parrott, D.M. 'Gnosticism and Egyptian Religion'. *NovT* 29 (1987) 73-93

– 'The 13 Kingdoms of the Apocalypse of Adam: Origin, Meaning and Significance'. *NovT* 31 (1989) 67-87

Pearson, B.A. 'Christians and Jews in First-Century Alexandria', in G.W.E. Nickelsburg – G.W. MacRae (eds) *Christians among Jews and Gentiles*, Philadelphia 1986, 206-16

– 'Earliest Christianity in Egypt: Some Observations', in Pearson-Goehring, *Roots*, 132-54

– 'The Figure of Melchizedek in Gnostic Literature', in id, *Gnosticism, Judaism,* 108-23

– 'Friedländer Revisited: Alexandrian Judaism and Gnostic Origins', in id, *Gnosticism, Judaism,* 10-28

– *Gnosticism, Judaism, and Egyptian Christianity* (SAC 5) Minneapolis 1990

– 'Jewish Elements in Gnosticism and the Development of Gnostic Self-Definition', in Sanders, *Self-Definition* 1, 151-60, 240-45

- 'Jewish Sources in Gnostic Literature', in Stone, *Jewish Writings*, 443-81
- 'The Pierpont Morgan Fragments of a Coptic Enoch Apocryphon', in Nickelsburg, *Studies on the Testament of Abraham*, 227-83
- 'Use, Authority, and Exegesis of Mikra in Gnostic Literature', in M.J. Mulder (ed) *Miqra* (CRINT II/1) 635-52
Pearson, B. – Goehring, J. (eds) *The Roots of Egyptian Christianity*. Philadelphia 1986
Perdrizet, P.I. – Lefebvre, G. (eds) *Les graffites grecs du memnonion d'Abydos*. Nancy 1919
Perkins, P. 'Apocalypse of Adam: The Genre and Function of a Gnostic Apocalypse'. *CBQ* 39 (1977) 382-95
- *The Gnostic Dialogue*. New York 1980
- 'Pistis Sophia', in *ABD* 5, 375f
- 'World, On the Origin of', in *ABD* 6, 972f
Piankoff, A. 'La descente aux enfers dans les textes égyptiens et dans les apocryphes coptes'. *Bulletin de la société d'archéologie copte* 7 (1941) 33-46
Pietersma, A. – Comstock, S.T. – Attridge, H.W. *The Apocalypse of Elijah* (SBLTT 19, Pseudepigrapha Series 19/9) Chico 1981
Pines, S. 'Eschatology and the Concept of Time in the Slavonic Book of Enoch', in R.J.Z. Werblowski – C.J. Bleeker (eds) *Types of Redemption* (NumenSup 18) Leiden 1970, 72-87
Places, É. des, (ed) *Jamblique Les Mystères d'Égypte*. Paris 1966
Pleyte, W. – Boeser, P.A.A. (eds) *Manuscrits coptes du Musée d'antiquités des Pays-Bas à Leyde*. Leiden 1897
Plöger, O. *Theokratie und Eschatologie*. Neukirchen 1959
Podemann Sørensen, J. 'Native Reactions to Foreign Rule and Culture in Religious Literature', in Per Bilde *et al* (eds) *Ethnicity in Hellenistic Egypt* (Studies in Hellenistic Civilization 3) Aarhus 1992, 164-81
Porcher, M.E. 'L'analyse des manuscrits coptes 131[1-8] de la Bibliothèque nationale'. *Revue d'égyptologie* 2 (1936) 65-123
Powell, D. 'Arkandisziplin', in *TRE* 4. Berlin – New York 1979, 1-7
- 'Tertullianists and Cataphrygians'. *VC* 29 (1975) 33-54
Préaux, C. 'Esquisse d'une histoire des révolutions égyptiennes sous les lagides'. *Chronique d'Égypte* 22 (1936) 522-52
Preuschen, E. *Origenes: Der Johannes-Kommentar* (GCS 10) Leipzig 1903
Priest, J. 'Testament of Moses', in *OTP* 1, 919-34
Prigent, P. – Kraft R.A. (eds, tr) *L'Épitre de Barnabé* (SC 172) Paris 1971
Puech, H.-C. 'The Pistis Sophia', in *NTA* 1, 250-59
Quibell, J.E. *Excavations at Saqqara* 1-8. Cairo 1907-35
Quispel, G. 'Judaism, Judaic Christianity and Gnosis', in Logan-Wedderburn, *New Testament and Gnosis*, 58-63
Rad, G. von, *Old Testament Theology*. ET New York – Evanston 1965
Rassart-Débergh, M. – Ries, J. (eds) *Actes du IVème congrès copte* 2. Louvain-la-Neuve 1992
Reeves, J.C. 'An Enochic Citation in *Barnabas* 4:3 and the *Oracles of Hystaspes*', in J. Reeves – J. Kampen (eds) *Pursuing the Text: Studies in Honor of Ben Zion Wacholder on the Occasion of His Seventieth Birthday* (JSOTSup 184) Sheffield 1994, 260-77
- *Jewish Lore in Manichaean Cosmogony: Studies in the Book of Giants Traditions* (HUCM 14) Cincinnati 1992
Reeves, J.C. (ed) *Tracing the Threads: Studies in the Vitality of the Jewish Pseudepigrapha* (EJL 6) Atlanta 1994
Regnault, L. *La vie quotidienne des pères du désert en Égypte au IVè siècle*. Paris 1990
Rehm, B. – Irmscher I. (eds) *Die Pseudoklementinen* I. *Homilien* (GCS 42) Berlin 1969
Reinink, G.J. 'Das Land "Seiris" (Sir) und das Volk der Serer in jüdischen und christlichen Traditionen'. *JSJ* 6 (1975) 72-85
Reymond, E.A.E. – Barns, J.W.B. *Four Martyrdoms from the Pierpont Morgan Coptic Codices*. Oxford 1973
Riddle, D.W. 'From Apocalypse to Martyrology'. *ATR* 9 (1927) 260-80

Roberts, A. – Donaldson, J. (eds) *The Ante-Nicene Fathers; Translations of the Writings of the Fathers down to A.D. 325* 1-10. Edinburgh 1868-72, rev repr Grand Rapids 1950-52
Roberts, C.H. *Manuscript, Society, and Belief in Early Christian Egypt.* London 1977
Robinson, J.M. (ed) *The Nag Hammadi Library in English.* New York – Leiden 1977; 3rd ed San Francisco 1988
Robinson, S.E. 'The Apocryphal Story of Melchizedek'. *JSJ* 18 (1987) 26-39
Römer, C. – Thissen, H.J. 'P.Köln inv. nr. 3221: Das Testament des Hiob in koptischer Sprache. Ein Vorbericht', in M. Knibb – P.W. van der Horst (eds) *Studies on the Testament of Job* (SNTSMS 66) Cambridge 1989, 33-45
Rosenstiehl, J.-M. *L'Apocalypse d'Élie: Introduction, traduction, et notes* (Textes et études 1) Paris 1972
Rousseau, P. 'The Formation of Early Ascetic Communities: Some Further Reflections'. *JTS* 25 (1974) 113-17
– *Pachomius: The Making of a Community in Fourth-Century Egypt.* Berkeley 1985
Rowland, C. *The Open Heaven.* New York 1982
Rowley, H.H. 'The Herodians in the Gospels'. *JTS* 41 (1940) 14-27
Rudolph, K. *Gnosis,* ET San Francisco 1983
– '"Gnosis" and "Gnosticism" – The Problems of Their Definition and their Relation to the Writings of the New Testament', in A. Logan – A. Wedderburn (eds) *The New Testament and Gnosis,* Edinburgh 1983, 21-37
Runciman, S. *The Medieval Manichee: A Study of the Christian Dualist Heresy.* Cambridge 1947
Russell, D.S. *The Method and Message of Jewish Apocalyptic.* Philadelphia 1964
Russell, N. *The Lives of the Desert Fathers.* London – Oxford 1980
Ruwet, J. 'Les "Antilegomena" dans les oeuvres d'Origène'. *Bib* 24 (1943) 18-58
– 'Les apocryphes dans les oeuvres d'Origène'. *Bib* 25 (1944) 143-66
Saldarini, A.J., 'Apocalyptic and Rabbinic Literature'. *CBQ* 37 (1975) 348-58
– 'Apocalypses and "Apocalyptic" in Rabbinic Literature and Mysticism', in Collins, *Apocalypse: Morphology,* 187-205
Sanders, E.P. (ed) *Jewish and Christian Self-Definition* 1-3. Philadelphia 1980-82
Schalit, A. 'Die frühchristliche Überlieferung über die Herkunft der Familie des Herodes'. *ASTI* 1 (1962) 109-60
Schepps, G. (ed) *Priscilliani quae supersunt* (CSEL 18) Vienna 1889
Schiffman, L.H. (ed) *Archaeology and History in the Dead Sea Scrolls* (JSPSup 8) Sheffield 1990
Schiffman L.H. – Swartz, M.D. *Hebrew and Aramaic Incantation Texts from the Cairo Genizah* (Semitic Texts and Studies 1) Sheffield 1992
Schlatter, A. *Der Chronograph aus dem zehnten Jahre Antonins* (TU 12.1) Leipzig 1894-95
Schmidt, C. 'Der Kolophon des Ms. orient. 7594 des Britischen Museums'. *SPAW* (1925) 312-21
Schmidt, C. – MacDermot, V. *The Books of Jeu and the Untitled Text in the Bruce Codex* (NHS 13) Leiden 1978
– *Pistis Sophia* (NHS 9) Leiden 1978
Schmithals, W. *The Apocalyptic Movement.* ET Nashville 1975
Schöne, K.I. *Die Weltchronik des Eusebius in ihrer Bearbeitung durch Hieronymus.* Berlin 1900
Schürer, E. *Geschichte des jüdischen Volkes im Zeitalter Jesu Christi* 1-3. 4th ed. Leipzig 1901-1909
Schürer, E. *The History of the Jewish People in the Age of Jesus Christ (175 B.C. – A.D. 135)* 1-3/2. rev ed G. Vermes – F. Millar – M. Goodman. Edinburgh 1973-1987
Schüssler Fiorenza, E. 'Apokalypsis and Propheteia: Revelation in the Context of Early Christian Prophecy', in id, *The Book of Revelation: Justice and Judgment,* Philadelphia 1985, 133-56
– 'The Phenomenon of Early Christian Apocalyptic: Some Reflections on Method', in Hellholm, *Apocalypticism,* 295-316
Schwartz, E. *Die Königslisten des Eratosthenes und Kastor.* Göttingen 1894
Scopello, M. 'The Apocalypse of Zostrianos [Nag Hammadi VIII.1] and the Book of the Secrets of Enoch'. *VC* 34 (1980) 376-85
– 'Le mythe de la "chute" des anges dans l'Aprocryphon de Jean [II.1] de Nag Hammadi'. *RSR* 54 (1980) 220-30

Segal, A.F. 'Jewish Christianity', in H. Attridge – G. Hata (eds) *Eusebius, Christianity, and Judaism*. Detroit 1992, 326-51

Selwyn, E.G. *The First Epistle of St. Peter*. London/New York 1947

Shaw, B. 'The Passion of Perpetua'. *Past and Present* 139 (1993) 3-45

Shelton, J.C. 'An Astrological Prediction of Disturbances in Egypt'. *Ancient Society* 7 (1976) 209-13

Sheppard, A.R.R. 'Pagan Cults of Angels in Roman Asia Minor'. *Talanta* 12/13 (1980/81) 77-101

Shirun-Grumach, I. 'On "Revelation" in Ancient Egypt', in S. Schoske (ed) *Akten des vierten internationalen ägyptiologischen Kongresses* 3 (Studien zur ägyptischen Kultur 3/3) Hamburg 1989, 379-84

Simmel, G. *Conflict and the Web of Group-Affiliations*. New York 1955

Smith, J.Z. 'Wisdom and Apocalyptic', in B.A. Pearson (ed) *Religious Syncretism in Antiquity*. Missoula 1975, 131-70; repr in J.Z. Smith, *Map is Not Territory: Studies in the History of Religions* (SJLA 23) Leiden 1978, 67-87

Smith, M. *Clement of Alexandria and a Secret Gospel of Mark*. Cambridge MA 1973
– 'On the History of ΑΠΟΚΑΛΨΠΤΩ and ΑΠΟΚΑΛΨΨΙΣ', in Hellholm, *Apocalypticism*, 9-20

Sparks, H.F.D. (ed) *The Apocryphal Old Testament*. Oxford 1984

Speyer, W. *Die literarische Fälschung im heidnischen und christlichen Altertum* (Handbuch der Altertumswissenschaft 1.2) Munich 1971

Spiegelberg, W. *Die sogenannte Demotische Chronik*. Leipzig 1914

Stäh* lin, O. – Früchtel, L. – Treu, U. (eds) *Clemens Alexandrinus* 1 (GCS 12) Leipzig 1936; vol 2 (GCS 15⁴) Berlin 1985; vol 3 (GCS 17²) Berlin 1970

Stark, R. – Bainbridge, W.S. *The Future of Religion*. Berkeley 1985

Stegemann, H. 'Die Bedeutung der Qumranfunde für die Erforschung der Apokalyptik', in Hellholm, *Apocalypticism*, 495-530

Steindorff, G. *Die Apokalypse des Elias, eine unbekannte Apokalypse, und Bruchstücke der Sophonias-Apokalypse*. Leipzig 1899

Stone, M.E. 'Apocalyptic Literature', in id, *Jewish Writings*, 383-441
– *The Armenian Version of IV Ezra* (University of Pennsylvania Armenian Texts and Studies 1) Missoula 1979
– *Fourth Ezra* (Hermeneia) Minneapolis 1990
– 'Lists of Revealed Things in the Apocalyptic Literature', in F.M. Cross – W.E. Lemke – P.D. Miller (eds) *Magnalia Dei. The Mighty Acts of God*. Garden City N.Y. 1976, 414-52
– 'Some Features of the Armenian Version of IV Ezra'. *Mus* 79 (1966) 387-400
– *Scriptures, Sects and Visions: A Profile of Judaism from Ezra to the Jewish Revolts*. Philadelphia 1980
– *A Textual Commentary on the Armenian Version of IV Ezra* (SBLSCS 34) Atlanta 1990

Stone, M.E. (ed) *Jewish Writings of the Second Temple Period* (CRINT II/2) Philadelphia 1984

Stone, M.E. – Strugnell, J. (eds) *The Books of Elijah* 1-2 (SBLTT 18) Missoula 1979

Strack, H.L. – Billerbeck, P. *Kommentar zum Neuen Testament aus Talmud and Midrasch* I-V. Munich 1922-61

Strobel, A. *Ursprung und Geschichte des frühchristlichen Osterkalenders* (TU 121) Berlin 1977

Stroumsa, G.G. *Another Seed: Studies in Gnostic Mythology* (NHS 24) Leiden 1984
– 'Esotericism in Mani's Thought and Background', in L. Cirillo (ed) *Codex Manichaicus Coloniensis*. Cosenza 1986, 153-68

Sturm, R.E. 'Defining the Word "Apocalyptic": A Problem in Biblical Criticism', in J. Marcus – M.L. Soards (eds) *Apocalyptic and the New Testament. Essays in Honor of J. Louis Martyn*. Sheffield 1989, 17-48

Swete, H.B. *An Introduction to the Old Testament in Greek*. Cambridge 1914

Tait, W.J. *Papyri from Tebtunis in Egyptian and in Greek*. London 1977

Talmon, S. *Jewish Civilization in the Hellenistic-Roman Period*. Philadelphia 1991

Tcherikover, V. – Fuks, A. – Stern, M., *Corpus Papyrorum Iudaicorum* 1-3. Cambridge MA – Jerusalem 1957-64

Thackerary, H.St.J. – Marcus, R. – Feldman, L. (tr) *Josephus, with an English Translation* 1-10 (LCL) Cambridge MA – London 1926-65

Tischendorf, K. von, *Apocalypses Apocryphae*. 1866 repr Hildesheim 1966
Torrey, C.C. *The Lives of the Prophets* (JBLMS 1) Philadelphia 1946
Trebilco, P.R. *Jewish Communities in Asia Minor* (SNTSMonSer 69) Cambridge 1991
Trevett, C. 'Apocalypse, Ignatius, Montanism: Seeking the Seeds'. *VC* 43 (1989) 313-38
Tromp, J. *The Assumption of Moses. A Critical Edition with Commentary* (SVTP 10) Leiden 1993
Turcan, M. *Tertullien: La toilette des femmes (De cultu feminarum)* (SC 173) Paris 1971
Turdeanu, E. 'Apocryphes bogomiles et apocryphes pseudo-bogomiles'. *RHR* 138 (1950) 21-52, 176-218
– 'La Vision d'Isaïe: Tradition orthodoxe et tradition hérétique', in id, *Apocryphes slaves et roumains de l'Ancien Testament* (SVTP 5) Leiden 1981, 160-64
Turner, J.D. 'Valentinian Exposition'. *ABD* 6, 781-83
Vaillant, A. 'Un apocryphe pseudo-bogomile: La Vision d'Isaïe'. *Revue des études slaves* 42 (1963) 109-21
– *Le Livre des Secrets d'Hénoch. Texte slave et traduction française*. Paris 1952
VanderKam, J.C. *The Book of Jubilees* 1-2 (CSCO 510-11, Scr. aethiopici 87-88) Louvain 1989
– *Enoch and the Growth of an Apocalyptic Tradition* (CBQMS 16) Washington 1984
– *Enoch – A Man for All Generations* (Studies and Personalities of the OT) Columbia SC 1995
– 'Enoch Traditions in Jubilees and Other Second-Century Sources', in P. Achtemeier (ed) *SBLSP* (1978) 1, 229-51
– 'Some Major Issues in the Contemporary Study of 1 Enoch: Reflections on J.T. Milik's The Books of Enoch: Aramaic Fragments of Qumrân Cave 4'. *Maarav* 3 (1982) 85-97
Veilleux, A. *Pachomian Koinonia* 1 (CSS 45) Kalamazoo MI 1980
Vermes, G. 'Josephus' Treatment of the Book of Daniel'. *JJS* 42 (1991) 149-66
Vielhauer, P. 'Apocalyptic', in *NTA* 2 (1965, 1976 ed) 581-600; rev by G. Strecker (1992 ed) 542-60
– 'Apocalyptic in Early Christianity', in *NTA* 2 (1965, 1976 ed), 608-642; rev by G. Strecker (1992 ed) 569-602
– *Geschichte der urchristlichen Literatur*. Berlin 1975
Violet, B. *Die Esra-Apokalypse, Teil 1: Die Überlieferung* (GCS 18) Leipzig 1910
Violet, B. – Gressmann, H. *Die Apokalypsen des Esra und des Baruch in deutscher Gestalt* (GCS 32) Leipzig 1924
Vivian, T. *Histories of the Monks of Upper Egypt and the Life of Onnophrius* (CSS 140) Kalamazoo MI 1993
– *St. Peter of Alexandria: Bishop and Martyr* (SAC 3) Philadelphia 1988
Vliet, J. van der, 'Chenouté et les démons', in Rassart-Déberg – Ries, *Actes* 2, 41-49
Volkmann, R. (ed) [Porphyry] *De Vita Plotini*, in *Plotini Enneades* 1. Leipzig 1883
Volkmar, G. *Das vierte Buch Esrae*. Tübingen 1863
Volz, P. *Die Eschatologie der jüdischen Gemeinde im neutestamentlichen Zeitalter*. 2nd ed Tübingen 1934
Waddell, W.G. *Manetho* (LCL) Cambridge MA 1940
Wakefield, W.L. – Evans, A.P. *Heresies of the High Middle Ages*. New York 1969
Walters, C.C. 'Christian Paintings from Tebtunis'. *JEA* 75 (1989) 191-208
Ward, B. *The Wisdom of the Desert Fathers*. Fairacres, Oxford 1975
Warga, R.G. 'A Coptic Letter'. *BASP* 29 (1992) 79f
Waszink, J.H. – van Winden, J.C.M. *Tertullianus: De idololatria* (Supplements to VC 1) Leiden 1987
Weill, R. *La fin du moyen empire égyptien*, Paris 1918
Weinel, H. 'Die spätere christliche Apokalyptik', in H. Schmidt (ed) *Eucharisterion 2. FS Hermann Gunkel* (FRLANT nF 19) Göttingen 1923, 141-73
Wendland, P. (ed) *Hippolytus Werke* 3 (GCS 26) Leipzig 1916
Wevers, J.W. (ed) *Genesis* (Septuaginta: VT graecum auctoritate Acad. Scient. Gottingensis editum, vol 1) Göttingen 1974
Wewers, G.A. *Geheimnis und Geheimhaltung im rabbinischen Judentum*. Berlin 1975
Wickham, L.R. 'The Sons of God and the Daughters of Men: Genesis VI:2 in Early Christian Exegesis'. *OTS* 19 (1974) 135-47

Wiesmann H. *Sinuthi archimandritae vita et opera omnia* (CSCO 108, Scr. coptici 12) Louvain 1952

Wilken, R.L. *The Land Called Holy: Palestine in Christian History and Thought.* New Haven – London 1992

– 'The Restoration of Israel in Biblical Prophecy: Christian and Jewish Responses in the Early Byzantine Period', in J. Neusner – E. Frerichs (eds) *'To See Ourselves as Others See Us': Christians, Jews, and 'Others' in Late Antiquity.* Chico 1985, 443-71

Williams, D.H. 'The Origins of the Montanist Movement: A Sociological Analysis', *Religion* 19 (1989) 331-51

Williams, F. (tr) *Epiphanius Panarion. Book 1* (Sects 1-46). Leiden 1987

Williams, M.A. 'The *Life of Antony* and the Domestication of Charismatic Wisdom', in id (ed) *Charisma and Sacred Biography* (JAAR Thematic Studies 48, 3-4) Chico 1982, 23-45

Wilson, R.M. 'Gnosis, Gnosticism, and the New Testament', in Bianchi, *Le origini*, 511-26

Winstedt, E.O. 'Coptic Saints and Sinners, III. St. Matthew the Poor'. *Proceedings of the Society of Biblical Archaeology* 33 (1911) 113-20

Winterbottom, M. (ed, tr) *Gildas: The Ruin Of Britain and Other Works* (History from the Sources) London – Chichester 1978

Wintermute, O. 'Apocalypse of Elijah', in *OTP* 1, 721-53

Wipszycka, E. 'Le nationalisme a-t-il existé dans l'Égypte byzantine?' *Journal of Juristic Papyrology* 22 (1992) 83-128

– 'La valeur de l'onomastique pour l'histoire de la christianisation de l'Égypte: à propos d'une étude de R.S. Bagnall'. *ZPE* 62 (1986) 173-81

Wisse, F. 'The Apocryphon of John (II,*1*, III,*1*, IV,*1*, and BG 8502,2)', in *NHL*, 104-23

– 'John, Apocryphon of', in *ABD* 3, 899f

Worrell, W.H. *Coptic Texts in the University of Michigan Collection.* Ann Arbor MI 1942

Wright, W. 'Two Epistles of Mar Jacob, Bishop of Edessa'. *Journal of Sacred Literature and Biblical Record* 10 (1867) 430ff

Young, D.W. 'The Milieu of Nag Hammadi: Some Historical Considerations'. *VC* 24 (1970) 127-37

Youtie, H.C. 'AGRAMMATOS: An Aspect of Greek Society in Egypt'. *HSCP* 75 (1971) 161-76

– 'HYPOGRAPHEUS: The Social Impact of Illiteracy in Graeco-Roman Egypt'. *ZPE* 17 (1975) 201-21

Zandee, J. *Death as an Enemy, According to Ancient Egyptian Conceptions* (NumenSup 5) Leiden 1960

Zauzich, K.-T. 'Das Lamm des Bokchoris', in *Papyrus Erzherzog Rainer (P.Rainer Cent.) 1.* Vienna 1983, 165-74

Ziegler, J. *Susanna, Daniel, Bel et Draco. Septuaginta: Vetus Testamentum Graecum* 16/2. Göttingen 1954

Index of Sources

For greater effectiveness, the source index is selective. 1 Enoch is not indexed for Chapter Two, nor are other apocalyptic texts treated thematically in that chapter and announced as such in the table of contents. The same goes for 4, 5 and 6 Ezra in Chapter Three and Daniel 9 in Chapter Five. Division:

1. Hebrew Bible
2. Greek Bible
3. Jewish and Christian Biblical Pseudepigrapha
4. Qumran Texts
5. Philo
6. Josephus
7. New Testament
8. Other Early Christian Writings
9. Gnostic Texts from the Nag Hammadi, Berlin and Askew Codices
10. Rabbinic Literature
11. Other Ancient Writings
12. Unnamed Manuscripts

1. Hebrew Bible
(Masoretic order)

Genesis		Exodus	
1-2	73	7:17	91
3	69, 73, 76, 79	7:19	91
5	36, 89	32:7	38
5:21-24	42, 88, 100	34:28	38
5:22	88	49:10	232
5:24	88		
6	24, 59, 67, 69	Numbers	
6:1f	69	35:30	91, 100
6:1-4	41f, 60, 67f, 70, 73, 76, 79f, 83, 87, 100f, 159	Deuteronomy	
6:2	60, 81, 86	4:26	170
6:4	86	17:6	91, 100
41:46	108	19:15	91
49:10	232-236, 238	30:19	170

8. Other Early Christian Writings (Alphabetical order)

Index of Names, Places and Subjects

Names of literary works and documents are italicized.

Catch words which appear in the table of contents are excluded. So are instances which may be found through the index of sources.

Index of Modern Authors